D1636763

Making a Life in Multiethnic Miami

LATINOS:
EXPLORING DIVERSITY AND CHANGE

Making a Life in Multiethnic Miami

Immigration and the Rise of a Global City

Elizabeth M. Aranda
Sallie Hughes
Elena Sabogal

LYNNE
RIENNER
PUBLISHERS

BOULDER
LONDON

857743835

Published in the United States of America in 2014 by
Lynne Rienner Publishers, Inc.
1800 30th Street, Boulder, Colorado 80301
www.rienner.com

and in the United Kingdom by
Lynne Rienner Publishers, Inc.
3 Henrietta Street, Covent Garden, London WC2E 8LU

Library of Congress Cataloging-in-Publication Data
Aranda, Elizabeth M., 1973–
    Making a life in multiethnic Miami : immigration and the rise of a global
city / Elizabeth M. Aranda, Sallie Hughes, and Elena Sabogal.
        pages cm. — (Latinos: exploring diversity and change)
    Includes bibliographical references and index.
    ISBN 978-1-62637-041-8 (hc : alk. paper)
    1. Immigrants—Florida—Miami. 2. Latin Americans—Florida—Miami.
3. Multiculturalism—Florida—Miami. 4. Miami (Fla.)—Ethnic relations.
5. Miami (Fla.)—Emigration and immigration. I. Hughes, Sallie.
II. Sabogal, Elena. III. Title.
    F319.M6A69 2014
        975.9'381—dc23

                                                                2013035073

British Cataloguing In Publication Data
A Cataloguing in Publication record for this book
is available from the British Library.

Printed and bound in the United States of America

5   4   3   2   1

*To the immigrants who shared their stories with us
and all who are fighting for immigration reform*

Contents

List of Tables and Figures   ix
Acknowledgments   xi

1 Immigration in the Age of Global Insecurity   1

2 The Contexts of Departure   45

3 The Context of Reception   79

4 Inequalities and Perceptions of Social Mobility   111

5 Politics, Membership, and Representation   161

6 Race, Discrimination, and Ethnic Rivalries   199

7 Immigrant Emotions and Strategies of Co-Presence   243

8 Translocal Placemaking and Belonging   281

9 The Security of Home in a Global Era   319

References   335
Index   361
About the Book   367

Tables and Figures

Tables

1.1 Race and Hispanic Origin of Persons in Miami-Dade County
 and Rate of Change, 1990, 2000, and 2012 22
1.2 Select Groups by National Origin in Miami-Dade County
 and Percent Change, 1990–2000 and 2000–2012 24
1.3 Qualitative Interview Sample Descriptives 34
1.4 Characteristics of Focus Group Participants 35
1.5 Descriptive Characteristics of ITMI Quantitative Sample 36
2.1 Income Distribution by Quintile and Rate of Change in Peru,
 the Dominican Republic, and Colombia 52
2.2 Foreign-Born Population of Twelve Latin American Countries
 in the United States 55
2.3 Remittances Sent by Immigrants Abroad 56
2.4 Reasons for Immigrating to the United States by Country/
 Region of Origin and Gender 58
4.1 Median Household Income and Rate of Change by Quintile,
 Miami-Dade County 118
4.2 Perceived Upward Social Mobility by Country/Region
 of Origin 129
5.1 National Origin/Ethnicity of Elected Officials in
 Greater Miami, 2010 169
5.2 Size of Represented Constituency 170
5.3 Immigrant Community Political Incorporation 187
6.1 Perceived Racial Discrimination by Country/Region
 of Origin 217
6.2 Perceived Everyday Discrimination by Country/Region
 of Origin 219

6.3 Perceived Employment Discrimination by Country/Region
       of Origin   220
7.1 Frequency of Visits to the Home Country   253
7.2 Frequency of Communication with People in the Country
       of Origin   256
7.3 Effect of Embodied Co-Presence on Happiness   269
7.4 Effect of Virtual Co-Presence on Happiness   271
7.5 Effect of Co-Presence by Proxy on Happiness   275
8.1 Reasons for Migrating to Miami Compared to Reasons
       for Migrating to the United States   287
8.2 Reasons for Moving to Miami by Country/Region of
       Origin and Gender   288
8.3 Definite Plans to Stay or Not in South Florida
       for Ten Years or More   293

Figures

2.1 Concern for Being Left Unemployed by Country, 2005   60
2.2 Top Two Most Important Problems in Latin America
       by Country, 2005   66
4.1 Distribution of Household Income for Miami, Florida,
       and the United States, 2005   117
4.2 Income Distribution in Miami by Race and Ethnicity, 2005   121
4.3 Perceived Social Mobility by Country/Region of Origin
       and Gender   127
5.1 Ethnic Political Representation, 2010   173
6.1 Residential Clustering of White Non-Hispanics
       in Miami, 2010   209
6.2 Residential Clustering of Black Non-Hispanics
       in Miami, 2010   210
6.3 Residential Clustering of Hispanics in Miami, 2010   211
7.1 ABS (Happiness) Scores by Country/Region of
       Origin and Gender   267

Acknowledgments

The seeds for this project were sown when the three of us met in the fall of 2002 as new hires at the University of Miami (UM). Little did we know at the time how many back-and-forth e-mails, visits, and conference calls would take place across the years, spanning several states and countries as one or another of us eventually moved on to new positions, went abroad to do other research, or once in a while even attempted to go on "vacations." What held us together during a decade of field research, analysis, and writing was that we believed in this project, that the unique talents that each one of us possessed would contribute to make the final product better than the sum of its parts, and that someday our efforts would bear fruit. Eventually, as most long-term academic projects do, this research would grow beyond the three of us and our respective universities and include many more institutions and people to whom we are indebted for financial support, wise advice, and encouragement.

We owe an enormous thank you to Chris Bose and Edna Acosta-Belén, editors of the series titled Latinos: Exploring Diversity and Change (of which our book is a part), for their excitement for the project, encouragement throughout the years of writing, and constructive comments on the book chapters as they went through various stages of maturation. Above all, we are very grateful for the faith they showed in our work and in our ability to pull the project together. Likewise, we appreciate the dedication and talent of our editor, Andrew Berzanskis, at Lynne Rienner Publishers, as well as Lynne Rienner herself and all the talented people in her organization. Along with two anonymous reviewers, they have made this a better book.

The institutions whose financial support made this book possible include the University of Miami's Center for Latin American Studies, which funded initial interviews and focus groups for the study; the College of Arts and Sciences at UM for a larger grant that allowed us to finish the qualitative interviews and focus groups; and the UM Provost's Office for several competitive summer research grants to Hughes and Aranda. Additionally, William Paterson University gave Sabogal an Assigned Release Time Award and initial summer funding, and the University of South Florida (USF) provided release time and support for Aranda to make progress on the research.

The book benefited from two external grant-making institutions whose support during economically turbulent times was vital to the continued production of knowledge on immigration and ethnic media, not only for our project but for many others as well. The National Science Foundation (NSF), Proposal No. 0752644, funded the Immigrant Transnationalism and Modes of Incorporation quantitative survey on immigration and transnationalism. We are grateful to Elizabeth Vaquera, with whom we collaborated to receive this grant and who has been supportive of the project throughout and encouraged us to use these data in our book. Importantly, the McCormick Foundation funded an interview project with Haitians in Greater Miami that supplemented our initial sample and allowed us to further explore the importance of ethnic and transnational media for immigrant settlement. Lilia Santiague, Yves Colon, and Tsitsi Wakhisi, who worked with Hughes collecting the interviews, generously agreed to let us use these data. We are equally indebted to the Department of Sociology and the College of Arts and Sciences and its Office of Research and Scholarship at the University of South Florida for their support of the NSF application, as well as other general research expenses, and the Department of Journalism and Media Management and the School of Communication at UM for their support of expenses related to the McCormick study.

This book could not have been completed without the help of diligent graduate and undergraduate students at the University of Miami and the University of South Florida, who helped us collect data, transcribe interviews and focus-group recordings, code and analyze qualitative data, and conduct statistical analyses. Their national origins reflect the makeup of Miami and, given the nature of our study, we were truly fortunate to have such a diverse and capable group of research assistants. They include Andrew Greenlee, a native Floridian who as a Center for Latin American Studies graduate assistant coauthored with us a preliminary grant proposal. In the School of Communication, we thank former doctoral students Jesus Arrollave, a Colombian native, for coordination and recruitment of South American focus groups; Yvette Bueno, of Dominican origin, and Puerto Rican María Elena Villar for interviewing, transcribing, and coordinating focus groups with Dominican and Puerto Rican participants; Danielle Rio-Rivero for conducting interviews with Cuban immigrants; and Randall Martínez and Zahra Shekarkhar, Cuban Americans, for their research assistance at various stages of the project. We also thank Abelardo Rodríguez, a

Mexican doctoral student in the Department of International Studies, who helped with interviewing, transcribing, and recruiting focus groups with Mexican participants, as well as Ashley Atwell and Bryn Hafemeister for also conducting interviews. In the Department of Sociology at UM we owe special thanks to Venezuelan doctoral student Rosa Chang, who conducted data coding and analysis of most of the qualitative data, helped us with interviews, and continued to provide research assistance to us even when some of us had moved on from UM. University of Miami undergraduate students who also deserve thanks are Sahily Serradet, for interviewing Cuban immigrants and transcribing the interviews, and Emanna Louis, for our initial Haitian-language interviews and their transcriptions and translations. Chris Hanson, UM's very capable Geography Department lab tech, created the politics maps from our original data, and Romina Herrera, a talented Florida International University student, created the ethnic and racial maps from Miami-Dade County census data. Hilary Dotson, a sociology doctoral student from the University of South Florida, provided research assistance, particularly with the analysis of quantitative data as we completed the manuscript. Likewise Rory Kramer provided valuable assistance with compiling US Census Bureau data. We are also thankful to Maria Patricia de Arrollave, who transcribed focus group recordings, and Carmen Longnecker, who transcribed and translated into English many of the Spanish interviews. We also owe a debt of thanks to the following individuals who were instrumental in helping us to secure funding for the quantitative portion of the study: Maralee Mayberry, Peter Kivisto, Silvia Pedraza, and Jorge Duany.

To our colleagues, friends, and family, who went above and beyond what "normal" colleagues and kin do, we send our great thanks and appreciation for their encouragement throughout the project, for providing feedback on grant proposals, for recommending readings to broaden the interdisciplinary scope of the book, and for reading selected chapters at various stages of manuscript completion: Suzanne Oboler, George Yudice, Steve Stein, Miguel Kanai, Giovanna Pompele, Margarethe Kusenbach, Tanya Golash-Boza, and Domenic J. Casenelli. We also thank our colleagues at the Institute for Public Opinion Research (IPOR) at Florida International University: Hugh Gladwin, Ann Reeder Goraczko, Suzanna Mic, Emma Ergon, and all of the IPOR staff and interviewers who assisted with the telephone interviews for the quantitative data collection. We further thank Elizabeth Vaquera, coprincipal investigator on the Immigrant Transnationalism and Modes of Incorporation (ITMI) project, who performed much of the quantitative data analyses employed in the book, assisted with the interpretations of findings, and painstakingly read through the entire manuscript and provided insightful comments throughout. Completion of this book would not have been possible without the support, assistance, and encouragement of this collection of colleagues and friends.

Finally, we all have personal thanks to make. Aranda would like to thank her coauthors, Sallie and Elena, for their patience and understanding through some difficult times and for their collaboration on such an important project. To her parents, siblings and their spouses, nieces, and nephews, Aranda offers thanks for their understanding when she missed many family functions due to "the book." She is particularly grateful to her father, Juan Aranda, who so closely has monitored and taken interest in her career, and to her mother, Carmen, who has provided emotional support throughout. Aranda is also grateful for the support provided by the Department of Sociology at USF, in particular the sense of community that prevails and the comfortable environment that is so important to scholarly productivity. It is a privilege for her to be part of this intellectual home. Aranda is deeply thankful to Elizabeth Vaquera and Kristin Carbone-López; their willingness to always review, comment, and support this research was invaluable. They are not just colleagues who made this work better, but true friends through and through. Last, but certainly not least, Aranda thanks Ray Eckstein and her children, Isabel and Andrew, for their unrelenting support; the book became another family member for a while, and she is truly appreciative for their understanding of the amount of time and effort this research took from them. She thanks them deeply for turning their home into not just an "oasis of productivity," but also a place of warmth and comfort. Finally, Aranda is thankful to Ray for the many days and nights that he took over care of the children and the home. His love and support carried her through a ten-year process of highs and lows—she dedicates her portion of this book to him.

Hughes first wants to thank Elizabeth and Elena, for their friendship, their patience, and a collaboration that has made her a better academic and person. Among colleagues she would like to single out are Leonardo Ferreira and Lillian Manzor, who remained important sources of encouragement during the many years of work on the book. Her personal gratitude goes to a group of amazing women: Jane, Cindy, Leigh Ann, and Yeidy. Their support and constant "presence" while physically far away allowed her to make a happy life in Miami. Hughes also owes thanks to all her wonderful friends in Miami and Mexico City, as well as her Reid family cousins. All were supportive and patient when she worked on weekends, missed e-mails, or left town for months at a time. Her niece and nephews, Domenic, Ragan, and Reece, perhaps played the most important role: they kept her real during this last decade, or at least as real as an academic can be. Finally, Hughes is grateful for the years she shared with her brother, Miles William Hughes. His commitment to social justice, public education, and the politics that support them will always be an inspiration and a cherished part of her being. She misses him enormously. She dedicates her portion of this book to his life, and to Leigh Ann, Ragan, and Reece Hughes, who carry his indomitable spirit within them. They are stronger than they know.

Sabogal would like to dedicate her part of the book to the loves of her life: her sons, Andrew and Patrick, for their love, support, and encouragement; her mother, Elena Seminario, for her nurturing; her sisters, Maria Luisa, Delfina, and Maricarmen; her brother, Enrique; and her in-laws, Giuliana, Juan Manuel, and Rodolfo, along with their children, Maria Fernanda, Josu, Jose Ignacio, Enrique, Alejandra, and Ximena. At critical moments, her family members have each taken turns being kind and understanding when she needed it the most. The book is also dedicated to the memory of her father, Polo, who had his ways of letting her know he was always there. Her family in Lima provided the cultural bridge she needed to live in South Florida and later New York, as well as the moral support and practical accommodations that a life lived traveling between two countries requires. Having emigrated from Peru as a young adult, she has always felt she has many "homes." Her mother, as well as her sister, Maria Luisa, and brother-in-law, Rodolfo, opened their homes so she could spend summers in Lima working on the book. She wishes to thank Liza and Sallie for their collaboration on this important project and all of her friends and colleagues in Lima, Florida, New Jersey, and New York for their love and support throughout the years that it took to complete the book. They are too numerous to mention individually, but they know who they are.

Finally, we owe our biggest debt of gratitude to the participants in this study. We hope that in some small way we help make their voices heard and better understood as our political elites once again debate their future without considering the full scope of their personhood in the discussions. At this writing, it seems likely that any meaningful immigration reform will fail, which means that some immigrants, including those whose stories are told in this book, will continue to lead lives that are marred by insecurity. It is our hope that future attempts to reform US immigration will be rooted in a recognition that policy should respond to not just the labor needs of a country, but also to the human needs of immigrants and their families. We believe that immigration reform is not just a civil rights issue, but is, moreover, an issue of granting basic human rights. Our hope is that this book will allow those who are removed from the lived experience of immigrants to better understand what it is like to navigate through the trenches of economic globalization. Their stories are the stories of all of us because although globalization may affect different groups in contrasting ways, it leaves no one untouched.

—*E. M. Aranda, S. Hughes, and E. Sabogal*

1

Immigration in the Age of Global Insecurity

Alejandra, a Colombian national, was born in 1954 in one of the country's main industrial cities. The daughter of an architect and a housewife, Alejandra enjoyed an upper-middle-class lifestyle growing up. Having earned a university degree in the late 1970s, she settled in Bogotá and worked as an executive in corporate sales. In spite of being divorced with two children, she was able to send them to good schools.

In 2001, when her children were ages sixteen and seventeen, Alejandra decided to move to Miami[1] with her mother, in search of a higher income and what she called *el sueño americano* (the American Dream). She had traveled to the United States many times since age thirteen and was familiar with Miami. Having been educated in Colombian bilingual schools, she also spoke English. To further make the change easier, she had a sister who lived in South Florida. Through her, Alejandra gained the necessary sponsorship to obtain a visa that allowed her to work in Miami.[2] After only four years of living in the United States, when asked if she regretted immigrating to this country, Alejandra answered, "Yes! (laughs) I have regretted it because first, leaving my children has been the most important factor. . . . [I]t has broken up a home, [and] it has broken up a family, because my children are twenty and twenty-one years old and studying at the university. I know they cannot come here because they are studying in the best universities there, and I don't have the money for them to study here. So I cannot sacrifice that they come here and stop studying just to be with me. So I have sacrificed one thing for another."

In discussions of global migration, the prevailing cultural assumption is that immigrants improve their lives (and those of their children) by moving from one country to another. In the case of immigrants to the United States, the notion of striving to achieve "el sueño americano" suggests that what lies ahead are positive outcomes, such as access to education, the opportu-

1

nity to make a better living, the possibilities for personal growth and esteem, and the idea that this new lifestyle can be sustainable, if not for oneself, then for one's children. We hear countless tales of immigrant success stories, from former US secretary of state Madeleine Albright, who moved as a teenager from Czechoslovakia, to former Miami Marlins manager Ozzie Guillén, who moved from Venezuela. In Alejandra's case, although she had only been in the United States for four years at the time of her interview, she did not exhibit the response predicted by the assumption that the benefits of migration outweigh its costs, and that mobility is natural and unproblematic.[3] Alejandra had moved with her elderly mother and settled in an area where she had a sister living nearby. Those factors that made her mobile (e.g., having grown children, a visa, and good English skills) and facilitated settlement (e.g., accessibility to kin) also divided her own family in the process as her children stayed behind.

Historian Susan Matt writes that "the idea that we can and should feel at home anyplace on the globe is based on a worldview that celebrates the solitary, mobile individual and envisions men and women as easily separated from family, from home and from the past."[4] Homesickness, a consequence of mobility, once a medical diagnosis in the United States, historically has been transformed into a taboo emotion to be suppressed by the modern individual, who was expected to unproblematically transfer loyalties from families, homes, and communities to employers and the government.[5] The enlightened individual (understood to be white men during colonial times) embraced mobility to maximize individual material happiness and "became less willing to submit to communal imperatives that dictated their location, and they manifested a new spirit of autonomy as they searched for contentment."[6] The assumptions guiding the mobility of early internal migrants in the United States have endured; only now mobile populations vary in origins, gender, and the scale of their mobility.

Thus, in modern times, a break with the past is expected not to deter the true "cosmopolitan" immigrant. Advances in technology, travel, and forms of communication suggest that the emotional costs of migration have been minimized since immigrants have more opportunities to maintain ties to loved ones than in the past. Yet, even when mobility decisions are freely made, they come at high emotional costs, particularly when families are separated.[7]

Typical tales of immigrant success do not often draw attention to these costs. Nor does the figure of the enlightened cosmopolitan migrant reflect the kind of experience that an immigrant such as Alejandra faced. Mobility *is* problematic for her. Emigrating at the age of forty-seven with her elderly mother, Alejandra was not just looking for a higher income. She felt strongly that in Colombia, "the bad thing about one's country is insecurity. The belief that once you are forty years old, you are worthless." Alejandra's sense of job security was threatened by perceived age discrimination in Colombian society, compounded by a particular characteristic of gender inequality that imposes earlier retirement expectations on women.[8] In addition to her increasing sense of professional and social insecurity, Alejandra felt that as a divorced woman, her chances of finding a romantic partner in Colombia were limited. Research on Latin American women indicates that those whose future economic prospects are uncertain are at a disadvantage when it comes to forming a union.[9] And, in Bogotá, Alejandra felt lonely. Urban environments in Latin America diminish women's connections to kinship networks; thus, migration is used to achieve family and kinship objectives.[10] However, her hope that migration would bring to her more money, a stable job, and a partner had recently waned since her breakup with the man she had been dating in Miami. On the day we spoke, Alejandra suggested that in her efforts to fulfill her financial and social aspirations, she wrecked her family and felt as alone as she did in Bogotá.

As stigmatized emotions, loneliness and homesickness are related, and throughout history, they have been viewed as signs of immaturity and dependency.[11] As Matt argues, they threaten "individual and social progress" because they accompany "the temptation to return home." These feelings undermine the capitalist expectation that individuals are interchangeable, thereby affecting the fluidity of this economic system.[12] Regardless of the stigma attached to these emotions, like many immigrants, Alejandra pondered what returning to Colombia to reconstitute her family would take. She concluded that a well-remunerated job was vital, because if things did not work out, she could not reenter the United States because she had not yet secured permanent residency. When asked how she felt about these mobility constraints, she said, "Very bored, very depressed, very out of place, and that affects you a lot."

Like Alejandra, many immigrants come to Miami searching for various forms of security and stability in a rapidly changing world. A pervasive condition of modernity is the movement of people and their detachment from territorialized social relations.[13] Modernity requires individuals to accept the loss of the past and to learn the "habits of individualism" that ultimately support global capitalism.[14] For many we interviewed, however, the process and consequences of migration brought emotional costs that challenged the idea that breaks with the past are unproblematic; moreover, these costs called into question the assumption that the outcome of mobility is progress when one considers the psychic energy required to adapt to the ambivalence of migration or to "subordinate the desire to stay behind to the goal of getting ahead."[15]

The immigrants whose stories are told in these pages reported leaving behind communities in which they experienced threats to their individual financial, physical, psychic (psychological), and social sustainability and that of their families. These threats resulted in perceptions of human insecurity from various sources that were undermining a "sustainable form of life."[16] Their stories illustrate how economic globalization and regional geopolitics restructured social conditions across space, creating new forms of security and insecurity that immigrants embody in lived spaces that include their home countries and, as we will show, Miami.

Why Miami?

Why is studying immigrants in Miami important? Saskia Sassen estimates at least seventy cities can be labeled as "global," and that the number is growing because of the compatibility of their roles in the global economy. With weaker global connections than New York, London, or even "second-tier" global cities such as Chicago and Toronto, Miami is one of many rising "minor" or "third-tier" global cities that are less studied sites for the materialization of global processes.[17]

Miami articulates regionally organized patterns of globalization that are most intense on a hemispheric scale rather than a global one. Its rise to global city status by linking regions across the Americas distinguishes Miami's global functions and highlights the specialized roles global cities play.[18] As Jan Aart Scholte notes, regionalization has occurred concurrently with globalization,[19] and regional nodes such as Miami, Dubai, Singapore, or Hong Kong play important roles in the global city system.[20] The social structures and cultural character of these cities are worthy of deeper study for what they can tell us about their residents' on-the-ground experiences of globalization.

Miami's particular multiethnic mix is another reason for studying the city. Miami is a "zone of contact"[21] for cultures from across the Americas, housing US natives and immigrants of many kinds. The city has been envisioned by Latinos/as as friendly to Spanish speakers and Latin American/Caribbean traditions, and also as a place where immigrants can "make it," an idea propagated by the success stories of the first waves of Cuban immigrants.[22] Yet, at the same time Miami houses complex social hierarchies that sort immigrants' life chances unequally and reflect Miami's bimodal economic structure, US racial ideologies and geopolitical projections, and cultural norms transplanted from places of origin.

Another of the lessons drawn from Miami's transformation is how the global city materializes transnational ideologies that have an impact on lives across multiple geographic sites. What we mean is that global Miami's economic structure reflects hemisphere-wide consequences of the neoliberal economic turn in the 1980s and 1990s, and its residents embody these effects in their social positions and life chances whether or not they are immigrants. Briefly, *neoliberalism* refers to a political and economic movement calling for a form of laissez-faire capitalism in which markets are deregulated, government social spending is curtailed, and state holdings are privatized, all in an effort to create export-based market economies to bring down foreign debt. In the process, although unevenly across countries, the initial results were increased impoverishment, slashed formal sector jobs, decreased real wages, and fewer social protections for citizens. When neoliberal economic restructuring after 1982 increased flows of direct foreign investment to and across Latin America and the Caribbean, much of it passed through Miami's expanding banking and trade infrastructure.[23] As the city became an interregional hub for "command and control" of financial and trade flows across the 1990s, demand increased for low-skilled laborers to service a growing international managerial class that in turn helped launch a real estate pricing boom and drove away portions of the middle class.

Concurrently, the implementation of neoliberal economic policies across Latin America created a pool of potential new immigrants by shrinking social safety nets, public security, and formal sector labor markets as states withdrew from economic production, disaster management, and social programs such as public education, health care, and pensions. Seeking greater human security (economic, physical, psychic, social), immigrants were drawn to Miami by jobs, social networks, and the city's geographic proximity and similarities to their places of origin. While the elite arrived with jobs in the new Miami offices of multinational corporations and specialized service firms, immigrants who had been caught in the squeeze of economic restructuring and rising insecurity of many kinds faced greater difficulties if they arrived in Miami without legal status or transferable professional credentials. In summary, global Miami reflects conditions stimulated by the implementation of the transnational economic ideology of neoliberalism and taking form within a particular set of historical-institutional structures associated with both US history and immigrants' places of origin.

How these dynamics play out in immigrant lives is the subject of this book. Miami is a rising global city that articulates regional flows most intensely, for three reasons: (1) it is multiethnic but predominately Latino/a and, within that, predominately Cuban; (2) it is polarized by wealth and other social disparities; and (3) its metropolitan area has the largest proportion of immigrants in the United States.[24] For all of these reasons, Miami is a case worthy of study, particularly since the last detailed account of the city was published in 1993 by Alejandro Portes and Alex Stepick. Since then, the city, its inhabitants, and the world have all changed in many ways. Risk and human insecurity, as factors leading to global population movement and conditioning settlement, especially beckon further elaboration.

Why Focus on Human Security?

In the 1990s, Anthony Giddens followed Ulrich Beck in conceptualizing the linkages among reflexivity, modernity, and risk.[25] Perhaps not coincidentally, within the system of global capitalism being manifested at that time, underemployment and labor "flexibility," weak state capacity to prevent disaster, and the linkages between rising crime and failing social programs raised for many Latin Americans the specter of risk to the sustainability of their lives and lifestyles. Faced with these conditions, Miamians, as we show in this book, engaged in migration and transborder ways of belonging as strategies to relieve the negative effects of human insecurity in their original homes while attempting to create more secure lives in new destinations. Although strategic, manifestations of agency through immigration and settlement decisions remain conditioned by immigration policies, class, gender, and racial hierarchies. Thus, for those like Alejandra, feelings of insecurity in the place of origin compel migration decisions, while attempts to reestablish the emotional security of home elsewhere carry other challenges.

Giddens developed the concept of ontological security to refer to a sense of safety in the world and confidence that one's reality is, in fact, what it appears to be. This sense of safety, sometimes experienced as feelings of comfort, is contingent on trust.[26] Whether we are talking about trust in individuals, groups, organizations, or institutions, trust acts as a mechanism that curbs existential anxiety and sustains ontological security. When trust in relationships, taken-for-granted social norms, and societal institutions erodes, ontological insecurity rises. We argue that, under these conditions, the need for ontological security, as much as other dimensions of human security such as physical safety and social security, influences choices about settlement and incorporation.

Ontological security also emanates from the reassurance of being embedded in stable and affirmative relationships.[27] These relationships, in turn, are uniquely related to particular places: built or natural spaces that are socially constructed and culturally imbued with meaning.[28] The desire to be physically present in the homeland, and particularly the hometown, is an emotional need we document across many migration experiences in this book. This phenomenon may come about because, as David Conradson and Deirdre McKay write, place plays "a major role in the ongoing constitution of identity."[29] Migration, thus, represents a disembedding mechanism that can shock place-based identities. From this perspective, mobility is paradoxical because it represents a search for greater security in some domains but embodies greater insecurity in others.

For immigrants who have been exposed to the United States through travel or US cultural exports and, like Alejandra, have family already living there, migration comes to represent a viable alternative to human insecurity. This familiarity diminishes, although does not erase, the uncertainties of mobility. In this book, we show, however, that once in Miami, immigrants find that migration acts as a prism through which prior forms of insecurity are refracted onto new experiences that carry new vulnerabilities. Some immigrants become (or continue to be) racialized actors, subject to growing levels of social scrutiny and state regulation in a city that is increasingly perceived to be for the "haves" and not for the "have-lesses." Others perceive a loss of social status associated with downward occupational mobility and disruptions of class-based networks back home. Most obviously, some immigrants lack a political voice or are even forced to remain in the civic shadows because they lack formal legal authority to be present and heard in the United States.

Further, in the first decades of the twenty-first century, immigrants to the United States again were portrayed as suspect in key public arenas such as mass media or electoral politics.[30] In seeking greater human security, many of Miami's immigrant residents arrived in yet another period of US insecurity, post–September 11, 2001, during which, to right-wing extremists or fearful natives, immigrants represented social, cultural, and national security threats to US society.[31] This shift in attitude has created insecure environments for immigrants, particularly those with temporary legal statuses or who are out of status altogether, resulting in contradictions whereby immigrants end up trading one source of insecurity for another.

Focusing on ontological security captures the range of contradictions that emerge when we consider that although mobility is expected to lead to positive outcomes for immigrants, the emotional costs, such as those we illustrate in Alejandra's case, beg for problematization. Moreover, does migration have other hidden costs? The human need for ontological security and the sense of assurance it instills best capture the paradoxes immigrants confront as they traverse the web of global capitalism.

Central Argument and Conceptual Development of the Book

The central argument that we present in this book is that migration in late modernity reflects the need to stabilize multiple dimensions of human security. Based on evidence from a wide sample of migration experiences from Greater Miami since the late 1980s, we argue that the immigration process often involves exchanging ontological security, as a form of emotional security anchored in relationships and worldviews formed at home, for other forms of security that are perceived as more immediately necessary for survival and that were threatened in our participants' places of origin. A corollary to this argument, which emerges from an examination of the same migration experiences, is that immigrants exhibit agency when faced with emotional disruptions endemic to migration. We argue that immigrants combat threats to ontological security by embedding themselves in relationships with emotionally significant people and places that are territorially positioned in the country of origin and in Miami, which constitute two poles of a translocal space. They do so to extend the comfort and support of the natal home to the immigrant destination through what we call "translocal social citizenship."

In most of the immigration stories we analyzed for this book, migration to Miami over the last thirty years involved exchanging forms of insecurity perceived as threatening to life projects in the home country for other forms of insecurity associated with the post-9/11 US national security state, the economic and political hierarchies of a global city, and the particular intraethnic and racial exclusions of a minority-majority (in this case, Latino and, more specifically, predominantly Cuban) city. These place-based conditions in Miami were experienced as immigrants dealt with separation from close social networks located in the place of origin. To confront the ambiguity of increased life chances (or the perception of those opportunities) with reshuffled social positions and potential detachment from supportive relationships, immigrants enacted a multisite mode of belonging that effectively merged places of significance with their individual and group identities into one cross-border *locality*, or translocal version of home. We argue that through reenactment, evocation, and direct social contact with their original homes and home lives, immigrants in Miami create a substantive form of citizenship that claims inclusion across territories based on participatory contributions to geographically separated social groups and communities rather than legal authorization from a state.[32] Miami's facilitation of translocal social citizenship attracted Latin American and Caribbean immigrants who were uprooted from the support of hometown networks and comforts by structural economic change or the public insecurity often associated with it. Thus, immigrants' experiences of life in Miami are negotiations of varied and overlapping forms of inclusion and exclusion within a place that is culturally inscribed by and socially constructed across multiple geographic locations.

In the remainder of this chapter, we present the basis of the arguments developed in the book. We address how neoliberalism reshuffled contexts of human insecurity that conditioned Miami immigrants' decisions about departure and settlement. We address Miami's transformation from a segregated southern US resort to the "Capital of Latin America" and the ensuing development of the city's income structure, ethnic composition, and residential segregation patterns. We pay close attention to how earlier Cubans shaped the cultural and political institutions met by the immigrants in our study, and how media-inspired imaginings of the city as welcoming to immigrants and Latinos/as specifically structured migratory pathways. We lay the groundwork for discussions of discrimination in a minority-majority city with immigrants making up 51 percent of the population, but also in which Cuban and Cuban American culture prevails, even though Cubans and Cuban Americans are only one-third of the population.[33] Finally, we turn to immigrants' multilocal strategies for gaining ontological security and argue that cross-border yet local strategies of social participation and membership represent forms of substantive citizenship.

Globalization and the Creation of Neoliberal Environments of Insecurity

The links between immigration and security have intensified in an era in which nation-states are shifting their economies toward greater integration. As Douglas S. Massey, Jorge Durand, and Nolan J. Malone have shown, these currents are working against each other.[34] Integration projects such as the North American Free Trade Agreement (NAFTA) increased labor emigration pressures at the same time that US border enforcement efforts skyrocketed.

The heightened perception of physical insecurity in the United States after 2001 is a context familiar to many countries around the world.[35] From the 1980s until the 2000s, many of those in our sample experienced various forms of human insecurity in their countries of origin. But the prevalence of insecurity in countries such as the Dominican Republic, Peru, and Mexico did not just involve threats from external agents of violence or even enemies from within. Many immigrants faced insecurity rooted in neoliberal economic policies that had multiple effects over economic, social, and, ultimately, political life in their home countries, as well as in the receiving environment of Miami.

Global Economic Integration and Structural Adjustment in Latin America

US-led banking responses to the foreign debt crisis in Latin America and the Caribbean in the 1980s and 1990s pressured national governments to enact structural transformations and implement economic policies rooted in laissez-faire market economics. Many of these changes undermined formal sector employment with good wages and health benefits. Specifically, while slashing social programs, governments ended trade protections for domestic business and sold off state assets, ultimately encouraging market consolidation with fewer firms and, consequently, fewer well-paying jobs. These policies uprooted people in the middle economic sectors who had relied on the state or domestic business for jobs. For those in rural areas, trade agreements lowered barriers to mass-produced corn and other grains from the United States, while cutting domestic crop subsidies. This loss of government protection stimulated large commercial agricultural production but destabilized small-farm economies.

Immigration as a family survival strategy resulted from lost employment or farm income, of course, but other causes were less obvious. First, employment in the urban informal sector grew; people had to work more hours for less pay and with fewer risk-diminishing benefits such as health insurance or pensions. Additionally, those with jobs saw their aspirations for career ascendancy put on hold or dashed. Perceptions of economic stagnation and worries about future economic security motivated a number of younger and midcareer people in our sample to emigrate to improve their current conditions and their chances for future security.

Second, debt increased while the ability to pay diminished. Alberto Mayol identifies a cultural component to indebtedness in his study of the Chilean student protests of 2011 that we noted as important to our study participants—social stigma and the equation of indebtedness to sin.[36] While we did not interview Chileans for our qualitative sample, Peruvians and Colombians in our study spoke of guilt and public humiliation associated with being late with payments.

An additional source of insecurity related to neoliberal transformations is that many families that were already stretched thin prior to the 1990s had little savings, crop insurance, or other support when faced with natural disaster or climate transformations, and this fragility was compounded by weakened state capacity for response, planning, and prevention in the face of budget cuts and deregulated farm markets. With little or no safety net, Central Americans headed to the United States in record numbers when neither state nor international responses could compensate for destroyed crops and business income after Hurricane Mitch in 1998 and Hurricane Stan in 2005, and extended drought has become a source of immigration pressure from northern Mexico. A series of hurricanes prior to the 2010 earthquake in Haiti created conditions that drove many there to seek residence elsewhere. Finally, along with economic insecurity, public insecurity including crime and police abuses increased in urban areas across the region. Among some of the less recognized causes for emigration, experts identify military demobilization without adequate employment opportunities, youth gang members deported from the United States to home countries they barely knew, and worsening conditions for youths as parents took on two jobs and public school education deteriorated. A number of people in our study mentioned these forms of insecurity as contributing factors in their decisions to migrate. Not until the Chinese import commodity boom of the mid-2000s did many countries stabilize, but crime and public insecurity in urban areas were still serious threats, the financial prospects of those in the middle economic sectors remained fragile thanks in part to unrelenting economic inequality, and the poor had lost a decade or more of social progress.

The social weaknesses of neoliberalism carried political implications that affected Miami's immigration stream. Mobilization of the increasingly detached poor, working class, and lower middle sectors affected conditions in a number of countries, each with their own particular political environments. In Haiti, which is particularly important to Miami, upper-class resentment against the increasing populism of President Jean-Bertrand Aristide resulted in a coup that removed him from power. In Venezuela, and a few years later in Ecuador, professionals faced a surge in populist policies and antirich rhetoric from elected presidents. In Colombia, Mexico, and more recently Puerto Rico, political and drug violence joined economic tightening, and in El Salvador and Honduras, violent youth gangs, many who were deported from the United States, complicated political and economic stabilization. All of these countries faced crime surges in the 1990s and early 2000s, compounding feelings of insecurity.

Macrolevel processes created "environments of insecurity"[37] in which potential emigrants and their families either accepted the instability and the ensuing threats to sustainability in their countries or left in search of more secure and stable environments. Some of the immigrants in our study were detached from their homeland economies and social contexts as the Cold War ended and countries with state-centered capitalist systems began to transition. Free market economies with electoral democracy emerged, but with concentrated wealth and economic opportunity, as well as deficits in democratic accountability, representation, and equal protection under the law. The model of deregulated markets, free trade, and elections without similar emphasis on social justice outcomes, which were assumed to be natural outcomes of liberalized states and markets, was supposed to solve the international debt crisis of the 1980s by tying the region to a form of laissez-faire capitalism that the United States and Western Europe had rarely experienced in their histories, but that dominated thinking in international financial organizations in the 1980s. Economic adjustment slashed support for human development, privatized state firms, and eventually balanced budgets in many countries. But, by the early 2000s, neoliberalism and elections that did not guarantee equal political representation, social opportunities, or the due process of law for poor majorities, women, or ethnic minorities had in most places led to greater wealth concentration with increased or stubbornly high inequality and opened the region to global financial shocks that produced the Tequila Effect in Mexico (1994), the Samba Effect in Brazil (1999), the Tango Effect in Argentina (2001), and other external jolts to real wages and dreams of economic well-being. Some countries made the economic transition better. However, neoliberalism exacerbated a crisis of labor incorporation and fueled criminal violence into the 2000s by increasing underemployment and perpetuating inequality.[38] The public security apparatus of the region did not transition well, and human rights abuses and corruption were common. Latin America became one of the most violent regions in the world.[39]

Economic shifts eroded financial and social benefits as well as social rights, especially for the middle class.[40] Violence increased the sense of risk. These changes, in turn, led to the deterioration of life chances (to varying degrees, depending on the country), thereby creating environments of insecurity.[41]

"Environments of Insecurity" and Emigration

Ibrahim Sirkeci argues that an environment of insecurity serves as an "opportunity framework for those who [have] existing migration 'plans.'"[42] We argue that neoliberalism's effects on social infrastructure and public safety nets across Latin America and the Caribbean engendered various forms of conflict and instability that affected the people living there and exacerbated insecurity. Two factors in particular contributed to the creation of environments of insecurity: material conditions characterized by poverty, deprivation, or conflict, and nonmaterial environments that generated fear of persecution or discriminatory practices.[43]

Protection of human rights and access to resources to meet basic needs are central to human security.[44] We see how neoliberal policies created environments of insecurity in the experiences of study participants who reported that their families experienced threats to their abilities to secure these rights and resources. Threats took the form of economic and social insecurity (e.g., job loss, downward mobility, and discrimination based on age, gender, race, and sexual orientation) and physical insecurity (e.g., exposure to crime, violence, and political unrest).

The conditions that created threats to human security also eroded the sustainability of kinship groups. Based on Giddens's work, scholars have argued that globalization and migration can undermine important relationships and result in feelings of ontological insecurity and existential anxiety.[45] As stated earlier, the ability to maintain trust and confidence in individuals and relationships as well as in institutions is essential to avoiding existential anxiety.[46] In Latin America, social trust is low and social exclusion has broadened outward from traditionally excluded minorities. The Inter-American Development Bank reported in 2007 that after twenty-five years of neoliberalism and advances in the procedures of electoral democracy, formal political inclusion in elections had increased, while social inclusion had "mixed results":

Who are the excluded in Latin America and the Caribbean today? Certainly they include members of traditionally stigmatized groups such as blacks, the indigenous and women. But they also include people who have been left on the sidelines as their societies speed along in the race to modern, globalized economies. . . . For instance, women have been included in some dimensions (formal political representation and education) but are still segregated in worse jobs than men. Contrastingly, entire sectors of the population have been excluded from formal jobs and their associated social insurance protection by slow growth and unemployment.[47]

In these particular contexts, the individuals and families in our study deliberated on the decision to emigrate. Migration decisions are multidimensional, often involving overlapping concerns reflecting a mix of structural constraints and individual and household considerations.[48] The formation of environments of insecurity shaped the context in which our participants' migration decisions were made. The initial goal of Miamians we interviewed who arrived after 1986 was to achieve forms of security for themselves and their spatially extended families.

In the mid-2000s, regional development shifted away from the United States and neoliberalism. Social democratic governments emerged and benefited from Chinese raw materials imports. Some Miamians returned to more institutionalized democracies in Brazil, Uruguay, Argentina, and Peru, where economic security seemed more attainable. Other governments espoused populism, socialism, and personalized presidential power, stimulating new flows of immigrants to Miami from Venezuela and Ecuador. Colombians, Nicaraguans, Dominicans, Puerto Ricans, Hondurans, and Mexicans continued to come in search of greater security.

Although migration is undertaken to achieve a greater sense of human security along multiple measures, immigrants found their presence was sometimes seen as a threat to current US residents' perceived ontological security through multiculturalism and, more broadly, to US national security.

Securitization of US Immigration Policy

Immigration has long threatened US residents' sense of cultural identity, challenging an Anglo, Protestant, English-speaking narrative of the nation with multicultural perspectives, experiences, and norms. The increase in the number of Spanish-speaking immigrants to the United States in recent decades has exacerbated these xenophobic fears.[49] In 2004, Harvard scholar Samuel Huntington gave a scientific stamp of approval to these perceived threats when he argued that Hispanics posed a challenge for the United States, in that a large number of immigrants could dominate cities such as Los Angeles and Miami, causing a "cultural division between Hispanics and Anglos," which could become "the most serious cleavage in U.S. society."[50]

Warnings of an immigrant takeover often cited Miami as the example the rest of the nation should avoid, as congressional representative Tom Tancredo did while seeking the 2008 Republican presidential nomination. Tancredo stated many times that a high immigrant-receiving area such as Miami "[had] become a Third World country." According to Tancredo, "the sheer size and number of ethnic enclaves devoid of any English and dominated by foreign cultures is widespread," and "until America gets serious about demanding assimilation, this problem will continue to spread."[51] When then Florida governor Jeb Bush, a Republican who is married to a Mexican and lives in Miami, protested, Tancredo responded he was calling "attention to a real problem that [could not] be easily dismissed through politically correct happy talk."[52]

Although Cubans and Cuban Americans are often considered to be among the most advantaged US Latino groups, these xenophobic fears target Latino and Cuban culture given how prevalent these groups are in Miami. As much as Cuban migration has been thought of as an "actively supported" population movement,[53] Cubans are not immune to Latino racialization, including perceptions of Latino (or Cuban) spaces as threats to the nation's cultural identity.

John Tirman argues that "migration has long had security implications, but mostly linked to 'social' security—jobs, welfare, etc."[54] Immigrants have been perceived as drains on local and state coffers, this perception resulting in proposals such as Proposition 187 in California (the "Save Our State" initiative) that aimed to bar undocumented immigrants from receiving public services (including public education). Immigrants were deemed to be "undeserving" of benefits, a theme that also surfaced in the Illegal Immigration Reform and Immigrant Responsibility Act of 1996, which made undocumented immigrants ineligible for social security benefits even if they paid the required taxes. That same year, the Personal Responsibility and Work Opportunity Reconciliation Act of 1996 also passed, essentially barring undocumented immigrants from most federal, state, and local public benefits, in addition to denying federal assistance to millions of *legal* immigrants.[55] Some even called for sharp reductions to the number of legal immigrants to the United States during this time.[56]

Anthropologist Leo Chavez argues that anti-immigrant discourses in the 1990s targeted anyone who looked, acted, or spoke like a foreigner and expressed nativist anger about demographic changes that were viewed as a "threat to the 'nation' that is conceived of as a singular, predominantly Euro-American, English-speaking culture." He continues, "By eliminating or reducing these stigmatized groups, immigration reform would, in theory, 'do something' about the source of the 'problems' facing US citizens, problems in the economy, education system, health care, and even the relations of local governments with the federal government."[57]

If, in the mid-twentieth century, immigrants symbolized this country's immigrant heritage, then by the latter part of the twentieth century, migration was linked to US residents' increased sense of insecurity due to cultural and social changes, which were perceived as threats to the established order and ethnic worldview. By the early 2000s, though, unease from growing multiculturalism was compounded by "the threat of terrorism" that additionally framed the immigration debate.[58] Efforts to link immigration to national security efforts are not new,[59] dating all the way back to the Alien and Sedition Act of 1798.[60] In the current period, restrictive immigration measures enacted in the mid to late 1990s as a response to the identification of immigrants as cultural and social threats facilitated the creation of the legislative infrastructure that has recast immigrants after 9/11 as threats to US national security.[61]

In sum, nativism, xenophobia, and general hostility toward newcomers are not exclusively modern phenomena, nor are they particular to the United States.[62] But, just as fearful natives or calculating politicians have called Miami a multicultural nightmare, the city is understood quite differently in the context of the Americas as a whole.

Marketing Miami: Social Remittances and the (Latino) American Dream

Portraits of comfortable lifestyles in the United States and the status symbols deployed in the marketing of US products and consumption practices are transmitted throughout the world through global media and the export of US cultural products. Miami, when viewed as a city of leisure friendly to immigrants, has its own place among these circulations. In recent decades, the promotional machinery that created a "Magic City" from a city of racial segregation and hurricanes has modernized and internationalized.[63] The glamour of Miami's promotional past fused with a Latin American cultural ethos projected itself across the hemisphere through transnational media spectacles aimed at Latin America and the US Latino market. Global media representations of Miami exported the idea of the Latino American Dream, seen in high-profile showcases of Latinos such as Emilio and Gloria Estefan, the Latin Grammys, telenovelas filmed in Miami, and parades of Latino pop star weddings and childbirths featured in glossy magazines such as *¡Hola!* Once unhooked from homeland safety nets, some immigrants to Miami followed discourses that synthesized the promotional frames embedded in Miami's "Magic City" and "Capital of Latin America" monikers.

The ideology of the American Dream and the marketing of this dream to Latin Americans are both cultural products and social remittances that, along with visits from seemingly "successful" immigrants back home, are collectively thought to entice nonmigrants to enter into global mobility circuits.[64] Mediated or interpersonally transmitted stories of the successful Latino population have continued to lure immigrants to Miami in what is now considered to be a process of "cumulative causation" in which migratory flows are sustained regardless of whether the original motives for migration remain. This phenomenon helps to explain why the more members of different Latin American communities gain US migration experience, the more likely nonmigrants from those very communities will embark on their first trip.[65]

Though, for some, the repatriated American Dream is a misrepresentation of what life in the United States is like, the prevailing assumption prior to immigration is that hard work results in greater levels of economic and social security and material comfort. Moreover, potential immigrants are exposed to other US ideologies. Among these is the notion that, for women in particular, the United States offers opportunities that may not be available in their home countries. As Alejandra indicated, the idea that age might not hinder women's opportunities in the United States to the same extent as in Colombia reinforces meritocratic and egalitarian ideals. Thus, information streams from media and immigrant relatives or friends can create hope that migration will yield higher levels of human security across its many dimensions.

Immigrants' willingness to pursue the American Dream, which rests on assumptions of equal opportunity and perceived access to resources in the United States, suggests that immigrants place confidence in US meritocratic ideals. Thus, migration represents the embodiment of trust that immigrants' efforts will be rewarded and of faith in a system of equal opportunity that is carried by social remittances and marketed through global media. This contrasts with their experiences of stagnated social mobility in their home countries.

As Giddens argues, this trust becomes a form of emotional inoculation against the existential anxieties that might develop from the process of contemplating migration and the experience of migration itself. This trust "allows the individual to sustain hope and courage in the face of whatever debilitating circumstances she or he might later confront."[66] Alejandra's comments about her expectations before migrating illustrate these expectations: "What was I expecting? That it would be easier to accomplish things; I was going to have a good income." Overall, for immigrants headed to Miami, one of the appeals was the idea that success stories indeed existed in the city, with the Cuban success story in particular being held up as a model for other immigrants to emulate, and the city's cultural diversity served as a magnet to populations who wished to follow in their footsteps.

To further understand the context that greets contemporary immigrants to Miami, however, we need to examine the city's past and its evolution into the multiethnic, global metropolis it is today. We look at the history of immigrant incorporation in the city and focus on its two largest national-origin populations to illustrate the different trajectories immigrants' experiences can take. These trajectories depend on various factors, among them, the countries from which they emigrate and the policies that receive them upon arrival.

Origins of Exclusion in Miami

Most studies of immigrants and their modes of incorporation in Greater Miami have focused on Cubans and Cuban Americans, although others have contrasted the arrival of groups such as Haitians and Nicaraguans to the Cuban success story.[67] Immigrants arriving in Miami face the material and ideological legacies of a US racial project that outdates and, in some important ways, has outlived the Cuban transformation of the city. Miami's history includes material and ideological legacies of white supremacy that were fairly typical of many southern US cities, but with the distinction that civil rights era reforms, which politically empowered African Americans in urban areas across the South in the late twentieth century, had a different outcome in Miami: they helped to empower early waves of Cubans who arrived with high levels of human capital, entrepreneurial skills, and an ability to frame themselves socially as white.

Racial Segregation and Racial Projects

Throughout its history, Miami has been among the most racially segregated cities in the United States, a condition that spanned two decades of riots (the 1960s and 1980s) and that lasted long after white supremacist doctrines were officially removed from federal and local law.[68] Through the majority of the twentieth century, African Americans in Miami were confined to overcrowded neighborhoods by legal statute, federal government housing policies, and real estate practices that drew a "red line" around areas in which blacks were allowed to purchase homes. The use of extreme violence against blacks to stop neighborhood desegregation prompted federal investigations as late as the 1950s. When Cubans arrived en masse in the 1960s, white elites had finally achieved a three-decade-long project of removing African Americans from the original "Colored Town" area west of the central business district to a "second ghetto" that was created with federal funds five miles away around a housing project called, ironically enough, Liberty Square.[69]

For years, local civic leaders wanted to remove blacks from the city's original black neighborhood, now called Overtown, so that Miami's business district could expand. The construction of the interstate system in the county in the late 1960s gave them the opportunity, and an estimated 40,000 African Americans, Bahamians, and other black Miamians were displaced from the commercial and cultural heart of black life, also called "The Harlem of the South." The first riots in black areas of Miami surged in the neighborhood of Liberty City in the 1960s. Many in both white and black elite circles blamed Cuban immigrants for labor force displacement, but later evidence cast doubt on this claim. Cubans built their own residential and economic enclaves in the 1960s and 1970s rather than displacing blacks, but the difference in treatment between repressed African Americans and government support for Cuban newcomers heightened the sense of injustice.[70]

Legacies of Miami's legally enshrined white racism continue to be manifested in residential patterns, municipal boundaries, and electoral districts. We argue that these are the outward signs of racial projects of the state, or what Michael Omi and Howard Winant refer to as worldviews linking representations and significations of the human body with organizational structures and institutional forms that naturalize a social order based upon body characteristics.[71] Racial projects that guided Miami's foundation in the early part of the twentieth century remain most visible in residential living patterns (where blacks live in more segregated areas compared to other groups), as well as court-ordered electoral districts based upon segregated neighborhoods as a way to ensure "minority" representation on governmental boards. As we will see in Chapter 5, redistricting produced districts that some politicians claimed for their own ethnicity over the years, whether as an "African American," a "Cuban," or an "American" (read: white) seat. This facilitated the political incorporation of Cubans and African Americans in local politics on a geographic basis but disadvantaged later immigrant groups. While in the 2000s, Cubans were overrepresented in relation to their percentage of the overall population, redistricting also pitted African American candidates against Haitian ones and may have contributed to the withdrawal of Anglos and Jews into small, newly incorporated municipalities, such as Aventura and Palmetto Bay (incorporated in 1995 and 2002, respectively).

The Cuban transformation of Miami occurred within this set of racialized political institutions, flowing through them rather than radically altering them.[72] In other words, US political, governmental, and educational institutions indeed became more populated with Cubans and Cuban Americans, and the percentage of African Americans in these organizations also greatly increased, but the racialized institutional structures themselves lived on.

Although US institutional structures remained intact in most cases, the Cuban transformation of Miami included cultural shifts with implications for the feel of inclusiveness in the city compared to the rest of the country. Speaking Spanish or accented English no longer was a marker of *alienness* in Miami. Black-white dichotomies in US racial codes were also blurred, though never erased, and other forms of national-origin, class-based, and legal hierarchies supplemented them.

Immigrant Incorporation in a Racially Segregated City

Cuban immigrants in Miami transformed from a refugee community into one that, over the years, eventually came to lead many arenas of local social, cultural, and political life.[73] As the seminal work on Miami, Alejandro Portes and Alex Stepick's *City on the Edge* documents the rise of Cubans as a locally focused political and cultural force in the 1980s.[74] Through their opposition to xenophobic political initiatives, the educational and entrepreneurial experiences they brought from Cuba, the household structure of earlier waves, rates of female labor force participation, and the character loans received from coethnics in banks, Miami's Cubans developed an enclave where the culture and institutions of Cuban society were re-created in the United States.[75]

The geography of race in Miami was set when Cubans arrived. In a segregated city and county, they settled in an area south of Overtown, later known as Little Havana, and in the working-class white city of Hialeah. As their numbers grew, Cubans expanded around the perimeters of Overtown and Liberty City, where blacks had been legally confined until the 1950s and then extralegally corralled through violence when they tried to move "across the color line" into white neighborhoods.[76] While Cuban households came to mix with those of native-born whites as their income levels grew, they rarely entered black neighborhoods.[77]

At the same time, the new immigrants had to negotiate discourses among the native white population that oscillated between defining them as an alien invasion or as a hardworking, entrepreneurial group and "one of us." Referred to as the Golden Exiles, the initial waves of Cuban immigrants arrived in the early 1960s with education and entrepreneurial experience.[78] In contrast to immigrants from other countries, and to help boost entrepreneurial activities in the enclave, Cuban immigrants arriving prior to 1980 received unprecedented government aid to resettle with the intent of draining the Castro regime of human capital and creating a "symbolic showcase" to promote capitalist ideology in the Caribbean.[79]

Some elite members of Miami's business community worked to create a positive discourse about the new arrivals. White business elites benefited from the 1960s construction boom that occurred after the exiles' arrival and had acquaintances among the exiles because of Miami-Havana business dealings prior to the Cuban Revolution.[80] These factors and the exile community's business success convinced elite whites to define Cubans as one of "us." The white welcome suited Cuban immigrants who "wished for acceptance in a racially divided, color conscious society," a description that particularly fit Miami, which was at that time under court order to desegregate its schools after being found in violation of the 1964 Civil Rights Act in 1969.[81]

Initial waves of Cubans in Miami also were contrasted with Afro-Cuban coethnics in Tampa and other Latin American and Caribbean groups (e.g., Mexicans and Puerto Ricans) across the United States, who had been legally racialized as black in other parts of the country.[82] Blackness became synonymous with being racially inassimilable, and in some cases, Latino groups such as Mexican Americans were considered "alien citizens."[83]

By the early 1980s, US relations with Cuba and the sociopolitical profile of Cuban immigrants had changed. In this period, about 125,000 Cubans, many considered to be poor and nonwhite, arrived via an exile-organized boat lift from the port of Mariel. Differences in demographics and political experience, as well as poor US press treatment linking them to crime and the emptying of Castro's jails, weakened the Cuban in-group solidarity that had helped create an enclave economy.[84] The negative press discourse also turned the entrepreneurial and political capacity of early Cubans toward politics in Miami through the process of reactive identity formation. The notion that ethnic identities intensify when individuals perceive prejudice and discrimination foreshadowed trends to come,[85] including Cubans' political transformation of Miami in the 1990s, remaking the city into a cultural pole of attraction for Spanish speakers.

Since 1995, the automatic legal status enjoyed by earlier groups of Cubans has been guaranteed only for a small group of visa seekers selected by lottery in Cuba and for those ingenious enough to make it to US soil. Public assistance also has been greatly reduced. Today, daily life in Miami, including for recent Cuban immigrants, involves navigating through the formal and informal mechanisms of inclusion and exclusion in a city that remains anchored in US racial projects of the racist past and "colorblind" present. Later-arriving Cubans as well as non-Cuban immigrants often find the institutional support mechanisms that were extended to Cubans in previous decades lacking. The reception of Haitians, the second-largest immigrant group in Miami-Dade County, provides the starkest contrast.

Miami's Haitian community was small until deteriorating conditions in that country spawned a mass exodus by boat toward the Bahamas and South Florida in the late 1970s.[86] Special programs were set up to quickly deport the Haitians, and the Reagan administration deployed the Coast Guard to stop immigrant arrivals at sea for the first time in US history.[87] In a second wave of mass immigration during the political instability and violence that characterized the postdictatorship political transition in Haiti from 1992 to 1995, 67,190 Haitians were intercepted at sea and returned to Haiti.[88]

Haitians met a cold US reception in the 1980s and 1990s, facing pervasive negative stereotypes, a stagnant economy, and a federal government resolved to block entry and settlement.[89] Trends continued into the 2000s, when after September 11, 2001, Attorney General John Ashcroft implied terrorists might pose as Haitians in order to sneak into the country by boat. He ordered Haitians who passed the standard "credible fear threshold" for political asylum to be detained until their court hearings, while immigrants from other countries in similar situations were typically paroled to the community.[90] Lawyers representing Haitians met restricted visitation hours and scarce visitation space.[91] More recently, with about 55,000 Haitians approved for family reunification visas but still facing up to seven years' wait on the first anniversary of the devastating earthquake of January 2010, community advocates made the comparison to Cuban émigrés approved for expedited family reunification three years earlier based upon, among other things, urgent humanitarian reasons.

By the 2010s, Greater Miami's Haitian community had created its own civic organizations, advocacy groups, and bloc of local officials. With professional and middle-income Haitians becoming more numerous, the Haitian community in Miami has set down deep roots and grown to be the largest community of Haitians in the United States. However, recent decades have seen the growth of other immigrant communities in Miami, an issue we turn to next.

Immigrant Diversification and Multiethnicity in Miami, 1990s–2000s

The theoretical implications of *City on the Edge* suggest that an immigrant group (e.g., Cubans) could be successful in this country without having to acculturate to white, Anglo American society.[92] The analysis, however, uncovered troubled relations among whites, African Americans, and Cubans, questioning whether these groups would come together. Contemporary Miami is predominantly Latino, with Cubans making up the largest Latino group. The city overall, however, is increasingly multiethnic in its demographics. Table 1.1 shows how in 2012, Cubans were 35 percent of Miami-Dade's population, non-Hispanic whites were 16 percent, and non-Hispanic blacks made up 17 percent. Thirty of the remaining 32 percent consisted of mostly non-Cuban Latinos.

Cubans as a percent of the Latino population in Miami-Dade County declined slightly from 1990 to 2000, rising again in 2012. At the same time, the Hispanic-origin population was 64 percent of the total Miami-Dade

Table 1.1 Race and Hispanic Origin of Persons in Miami-Dade County
and Rate of Change, 1990, 2000, and 2012 (percentage)

Race/Ethnicity of Population	1990	% Change	2000	% Change	2012[a]
Non-Hispanic whites	30.2	−31.5	20.7	−22.7	16.1
Non-Hispanic blacks	19.1	−0.5	19.0	−10.0	17.1
Hispanics	49.2	16.5	57.3	12.2	64.3
Cuban	29.1	−0.7	28.9	19.4	34.5
Non-Cuban Hispanic	20.1	41.3	28.4	4.9	29.8
Other	1.4	21.4	1.7	11.8	1.9
Multiracial	n.a.	n.a.	1.4	−57.1	0.6
Total[b]	100.0		100.0		100.0

Sources: US Census Bureau (1990, 2000, 2012).
Notes: a. Given that the difference between the 2010 Decennial Census and the 2012 ACS ethnic group proportions are very similar, the most recent data are reported in this table.
b. Totals may not add up to 100% because of rounding.
n.a. = not applicable.

County population in 2012, up from 49 percent in 1990 and 57 percent in 2000. As Cubans continued relocation to Miami, the non-Cuban Latino and Caribbean populations increased at a much faster pace during the 1990s, slowing considerably in the 2000s, but not without diversifying the area (see Table 1.2).[93] The diversification of Miami's immigrant community includes South American professionals seeking physical, economic, and social security; Haitians seeking political stability and economic security; and Mexicans and Central Americans fleeing both physical violence and economic insecurity. Venezuelans, some of whom describe themselves as political exiles, flee all of the above.[94] Puerto Ricans, though technically not immigrants, undergo similar transitions by crossing cultural, racial, and geopolitical borders.[95] Their experiences are included for these reasons, particularly given the acceleration of migration in the 2000s due to government layoffs, a drug-related crime wave, and US job recruitment targeting professional and service workers. In addition to these groups, the ultra-wealthy from all over the world have homes in Miami, as do celebrities seeking the city's glitzy media spotlight. By the 2000s, Miami was no longer an ethnic enclave in the sense of an economically and geographically bounded ethnic neighborhood, but rather an immigrant metropolis where Hispanics dominate and African Americans and other blacks are residentially concentrated. White non-Hispanics also cluster but mix much more with Hispanics than blacks.[96]

In the mid-1990s, scholars debated the implications of increasing immigrant concentration because it appeared to be related to the acceleration of out-migration from the city of low-income and less-skilled domestic internal migrants, leading to what William Frey called a "demographic balkanization" across many regions of the country.[97] Patricia Zavella researched how global economic restructuring led to similar characterizations of California's demographic transition and a sense of "paradise lost" by white citizens in the 1990s.[98] "White flight" occurred in parts of California given the cultural anxieties caused by increasing Latin American populations. The patterns of emigration of whites from Miami mirror these dynamics.

Rather than use the term *balkanization*, which suggests the entrenchment of ethnic groups, we argue that Miami and perhaps other minority-majority cities instead have been *ghettoized* in the collective imagination of the US citizenry, leading to the racialization of places in the discourse of conservatives and others alarmed by demographic shifts. Thus, immigrants are not necessarily closing off their communities, but instead native whites and blacks who perceive the browning of Miami further reinforce patterns of out-migration from the city. What is "new" about this trend is, according to Frey, "its geographic scope." In contrast to segregation patterns across neighborhoods or between cities and suburbs, "the emergence of entire metropolitan areas or labor market regions that are distinct from the rest of the country in their race, ethnic, and demographic makeup introduces a new dimension."[99] Thus, particular regions of the country are becoming racialized spaces.

Miami's cultural diversity and the political ascendancy of Cubans are not lost on immigrants who have come since the late 1980s. Immigrants we interviewed who had been in other areas of the United States reported many experiences of white racism prior to relocating to Miami.[100] Jaime, a forty-seven-year-old mortgage officer, traveled around the United States for ten years before settling in Miami in the early 2000s. The potential for greater cultural acceptance drew him to Miami: "People are more friendly here. It makes it easier to be in the United States. When you land in places like New England, the first day I arrived there and rented a car. . . . I put the date with the day before the month . . . [and] the woman said, 'What did you put here?' And I said, 'In my country we put the day first.' And then she tells me, 'Now you are in America!'" In other parts of the country, Jaime believed, "They are always insulting you." He continued, "When they see I look more American than Hispanic but I had an accent, they would ask, 'Where are you from?' And I [answered], 'Dominican.' Oh, you noted the difference, the rejection." Jaime had lived in Connecticut, Rhode Island, Maryland, and Virginia. "And when I came here to Florida, Florida is cosmopolitan. People are from all over, from Peru, from Ecuador. We accept each other and exploit each other every day."

The perceived acceptance of immigrant groups in Miami does not necessarily mean that one finds racial or ethnic mixing or even coethnic solidarity. The paradox that Jaime lays out is twofold: He rejects discrimination from whites, stating that, in Miami, he feels better. Yet the paradox is re-

Table 1.2 Select Groups by National Origin in Miami-Dade County and Percent Change, 1990–2000 and 2000–2012

Country of Origin	1990		Change in Population (percentage)	2000		Change in Population (percentage)	2012[a]	
	Number	Percentage		Number	Percentage		Number	Percentage
Cuba	561,868	29.0	15.8	650,601	28.9	37.4	894,168	34.5
Haiti	n.d.	n.d.	n.a.	95,669	4.2	28.6	123,001	4.7
Dominican Republic	23,475	1.2	55.3	36,454	1.6	78.3	64,991	2.5
Puerto Rico	68,534	3.5	17.0	80,327	3.6	12.8	90,646	3.5
Mexico	23,193	1.2	64.3	38,095	1.7	53.0	58,291	2.2
Central America	119,534	6.2	7.8	128,903	5.7	73.0	222,992	8.6
Nicaragua	74,244	3.8	-6.7	69,257	3.1	63.9	113,501	4.4
Honduras	18,102	0.9	48.2	26,829	1.2	100.1	53,691	2.1
El Salvador	7,339	0.4	24.2	9,115	0.4	132.8	21,218	0.8
Guatemala	8,242	0.4	17.4	9,676	0.4	86.4	18,035	0.7
Panama	6,729	0.3	-12.9	5,863	0.3	40.5	8,235	0.3
Costa Rica	4,743	0.2	-0.8	4,706	0.2	66.5	7,835	0.3
Other Central America	135	0.0	2,460.7	3,457	0.2	-86.2	477	0.0
South America	108,498	5.6	51.4	164,228	7.3	91.6	314,640	12.1
Colombia	53,582	2.8	30.8	70,066	3.1	85.5	129,981	5.0
Venezuela	5,846	0.5	119.3	21,593	1.0	122.4	48,025	1.9
Peru	16,452	0.8	41.8	23,327	1.0	105.0	47,811	1.8
Argentina	8,585	0.4	55.4	13,341	0.6	104.7	27,312	1.1
Ecuador	7,986	0.4	32.2	10,560	0.5	104.1	21,554	0.8
Chile	7,928	0.4	-0.2	7,910	0.4	34.4	10,632	0.4
Uruguay	1,482	0.1	23.4	1,829	0.1	251.7	6,432	0.2
Bolivia	2,309	0.1	4.7	2,418	0.1	148.0	5,997	0.2
Paraguay	166	0.0	161.4	434	0.0	155.5	1,109	0.0
Brazil	n.d.	n.d.	n.a.	9,880	0.4	56.2	15,432	0.6
Other South America	161	0.0	1,682.6	2,870	0.1	-87.6	355	0.0

(continues)

Table 1.2 continued

Country of Origin	1990		Change in Population (percentage)	2000		Change in Population (percentage)	2012[a]	
	Number	Percentage		Number	Percentage		Number	Percentage
Other Hispanic	44,498	2.3	356.2	203,009	9.0	–82.2	36,232	1.4
Jamaica	n.d.	n.d.	n.a.	41,576	1.8	–5.7	39,217	1.5
Bahamas	n.d.	n.d.	n.a.	8,924	0.4	–5.0	8,477	0.3
Total Latin America and the Caribbean[b]	1,061,669	54.8	35.8	1,442,019	64.0	27.4	1,837,223	70.9
Total	1,937,094		16.3	2,253,362		15.0	2,591,035	

Sources: US Census Bureau (1990, 2000, 2012).
Notes: a. ACS data are based on estimates. As such, the total sum of the estimates for individual countries of origin may not match the estimate for the particular region in which the country is located.
   b. Total numbers include countries of origin not included in this table (e.g., Virgin Islands).
   n.d. = no data.
   n.a. = not applicable.

vealed in his statement, "We accept each other and exploit each other every day," a statement illustrative of the notion of inclusionary discrimination in which "racial and ethnic inclusion [exist] alongside discriminatory practices."[101] The question is not so much about whether racial exclusion exists; the issue is, rather, that race sets the *terms* of inclusion.

In addition to immigrant diversification, since the late 1980s, many other national and global developments transpired, forming the contextual layers undergirding the contemporary experiences of US immigrants. On top of the immigration debates of recent decades, the city also reflects economic bifurcation and the compression of the US middle class.

Economic Polarization, Labor Market Segmentation, and Neoliberal City Policies

As the gateway to the Americas, Miami's economic and ethnic structures exhibit patterns associated with a global city, revealing a confluence of cultures and peoples that includes highly mobile executives and professionals earning high wages (who presumably have legal status) and others who are placebound as a result of their unauthorized status or lack of financial resources. The latter usually work in low-wage jobs and oftentimes cannot transfer their occupational statuses from their home countries, leading to a city of contrasts where class has multiple dimensions and where poverty rates are among the highest in the United States. In this context, finding a middle-class job is hard, although more than economic structures are at work. Economic troubles occur when immigrants cannot transfer professional credentials and educational degrees, or when language impedes passage of licensing requirements, in addition to the issue of whether one has the legal residency necessary to work in a professional job or seek higher education. In the case of women, who may come as dependents of their husbands recruited through occupational preference categories, they may not have work permits, rendering them confined to the domestic sphere of the home in spite of their former occupational statuses and levels of education. For those who do attain work permits, gendered occupations and inequality in pay result in greater levels of economic vulnerability among older women in particular, and this vulnerability most negatively affects women heading single-parent households.

Many immigrants in our sample felt that the United States was indeed a country where they could work; however, the nature of their jobs in low-skill service industries left no time or energy to focus on family or social relationships. In spite of full-time work, and in some cases due to barriers to finding jobs that would provide sufficient work hours, some felt misled by what they heard about the American Dream because their hard work did not substantially raise their standard of living beyond the status of the working poor. Among others entering with high levels of human capital, many felt their material goals were seriously compromised by downward mobility in other interrelated statuses, including lost political status (denial of political voice, fear of incarceration, and threat of deportation), deteriorated economic and social class status (downward mobility for professionals or the homeland upper middle class), and a perception of lower racial standing when compared to mixed race societies of the Caribbean and regions farther south. Altogether, the downgrading of social statuses led to feelings of despair.

In this regard, while many immigrants fled environments of insecurity stemming from the effects of neoliberalism, they entered a global city that was also affected by economic globalization and was developing equally troubling sources of insecurity. As Jan Lin has argued, parallels exist between the neoliberal city of the global North and neoliberalism in other countries, including "devolution from public financing of urban infrastructure and services in favor of privatization and public-private partnerships." He adds that this shift is "akin to the neoliberal economic strategies pursued by developing countries that invite foreign investment through tax holidays and free trade zones."[102]

The toll that neoliberal policies have taken on the city and the visible signs of growing levels of income and wealth inequalities in Miami were noted by immigrants, particularly those who had established histories of periodically visiting Miami to see family members or as tourists prior to settlement. Even Alejandra, the Colombian immigrant whose narrative opened this chapter, noted the deterioration of the city's infrastructure when comparing the current situation with her recollection of Miami in trips prior to emigration. It was "completely different. . . . Now I see a very poor city."

In spite of being an immigrant herself, Alejandra and others in our sample often placed some of the blame for these negative changes on increased immigration to the area. "You did not see so many immigrants. . . . [I have witnessed] quite a lot of poverty and deterioration in Miami, a lot with respect to what it was before. . . . And [when I] speak to everyone about this so-called American Dream, [I hear] the struggles and the indecisions of all those who regret coming."

Alejandra also highlighted the positive side of migration and life in the United States: "The only good thing is that there are opportunities to work and that here, you do not grow old as quickly as you do in our countries, and that is an advantage." Although these quotes reveal the contradictions that Miami, and the United States in general, represent (e.g., struggle versus opportunity), they also illustrate feelings of ambivalence toward migration. Immigrants recognize how migration has brought greater security in some respects, but also how new forms of insecurity plague their lives in the global city. For some, these insecurities are financial; for others, they are related to temporary or liminal legal statuses; and for still others, they are tied to new experiences as racial minorities in a land that is not their own.

As a result of barriers to full incorporation, recent decades have ushered in accounts of immigrants who work hard to maintain ties to their former countries. Although disagreement can be found about whether these ties are sustained mostly by those barred from opportunities to integrate into US society, or if those who maintain such ties do so because maintaining them becomes easier with full US incorporation, a consensus exists that many immigrant groups maintain cross-border linkages through remittances, contact with home country family members and friends, travel, and, in some cases, transnational businesses. What remains unclear is whether and how these transnational connections enhance the lived experiences of being an immigrant in a US global city.

Cross-Border Imagination, Adaptation, and Belonging

Scholarly debates about the declining role of states in the lives of immigrants became popular in the 1990s. Arguing that immigrants bypassed national boundaries by maintaining linkages to their home societies, researchers showed how immigrants worked to sustain ties through visits, remittances, cross-border community development and involvement, and entrepreneurial activities. This research challenged scholars to depart from the "container" approach to immigrants' lives toward a more dynamic view of immigrant communities and the processes through which immigrants engaged in transnationalism as an exercise of agency to combat sources of structural constraints in their lives in the United States.[103] Although since then many argued that transnational formations are not new,[104] others maintained that advances in technology, communications, and travel compressed time and space, leading to new social formations and patterns of adaptation.[105]

Subsequent years witnessed a surge in research on immigrant transnationalism leading to new conclusions about the nature of immigrant adaptation in a globalized world. Transnational perspectives were employed to further understand the situation of immigrants from Haiti, the Dominican Republic, Mexico, and Puerto Rico, among many other areas.[106] More recently, Jorge Duany has argued that transnationalism takes shape based on the character of the sociopolitical ties between sending and receiving countries.[107] He argues that, although cultural border zones encompass both sending and receiving countries, legal boundaries entrench divisions among transnational families.[108] This complicated situation results in emotional experiences of transnationalism that, although sometimes overlooked, are garnering increasing attention.[109]

This point takes us back to Alejandra's story. The conditions under which she immigrated illustrate the costs of migration that are borne by transnational families and those who live with heavy hearts given the legal boundaries that separate kinship groups.[110] Alejandra left her two teenage children in Colombia so they could get a college education. As they embarked on the path of early adulthood, Alejandra was coming upon her fifties and faced life as an immigrant in a new country. Migration appears to be turning the normative stages of the life cycle on their heads, in particular, the way in which young adults, in contrast to their parents, experience these life stages. As Alejandra's children stayed close to home to further their educations rather than going abroad, as many do, Alejandra was the one who left the household to increase her status and fulfill her desire for independence, in contrast to many parents of adult immigrants, who remain in the home country when their children depart.

Just as experiences of life cycle stages are shifting, so too are the expectations of how to "accomplish" gendered social roles. Carlos, a Dominican immigrant, recounted in a focus group how migration changed the way he approached fatherhood: "I was raising my son and suddenly the decision is made to come here and there is a physical bond, a personal bond, that is going to break. . . . I did not want him to feel it. . , , So that is why I stay in touch. He is eight years old. . . , I call every day. I ask him, 'How are you? What did you do today? They said you did this or that thing at school. What did you have for supper? Did you eat your meat?'"

Although scholarship on transnationalism emphasizes the agency of actors over state controls, our research reveals that transnational families are subject to high levels of state regulation that (1) keep families apart because of legal restrictions on entry and reunification, (2) dissolve families' abilities to engage in face-to-face interactions and care work through restrictions on exit and reentry for certain kinds of visa holders and long delays in review of applications for family reunification visas, and (3) separate families through detention and deportation procedures, regardless if any member of the family has US citizenship. Similar to feminists' critiques of state efforts to control women's bodies, immigration policies are increasing state regulation of immigrant families.[111]

If we return to our opening discussion of homesickness and loneliness among migrants and consider how the lives of transnational families are increasingly subject to state restrictions, we see how the social, cultural, political, and economic trends we have discussed thus far come to weigh on the shoulders of immigrants and those they leave behind. In this book, we explore the nature of such struggles, particularly the emotional toll that ambivalence toward migration takes on immigrants and the strategies that immigrants employ to combat these dislocations. We illustrate how immigrants construct spaces of belonging that nurture lives that are embedded simultaneously within Miami and their places of origin. The richness of their trans-border experience varies, but their efforts clearly challenge conventional approaches to citizenship by weaving together practices of emplacement and belonging that blend the original and new home.

The strategies immigrants use to manage the emotional challenges of migration involve practices that make them feel as if they are socially and sensorially embedded in two places at the same time. These strategies enact a form of being and belonging, which we call *translocal social citizenship,* that claims simultaneous social membership in two local spaces.

Locality is a quality of place, or a "structure of feeling," associated with a locale. For geographer Doreen Massey, locality results from face-to-face encounters, or physical co-presence, in a place that is socially constructed and imbued with meaning through experience, the ongoing construction of social relations, and the shared feelings and understandings associated with those relationships. Another key thinker on space and place, anthropologist Arjun Appadurai, extends the notion of locality to include not only feelings associated with places that are socially constructed through face-to-face co-presence, but also virtual places created through the use of communications technologies or media that facilitate social immediacy and interaction in imaginary or virtual modes of co-presence. For Appadurai, locality has a variable quality that is constituted by social immediacy and interaction within a range of contexts that must be constantly "worked" to maintain their meaning.[112] Our research shows that immigrants' routine communicative and imaginative practices extend social relations and subjectivities from the place of origin to the place of settlement, creating a translocal place that fuses the relationships, emotions, and even bodily sensations associated with the original home with the immigrant destination.

Citizenship studies have recognized how immigrants make many claims for belonging beyond those of formal legal membership. Our use of social citizenship draws on notions of substantive citizenship, which bases claims to belonging on participation in the social life of a place rather than on a legal right.[113] Unlike formal citizenship claims, immigrants' substantive citizenship practices are usually translocal rather than transnational. Someone may be a formal citizen of Colombia living in the United States, but that person makes his or her strongest claims for social belonging and inclusion in intimate networks based in the Colombian hometown and Miami.

Translocal social citizenship thus emphasizes the lived condition of membership in intimate groups and cultural collectives that are emplaced in geographically separated locales that immigrants connect by engaging in everyday practices of belonging. The first set of practices we identify maintains immigrants' memberships in significant social groups from the place of origin by finding ways to sustain and nurture relationships, in person or through mediated forms of communication. Media scholars have argued that consumption of television content about faraway places can extract viewers from their geographical locations, at least through the imagination.[114] We find that many immigrants in Miami use synchronous communications technologies (texting, telephone, Internet video conferencing, or any social interaction that occurs in real time), as well as ethnic community or transnational media from the country of origin, to *remain* embedded in homeland cultures and comforts while residing elsewhere. The second set of practices involves experiencing the comfort and security of the natal home in Miami by engaging in translocal placemaking. Immigrants create sensorial approximations of the original home by engaging in habitual practices and attitudes associated with the original home, and creating group memberships based on shared cultural understandings or practices. Moreover, for many, the built and natural environments of Miami, as well as the circulations of people, products, and information between Miami and their home countries, enhance feelings of comfort and social belonging because they remind immigrants of original homes where individual and group identities were formed.

Immigrants from a wide variety of backgrounds expressed that Miami felt like home, in spite of the mechanisms of exclusion that they faced. Thus, if legal citizenship includes formal citizenship rights, such as legally protected presence, a public voice, the possibility of naturalization, and the possession of voting rights, then translocal practices are attempts to compensate for the ontological consequences of the denial of these things through constructions of social embeddedness in two places merged as one translocal home.

In this book, we build each chapter on the previous, culminating in our argument that citizenship is a multidimensional status of membership with varying layers of inclusionary and exclusionary categories and practices.[115] When barred from legal citizenship, Miami's residents have staked claim to substantive citizenship through their mundane participation in cultural collectives grounded in Miami, as well as in translocal networks of comfort and caring. Miami's structurally excluded residents enact membership by seeking paths through which to overcome exclusion. Some have obtained legal residency or formal citizenship, well-paid and meaningful work, or political incorporation through substantive representation by elected officials. Many, however, have not obtained the illusive goal they still call "el sueño americano," which, in immigrants' constructions of Miami, bundles their hopes for security, well-being, and social inclusion in the place they live in and sometimes call home.

In the following pages, we examine the cases of immigrants to Miami by empirically supporting the interpretations and arguments that we have laid out in this chapter and will develop throughout this book. The hierarchies, experiences, and strategies we identify should be viewed as a set of intersecting planes through which immigrants traverse. We hope that our research can shed light on immigrants' experiences of these journeys and the tools and strategies that they employ to navigate through the pockets of globalization, and in the process, seek and create meaningful lives in Miami and other global cities.

Data and Methodology

Making a Life in Multiethnic Miami contains descriptions of life in Miami from the perspective of participants' perceptions and experiences, immigration research spanning several disciplines, and insights from unstructured participant observation over the course of ten years by the authors, who all live or have lived in Miami. By placing immigrants' lived experiences and expressed interpretations of reality within a sociohistorical framework, we can better understand what happened to these people and the city they helped invigorate and sustain. Grounding our analysis in a constructivist paradigm of social inquiry, we describe how immigrants seek, negotiate, and engage possibilities to assert agency as global and local forces prompt their departure from home and suggest that Miami offers possibilities of membership in a more economically and physically secure community. We hear in their voices how embeddedness in transborder social groups allows them not only to maintain identities and statuses that mitigate marginalization and feelings of exclusion in Miami but also to continue to search for a multidimensional condition of human security through a strategy of immigration.

We define participants in the qualitative sample of our study as those arriving after the immigrant amnesty and legalization programs of the mid-1980s, such as the Immigration Reform and Control Act of 1986, and include in this sample interviews and focus groups with Miamians from Colombia, Cuba, the Dominican Republic, Haiti, Mexico, Peru, and Puerto Rico. Rather than selecting countries of origin based upon the size of a national-origin group in Miami, we selected this sample in order to compare conditions of departure and reception for a wide range of nationality groups holding varied social statuses (e.g., race, citizenship, maturity of the receiving immigrant community, and class of origin).

This research follows the philosophy and method Michael Burawoy developed as the extended case study.[116] In the extended case study method, researchers examine how external forces shape the social situations of individuals and groups yet also consider how the actions of these individuals and groups stabilize (and destabilize) macrostructures. Using participant observation as well as in-depth interviews and survey data, the inquiry extends from the microexperiences and processes of immediate, intimate daily life to the macroforces of global economics, geopolitics, and many forms of nation-state regulation, recognizing, as Burawoy has stated, that "there can be no one-way determination between processes and forces."[117] Burawoy explains that the extended case method allows researchers to "emphasize the way the external 'system' colonized the subject lifeworld and how the lifeworld, in turn, negotiated the terms of domination, created alternatives, or took to creative protest."[118]

Our case study employs a mixed method design, in which unstructured observation and participation were sequentially overlaid with semistructured in-depth interviews, focus groups, and, ultimately, a random sample survey that allowed for statistical testing of some of the findings that emerged from our qualitative analysis, as well as census data. Rather than using this method as strict hypothesis testing, we use the quantitative study as a form of triangulation of the findings in the qualitative study, as well as a way to deepen the understanding that resulted from the overall inquiry and to confirm the extent to which qualitative findings could be generalizable. The validity of the study's findings is based upon collection of rich data, triangulation of data sources, and peer checks of researcher interpretations. Study team members engaged in internal peer-checking processes that resulted in each of the researchers analyzing data separately. Analyses and interpretations of the rich qualitative data, which produced more than 1,000 pages of transcripts, were then jointly corroborated, revised, or refined in regular group meetings that spanned several years. Further, comparison across data sources allowed trends to be juxtaposed and anomalies to be identified, scrutinized, and used to refine theory.

The project draws from interdisciplinary scholarship and five sources of data, as well as participant observation during the three authors' many years of living in Miami-Dade and Broward counties. Typical of interdisciplinary ethnographic work, this approach draws its strengths from the immersion of researchers in the cultural group under study, as well as the use of multiple sources of data.[119] One of the authors is a broadly trained anthropologist and sociologist, who is also a naturalized US citizen from Peru who initially migrated with an H-4, nonworking visa in 1985. Another is a sociologist and daughter of Puerto Rican return migrants to the island, who, in turn, left the island for a US undergraduate education in 1991 and stayed. The third is a bilingual Anglo who has lived in Mexico and is an interdisciplinary social scientist trained in Latin American studies. As a communications scholar, her work encompasses both ethnography and audience reception research.

The first two data sets were collected in a purposive, nonrandom, snowball sample of 101 in-depth interviews and fifteen focus groups with

Table 1.3 Qualitative Interview Sample Descriptives

	Colombia	Cuba	Dominican Republic	Haiti	Mexico	Peru	Puerto Rico	Total
Gender								
Male	8	2	5	9	9	9	8	50
Female	6	10	8	4	7	7	9	51
Mean age	45.6	41.5	42.6	39.3	40.2	49.3	45.4	43.4
Educational attainment[a]								
Some high school	0	2	0	3	6	1	2	14
High school diploma	0	0	2	1	0	3	0	6
Some college	4	5	8	4	5	2	2	30
College degree	4	4	3	2	1	6	5	25
Graduate	5	1	0	0	3	4	7	20
Country where highest educational degree was attained[a]								
Country of origin	10	5	5	5	9	9	6	49
United States	3	7	8	8	6	4	9	45
Preferred language[a]								
Spanish	13	10	12	0	13	16	9	73
Creole	0	0	0	9	0	0	0	9
English	1	2	1	3	2	0	8	17
Mean years in the United States	5.9	11.8	10.9	14.3	11.7	8.2	8.5	10.2
Marital status[a]								
Married	5	0	8	4	9	8	9	43
Single	7	6	4	9	5	6	4	41
Divorced	2	4	1	0	0	2	2	11
Widowed	0	2	0	0	0	0	1	3
Have children	6	5	10	5	9	10	10	55
Mean number of children	1.34	2.6	2.4	1.4	2	2.2	2.3	2
Total by country of origin	14	12	13	13	16	16	17	$N = 101$

Note: a. The N for some descriptives may not match up to the subsample N due to missing information.

recent immigrants in Miami carried out from 2003 to 2006. Herein referred to as the "qualitative sample," open-ended questions and discussion rather than tests of a priori categories were used by researchers to understand immigrants' experiences and perceptions. Table 1.3 breaks down individual characteristics of the interview sample and Table 1.4 breaks down characteristics of participants in the focus groups.[120]

To expand the only non-Latino-origin group, we drew from a second qualitative data set that Sallie Hughes designed and oversaw. It includes sixty-nine in-depth interviews and five focus groups with a purposive, non-random sample of self-identifying Haitians and Haitian Americans. The data include immigration histories, perceptions of belonging in Miami, and

Table 1.4 Characteristics of Focus Group Participants

Characteristics	Number
Gender	
Women	55
Men	55
Country of Origin[a]	
Colombia	23
Cuba	14
Dominican Republic	25
Mexico	15
Peru	21
Puerto Rico	11

Notes: a. *N* – 109 in this section due to missing information from one focus group participant. *N* = 110.

patterns of consumption (choice, use, reaction, and interaction) of Haitian ethnic community media and mainstream US media in Miami in 2008 and 2009.[121]

The fourth data set is derived from a telephone survey administered by the Institute for Public Opinion Research at Florida International University in 2008 to a random sample of 1,268 South Florida immigrants about issues of immigrant adaptation, subjective well-being, discrimination, measures of assimilation, and transnational participation. With the support of the National Science Foundation and in collaboration with our colleague Elizabeth Vaquera, we created this survey, which we call the Immigrant Transnationalism and Modes of Incorporation (ITMI) Quantitative Survey,[122] to examine first-generation immigrants from over eighty countries (both long-established settlers and newcomers). The qualitative findings were used to develop the survey questions that tested whether the information gained through the qualitative study was supported by data from a larger random sample of immigrants.[123] Table 1.5 contains the demographic characteristics of the quantitative sample.

Last, we draw from the US Census of 1990, 2000, and 2010, and 2012.[124] Like all social scientific inquiry, our training, values, research paradigms, and choice of methodology have influenced the results, but through a multiauthored method and the validation checks mentioned above, we have tried to make our interpretations transparent and internally consistent, while basing them upon participants' stories of their lived experiences.

Structure of the Book

We begin by discussing the globalization of environments of insecurity. In Chapter 2, we document why and how immigrant Miamians left their

Table 1.5 Descriptive Characteristics of ITMI Quantitative Sample

Characteristics	Percentage
Female	52.5
Age (mean)	48.6
Country/region of origin	
Cuba	35.8
Colombia	7.0
Haiti	7.4
Non-Spanish Caribbean	9.3
Spanish Caribbean	9.1
North/Central America	12.7
Other South America	12.2
Other non-Hispanic	6.5
Marital Status	
Married	59.7
Single	18.4
Widowed	6.5
Divorced	15.5
Education	
Less than high school	24.6
High school	29.2
Some college	22.3
College	15.7
Graduate school	7.6
Household annual income (US$)	
19,999 or less	24.6
20,000–39,999	32.1
40,000–59,999	21.1
60,000–79,999	6.2
80,000 +	16.0
Years in the United States (mean)	21.9
US citizenship	54.0
Perceived English fluency	
Does not speak English well/at all	34.1
Speaks English well	30.4
Speaks English very well	36.0

Source: ITMI Quantitative Survey.
Notes: $N = 1,268$. Some measures have between 0 percent and 1 percent of missing values, except for citizenship ($N = 1,194$) and income ($N = 906$).

homelands in the 1990s and 2000s, driven away by varying forms of insecurity. Sometimes, study participants perceived themselves to be targets of violence in various forms. Other times, they personally embodied labor redundancy because they could not find secure employment, or their businesses failed during the economic restructuring associated with neoliberalism. At the same time, they were attracted to discourses of material well-being, individual freedom, and greater quality of life in Miami.

In Chapter 3, we examine the context of reception for immigrants with precarious, temporary, or no legal status. We argue that post-9/11 policies have criminalized immigrant groups even as they are deployed according to the needs of capital. We show how their lives increasingly are regulated by the state and how state policies made their liminal statuses untenable to them despite their economic contributions to the US economy. We demonstrate how immigration enforcement policies of the last two decades enhanced threats of deportation, spawning intense feelings of psychological insecurity for some immigrants and their families.

In Chapter 4, we illustrate how globalization and neoliberal city politics have led to economic bifurcation and a demand for flexible immigrant labor. Changes in social class status upon migration are examined by comparing perceived class status before and after migration. In this chapter, we pay close attention to factors that both contribute to and detract from the likelihood for upward social mobility once immigrants are in the United States. Analyses are focused particularly on how mobility is experienced according to gender, country/region of origin, and legal status. They are also used to examine how perceived social status relates to immigrants' identities and esteem. We conclude with a discussion of how unionization drives in Miami can raise wages and uplift the lives of the city's low-wage workforce.

In the next part of the book, we show how Miami's legal, political, and racial structures configure mechanisms of inclusion and exclusion that translate into the privileging of some immigrant subgroups and national cohorts. National origin, legal status, gender, race, and power provide the contours for the boundaries of groups, locating them into hierarchies that are sustained by global capitalism as well as local and state racial projects. In Chapter 5, we examine how formal citizenship shapes opportunities for legal inclusion by analyzing patterns of ethnic group political incorporation. We see how Cubans and Cuban Americans have mobilized their citizenship rights to obtain political representation beyond even what their comparatively large numbers would suggest, while first- and second-generation Haitians, Colombians, and Nicaraguans have even less formal representation than what their smaller numbers suggest. We show how non-Cuban immigrants perceive that political inequality sustains their economic and legal precariousness, as well as intraimmigrant social hierarchies.

In Chapter 6, we examine racial formations in Miami from a transnational perspective. Breaking open the category of Hispanic, we show how transnational racial meanings converge to privilege certain groups over others. Country of origin is a mechanism of stratification, but ethnocentrism reveals underlying racial dynamics rooted in Latin American and Caribbean racial hierarchies that reify the statuses of Afro-Latinos, Afro-Caribbeans, people of indigenous roots, and colonial subjects toward the bottom of the local ethnic and racial hierarchy. We also show how interethnic and interracial differences are exacerbated by inequalities coded into formal immigration law and into informal class and cultural distinctions and appraisals of race. We illustrate how legal status has become conflated with race, representing a contemporary US racial formation that is reproduced within Miami's immigrant population.

In the last part of the book, we look at how immigrants develop strategies in their daily lives to contend with emotional struggles of immigration including reshaped mechanisms of inclusion and exclusion. In Chapter 7, we show how immigrants carve out ways of belonging to soften the effects of exclusion. Their search for belonging and inclusion results in strategies of transborder co-presence that contest dominant forms of citizenship grounded in formal membership in the nation-state. Translocal connections, including social participation in the hometown networks and relationships of care, occupy a central position among immigrants' strategies for belonging. Driven by affective dimensions of the human experience, we show how advances in technology and the expansion of transnational media and coethnic media in Miami have ushered in new ways for maintaining substantive forms of citizenship in a locality that crosses state boundaries.

In Chapter 8, we look at how immigrants construct belonging in Miami through sensory experience, memory, thoughts, and behaviors associated with their places of origin that allow them to reenact and reexperience the comforts of home in the geographic space of Miami. We argue that, along with co-presence practices, translocal placemaking is a better way to conceive of belonging in a mobile world. Through translocal social citizenship, immigrants seek to counteract formal mechanisms of exclusion and discrimination. In short, sustaining membership or social citizenship in the original home and the new home results in feelings of belonging that help compensate for experiences of marginalization within their daily lives in Miami.

In Chapter 9, we conclude with several narratives of immigrants— some who have remained in the United States and fought for social inclusion and others who, coming from different social class backgrounds, have returned to their countries of origin under very different circumstances.

At a broad level, the material in this book is used to illustrate that immigrants construct human security simultaneously in multiple dimensions and on multiple scales; the exclusions experienced in one domain or at one scale are compensated for by seeking belonging in others. Findings suggest that belonging is not structured by a global versus local logic; moreover, global mobility does not necessarily dislocate its subjects, rendering them homeless and without agency. Mobility with connectivity engenders forms of belonging that coexist but also challenge exclusionary structures in overlapping scales and domains on a daily and ongoing basis. Immigrants, and probably others living mobile lives, seek to shape these experiences with all the emotional, material, and mental resources they can muster in the pursuit of the full experience of human security.

Notes

1. When we refer to Miami in this book, we are talking about the geocultural region including Miami-Dade County and southern Broward County, rather than only the incorporated city of Miami. This practice follows vernacular uses in Latin America and the Caribbean and also follows local media markets and circulations for employment and residence. While most interviews are with Latin American and Caribbean immigrants who live in Miami-Dade County, some people work in Miami-Dade County but live in portions of southern Broward County.

2. Alejandra's interview did not reveal whether her sister arranged for her employer to sponsor Alejandra's migration or if she helped her to immigrate through other channels. What is clear from the interview was that Alejandra had a legal work permit; however, she stated that she could not leave the country because she lacked permanent residency.

3. Matt 2011, p. 4.

4. Matt 2012, p. A31.

5. Matt 2011.

6. Ibid., p. 4.

7. Dreby 2010; Matt 2011.

8. In the 1980s to the mid-1990s, the retirement age in Colombia for women in the public sector (which is lower than that for men) was age fifty, and in the private sector, age fifty-five (Clavijo 2009).

9. Parrado and Zenteno 2002.

10. Heaton, Forste, and Otterstrom 2002; Parrado and Zenteno 2002.

11. Matt 2011.

12. Ibid., p. 252.

13. Giddens 1990.

14. Matt 2011.

15. Ibid., p. 7.

16. Huysmans 2006, p. 7.

17. Sassen 2009. Abrahamson (2004) describes global cities as those that successfully recruit multinational corporations and specialized service firms while providing cultural attractions to draw international tourists. He layers global cities in tiers (first, second, and third) depending on their level of global connectivity in these domains. Sassen (2009), more interested in economic functions than cultural attributes, describes global cities as "major" or "minor" depending on the intensity and geographic diversity of the cross-border financial and business circuits they facilitate. Sassen (2011) describes Miami as an infrequently studied global city worthy of further investigation.

18. Sassen 2009.

19. Aart Scholte 2005.

20. Singapore and Dubai also pursued regionalized paths to the global economic and cultural arena (Sassen 2011), and as Hong Kong gained global city status, it attracted immigrants from the less-developed countries of the Asian Pacific region to work in low-wage jobs supporting finance and trade managers (Chui and Lui 2009; McKay 2006b).

21. Pratts (1991) developed the term *contact zones* to describe interaction in the multicultural classroom. She defines them as "social spaces where cultures meet, clash, and grapple with each other, often in contexts of highly asymmetrical relations of power, such as colonialism, slavery, or the aftermaths as they are lived out in many parts of the world today" (p. 34).

22. Portes and Stepick 1993.

23. Sassen 2011.

24. Henderson 2003.

25. See particularly Giddens 1990 and 1991.

26. Giddens 1991.

27. Giddens 1990.

28. See Low (1994) for a parsimonious description of place:

Place is space made culturally meaningful, and in this context it provides the context and symbolic cues for our behavior. Place, however, is not just a setting for behavior but an integral part of social interaction and cultural processes. An understanding of place cannot be separated from how people live their lives or from the historical moment and sociopolitical institutions that structure those lives. Further, place links local identity and its specificity with the globalization and interdependency of the modern world. (p. 66)

29. Conradson and McKay 2007, p. 168.

30. Noriega and Iribarren 2011; Santa Ana and González de Bustamante 2012.

31. See García y Griego (1980) for cyclical accounts of inclusion and exclusion of immigrants.

32. See Glenn (2011) for a place-based discussion of substantive citizenship; see Glick Schiller and Caglar (2008) for a discussion of substantive citizenship on a transnational scale.

33. US Census Bureau 2012.

34. Massey, Durand, and Malone 2002.

35. Kinnvall and Lindén 2010.

36. Mayol 2012.

37. Sirkeci 2005.

38. Luna and Filgueira 2009; Massey, Sanchez R., and Behrman 2006.

39. Portes and Hoffman 2003, in Sanchez R. 2006.

40. Almeida 2007.

41. Sirkeci 2005.

42. Ibid., p. 199.

43. Sirkeci (2005) clarifies, however, that the option to exit is unlikely to be available to those who are in the most danger. Other research has identified women as a group that is particularly vulnerable to insecurity (Freedman 2003) and who have fewer options to exit such environments given that they may not have access to the same opportunities for labor migration as men and, thus, must rely on family reunification for migration and legal status.

44. Huysmans 2006.

45. Kinnvall and Lindén 2010; Giddens 1990, 1991.

46. Giddens 1991.

47. Inter-American Development Bank 2007, p. 1.

48. Aranda 2007; Grasmuck and Pessar 1991.

49. Tirman 2006.

50. Huntington 2004, p. 40.

51. Clark 2006, p. 1B.

52. CBS News/Associated Press 2009.

53. Portes and Rumbaut 2006.

54. Tirman 2006, p. 2.

55. Massey, Durand, and Malone 2002.

56. Chavez 1997.

57. Ibid., p. 62.

58. Tirman 2006, p. 2.

59. Martínez 2009.

60. See primary documents from the Library of Congress, http://www.loc.gov /rr/program/bib/ourdocs/Alien.html (accessed September 27, 2012).

61. We see this in the legislation known as Illegal Immigration Reform and Immigrant Responsibility Act that added Section 287(g) to the Immigration and Nationality Act laying the groundwork for the "vertical" integration of local, state, and federal law enforcement (Marrow 2012). Through "memoranda of understandings" between Immigration and Customs Enforcement (ICE) at the federal level and state and local officials in the 2000s, these agencies were allowed to jointly pursue the apprehension of undocumented immigrants. These partnerships eventually would lead to the recruitment of local officials to carry out federal immigration enforcement.

62. See Duany 2006; Higham 2002 [1955]; Perea 1997; Perlmann 2005; Roediger 2005; Zolberg and Litt Woon 1999.

63. The Magic City was an invention by a railroad publicity agent at the end of the nineteenth century who hoped to combine the allure of technological spectacle, natural beauty, and a myth of abundance to attract visitors and investors to a "New South" city combining wealth and racial exclusion (see Bush 1999). Historian Ira de Augustine Reid quotes a Bahamian resident of Miami in 1939 as follows: "Colored Miami certainly was not the Miami of which I had heard. It was a filthy backyard to The Magic City" (quoted in Mohl 1989, p. 68).

64. See Lin (2011) on cultural products. Levitt (2001) describes social remittances as values, ideas, and cultural norms that immigrants transmit to kinship networks in home countries.

65. Fussell 2010.

66. Giddens 1991, p. 39.

67. García 1996; McHugh, Miyares, and Skop 1997; Portes and Stepick 1993; Stepick et al. 2003.

68. Mohl 1989; Moore 2004; Winsberg 1979.

69. Mohl 2001.

70. Croucher 1997; Stepick et al. 2003.

71. Omi and Winant 1994.

72. Stepick et al. 2003; Stowers and Vogel 1994; Warren and Moreno 2003.

73. This section is adapted from Hughes et al. 2012.

74. Portes and Stepick 1993.

75. Ibid.

76. Mohl 1989, 1990, 2001; Pérez 1990.

77. Winsberg 1979, 1983.

78. Portes 1969.

79. This aid included automatic legal immigration status and access to fast-track paths to citizenship; occupational training; scholarships for higher education and low-interest educational loans; English lessons and expedited entry into US medical professions for health-care workers; and hundreds of millions of dollars to establish

businesses (Pérez 2003). Also see Alberts (2005), Grosfoguel (2003), and Pedraza (2004).

80. Croucher 1997; Winsberg 1979.

81. Croucher 1997, pp. 182–183; see also Moore 2004.

82. Greenbaum 2002; Ngai 2004.

83. Ngai 2004, p. 8.

84. Alberts 2005.

85. Portes and Rumbaut 2001; Portes and Stepick 1993.

86. Brookings Institution 2004.

87. C. Charles 2007; Marcelin 2005.

88. C. Charles 2007.

89. The US Centers for Disease Control designated being Haitian a risk factor for contracting HIV and quarantined Haitians in hospitals (the phrase "three Hs" was coined to identify those with elevated risk of having the human immunodeficiency virus (HIV)—hemophiliac, homosexual, and Haitian) (C. Charles 2007; Marcelin 2005). Even though they were fleeing a brutal dictatorial regime, only 11 out of 22,940 Haitians interdicted at sea from 1981 to 1990 were considered by US immigration officials to be qualified to apply for asylum (Wasem 2010).

90. Little and Newhouse al-Sahli 2004.

91. See Wasem 2010. Among the infamous detention centers is Krome in Miami-Dade County. Formerly a Cold War missile base, Krome Detention Center, in recent years, has been plagued by charges of abuse and human rights violations, which in one case led to the death of a detainee. The center currently only houses male detainees after two Immigration and Naturalization Services officers were indicted in 2001 on charges of sexual abuse of female detainees.

92. See also Stepick et al. 2003.

93. Advocates for Miami's smaller ethnic communities argue US Census figures undercount undocumented immigrants and other disadvantaged groups. For example, the 2000 census counted about 96,000 Haitians in Greater Miami, but community organizers believe they undercounted Haitians due to language differences, poor outreach, and Haitians' distrust of authorities. The 2010 census added Creole-speaking interviewers and Haitian media ads. We use the Census Bureau's Decennial Census and American Community Surveys because they offer the only detailed, empirical picture of South Florida's ethnic makeup.

94. Shumow 2010.

95. Aranda 2007; Duany 2002.

96. Moore 2004. See also Miami-Dade County, Department of Planning and Zoning (2010) for ethnic distribution maps from the 2010 census. For a historical view, see Winsberg (1979, 1983).

97. Frey 1996.

98. Zavella 1997.

99. Frey 1996, p. 742.

100. Feagin and Vera 1995.

101. Sawyer 2004, p. 19.

102. Lin 2011, p. 221.

103. Basch, Glick Schiller, and Szanton Blanc 1994.

104. Foner 2000.

105. Morley 2004; Portes, Guarnizo, and Landolt 1999; Vaquera and Aranda 2011.

106. On Haitian transnationalism, see Laguerre 1998; for Dominicans, see

Guarnizo 1997 and Levitt 2001; for Mexicans, see Smith 2006; for Puerto Ricans, see Duany 2002 and Aranda 2007.

107. Duany 2011.

108. Ibid.

109. Aranda 2007; Dreby 2010; Duany 2011.

110. Aranda 2007; Dreby 2010; Hondagneu-Sotelo and Avila 1997; Parreñas 2001, 2005.

111. Marrow 2012; Naples 2007.

112. Appadurai 1995, 1996; Massey 1993, 1994. See McKay (2006a) for a succinct discussion.

113. Glenn 2011.

114. Morley 2004.

115. Holston and Appadurai 1999; Reed-Danahay and Brettell 2008.

116. Burawoy 1991; Burawoy et al. 2000.

117. Burawoy et al. 2000, p. 28.

118. Ibid., p. 25.

119. Creswell 2007.

120. The individual interviews typically lasted approximately one to three hours, though some took longer. Focus groups were designed to take approximately ninety minutes but often exceeded this duration. The interviews combined life and migration histories with discussion of perceptions of individual and group relations in Miami. The focus groups discussed uses and reactions to mass media content as well as intergroup relations in the city. The language used in the individual interviews—either Spanish, Haitian Creole, or, in a few cases, English—was chosen by the participants. Transcripts of interviews carried out in Haitian Creole were subsequently translated into English. The authors translated excerpts of Spanish interviews used in this book. The focus groups were conducted in Spanish. They were organized by national-origin group, although several of them were diverse because respondents frequently brought guests from other backgrounds. We were not able to conduct focus groups with Haitians.

121. Half of the participants were male. Participants decided whether to be interviewed in English or Creole. This sample is the only one that includes the US-born second generation. Of the ninety-one participants in this data source, twenty-six were Haitian Americans. We take care to point out when we are drawing upon second-generation Haitian Americans, which happens infrequently. Participants in this group were recruited from at least a half dozen starting points around Miami, including through community churches, parks, universities, and relatives of Haitian interviewers. The sampling strategy sought sufficient numbers of Creole-speaking participants in addition to working toward gender, age, and occupational diversity.

122. Aranda, Vaquera, and Sabogal 2007. "Immigrant Transnationalism and Modes of Incorporation Study." Funded by National Science Foundation, Proposal No. 0752644.

123. The random digit dial sample included two components: one sample of land-line telephone numbers and a subsample of cell phone numbers. Out of the 1,268 completed phone interviews, 344 were conducted with cell phone users. The sample had an overall margin of error of plus or minus 2.8 percent. The survey was originally created in English, pretested, and translated into Spanish. It was pretested in Spanish, amended, and pretested a third time. It was also translated into Haitian Creole. The interviews were performed using computer-assisted telephone interviewing survey techniques. The cooperation rate was 87 percent—that is, of the

qualified respondents who heard the interviewer's introduction on the phone, 87 percent agreed to complete the survey. The response rate was 51 percent for landlines and 49 percent for cell phones (American Association for Public Opinion Research response rate #4), which is comparable to studies using similar methods and populations (American Association for Public Opinion Research 2011; Kasinitz et al. 2008). Analyses reported are weighted by age, gender, education, and country of origin to represent the proportions of each immigrant population based on data from the American Community Survey (2005–2007). Multiple imputation techniques were employed to deal with missing values on covariates in the analytical models. The *proc mi* and *proc mianalyze* commands of the SAS software were also used to deal with missing data. These statistical tools predict values for missing data by incorporating information from other attributes of individuals with some randomness built into the imputed values in order to account for the uncertainty of estimates (Allison 2002).

124. When data broken down by ethnicity or ancestry were not available from the US Census Bureau's 2012 American Community Survey one-year estimates, we drew from American Community Survey data from previous years to fill in the gaps.

2

The Contexts of Departure

Lola, a university-educated immigrant from Lima, followed her husband to Miami in 2001 after their small security guard business in Peru failed. Like many business sectors, even private security services in Lima were being absorbed into a few giant companies. She described a gradually declining economic status that undercut the family's economic well-being and threatened her children's future standing as tuition in private schools from which she graduated became unrealistic. "I swear I felt really uncertain," she explained three years later. "But the situation was so critical in Lima that we said, 'Enough, it is best that we go.' But it was a very, very difficult decision to make. At the beginning I did not want to. I was anguished, but my husband told me, 'Look, what are we doing? We cannot continue here.'" At that rate, she said, they would have defaulted on their rent and would have had to move in with family.

At age forty-seven, Lola came with her family to Miami on a tourist visa. She obtained a job in a Spanish-speaking telephone marketing company until pressure to increase her daily sales drove her away. Her family's hope to open a business in Miami never materialized, so Lola cleaned houses five times a week. With Lola and her husband's blessing, their daughter married a friend with citizenship to obtain legal residency. Her new status allowed her to pay in-state university tuition prices. Lola's son was getting good grades in a public high school when we interviewed her in 2006. Although her family found greater financial security upon moving to Miami, they now faced a new form of insecurity related to their undocumented immigrant status.

Lola and her family had, in effect, exchanged one form of insecurity for another. By insecurity, we mean the lived experience of economic, physical, social, or psychic vulnerability that threatens an individual and his or her family's livelihood or lifestyle. In this chapter and the next two, we show how various forms of human insecurity in the homeland make conditions ripe for emigration. However, once in Miami, immigrants face new forms of insecurity that shape integration experiences. Confronted with one or more of these vulnerabilities in their home countries, the immigrants in our sample could continue to live in states of insecurity, or alternatively, exit in search of stability and its sustainability in a new country.

In this chapter, we analyze the context of departure of immigrants arriving in Miami from the late 1980s through the first decade of the twenty-first century. Miami's newest residents come from a variety of emigration contexts, but common to most experiences were perceptions of vulnerability that arose during a period when most countries underwent severe economic restructuring programs associated with the laissez-faire economic ideology known as neoliberalism. Although late-arriving Cubans faced unique conditions for emigration (though they still faced economic insecurity in the early 1990s resulting from the fall of the Soviet Bloc and exacerbated by the US embargo),[1] what was common to other nationality groups was that immigration was a response to an overall sense of insecurity during and after implementation of economic reforms.

Neoliberalism and the Formation of Environments of Insecurity

As the consensus of core constituencies of international finance, neoliberalism was the economic policy response to the foreign debt crisis that enveloped Latin American governments in the early 1980s. In US policy circles, from neoliberal ideas emerged a set of economic measures that policymakers presumed would best remedy the debt, deficits, inflation, and lagging productivity that plagued many Latin American countries. In order to receive International Monetary Fund bridge loans to prevent default, Latin American governments, often supported by domestic finance ministers trained in US institutions, promised to change development paths from declining state-led capitalist models to deregulated, privatized, market-based economies. Although variations existed in different countries and regions, governments made huge cuts in spending, privatized state enterprises, deregulated banking and communications, freed currencies, and ended or lowered tariffs and other barriers to imports. The idea of the laissez-faire makeover was to retool economies for large-scale, export-oriented manufacturing and commercial agriculture. International investors joined with family owners of the largest domestic businesses to finance much of the makeover through direct investment in manufacturing plants, communications, banks, toll-based highways and seaports, and other enterprises formerly owned or regulated by domestic companies or governments.

Economic liberalization and open trade staunched inflation and curbed budget deficits in several countries, but by 2000, that balanced budgets and freer trade were not enough to spur economic development became apparent. By the mid-2000s, economic policies nicknamed "the Washington Consensus" and most of the domestic politicians who supported them were out of favor in Latin America. Carlos Santiso wrote, "From Venezuela to Bolivia, the depth of disenchantment with austerity budgets and neo-liberal economic policies is palpable. While the 1980s were a 'lost decade' marked by a debt crisis, stabilization packages and structural adjustment, the 1990s have largely been a 'disappointing decade' of recurrent turbulence and unmet expectations."[2]

Unemployment, poverty, and wealth gaps remained stubborn or increased. Analysis of the first fifteen years of neoliberalism found that in many countries pools of "redundant workers" displaced from secure, formal sector employment had been created, whereas on a macrolevel expanded global trade, investment, and communications had increased inequalities between nations.[3] This damaging economic shift occurred in an era where promises of developed-world status through market economics and free trade spawned aspirations to consumerist lifestyles and the achievement of the American Dream at home.[4] However, the reality for many of the immigrants in our sample was one of increasing insecurity in their lives.

The environments of insecurity that neoliberalism created extended "opportunity framework[s]" to those who had or were contemplating migration.[5] Our participants from Peru, Mexico and, to a lesser extent, Colombia reflected this phenomenon. For these countries and many others, evidence linked rising emigration to families' attempts to cope with the detrimental effects of neoliberal restructuring on their households' economic viability. The strengthening of international investment and informational and transportation linkages to the United States enhanced the conditions necessary for massive emigration.

With regard to Caribbean migration, movements of Puerto Rican and Haitian immigrants into Florida were particularly noticeable by the 2000s, although Dominican immigrants and those from other countries also began to favor Florida.[6] These Caribbean populations serve as examples of massive emigration during periods of structural transformation that resembled some aspects of neoliberalism but occurred earlier in the twentieth century.

Saskia Sassen argues that the pathway for Haitian immigration to the United States was opened not by ancestral poverty and population pressure, which had been present for decades if not centuries, but in the 1970s by a harbinger of the global neoliberal wave a decade later—a turn to export-oriented industrial production and commercial agriculture financed by US investors.[7] The shift from agricultural production for internal subsistence to externally focused manufacturing uprooted people from traditional rural livelihoods and created informational and transportation links to the United States. Displacement caused by changing production models and increasing links to the United States initiated mass Haitian immigration.[8] Once networks were firmly established, waves of political instability, criminal violence, and weather disasters deepened vulnerability and pushed migrants to the United States in greater numbers. Many of the Haitians in our qualitative sample immigrated to Florida after 1986 as children who were reuniting with parents. The parents had gone first, established residency, and then sent for them.

Similarly, poverty and economic stagnation were present in the Dominican Republic long before mass Dominican migration to the United States began, but not until the US military intervened in the country to unseat leftist president Juan Bosch in 1963 did a stream of middle-class refugees immigrate to the United States. This mass immigration, in turn, created family and personal networks that grew in number with the increase of US investment in the island. Most of the Dominicans in our sample followed family members or other network contacts to Miami.[9]

In some ways, Puerto Rican migration anticipated and outpaced the experiences of Haiti and the Dominican Republic. The Puerto Rican government in the 1940s planned for large-scale migration to be the safety valve that would ease the pressures of population growth and labor redundancy due to displacement by a massive state-led industrialization project.[10] With US citizenship, government sponsorship, and labor recruitment efforts on the island, Puerto Ricans began a mass exodus, mostly to the US Northeast and Chicago. Among these immigrants was a large proportion of the island's rural population. As Jorge Duany has shown, between 1948 and 1990, the government's Farm Labor Program recruited 421,238 Puerto Ricans to work on the US mainland, including in South Florida to pick avocados and lettuce.[11]

Over the decades, Puerto Rico industrialized and then moved into a postindustrial service-based economy, just as industrial employment and middle-sector wages in US urban centers slackened. US citizenship, increased bilingualism, and spatially expanded social networks eased the ability to move to and from the island as economic opportunities presented themselves in either location. In the late 1990s and 2000s, as economic conditions on the island eroded, migration pushed past the level of the government-sponsored "great exodus" in the 1950s.[12] However, the destinations of Puerto Rican migrants diversified, and Florida is now the second most popular state among mainland Puerto Ricans. Most have settled near Orlando, in Central Florida, but Puerto Rican communities also have grown in South Florida. Mainland-born Puerto Ricans who had migrated to Rustbelt cities also initiated patterns of secondary migration to Florida. In short, economic restructuring and direct economic and social linkages between the island and mainland have created a migration superhighway that hundreds of thousands travel. Recent evidence indicates that island migrants draw from higher socioeconomic statuses.

Industrialization and export-oriented production failed to produce sufficiently sustained and equitably distributed economic growth to keep large portions of Puerto Rican, Haitian, or Dominican populations from emigrating near the end of the twentieth century. In the 1990s, emigration continued at high levels from all three places, but similar to Puerto Rican migration, a major shift in the US destination of these Caribbean immigrants was under way. By the mid-2000s, Florida attracted more Haitians than any other state, and the Miami-Pompano Beach metropolitan area was home to the largest US concentration of Haitians. More Dominicans still migrated to the Northeast than to Florida, but their numbers in Florida grew exponentially.[13]

The history of emigration from Haiti, the Dominican Republic, and Puerto Rico could have suggested to policymakers in the 1980s and early 1990s that a shift away from traditional production activities to export-oriented manufacturing and large-scale commercial agriculture might uproot millions and spawn massive immigration streams. However, few members of Latin America's technocratic elite, the US government, or the World Bank and International Monetary Fund were paying much attention to history. Community-based development and stimulus for domestic production on par with exports were sought in a substantial way in only a few countries. Both former presidents Carlos Salinas of Mexico and Bill Clinton of the United States claimed that NAFTA would lower immigration to the United States.[14] Instead, Mexico and Latin America continued to export people, and in even greater numbers.[15]

Political crises responding to economic hardships caused by neoliberal restructuring and corruption among some of neoliberalism's most vociferous presidential proponents prompted many countries to turn strongly to the left in the 2000s. In Brazil, Uruguay, and to some extent Chile, social democratic political parties took power and led economic change. In Venezuela, Ecuador, and Bolivia, the turn pivoted on personalistic presidents who ruled through plebiscite with the support of the poor and use of populist rhetoric that scared the middle and upper middle classes. At the same time, countries with raw goods exports such as Brazil and Venezuela, and to a lesser extent Peru, experienced booms after 2000, fueled by the need for raw materials by industrializing China.

Although the percentage of the foreign born in Miami-Dade County remained consistent at around 51 percent between the 2000 and 2012 censuses (the Hispanic population grew to 64.3 percent of the population in

2012 from 57.3 percent in 2000), some shifts in residents' national origins occurred as conditions changed in Latin America. The Venezuelan presence in Miami doubled between 2000 and 2012 as business owners and professionals sought refuge from what many saw as a threatening political turn, as well as rising insecurity due to crime. Ecuadorans, although smaller in numbers, also dramatically increased their population in Greater Miami from 2000 to 2012 for similar reasons. And the origins of Miami's wealthiest immigrants diversified as capitalists from booming Brazil became noticeably more present in international banks, Port of Miami construction, the posh Brickell skyline, and other international businesses that invested in Miami after the 2008 recession.[16]

Thus, the contexts of security, or lack thereof, in Latin America and the Caribbean of the 2010s continued to shape the development of multiethnic Miami, and vice versa. But the period from 1986 to the present is when Miami's ethnic makeup and development path changed from a Cuban, Anglo, African American city that coordinated US penetration into the region to a multiethnic (but still predominantly Cuban) city that was at once a US and global node of capitalist command and control. We analyze this period in detail in the next section, explaining the contexts that led Miami's newest residents to emigrate north.

Detachment from the Formal Labor Market

Trends in employment, purchasing power, poverty, and inequality analyzed over a decade suggest that neoliberal policies increased the economic insecurity of potential immigrants and detached them from the social protections of their countries' formal economies. Purchasing power (real wages) declined in the 1980s and then stagnated in the 1990s; recessions ravaged household and small business income and planning; better-paid employment in traditional sectors declined without easy movement into new (but lower-paid) export industries; and the relative standing of lower- and middle-income households declined compared to the wealthiest. During this period—Santisi's "disappointing decade"—immigrants from across Latin America made Miami much more than a Cuban enclave community.

Economic output in Latin America grew 3.8 percent on an average annual basis between 1995 and 2005,[17] but output per person grew only an average of 1 percent annually, suggesting production growth did not keep pace with population growth. The worst performers were Haiti, Venezuela, Paraguay, Argentina, Brazil, and Colombia. At the same time, economic instability stymied business planning and forced households such as Lola's to make difficult decisions to compensate for eroded living standards. Considering population growth as well as economic output suggests that some populations reeled. In the same ten-year span, per capita gross domestic product declined seven of those years in Paraguay; six in Uruguay; five in Venezuela; four in Colombia, Honduras, and Mexico; three in Argentina, Bolivia, Brazil, Costa Rica, and Peru; and two in Ecuador, El Salvador, Guatemala, and Panama.

Purchasing power for urban formal sector workers grew on average 1.6 percent for twelve countries who reported data between 1995 and 2004, but we should view this achievement with caution. First, the differences across countries were extreme. Second, government real wage data do not adequately capture a large part of the population that works in the rural sector, less than full-time, or in the growing informal economy. Third, growth over a ten-year span masks huge year-to-year fluctuations due to counterinflationary policy.

Where economic growth could be found, skewed income distribution diluted potential positive effects. A look at how income distribution changed in three countries that were home to some of the immigrants in our qualitative study shows that lower- and middle-income sectors faced entrenched losses of economic standing across the period, while only the wealthiest quintile gained in relative terms. Table 2.1 presents the percent of income controlled by each quintile of the population and the changes in the distribution of income across time for Peru, the Dominican Republic, and Colombia based on World Bank data.[18]

With variable income gains and high levels of inequality, open unemployment grew.[19] The Economic Commission for Latin America and the Caribbean (ECLAC) reports the regional urban open unemployment rate went from 8.7 percent in 1995 to 10 percent in 2004, adjusting for mid-decade methodological changes in Argentina and Brazil.[20] However, the degree to which countries counted jobs in the informal sector (unstable, lacking benefits, fewer hours than full employment) varied. Moreover, rural households had fewer survival options when wage earnings declined and crops failed as happened during Hurricane Mitch in Honduras in 1998 or during Hurricane Stan in Guatemala, El Salvador, and southern Mexico in 2005. The highest average annual levels of urban unemployment were reported in Argentina (16 percent), Panama (15.9 percent), the Dominican Republic (15.5 percent), and Colombia (15.2 percent), but midlevel unemployment, in Venezuela (12.6 percent), Peru (8.9 percent), and Ecuador (10.7 percent), remained high in comparison with US levels of the time.[21]

With uneven results on wages, equality, and unemployment, the number of people living under the poverty line decreased only slightly across the region, and the variation between countries was extreme. From the early 1990s to the early 2000s, poverty declined a total of 3.6 percent across the eighteen-country ECLAC sample to an average of 46.7 percent.[22] Poverty increased the most from 1989 to 1990 and then again from 2001 to 2002 in South America: Argentina, Paraguay, Bolivia, and Venezuela. Poverty de-

Table 2.1 Income Distribution by Quintile and Rate of Change in Peru, the Dominican Republic, and Colombia (percentage)

Quintile	Peru			Dominican Republic			Colombia		
	1994	2003	% Change	1989	2004	% Change	1991	2003	% Change
Lowest 20%	4.9	3.7	−1.2	4.2	4.0	−0.2	3.6	2.5	−1.1
Second 20%	9.2	7.7	−1.5	7.9	7.8	−0.1	7.6	6.2	−1.4
Third 20%	14.1	12.2	−1.9	12.5	12.1	−0.4	12.6	10.6	−2.0
Fourth 20%	21.4	19.7	−1.7	19.7	19.3	−0.4	20.4	18.1	−2.4
Highest 20%	50.4	56.7	6.3	55.7	56.7	1.0	55.8	62.7	6.9
Total	100.0	100.0	n.a.	100.0	100.0	n.a.	100.0	100.0	n.a.

Sources: World Bank (1995), pp. 196–197; World Bank (2007), pp. 66–67.
Notes: Some totals may not add up to 100 percent due to rounding.
n.a. = not applicable.

creased the most in Chile, Panama, Brazil, Guatemala, and Mexico. We found no comparative figures for the Dominican Republic and Haiti.

Whether the Latin American and Caribbean region has ended a long period of downward adjustment and will move into sustained economic development with real gains in human development and social equality remains to be seen. In several places, restabilization occurred at lower levels of well-being and higher degrees of vulnerability for large segments of the population. The largest new population segment charted by the Inter-American Development Bank's exploration of the effects of the post-2000 export boom is one that is no longer poor but whose economic gains were not consolidated and are highly vulnerable.[23]

Because of its links to the United States, Puerto Rico's economy experienced the period differently, but with the same pressures. The island already had embraced export-oriented manufacturing decades earlier than the rest of Latin America and, by the 1980s, was dealing with a postindustrial transition and the advantages and disadvantages of being closely tied to the US labor market. Puerto Rico's golden age of industrial development occurred in the 1950s and 1960s, with unemployment rates and poverty declining steadily across two decades. The island became a showcase for free market, export-oriented industrialization. However, the economic engine ran out of steam by the 1970s when the US commonwealth moved into a postindustrial economic pattern. Services and tourism expanded but were not enough to prevent what Francisco Rivera-Batiz and Carlos Santiago called a protracted "crash of the labor market," particularly for younger workers.[24] Open urban unemployment reached over 20 percent in 1990, about four times the level of 1970. The US economic upswing of the 1990s helped push down Puerto Rican urban unemployment across the decade, but it still remained at a stubborn 15 percent, 6 percent higher than the US rate. Economic turmoil continued into the 2000s, and the island's economy experienced a prolonged recession from 2006 to 2011.[25] From 2000 to 2008, the island's urban unemployment rate was 11.3 percent, although youths age fifteen to twenty-four were twice as likely to be unemployed. Rural unemployment was higher. Poverty remained at stubbornly high levels.[26]

Immigration Trends Under Neoliberalism

While several waves of Latin American immigrants have come to the United States historically, the country experienced a sustained increase in immigration from this region from the early 1980s to the mid-2000s, with the only dip occurring after the attacks of September 11, 2001.[27] During this period, when neoliberalism was implemented and eventually moderated or abandoned depending on the country, the number of Latin Americans from a twelve-country sample who resided in the United States (and were counted by the US Census Bureau) rose 388 percent.[28] In Table 2.2, we show how El Salvador's population in the United States increased more than 1,000 percent. The number of Brazilians and Guatemalans in the country increased more than 750 percent. Mexico, the Dominican Republic, and Nicaragua's populations in the United States increased more than 300 percent, and the number of Ecuadorans rose 294 percent. The number of Hondurans and Colombians more than tripled, and the number of Argentines more than doubled. Although not reported in Table 2.2, migration from Puerto Rico accelerated to the point that between 2000 and 2010, the island actually lost 2.2 percent of its population.[29]

Another way to gauge changes in the levels of recent immigration from Latin America is through remittances sent by immigrants in the United States to their home countries. Remittances sent by those living abroad grew steadily for most of the countries in the region, an average annual growth rate of 22 percent between 1999 and 2004 for the countries listed in Table 2.3. The total of remittances increased 131 percent during the half decade. The increase in remittances sent home by Argentines was nearly 400 percent as professionals and blue-collar workers surged abroad once their businesses were lost during the 1999–2002 crash.

The makeup of the immigrant stream changed, becoming more urban and feminine. More women immigrated than men from Peru, Brazil, and the Dominican Republic, as many women as men from the Central American countries, and only slightly fewer women than men from Mexico.[30] Mexico City stopped attracting internal migrants and started sending more residents abroad.[31] Professionals and those from urban middle classes played larger roles in immigration, due especially to South American migration, creating urban and rural streams of migrants with different demographic profiles.[32]

Considering the uneven performance on economic growth, inequality, real wages, urban unemployment, and the population living under the poverty line, Latin America's economic progress was patchy and halting after the Washington Consensus was consolidated. In countries where real income and employment declined or failed to keep pace with population growth, and where the poor and middle-income sectors saw their relative economic standing erode, dreams, as well as living standards, were downsized. Instability suppressed modest economic gains in many countries, crushing hopes. In 2000, only 27 percent of Latin Americans polled in nineteen countries by "Latinobarometer" thought that their country was "progressing." In 2004, 55 percent thought their parents lived better than they lived at survey time, and only half expressed optimism for their children's future.[33] These sentiments correlate with the many reasons those in our sample gave for leaving their home countries.

Table 2.2 Foreign-Born Population of Twelve Latin American Countries in the United States (thousands)

Country of Origin	1970	1980	1990	2000	2001	2002	2003	2004	2005	% Change, 1980–2000	% Change, 1980–2005
El Salvador	16	94	465	837	846	868	1,019	955	1,121	790	1,093
Brazil	27	41	92	165	193	173	195	271	356	302	768
Guatemala	17	63	226	345	366	407	441	522	546	454	767
Mexico	760	2,199	4,298	8,393	8,855	9,659	9,967	10,453	10,805	282	391
Dominican Republic	61	169	348	726	646	652	719	631	695	330	311
Nicaragua	16	44	169	262	257	208	184	145	181	495	311
Ecuador	37	86	143	303	332	359	430	264	339	252	294
Honduras	39	109	107	262	257	208	184	145	379	140	248
Colombia	64	144	286	460	529	540	484	435	479	219	233
Argentina	45	69	93	91	137	128	143	141	145	32	110
Costa Rica	17	30	44	81	76	66	68	50	52	170	73
Panama	20	61	86	72	80	48	50	82	55	18	7
Total	1,119	3,109	6,357	12,006	12,574	13,316	13,884	14,094	15,163	286	388

Source: US Census Bureau and survey data reported in Burgess (2009).

Table 2.3 Remittances Sent by Immigrants Abroad (millions of US$)

Country	1999	2000	2001	2002	2003	2004	% Change, 1999–2004
Argentina	64.3	86.3	189.6	206.6	273.4	311.8	384.9
Bolivia	96.0	126.9	135.3	112.9	158.2	210.6	119.3
Brazil	1,862.0	1,649.4	1,774.8	2,449.0	2,821.3	3,575.1	92.0
Colombia	1,312.1	1,610.1	2,056.4	2,479.9	3,076.0	3,189.7	143.1
Costa Rica	126.5	136.0	198.4	250.6	320.9	319.5	152.6
Dominican Republic	1,631.1	1,838.8	1,981.8	2,194.3	2,325.4	2,501.2	53.3
Ecuador	1,089.5	1,322.3	1,420.6	1,438.0	1,633.4	1,838.0	68.7
El Salvador	1,387.3	1,765.4	1,926.0	1,953.7	2,122.4	2,564.1	84.8
Guatemala	465.6	596.2	633.8	1,600.2	2,147.0	2,627.5	464.3
Honduras	328.3	484.0	622.8	817.8	883.5	1,175.1	257.9
Mexico	6,648.6	7,524.7	10,146.3	11,029.4	16,653.7	19,861.7	198.7
Nicaragua	300.0	320.0	335.7	376.5	438.8	518.8	72.9
Panama	48.3	16.4	73.1	84.6	106.8	108.9	125.5
Paraguay	267.5	278.0	263.8	201.5	222.1	238.2	−11.0
Peru	670.0	717.7	753.2	705.4	868.5	1,132.7	69.1
Uruguay	n.d.	n.d.	0.0	36.1	61.8	69.9	n.d.
Total	18,296.1	20,472.1	24,512.4	27,938.6	36,116.1	42,246.9	130.9

Source: World Bank (2013).
Note: n.d. = no data.

Reasons for Immigrating to the United States

When we examine our quantitative sample to better understand the reasons that motivated participants' immigration journeys to the United States, we must keep in mind that contrary to the qualitative sample that comprised immigrants who had mostly come to this country since 1986, immigrants in the quantitative sample are more heterogeneous, for their arrival in many cases predates this cutoff. In spite of this difference, when we examine the trends underlying migration decisions, certain patterns emerge that are corroborated by our qualitative data. Table 2.4 breaks down the reasons for immigration to the United States for the quantitative sample and analyzes them by country or region of origin and gender.[34]

Upon examination of these data, several notable trends emerge. Cubans overwhelmingly report coming to the United States for political reasons. Although our qualitative data suggest that economic reasons have been more salient for recent immigrants, we must remember that Table 2.4 includes pre-1986 immigrants. With regard to Haitians, economic as well as political reasons are at work just as much as violence is a push factor; the issue is also expressed as a decision related to quality of life, particularly for Haitian women. With the exception of the non-Spanish-speaking Caribbean, South Americans (excluding Colombians), and other non-Hispanics, women are more likely to report migrating for quality-of-life reasons compared to their male conationals. At the same time, with the exception of the non-Spanish Caribbeans and other non-Hispanic groups, women are about as equally, if not more likely, to report coming to the United States for a job or investment opportunity. This finding challenges the assumptions that women are often tied migrants—in other words, their migrations are tied to the trips of men (e.g., husbands), thereby following men as dependents. No less important is that certain groups were more likely than others to report migrating because of violence in the home country or for economic reasons. Haitian women to a greater extent than Haitian men reported leaving Haiti because of violence. To a lesser extent than Haitians but important nevertheless, Colombian men and women and other South American men as well as non-Hispanic women also reported violence as a reason for leaving their countries.

Finally, men and women from Haiti, the Spanish Caribbean, North and Central America, and South America reported migrating for economic reasons to a greater extent than the sample mean. In the sections that follow, we illustrate how participants' framing of many of these responses invokes notions of insecurity, be they physical (e.g., threats to personal safety), social (e.g., inequalities and discrimination), economic (e.g., changing lifestyles and employment insecurity), or psychic (e.g., the uncertainty and the emotional tolls that other forms of insecurity take on emigrants and

Table 2.4 Reasons for Immigrating to the United States by Country/Region of Origin and Gender (percentage)

	All		Cuba		Haiti		Colombia		Non-Spanish Caribbean		Spanish Caribbean		North/Central America		Other South America		Other Non-Hispanic	
	Men	Women	Men	Women	Men	Women	Men	Women	Men	Women	Men	Women	Men	Women	Men	Women	Men	Women
Economics	30.3	26.7	26.7	23.2	37.2	34.4	31.2	26.4	25.7	19.1	31.0	29.1	43.2	34.5	33.2	33.5	18.7	14.4
Job or investment opportunity	24.4	24.3	12.9	11.8	18.3	25.0	22.9	32.9	36.2	25.5	41.5	40.8	27.3	31.5	26.2	29.1	53.9	27.0
Education	13.4	11.4	5.3	7.6	27.8	21.3	20.8	11.1	18.4	28.8	20.0	6.7	5.3	6.9	23.8	15.4	16.7	2.9
Political reasons	38.3	32.1	75.0	72.4	27.9	26.6	16.0	11.6	0.9	5.4	2.2	1.3	26.9	21.3	18.1	7.4	9.6	11.7
Friends/family in United States	17.7	16.4	11.6	12.0	25.3	17.3	20.1	24.7	27.8	26.8	29.5	8.6	12.6	12.5	23.9	21.1	11.8	22.7
The "American Dream"	7.8	5.9	4.1	4.3	9.6	4.7	12.9	14.3	9.4	9.6	15.5	5.9	9.0	4.8	3.2	5.1	15.4	2.6
Violence in home country	4.5	5.1	2.3	3.0	21.5	32.1	9.9	8.8	0.0	2.7	1.4	0.0	2.4	2.3	6.6	2.1	0.6	7.5
Quality of life	15.1	16.4	9.6	10.5	42.9	49.1	7.6	16.4	29.8	28.0	17.7	28.4	6.6	8.6	15.1	7.2	13.3	11.3
Curiosity	1.4	2.6	0.0	0.7	1.6	0.0	0.0	3.3	7.4	0.9	1.9	4.6	0.0	1.7	1.8	10.5	4.4	0.5
Not my decision	3.9	3.0	2.5	2.6	10.9	1.8	2.8	0.9	2.8	2.2	1.5	7.6	7.5	6.5	3.6	0.6	2.5	0.3
Other	6.6	14.1	5.9	6.7	13.1	21.1	4.9	15.0	4.1	13.5	0.1	17.4	10.1	15.0	6.0	17.4	10.3	33.7

Source: ITMI Quantitative Survey
Note: N = 1,268.

their families). Although our samples are different considering the recency of migration, the qualitative data largely corroborate the quantitative findings, with perhaps two exceptions: The levels of violence that the qualitative sample reports (especially among Colombians, Peruvians, and, to a lesser extent, Mexicans) appeared to be more salient than what appears in the quantitative sample. Secondly and as mentioned previously, recent Cuban immigrants seem to be searching for greater economic opportunities rather than migrating because of strong opposition to the political system, although they acknowledge that both factors are comingled. We examine the qualitative findings in the sections that follow.

Economic and Occupational Insecurity

Household studies in areas from which people emigrated in the early 2000s suggest that declines in job status and security, wage levels, and purchasing power prompted the immigration decisions of urban populations, while the loss of farm credits, insurance, and price supports increased farm family vulnerability. According to Corporación Latinobarómetro, in 2005, 75 percent of the region's workers were worried that they might become unemployed in the coming year. That was the fourth consecutive year that such a high proportion of the region's population expressed this anxiety.[35] As Figure 2.1 shows, perceived job insecurity is higher in some of the countries our participants emigrated from: 79 percent for Peru and 82 percent for Colombia and Mexico.

Declining living standards along with the emotional toll of perceived job insecurity also played roles in migration decisions. These emotions included pessimism and anxiety, as seen in Lola's story in the beginning of this chapter. These were some of the conditions that led urban professionals to migrate abroad in large numbers and prompted rural families and unskilled urban workers to send at least one household member in search of remittances.[36] For the poor, money sent home from abroad became essential to their families' survival.[37] For downwardly mobile professionals and middle-sector workers, emigration seemed to be their best chance to maintain current economic status and lifestyles for themselves and their children.

Poor Emigrants from Rural and Urban Sectors

Although neoliberalism lowered budget deficits and increased trade, it did so in part by ending state support for agricultural credits, crop insurance, price supports, and technical assistance for small farmers and stimulating export manufacturing at the expense of better-paid domestic production. Commercial agriculture tended to expand through the development of large farms outside of smallholder regions in areas such as the Mexican border

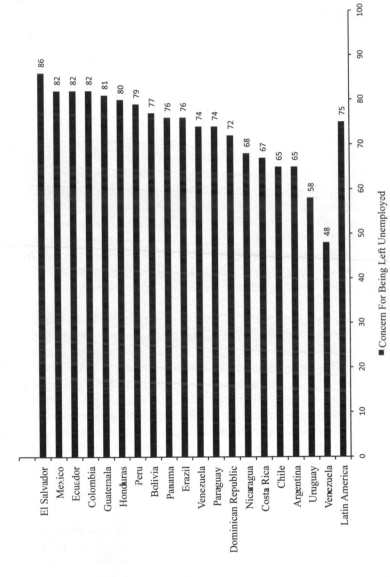

Figure 2.1 Concern for Being Left Unemployed by Country, 2005 (percentage)

El Salvador — 86
Mexico — 82
Ecuador — 82
Colombia — 82
Guatemala — 81
Honduras — 80
Peru — 79
Bolivia — 77
Panama — 76
Brazil — 76
Venezuela — 74
Paraguay — 74
Dominican Republic — 72
Nicaragua — 68
Costa Rica — 67
Chile — 65
Argentina — 65
Uruguay — 58
Venezuela — 48
Latin America — 75

■ Concern For Being Left Unemployed

Source: Corporación Latinobarómetro (2005).
Note: N = 20,207.

states of Sinaloa and Baja California, drawing migrants from southern Mexico to the border region.[38] Moreover, cheaper imported corn undercut domestic farm prices for that important Meso-American staple. The urban poor and lower middle classes lost access to formal labor markets as domestic manufacturing was replaced by more labor efficient export production. In Guadalajara, Mexico, for example, cheaper imports undermined traditional manufacturing in leather goods and textiles. New, smaller firms attempted to compete with lower wages and leaner production lines. By 1987, wages in the new plants—for a smaller number of workers—were 60 percent lower than those in older plants.[39]

As a result, poor households seeking to protect themselves in the face of waning employment, decreasing wages, and increasing agricultural prices turned to the international migration of family members for survival. If before, international migration was to improve well-being by taking advantage of previously created migration networks as formal sector jobs and other opportunities for wages became scarce, more recently, immigration became necessary for survival in sectors of both the urban and rural poor. We see this trend with Ignacio, a Mexican immigrant who worked at age sixteen as a welder in a factory. The low pay, in combination with an occupational accident, opened the door to migration in a town where going to "*el norte*" was increasingly becoming the norm: "What I made was not enough. . . . For me to sustain my family—I am talking [about] my brothers and my parents—it was in reality little money. You could not make money. . . . From my town, many people were coming [to the United States] and that is where I said, 'I am going too.'"

In the countryside, immigration replaced small-farm credit, price supports, and crop insurance formerly provided by the state. But domestic migration to big cities no longer produced income for struggling families in home communities, prompting international migration. Moreover, absent household members and the loss of their daily contributions made it harder to survive in Mexican cities.[40] For instance, Maruja illustrated this challenge when she explained why she did not migrate to Mexico City and instead went from her rural community directly to the United States: "My town does not have that custom of leaving your small town to go to the Federal District [Mexico City]." When asked the question, "What is the custom in your town?" Maruja responded, "[To] emigrate to the United States and earn dollars. . . . Earn dollars and send dollars. Once you have dollars you immediately have a house, you have a car very quickly, and you have luxuries very quickly. So I wanted to earn dollars and come to the United States. . . . Like people do. Because those ideas got in my head so much that I would see other persons who did it and I would say, 'I want to do it too.'" Thus, international migration spread from sender communities with immigration traditions stemming from the 1940s to communities that had never before seen such high levels of emigration. As Maruja's example shows, rather than a localized or regional occurrence with long tradition, emigration from Mexico became "a national phenomenon" that covered the country during the late 1990s.[41]

Digno, a Mexican construction manager, saw no future for himself in his country either and blamed it on government economic managers during a focus group of Mexican immigrants in 2004. "A while back we were talking about a future for Mexico," he said. "But Mexico is totally, terribly administered. Without a good administration, there is no work . . . so I came here because of secondary effects. All of us are secondary effects of a terribly administered future." Declines in state investment that directly and indirectly affected the lives of immigrants cast doubts on the citizenry's ability to trust government officials. Concerns about how governments managed national economies reverberated throughout our sample and were seen not just among the poor and working classes, but also the middle and upper middle sectors of Latin American countries. As Esteban, a Colombian, put it, "The problem with Colombia is basically the economic part, which is not doing well because of a lack of good governability. . . . Everything flows from the lack of good governing of the state. There is a lot of state corruption. Because of that it generates resentment in the lower classes, and because of that come problems with insecurity. It is all like one big chain."

Alejandro Portes and Rubén Rumbaut as well as Douglas Massey and his colleagues have argued that the poorest sectors of immigrant-sending nations do not emigrate because they lack the capital to finance the move.[42] Although we heard from many poor families who reported struggling economically in their home countries, many of these experiences were limited to Mexican immigrants and those from countries in the Caribbean. Although we heard from members of the middle and upper middle classes of these countries too, most of our qualitative sample participants from South America, in comparison, originated from the more privileged economic strata of their societies.

Emigrants from Middle- and Upper-Middle-Class Sectors

Structural adjustment led to a sharp increase in international migration from countries such as Colombia and Peru between 1988 and 2000.[43] In Peru, structural adjustment provoked inflation that averaged 4,000 percent between 1988 and 1990, devastating real wages. After 1993, economic recovery did not return employment to previous levels. Peru's economy eventually stabilized "with widespread impoverishment and underemployment. . . . [Structural adjustment] has tended to increase the economic vulnerability of Peruvians while reducing basic safeguards to a minimum."[44]

Both wages and employment fell to levels where families could not sustain themselves on the domestic labor market. Diego, a Peruvian immigrant, found no work in a new field of expertise in which he retrained after having to close down his business: "The possibilities of working in my profession were practically taken over. I worked hard on my own business, but it did not do well and I had to close. For four years I tried to make it work. The situation under Fujimori was good at first but fell [apart].[45] I am talking about 1997. The economic situation forced me to close my business. Then I worked for the government and after that I decided to study. When I finished my MBA [master of business administration], I realized that there were no job opportunities for a forty-four-year-old person."

Our interview with Joaquín, another Peruvian, stands out for the psychological toll that his family's financial insecurity took on him. Joaquín told us of the constant humiliation he experienced while living in Lima because his parents could not pay their bills. The shame he faced escalated after he started finding notifications from debt collectors taped to the front door of his house. He stopped bringing friends home to avoid feeling embarrassed. The pressure of not having money and the persistence and constant harassment of the debt collectors took its toll as he attempted to cope with a situation he could not control: "I had had personal problems and some notes on the door all day from the credit cards saying that we are debtors and all of that. Forget it, it was driving me crazy. I even had to go to a psychologist." Until recently, Colombia and Peru had companies that specialized in sending collectors dressed in unique costumes to the homes or workplaces of debtors. The idea was to shame the person to force them to pay the debt.[46] Those with resources and contacts abroad left. The rallying cry became "*Sálvese quien pueda*"—"Save yourself if you can."[47]

The increasing socioeconomic diversity of emigrants was not limited to Peru and others we have mentioned. Moreover, the number of US immigrants from most Latin American and Caribbean countries dramatically increased after 1986, even among countries with long-standing migration flows. Some countries in the region did not become major exporters of migrants until the 1980s and 1990s. Countries with the highest annual growth rates of populations in the United States in the 1990s were Brazil, Ecuador, Honduras, and Colombia.[48] In other cases, such as in Puerto Rico, already high levels of migration to the United States intensified. As mentioned previously, migration remained an escape valve during a period of "deep economic and social malaise" in Puerto Rico.[49] In the late 2000s, levels of out-migration rivaled those of the "great migration" of the 1940s and 1950s, and by 2006, more Puerto Ricans lived in the continental United States than on the island.[50] The strongest indicator of Puerto Rican out-migration is the unemployment differential with the United States.[51] For example, Hector, who arrived in 1989, decided to migrate to Florida because he lost his job in Puerto Rico. Some of his friends told him that in Miami, he would find more opportunities to make money and more jobs than in Puerto Rico, where the unemployment rate was so high. Because he believed finding a job on the island was going to be difficult, he decided to take the risk and stated, "This is why I am here. I just packed my bags and got on a plane."

Although Puerto Rican migrants consist largely of blue-collar and service workers, increasingly members of the island's middle class have left to look for education, greater financial security, and a better "quality of life."[52] Their social networks in Miami made their decisions easier, as in Paola's case: "In reality I chose Miami because of my education, but since I have an aunt, my mom's sister, well that facilitated it for me." Ruben, also Puerto Rican, alluded to the environment of public insecurity on the island: "[I needed] a change because things were getting very bad. Things were clearer here and there were more opportunities."

Dominicans also relied on social networks to come to the United States. Sometimes these networks led them to the Northeast, but within a few years, they would relocate to Miami. Economic insecurity related to austerity measures often prompted these moves. In the following example, Josue's migration was tied to mass layoffs in the phone company:

> The reason why I came here, first because people had talked to me about Miami as a very cosmopolitan city. . . . And they told me I would like Miami. Things are more or less on the go. . . . But the motive to come here was really economic. I worked at a large Dominican company, the phone company back then it was called [sic]. But, since during that time the country was undergoing a hard economic situation, they started cutting back personnel. Not just in our community but 7,000 employees in communities around the whole country. Four thousand employees remained. Those [layoffs] were in droves. In many of the large businesses too. . . . And they said to me, "You should go to Miami. You will like it more than New York."

In sum, among middle- and upper-middle-class sectors of Latin American and Caribbean societies, downward mobility, overall insecurity, and loss of hope for a more secure future influenced immigration decisions. Lola's company in Peru went under, and she worried about her children's future. In Colombia, twenty-nine-year-old medical school graduate Ariana saw a future that "was, with each day, more dark. . . . Instead of seeing that there would be a sun at the end of the tunnel, the tunnel closed each day more. Here I believe that hope persists. In Colombia, I feel that even hope has been lost." Some lost hope was rooted in a growing perception of physical insecurity related to increasing violence.

Citizen Insecurity and Violence

The waves of violence and public insecurity that have swept through many Latin American countries since the 1980s have several causes. Magaly Sanchez R. identifies different forms of violence that emerge from different historical periods:

> First came structural violence, the rampant economic inequality, social exclusion, and persistent poverty arising from the imposition of neoliberal economic policies. In response came two other kinds of collective violence, one political and the other criminal. As the urgency of circumstances facing middle- and working-class people increased, many turned to radical violence, leading to successive waves of strikes, demonstrations, and insurrections throughout the region. At the same time, the situation of the poor and the young deteriorated, and many of them turned to criminal violence in the form of youth gangs, criminal mafias, and drug cartels.[53]

As we have seen, economic insecurity is among the biggest sources of anxiety for Latin Americans. However, our participants also talked about crime in the form of violent armed robbery and kidnappings as their most common fears. Jaime, a Dominican in one of our focus groups, explained that not until the 1980s did migration begin to be considered as a strategy to combat not only political and economic insecurity but also fear tied to lack of physical safety:

> Every time we came for vacation we came here [Miami]. And we never thought of coming for a position . . . [because] the island was very calm. But after the eighties, the country started to change a lot and the quality of life was very difficult. . . . So right now, the country is exposed. I have a friend that was vice president of a bank and he was kidnapped and then they kidnapped his daughter. It has now been three years since I went back to the country. I don't know how it is but I have heard comments of how life is. It does not interest me at all to go back. . . . When things started to deteriorate at the beginning of the 1990s and in '91 and the situation was that everything was very expensive . . . [it was] hard and we decided to leave and sell our properties that we had there. And right in time because practically the ship has sunk from what I have heard.

Citizen insecurity, including crime and other street-level violence, was often cited among the reasons for leaving Latin American and Caribbean countries in the 1980s and 1990s. Surveys corroborate our participants' perceptions that in Latin America, crime is considered the second most important problem after unemployment (see Figure 2.2).

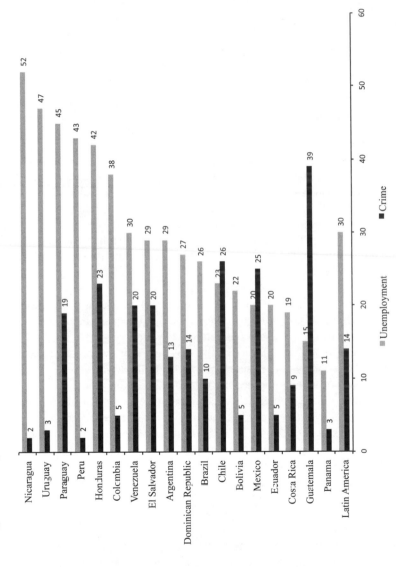

Figure 2.2 Top Two Most Important Problems in Latin America by Country, 2005 (percentage)

Source: Corporación Latinobarómetro (2005).

Latin America is not only the most socially and economically unequal region in the world but also among the most violent, particularly since the 1980s.[54] The United Nations Development Programme has linked this criminal violence and citizenry insecurity to social factors including social inequality and underemployment, among younger cohorts in particular,[55] which are rooted in the structural violence that Sanchez R. describes above. Structural violence is thus imposed through societal mechanisms (e.g., discrimination and exploitation) that lead to inequality.[56] Thus, contrary to the past, criminal violence is not necessarily politically motivated; Imbusch, Misse, and Carrión argue that this violence takes the form of "social, anomic, or criminal violence . . . [and] it is an expression of social and economic, but not of political conflict," becoming the leading cause of death for people ages fifteen to forty-four.[57] Together these serve as backdrops to insecurity and make up the social context from which emigrants departed.[58]

Participants in our study often expressed fear of kidnappings, which were quite common during the 1990s and early 2000s. A study conducted by Fundación Libre, a Colombian nongovernmental organization, shows that the number of kidnappings in Colombia started to increase around 1998, when a total of 2,860 cases were reported. By 2000, with a record 3,572 individuals kidnapped, Colombia was seen as "the kidnapping capital of the world." Many Latin American countries also started to experience record numbers of kidnappings in the late 1990s through the 2000s.[59] Today, Lola Viviana Esguerra Villamizar estimates that 75 percent of world kidnappings take place in Latin America and the Caribbean.[60] These record levels of violence throughout the region led many Colombians, Mexicans, Haitians, and Peruvians to flee their countries because they or their families were vulnerable to extortion and threats by common criminals, guerrillas, and paramilitary groups. Feeling that their governments could not protect them and lacking alternative solutions to living in fear, many of our interviewees arrived in the United States seeking asylum to protect themselves and their families.

Different kidnapping modalities proliferated in the region and affected the population as a whole, not just the direct victims. In Colombia, kidnappings were closely linked to armed conflict, political instability, and lack of state presence in rural areas. Kidnappings in Colombia occurred mostly in rural areas but involved urban victims so that hostages were often not residents of where the kidnapping occurred.[61] "Forced out" by the guerrillas in Colombia, Ivan, an upper-class Colombian in his final year of medical school, fled his homeland with his fiancée in 1999 due to guerrillas' threats against their lives. In order to complete his medical school training, Ivan was required by law to spend one year practicing medicine in a rural area. He was assigned to practice in a region controlled by the Fuerzas Armadas Revolucionarias de Colombia (FARC; Revolutionary Armed Forces of

Colombia), and as he explains, "the guerrilla there was used to being obeyed at gunpoint." Forced to treat patients for free in addition to having to provide them with free medicine, consultations, procedures, and surgeries, Ivan "obviously didn't agree; I simply did not agree with the way they made the laws. . . . That's how it [the threats against his life] all started." His fiancée was also sent to work for a year in the same rural area and ordered by the state to become an election official in a guerrilla-controlled zone. She, like Ivan, soon realized their lives were in danger since the state did not protect them. They ultimately fled to the United States because the threats not only affected their physical security but also their psychological well-being and stability. In his interview, Ivan stated,

> I think that the possibility of growing as a person, spiritually, religiously—I think that peace of mind is worth more than all the money in the world. Knowing that you're not going to be attacked tomorrow . . . that you will be able to eat tomorrow, that you will continue to rise and scale to new positions. . . . That tranquility, however difficult things are, however many battles there may be . . . I think that it makes a lot of people emigrate from their country, even those who have no reason to—having the tranquility of knowing that tomorrow, they can go on eating and living and working—and having a future.

In the rest of the region, kidnappings, the preferred mode to extort money by common criminals and even corrupt police officers, were mostly urban. While the wealthy had access to security or bodyguards to avoid high net-worth kidnappings, the middle class was unprotected and could not afford the services provided by companies such as the security company owned by Lola and her husband in Peru.

In the mid-1990s, a new modality of kidnapping emerged throughout the region as a result of the difficulty and resistance encountered by common criminals in attempts to rob banks or to kidnap wealthy businessmen. In general they became known as "express kidnappings," but were labeled *sequestro relâmpago* in Brazil [lightning-fast kidnapping]; *secuestro al paso* in Peru [kidnapping along the way]; *paseo millonario* in Colombia [millionaire's ride]; and *secuestro express* in Mexico [express kidnapping] and other countries.[62] In express kidnappings, people were surprised by two or three individuals who would either carjack them or get into taxis carrying passengers. They would reroute them to automatic teller machines (ATMs) throughout the city to get cash or go to their homes to steal jewelry, money, and other valuables. After a few hours, the targeted person would be left in the middle of a street unharmed. In Colombia, those who were affected by paseo millonario carjackings were most at risk while taking taxis. *El Tiempo*, a Colombian daily newspaper with the highest national circulation, described the process: "The passenger of a taxi is picked up, with the driver as an accomplice, by other delinquents that take him to ATMs to withdraw money and hand it over. In the *fleteo*, the delinquents intercept a person that previously took out money from a bank, to steal it."[63] Throughout Latin America, express kidnappings represented a constant threat to citizens at all times and hours; *Caretas*, a political magazine in Lima, noted in 1996,

> Business owners, businessmen, executives, professionals, homemakers, university students, whoever uses [a] new car or who appears to have a good economic situation can be kidnapped *al paso*. No matter the neighborhood, the time, or the abundance of people who transit in the area. A successful businessman from La Victoria or El Mercado Central can be temporarily kidnapped in the afternoon, upon leaving his/her business. A business owner could be intercepted on Colonial Avenue, in El Callao, or in Breña at 7 o'clock at night. . . . A housewife could be assaulted in La Molina or in San Borja in the afternoon. A student could be kidnapped in Surco when she leaves the university at any time of the day.[64]

This quote clearly emphasizes that not a single safe area could be found in Lima and everyone was at risk. Camila, a Peruvian in our sample, stated that as she talked with her friends, cousins, and family generally, the criminality prevented her from contemplating a return to Peru: "The social part, the insecurity. . . . It is the aspect of frequent criminality. In any zone, you don't have security. Kidnappings—there is no tranquility." From the introductory chapter, we know that Colombian Alejandra wanted to return to her native country to reunite with her children and because she sought the positive feelings this reunion would bring her. She understood these feelings would compensate for the economic hit she might take if she were to return. But, like Camila described above, she was afraid for her safety and worried about declining opportunities for her children: "The kidnappings that are going on in the schools, and obviously the possibility that, the same opportunities that we have, my children will not have. No, I mean, to live comfortably and accessing everything with education, being able to pay for universities, working where you truly want to be working, in your profession, that does not exist anymore. It is too difficult."

Caretas indicated that women in particular were at high risk from express kidnapping.[65] In this respect, rates of gender violence in Latin America and their escalation in the past two decades are palpable concerns for women in the region.[66] Small Arms Survey, an independent research project at the Graduate Institute of International and Development Studies in Geneva, Switzerland, notes that of the twenty-five countries with high and very high feminicide rates, over half are in the Americas (four in the

Caribbean, four in Central America, and six in South America). Moreover, regions with the highest rates of lethal violence are also those with the highest feminicide levels.[67]

El Salvador has emerged as the country with the highest feminicide rate in the world. Importantly, in El Salvador and Colombia (ranked first and tenth, respectively), the majority of feminicides are not committed by intimate partners, which is the case, for example, in the United States. Thus, feeling vulnerable to physical harm was particularly pronounced among women.

Citizen insecurity and violence should not be conceived of as a phenomenon separate from economics when looking for the reasons why record numbers of immigrants left Latin America and the Caribbean under neoliberalism. Economic forces that function as "push factors" for emigration are connected to citizen insecurity and criminal violence, something our participants seemed to intrinsically understand when they intermingled reasons for emigration while describing their departures as well as the reasons why they would not consider return.

Ozius, a musician, left Haiti unexpectedly when a US cruise line recruiter came to his village, but when asked what he would need to return to Haiti, he mentioned both professional resources and greater security. "If I return, you want to know if I need money, if I need a house, if I need two, three cars? Tell them that I want an entire music studio. And that I need ten security guards [and] three police dogs."

Damian, a Colombian trucking company executive who was threatened by the guerrillas, had always planned to come to the United States to work but moved up his departure after his family's company was targeted. Guerrillas had burned their trucks, stolen merchandise, and extorted money from them. Damian came from Colombia seeking "security, [and] tranquility. . . . It was terrible, terrible." As Ibrahim Sirkeci has noted in his research on insecurity and migration in Iraq, an "environment of insecurity" often accelerates migration for those who already were considering it as an option.[68] Ivan, also Colombian, and mentioned earlier, similarly moved up his plans to emigrate after being threatened by guerrillas. The psychic and physical insecurity were compelling reasons for immigrants to leave what they had attained behind: "There was a time when I felt trapped for six months in Bogotá," said Ivan. "I was even scared to answer the telephone. This was the last drop that overturned the cup."

In sum, in addition to issues of economic insecurity stemming from neoliberal policies, many middle-class professionals from our sample cited personal insecurity as a reason for departure. But often, physical insecurity and economic insecurity were interrelated. As Camila, from Peru, stated, "The bad part is . . . the political situation, the insecurity that there is, the lack of employment, that you don't know how long your job will last, that you cannot plan for the future, that you cannot plan for your children's future." She and her husband moved to Miami after he lost his job. She said both the economy and public insecurity prompted their decision.

Comingling of Political and Economic Instability

Katrina Burgess notes that even though political crises and instability were present in several immigrant-producing Latin American and Caribbean countries in the 1990s, economic push factors were common to all of them.[69] Criminal violence and political insecurity were the most mentioned reasons for exiting their country by Colombian and Peruvian participants in the qualitative sample. Our Haitian participants, however, who tended to migrate as youths in order to reunite with a previously departed parent, cited an overall sense of insecurity as the primary reason they would not return. Although applications for asylum on behalf of Haitians are frequently denied under the assumption that they are economic migrants, our data illustrate that the environments of insecurity that frame the conditions that expel Haitians are rooted in economic, social, *and* political instability, further complicated by natural disasters.

Gross domestic product in Haiti fell three of the nine years between 1997 and 2005. In addition, gross domestic product per capita fell five of nine years. Visas granted to Haitians to visit the United States, a common means of arriving and staying on without legal permission to immigrate, almost doubled between 1993 and 2000. Immigrant admission through family reunification and other legal means increased 61 percent between 1993 and 2008.[70] Migration was a way to escape not only declining economic conditions but political instability and social insecurity. As Patrick explained, "There was a political situation that happened in Haiti, [so] that I felt that I had to leave the country. I arrived [in] 1994. I arrived by plane. It was the three of us that arrived that sought political refuge together. . . . It was all a risk. Everyone was in danger. My political participation made it so that I had to leave and come to the United States so that I might not die. It was the military regime; you know that in 1991 there was a coup d'état that happened. Jean-Bertrand Aristide left the country, but the military was always there brutalizing and torturing people."

Around the same time that Patrick came to the United States, Deborah Sontag of the *New York Times* wrote about the Haitian diaspora in the United States. One statement that she made stands out for its on-point description of the Haitian case: "Every wave of migration from Haiti has come during political turmoil there, but economic malaise always accompanies such turmoil. So it is often difficult to distinguish political from economic migrants."[71] This logic applies to the following case, where Stephane told us that he had emigrated for economic reasons, but then followed up by saying, "Well, the reason that I felt like coming here is because I was in a [occupational] position, and I saw that the government was falling apart. And I felt I was not going to stay in the position that I was in, and I said I have to put wind in my wings [*put a pep in my step*] because I already have two children, so that I could raise my children."

For Haitians, as well as others in our sample, economic, political, physical, and social insecurity become conflated. Moreover, as seen in our Haitian sample, many families are forced to migrate in stages. For example, Stephane left his children when he came to the United States in search of greater economic security. Fredeline, on the other hand, lived with her grandmother in Haiti until her parents sent for her at age seven.

In short, political instability and ensuing violence have become part of daily life for Latin American and Caribbean populations. However, economic deprivation must take a central space in any analysis of its causes, and this realization brings the discussion back to the effect of the failures of neoliberal economic reforms. Sanchez R. argues that to enforce economic austerity, state force is implied, and "its ubiquity throughout the region suggests that, at the very least, it constitutes a necessary condition for the incorporation of nations into the global market economy under neoliberalism."[72] She also notes that the region's economically pressured middle and working classes have turned to repeated strikes and street demonstrations, toppling governments in Ecuador, Argentina, and elsewhere before eventually electing a new type of leader in many countries across the Americas that has turned away from neoliberalism and its unfettered faith in market economics. As conditions of the poor deteriorated, however, a number of the young shunned political protest to participate in gangs, criminal mafias, and drug cartels. Violence and criminal behavior have even been legitimized under conditions of extreme social exclusion and economic isolation. Thus, the violence that many immigrants in our sample fled from is rooted in structural violence through the imposition of neoliberal policies and the ensuing insecurity that resulted from various social groups' reactions to austerity measures. The way that those in our study responded to these social processes was by exiting those environments of insecurity.

Seeking Educational Opportunities and Individual Freedoms Abroad

As economic, political, and social factors become comingled, emigrants look toward possibilities for creating better futures, often framing their pursuits in terms of seeking greater educational opportunities and better quality of life. Ariana, a Colombian doctor, acknowledged the lack of economic opportunities, set against a background of physical insecurity, but also emphasized the anticipated gains of migration in terms of ensuring greater social security: "I decided to come initially because the situation in my country was becoming more complicated economically in the health area. I had just graduated in medicine, so I decided to come here, first to be able to do my specialization in this country because I consider the education here better than in Colombia at the postgraduate level, and also looking for new options to improve my life both economically and socially, looking for a better future for my children, and in general for all of the family, as well as fleeing the violence and all of the aggression that Colombia was living in that moment."

Within a context of growing insecurity, time and again, our participants voiced the desire to maintain their lifestyles in declining economic conditions by getting an advanced education, practicing their chosen profession, or participating in a consumerist lifestyle. At the same time, greater economic vulnerability and other forms of insecurity coincided with the spread of new communication technologies, increasing the economic, cultural, transport, and informational ties between the United States and Latin America.[73] "I am from Coahuila [a Mexican border state]," said Miranda, who immigrated in 1997. "I studied computer engineering and I came here supposedly for a year to save money to do my masters and to study English, but then I stayed on." Juan was from Mexico City and came "to find a job where I can develop in my career, a career similar to hers, in computers. . . . I have a [work] visa. I am trying to develop, to improve myself here. I am seeking a better economic future."

Amelia, from Colombia, explained that when she turned age thirty-two, she wanted to move out of her parents' house and live independently, but she discovered she had been out of college too long to find work in Cartagena in the year 2000. She had vacationed in Miami and thought she could find work there. "I began to look for work in Colombia, and it was really hard because in Colombia they want recent graduates," she said. "I had graduated a long time ago." Similarly, Dori, a Peruvian, alluded to the age discrimination in her home country that exacerbated feelings of insecurity: "[In the United States] one can work here and the work is hard but well paid," she said. "Everything is abysmal in Peru. From age forty on, there's no work for the old people."

The sense of social insecurity that emerges from our interviews is also related to perceptions of declining social rights in various countries. Neoliberal policies often are accompanied by cuts in public expenditures that erode the social safety nets designed to help populations survive in times of need. The resulting social insecurity and instability framed the kinds of decisions that Dori and others made. While Dori's decision seems rash (she came on a temporary visa and stayed), it highlights the perceived instability in her home country.

Puerto Ricans, because of their citizenship status and longer migration history, also show a pattern of coming to the United States to improve themselves through education. "In my case, it was that to obtain a better education we had to come to the United States," said Yolanda, who completed her doctorate and worked at a university. "And that was something in my house they explained to us since we were little. 'You have to get good grades. You have to study to get into a good university. It is going to be there [United States] and not here [Puerto Rico] because here things are worse off and you have to do your part to have a better future.'" When governments reduce debt by slashing social spending, environments of insecurity are more likely to form given resulting social unrest. Educational institutions are not spared. In countries such as Mexico and Nicaragua and in Puerto Rico, the mid to late 1990s and 2000s witnessed student protests over university tuition hikes that resulted from austerity measures. At times, these protests turned violent.[74] Both the causes and consequences of protest activities underscore the backgrounds against which migration decisions are made.

In the case of Cubans, the pursuit of individual freedom and the desire to better themselves led many to decide to leave. For example, Ernesto reported that his financial situation was the primary motivator for migration, but when he elaborated on his response, he described what was really a desire for individual accomplishment: "The economic situation was really one of the principal causes. But in my case, the fact that I worked at a place that was supposedly pretty good, that influenced a lot. But I had no opportunity to study more, I had to dedicate myself 100 percent to my job, and what else was I going to study? It was difficult. That influenced me a lot that I didn't have a way to continue developing. . . . [You could not develop] if you did not belong to the Communist Party's organizations, to organizations such as Communist Youths, which I never . . . belonged to."

Rodolfo, who was part of the wave of *balseros* (rafters), left Cuba in August 1994 but arrived in the United States in April 1995. He left Cuba on a raft and almost made it to Key West. There were eight people in the raft including himself and his brother. The raft was intercepted at sea by the US Coast Guard nine miles from land, so they were all taken to a camp in Guantanamo Bay, where he spent nine months. During our interview, Rodolfo emphasized that he had left Cuba primarily for economic rather than political reasons: "Basically, for economic reasons. I would say I disagree when someone asks me if I left for political reasons. Although I had political reasons for coming I don't think they were my main motivation to come here." He continued, "Because it is a combination of elements. The economic sector makes room for other factors and then . . . the way in which you feel. The way in which one analyzes things comes from those economic roots. It leads you to conclusions that are political, conclusions about how society is organized and how one would want to become organized in that society, how one would want to live in that society."

Individual aspirations often emerged from consumer desires. Alvaro, a Dominican, talked about moving to the United States given the ideology that a professional should, in theory, be able to afford a consumerist lifestyle: "In Santo Domingo you can say that the person 'can live' but . . . does not have . . . rights to obtain things like a house or a car. . . . If you are a professional, you can work and live, but the possibility of obtaining those things is very difficult."

Decisions to move were commonly facilitated by social networks in the United States, particularly in the case of more mature immigrant communities, as seen in these Caribbean cases. At the same time, while many sought to reunify with family members who had already left for the US mainland, others sought independence from their kin in the home country, highlighting again migration as a vehicle to pursue individual freedom with the household representing the mediating institution that promotes or hinders migration chances. One of the participants in our Dominican focus group discussed how migration gave her and her spouse the space to develop as a couple, given that in Santo Domingo, they lived with her parents: "There are things that a marriage needs per se. In Santo Domingo, we were not achieving these. It was principally independence in our marriage, and we decided, 'Let's emigrate because the first thing we are going to accomplish is that. Being independent.'" Paradoxically, although they came to the United States searching for independence, they had to rely on US kin to access opportunities: "Well, because in reality we have family here, principally, next to me, and they opened their doors. When we came here, we came to their house." Yanira, a Puerto Rican, also came to Miami seeking a similar type of independence from her parents: "I wanted to study here. I wanted to know something different. . . . In reality it was that my parents were not letting me leave, and I wanted a bit more space."

Households represent the mediating structure by which migration decisions are made. At the household level, environments of insecurity come to intrude on individuals' perceptions of stability and the likelihood of sustaining what at one point in life might have been stable lifestyles. Although not all households migrate as a unit, the kind of migration (individual versus household) certainly shapes perceptions of security in the United States as well as the process of incorporation. We examine these in subsequent chapters.

Conclusion

For many immigrants from Latin America and the Caribbean, neoliberal reforms of the 1980s and 1990s resulted in economic instability and limited state capacity to provide adequate social safety nets in their respective countries of origin. Environments of insecurity formed in many countries in which citizens increasingly felt physically, financially, and socially vulnerable to instability. These economic transformations also affected political stability in many cases, all of which led to widespread feelings of psychic insecurity in which trust in public institutions eroded and citizen insecurity increased. This context of departure, a product of structural violence, prompted many to leave their homelands. Did immigrants find greater security when they left their home countries for Miami? Or did they trade some sources of insecurity for others? The context of reception is vital to understand how, in some cases, security was attained, but in others, the nature of insecurity changed. We turn to this in the next chapter.

Notes

1. The Cuban economy lost between $3 billion and $6 billion yearly in aid and subsidies that had been provided for decades by the Soviet Union (Purcell 1996). On the US embargo, see Nackerud and colleagues (1999).
2. Santiso 2004, pp. 828–829.
3. Cohen and Centeno 2006; Sánchez R. 2006; González de la Rocha 2006.
4. Suárez-Orozco 2005.
5. Sirkeci 2005, p. 199.
6. Duany 2011.
7. Sassen 1998.
8. Ibid.; see also Suárez-Orozco 2005.
9. Although our focus groups targeted post-1986 immigrants, participants in one of our Dominican groups invited coethnics to attend, and some of them had arrived before 1986.
10. Duany 2004.
11. Duany 2011.
12. Duany 2004; Meléndez 2007.
13. These data come from state-level comparisons of ancestry data from the US Census in 1980, 1990, and 2000.
14. Zabin and Hughes 1995.
15. Passel and Suro 2005.
16. "Foreigners Responsible" 2012; Whitefield 2012.
17. The data come from the Economic Commission for Latin America and the Caribbean (ECLAC 2005). The countries include Argentina, Bolivia, Brazil, Chile, Colombia, Costa Rica, the Dominican Republic, Ecuador, El Salvador, Guatemala, Haiti, Honduras, Mexico, Nicaragua, Panama, Paraguay, Peru, Uruguay, and Venezuela.
18. We are interested in the patterns of change for differing quintiles across a period of neoliberal consolidation. The World Bank cautions against quantitative comparison of levels of inequality between countries because of differing methodologies.
19. Open unemployment does not include those who work part-time or without benefits.
20. ECLAC 2005.

21. Ibid.
22. Haiti data come from the United Nations Development Programme (2008). The remaining data come from ECLAC (2005).
23. Ferreira et al. 2012.
24. Rivera-Batiz and Santiago 1996, p. 5.
25. Duany 2011.
26. Data come from Rivera-Batiz and Santiago (1996) and the US Department of Labor and Human Resources, Bureau of Labor Statistics, Household Surveys, 2003–2013. The data show that 2008 was a peak year for unemployment, because after that the labor force began to diminish through migration; see also Duany 2011.
27. Passel and Suro 2005.
28. Burgess 2009.
29. Duany 2011.
30. Durand and Massey 2010.
31. Burgess 2009.
32. Durand and Massey 2010.
33. Corporación Latinobarómetro 2005.
34. For groups in the ITMI Quantitative Survey with sufficient respondents, we analyze them by country of origin. However, when the numbers for particular countries are small, we aggregate respondents by region of origin instead. The country/region of origin category is used throughout the book.
35. Corporación Latinobarómetro 2005.
36. Burgess 2009; González de la Rocha 2006; Massey and Capoferro 2006; Plaza and Stromquist 2006.
37. Massey, Sanchez R., and Behrman 2006.
38. Zahin and Hughes 1995.
39. González de la Rocha 2006.
40. Ibid.
41. Burgess 2009, p. 180.
42. Portes and Rumbaut 2006; Massey, Durand, and Malone 2002.
43. Massey and Capoferro 2006.
44. Plaza and Stromquist 2006, pp. 105–106, 112.
45. Alberto Fujimori was president of Peru 1990–2000.
46. In Colombia, the *chepitos* (debt collectors) were men dressed like Charlie Chaplin (in black tuxedos) carrying briefcases along with large signs that stated *deudor moroso* (late payer). The chepito would stand all day outside the office of the debtor. Similarly, in Peru, the *hombrecitos amarillos* (little yellow men) were hired to harass anyone delinquent on a debt. Like chepitos, they were highly identifiable as debt collectors and would follow their victims from home to work using techniques that included leaving notifications on doors (such as the ones Joaquín used to find), calling at midnight, and putting notifications in major newspapers to pressure the debtor into paying to avoid further embarrassment and humiliation. Colombia outlawed this practice in 1992, and in 2004, it was declared unconstitutional in Peru where a judicial court ruled that the use of intimidating techniques violated the fundamental right to a good reputation among alleged debtors. However, the use of debt collectors is still legal in Venezuela, where more sophisticated versions of these companies are found. *Dr. Diablo* (Dr. Devil) has slogans such as "delinquency leads to hell" and "shame pays." To attack the morale and reputation of the victim, this agency sends mobile "commando" units that include a driver and young, sexy models dressed as demonettes, in addition to Rottweilers and monkeys, along with a lawyer, bodyguards, and a man dressed as the devil. They use speakers

to draw public attention. A new variant are the *mariachi diablos* (mariachi devils), whose music is used to celebrate the anniversaries of older, unpaid debts. The mariachi diablos compose and sing songs with clear allusions to the unpaid debts (Brachfield 2010).

47. Massey and Capoferro 2006.
48. Burgess 2009.
49. Rivera-Batiz and Santiago 1996, p. 5.
50. Irizarry 2008.
51. Meléndez 2007.
52. Duany 2011.
53. Sanchez R. 2006, p. 179.
54. On inequality, see Gootenberg 2010; Portes and Hoffman 2003. On violence, see Imbusch, Misse, and Carrión 2011; Muñoz 2011.
55. Muñoz 2011.
56. Menjívar and Abrego 2012.
57. Imbusch, Misse, and Carrión 2011, p. 96.
58. Muñoz 2011.
59. Esguerra Villamizar 2011.
60. Ibid.
61. Rubio 2004.
62. See Esguerra Villamizar 2011; "Se Dispara el Paseo Millonario" 2000; "Secuestro al Paso" 1996.
63. See "Se Dispara el Paseo Millonario" 2000.
64. See "Secuestro al Paso" 1996. Coauthor Hughes was express kidnapped while in Mexico City doing dissertation research in 1999. It unfolded in much the same way these press accounts describe.
65. Ibid.
66. Fregoso and Bejarano 2010.
67. Alvazzi del Frate 2011, p. 116, quoted in "Femicide: A Global Problem," Small Arms Survey 2012.
68. Sirkeci 2005.
69. Burgess 2009.
70. US Department of Homeland Security 2007; US Department of Justice 1997.
71. Sontag 1994.
72. Sanchez R. 2006, p. 178.
73. Suárez-Orozco 2005.
74. Almeida 2007; Lewin 2011.

3

The Context of Reception

The only problem here [in the United States] is the illegality. . . . Because we are not bad people and the only thing we want is to get ahead.
—Joaquín, Peruvian immigrant

Joaquín, quoted above, found some degree of economic security in the United States, leaving behind the debt and humiliation that he experienced in Peru due to the tactics of debt collectors. In the United States, though, he lacked legal authorization to work, and as we showed in the previous chapter, even though he had found a certain degree of financial stability, Joaquín felt that his wages did not reflect his worth. He attributed this discrepancy to his undocumented status, which, he believed, made him vulnerable to employment discrimination as reflected in his compensation. His legal status constrained the degree to which he could improve himself financially, and his employer profited from his vulnerable status. Joaquín essentially traded economic insecurity in Peru for legal insecurity and financial vulnerability in the United States.

Like Joaquín, upon their arrival in Miami, immigrants experienced new forms of social insecurity tied to immigration policies determining legal categories of admission. This insecurity involved their abilities to transition into more stable legal statuses and the specter of suspicion that has been cast on all immigrants after the terrorist attacks of September 11, 2001.[1] Thus, in many ways, the context of reception shaped their experiences of incorporation into the United States. More specifically, the *legal* context of reception that greets today's immigrants is one that Cecilia Menjívar and Leisy Abrego argue is a "multi-pronged system of laws at the federal, state, and local levels that promotes a climate of insecurity and suffering" that exposes immigrants and their families to "legal violence."[2] They describe the hidden and violent effects of the "underside" of these laws that essentially keep immigrants (both documented and undocumented) from access to the resources and services they need to successfully incorporate into US society. Menjívar and Abrego further argue that the blurred lines between immigration and criminal laws have "fashioned a violent context for immigrants already in the country, where social suffering becomes commonplace, normalized, and familiar."[3] They identify how legal violence exacerbates the vulnerabilities of immigrants and their families to exploitation from coethnics in the process of crossing the border; abuse from employers in the context of work; and feelings of terror that haunt immigrants when they consider that they or any individual family member could be deported at any time given the surge in raids by ICE since the mid-2000s.[4]

We argue that the context of reception is also a racialized one. In a racialized social system[5] in which corporate interests lie in the extraction of immigrants' labor from the totality of their personhood, the objectification of immigrants as labor to be deployed according to the needs of corporate and government stakeholders continues a legacy of incorporating immigrants into the United States as racial subjects. However, instead of being subjected to Jim Crow–style segregation based on race, legal status and legal violence have become the colorblind mechanism used to manipulate the conditions under which immigrant labor is deployed, retained, or expulsed according to the needs of business. In this way, immigrants' legal statuses, or their "liminal legality," that is, the "spaces between conventional legal categories" that often result in long-term states of uncertainty,[6] and immigration policies in general maintain the structure of the global city and the racial hierarchy of workers. In this chapter we examine recent changes in immigration policies and how they have shaped the context of reception in Miami. We illustrate how these policies have been key to infusing insecurity into the lives of immigrants, reminiscent of the uncertainties and anxieties of the lives they left behind.

Context of Reception and Its Sociolegal Dimensions

Adrian, who is Mexican, lived in a state of psychological uncertainty and insecurity stemming from his immigration status. He felt bitter about not being able to remain in his home country and also about the prospects of being deported from the United States on a moment's notice, particularly since he felt that migration was the only way he could sustain his economic livelihood: "All of us who came here experience bitterness because we cannot be there, in our land. We did not come by choice nor did we come as tourists. We came because of a pretty grim economic situation. And our bitterness, the most profound, is not to be able to live in our own country. To live here, always in danger of getting thrown out any day they want. This is the bitterness we live with."

The uncertainty of not knowing whether *la migra*[7] would put an end to Adrian and his family's American Dream had an enormous impact on his psyche. He felt a lack of control over his situation, clearly articulating that if he had the opportunity to give his family a better life in his homeland, he would much prefer to be in Mexico rather than to live with the uncertainty of whether they would be rounded up and deported. Thus, the sociolegal context of reception is key to understanding his lived experience.[8]

The context of reception involves multiple dimensions, including the immigration policies that shape immigrant incorporation. Policies toward various populations have the effects of either actively encouraging, passively accepting, or outright excluding immigrant groups, depending on the country of origin and its relationship with the United States.[9] The changes in immigration policies that took place in the 1990s and 2000s, particularly the draconian enforcement of immigration policies and programs after 9/11, hampered the efforts of some immigrant groups to attain security and stability in Miami. While domestic policies launched state and local-level programs, they were fueled by global events and conceptions of "threat" that transcended the state but nevertheless scapegoated various ethnic and racial minority groups within the United States.[10] We examine some of these policies next.

Securitization of Migration After 9/11

After 9/11, certain ethnic and racial minorities and immigrant communities came to be defined as threats to national security.[11] The politics of insecurity implore us to consider the definitions of who and what are defined as "threats," the perceived severity of the threat, and the conditions under which the discourse of insecurity is deployed, particularly as tools of government. Each of these—definitions, policies, and the discourses that support them—are socially constructed, politicized, and subject to contestation.[12]

The discourse of national security after 9/11 supported legislation that intended to identify menaces to the nation from within and included domestic policies focused on internal surveillance of immigrant communities.[13] Initially, many of these efforts targeted Muslims and Middle Easterners, and the organizations that served them, illustrating the erroneous assumption that US-based ethnic groups would support the presumed terroristic activities of their conationals. Suspicion eventually extended to immigrants coming from south of the US-Mexican border and parts of the Caribbean.[14] Thus, migration and security issues became conflated.[15]

The social construction of immigrants as threats flourished as Miami became more dependent on flexible immigrant labor. In the early 2000s, buzzwords like *border security* rallied individuals and agencies in efforts to reassure the US electorate that the country's international boundaries were not as porous as they were perceived to be. The logic behind immigration policies at that time was to make coming to the United States more difficult for labor migrants and international students; tougher entry policies would, in theory, keep terrorists out.[16] Even asylum policies toward certain groups were shaped by warnings that terrorists would gain entry to the country through refugee routes.[17] Moreover, domestic programs increasingly took on the approach of "attrition through enforcement—making life as difficult as possible for unauthorized immigrants to force self-deportation from the United States."[18]

Fears tied to border security exacerbated the already existing perceptions that immigrants represented cultural and social threats. Nancy Naples has shown that the formal regulatory role of the state in terms of surveillance of immigrants' lives enhanced and normalized "less formal local practices associated with the social regulation of community."[19] Examples range from state efforts to deputize community members as enforcers of immigration policies to social regulation of immigrants who are scrutinized in public when speaking their native language, Spanish.[20] As migration became conflated with national security, policies already placed in motion in the 1990s were ratcheted up in the wake of 9/11, creating new sources of insecurity for immigrants who were defined as "the other" and, in some cases, were treated as criminals.[21]

State regulation has extended to the lives of immigrants, both legal and undocumented, given the levels of restrictions placed on their abilities to engage in activities such as work, voting, education, free speech, renting an apartment, and even the use of public transit.[22] Considering the state's power to regulate the lives of those whose very existence is defined by the legal code, we absolutely must examine the policies that go into state definitions of not only who is or is not a full member but also whose presence will be acknowledged, who will remain invisible, and which categories of membership will be afforded different types of social rights.

Miami contains extreme diversity regarding the legal statuses of various immigrant populations.[23] Among these categories of membership, citizenship is typically thought of in terms of an individual's relationship to the state as a member or a "guest." Daiva Stasiulis and Abigail Bakan have argued that we often "presume that there is an ideal of citizenship which is fair, inclusive and, if not necessarily fully universal, at least constructed in such a manner that it could be reformed or adapted to incorporate differences in an egalitarian manner."[24] However, citizenship at best is an ideological construct "rather than a lived reality."[25] We see this difference between theory and practice in the erosion of social rights afforded to different groups depending on their relationship to the state. For example, new immigrants from poor, underdeveloped countries often struggle to obtain minimal privileges sometimes regardless of citizenship status.[26] Yet global capitalists often enjoy most of the privileges of formal state membership, even if they do not hold citizenship status.[27] Rather than assume social and economic outcomes are tied to a dichotomous status of citizen or noncitizen, we should examine the extent of state and social regulation of those who hold legal statuses that fall along a spectrum of membership, or as Menjívar states, in liminal spaces, which in turn is attached to varying levels of rights, benefits, and responsibilities.[28]

For some immigrants, the lack of authorization to live and work in their host countries created for them impossible situations where they were "barred from citizenship and without rights" or where they had access to formal rights but were barred from substantive rights.[29] James Holston and Arjun Appadurai claim that "the formal refers to membership in the nation-state and the substantive to the array of civil, political, socioeconomic, and cultural rights people possess and exercise."[30]

Not all citizens have access to the same rights, as seen in the historical social, cultural, and legal exclusion of African Americans, Puerto Ricans, Mexican Americans, and others, yet the promise of permanent legal status was constantly on the minds of those in our sample who lacked it. Adding to the complexity of admittance, the categories of admission that are folded into immigration policies perform the function of sorting populations into varying categories of membership in the nation-state—with greater or lower levels of psychic insecurity attached to them. In spite of the variation in these modes of entry, we argue that the trend of criminalizing immigrants, which accelerated in the 1990s and intensified in the 2000s, is one in which immigrants in general have come under scrutiny to the point where the status itself has been infused with criminal meanings. Although undocumented immigrants, such as visa overstayers and those who arrived with no entry authorization, are most likely to be criminalized in this environment, the suspicion is extended to other immigrants, based on physical appearance or use of Spanish or Haitian Creole, regardless of what their legal status actually is.

Criminalizing Immigrants and the Stigma of Illegality

When we began our study in 2003, the post-9/11 anti-immigrant movement was well under way and very much felt in Miami. For that reason, and to protect participants in our study, we avoided questions or issues related to legal status in our qualitative interview guide as well as our phone survey, the former of which included over 60 questions, and the latter, over 130. We were thus quite surprised by the large number of our interviewees who spontaneously started talking about their status during interviews, focus groups, and in participant observation settings, both private and public (dinner parties, Tri-Rail,[31] Metrorail,[32] etc.). Even in the 2008 phone survey that we conducted, in spite of never asking about legal status, at least 50 of 1,268 participants volunteered that they were or had been undocumented at some point.

During a focus group conducted with Peruvians and Colombians in 2005, the participants discussed the topic of "illegality" and criminality, a conversation that emerged after talking about why they had immigrated to the United States. Ernestina said, "It is an offense to come. For example, I have committed an offense because I came as a tourist and I am lying. When I decided to come to work, I knew I would be committing an offense." Mario added, "But it is a worse offense to stay in my country and not be able to feed my children." Dulce pointed out, "But the jobs we all do here are the jobs that nobody wants!" And Guillermo finished the conversation by saying, "And the people from here, the natives will not do them. And if they decide to do them, it would cost the state a lot more [than to hire us]. . . . I believe that here you work hard, here or back in Peru. We are not taking anything from anyone."

This spontaneous exchange illustrates the mixed feelings of the participants regarding their immigration statuses. When Ernestina stated that she had committed an offense by coming to the United States without authorization, the others, probably thinking about themselves, offered explanations for why she (and they) had done so as well. John Morton, assistant secretary for ICE, stated during an interview in February 2010 that "immigration laws are civil in nature," and as a result, an immigrant could be in the country unauthorized without making an "illegal" entry or using fraudulent documents if he or she overstayed a visa.[33] However, the policies of recent years have escalated legal penalties for being undocumented, as seen in the many efforts to cast immigrants as committing criminal offenses by being out of status. In the exchange above, however, the discourse reveals that the kind of law that participants had the most respect for was natural law, acknowledging, perhaps from their experiences in their countries of origin and now in the United States, that man-made laws that limit human rights are illogical and illegitimate, and that the obligation to feed one's family is ultimately the highest form of law by which they should abide.

As important, this exchange shows that, for immigrants, lack of legal status is a painful issue as well as a constant reminder of their lack of rights in US society. Endemic to the experience of being undocumented is to not internalize the constructions of criminality that abound in the media and the stigma attached to immigrants generally. Increasingly, it involves managing the fear and anxiety invoked by rumors of government raids and stories of detention or, worse, deportation of community members.

In 2003, ICE, the largest investigative branch of the Department of Homeland Security, devised a new strategic plan, known as Operation Endgame. Operation Endgame called for expedited efforts to apprehend and remove the backlog of "alien fugitives" from the country by 2012.[34] Operation Endgame resulted in a record number of deportations under the administration of George W. Bush and only intensified under the administration of Barack Obama.[35] Moreover, the process of immigrant removal increasingly came to rely on immigrant detention.[36] Thus, we see how the criminalization of undocumented immigrants embodies efforts to convert what was considered to be a civil offense into a criminal one.[37] As Mateo, a Peruvian, put it, "We are not bad people. Maybe the only bad thing we have done is to come here illegally. But illegally for what? To work."

In addition to detention, the criminalization of immigrants involves recruiting local and state law enforcement to carry out immigration laws, and increasingly it relies on getting bureaucrats and civilians (e.g., hospital workers, teachers) involved in the common goal of identifying and removing undocumented immigrants from their communities. This approach will make us all, in Helen Marrow's words, the "immigration police."[38]

The criminalization of immigrants has been at the forefront of policies and pilot programs carried out in the state of Florida. As the nation's "testing ground for anti-immigrant measures and enforcement ideas," attorneys from the former Florida Immigrant Advocacy Center (currently known as Americans for Immigrant Justice) have argued that "much of what happens in Florida has a rippling effect nationally."[39] In 2002, the state was the first to sign a memorandum of agreement (MOA) with the Department of Justice in which a number of Florida's state and local law enforcement officials were deputized to perform immigration enforcement functions, including the right to access immigration databases and to question and detain immigrants.[40] The deputized officers received a mere six-week training course to educate them on the intricacies of immigration law, according to some, a set of laws more complex than the US tax code, with over twenty-five different types of nonimmigration visas alone.[41] Moreover, local police in the state were found to be "arbitrarily turning immigrants over to Border Patrol after stopping them for routine traffic violations or, worse, stopping them for no reason at all other than that they 'look' and 'speak' like foreigners."[42] With the full support of then governor Jeb Bush, this pilot program brought to life Section 287(g) of IIRIRA; since then, 287(g) MOAs have been extended to jurisdictions all over the country.[43]

Although the argument can be made that in Miami, this kind of racial profiling could be impossible due to the large Latino population, profiling can rely on more than race, such as perceived class status, and can occur at different scales. At the macrolevel, the South Florida region is singled out as a testing ground for new immigration programs precisely because of the high concentrations of Latino and immigrant populations. As such, Miami as a place has been racialized and can be considered to be racially profiled, by being a consistent target for pilot testing. At a microlevel of analysis, as we will see in Chapter 6, within the Latino population, the poor as well as Latinos who "look Mexican" have become proxies for undocumented populations, reflecting how race, class, nationality, and illegality have become conflated not just in the eyes of non-Latinos, but precisely within the Latino population itself. Although racial profiling efforts are more easily identifiable in mostly white areas of the country, in a multiethnic metropolitan area with a high concentration of immigrants, other factors, such as markers of class status and nationality, emerge as ways to profile populations based on conceptions of race that encompass other social attributes.

For immigrants, the stakes are high in the game of racial profiling, largely due to the federal program known as Secure Communities that was implemented in 2008 under the Bush administration and expanded during the first Obama presidential term. This program created government partnerships with a number of local jurisdictions around the country that involved information sharing between the Federal Bureau of Investigation and ICE.[44] Two rounds of data sharing aiming to match the fingerprints of suspects with those contained in immigration databases resulted in ICE having the authority to instruct local authorities to detain individuals in question until federal officials could initiate removal proceedings.

Although in 2011 President Obama ordered the use of prosecutorial discretion in determining whom to detain for deportation, large numbers of noncriminal individuals have been deported through the Secure Communities Program in Florida.[45] The percentages of immigrants without criminal backgrounds who were deported through the program in South Florida included 62 percent of those apprehended in Palm Beach County, 57 percent in Broward County, and 51 percent in Miami-Dade County.[46] Many were arrested for minor offenses such as driving a car with a broken taillight.[47] Some believe that the program *encourages* racial profiling, considering that 93 percent of those apprehended under Secure Communities at a national level were Latino, even though Latinos made up 77 percent of the undocumented immigrant population.[48]

In addition to local police turning immigrants over to ICE and the immigration checks that were implemented for driver's licenses as of 2005, stepped-up enforcement targeting immigrants included militarized tactics reminiscent of large-scale operations used to arrest gangs or armed criminals. Some of the lexicon employed by immigration enforcement agencies suggests a militarized worldview that contributes to the construction of immigrants as the enemy within. The Department of Homeland Security, through ICE, launched the National Fugitive Operations Program in 2003, the year we began our interviews. The program was advertised as being designed "to dramatically expand the agency's effort to locate, arrest, and re-move fugitives from the United States."[49] ICE defines a fugitive as "an alien who has failed to leave the United States based upon a final order of removal, deportation, or exclusion; or who has failed to report to ICE after receiving notice to do so."[50]

The primary mission of ICE's "fugitive operation teams" is ostensibly to apprehend aliens considered to be a threat to national security, including members of transnational street gangs, child sex offenders, and aliens with prior convictions for violent crimes. However, in reality, agents often seek to apprehend otherwise law-abiding families who have ignored deportation orders. Researchers from the Migration Policy Center found that almost three-quarters (73 percent) of the individuals apprehended in fugitive oper-ations between 2003 and 2008 had no prior criminal history.[51]

Psychic Insecurity Tied to Immigration Enforcement and Anti-Immigrant Discourse

The implementation of driver's license checks, local-federal information sharing, and news, rumors, or concrete experiences with militarized raids made immigrants' lives less secure by instilling in them fear of the police and immigration officials. This distrust led to immigrants' reluctance to re-port crimes and to come forth as either victims or witnesses to crime; fur-thermore, evidence suggests that some are even turning to legal immigrants to report these crimes for them or to have them conduct any business with government officials for them so as to remain "under the radar."[52] The fear of being detained or deported was palpable among some of the immigrants in our research. As one of our respondents, Lola, a Peruvian, put it, "I think that the principal problem here [in South Florida] is to have a fear of the police . . . fear that they will grab you, that they will deport you, that they will harm you in some way . . . but at least you can walk freely through the streets without fearing that you will be robbed or held up or anything else."

As Lola's comments suggest, moving to Miami meant that she no longer feared being victimized by crime like she had been in Peru; how-ever, like many other undocumented immigrants, she also suggested that they themselves have been labeled as criminals in the United States. The greatest fear for many of those we interviewed whose legal status was un-certain was to be pulled over by a police officer while driving, not be able to produce the proper documentation, and possibly be jailed or deported altogether.

Living with these fears created a new sense of vulnerability and inse-curity in immigrants' lives. One of the coauthors of this book, Elena Sabo-gal, who interviewed many of the undocumented immigrants in our sample and who was invited on multiple occasions to dinner parties with participants and their friends and families, witnessed firsthand the terror that immigrants felt, particularly when they needed to go out in public, drive, or even take public transportation. At one of these dinner parties, one of the guests told of being pulled over for a minor traffic infraction. He recounted the terror he felt when a highway patrol officer asked for his driver's license and how the stress of that encounter led him to believe he was going to go into cardiac arrest. Similarly, on another occasion, Martin, a Peruvian participant in one of our focus groups, explained that he was fearful of driving because he already had been pulled over once and was asked for proof of residency.

High-profile cases of seemingly arbitrary detentions heightened these fears. One such case, involving Peruvian immigrant Lourdes Sandivar, was closely followed by participants and other Miami immigrants because it was widely publicized in Spanish-language media in 2004. Sandivar was a clear example of the program's efforts to arrest people who did not comply with removal procedures but who had no prior criminal history.[53]

In early 2004, the *Miami Herald* reported that Lourdes Sandivar was followed by federal agents to her house after she dropped off her children at school. The officers then ordered her to contact her husband, José, at his place of work to ask him to come home. Although neither of the Sandivars had a criminal record, José was taken to Krome Detention Center in Miami, while Lourdes was allowed to stay home on the condition that she wore an electronic monitoring device on her ankle.[54] In addition, Lourdes was not allowed to leave Broward County without permission and had to remain in her home between 5 p.m. and 6 a.m. Her phone calls were monitored, and she was asked to remove the answering machine, caller ID, and call-waiting phone features. Lourdes was randomly selected to participate in the Electronic Monitoring Program, a pilot program being tested in Florida by Homeland Security. Since then, the use of ankle monitors has expanded to the rest of the country to allow immigrants to stay at home while they wait for their cases to be heard in defensive procedures.[55] The Sandivars were not successful in securing asylum. After eleven years of building lives in the United States, the couple was deported to Peru in 2004, leaving the country with their two US-born children.

Our participants heard of these and other similar traumatic experiences through local media. These ordeals demonstrated to them that even though they upheld the law and tried to participate in the social life and economic development of the community, they still could be detained or deported without warning. The threat of deportation illustrates how legal violence shaped their everyday lives by not only engendering a sense of uncertainty and insecurity, but also increasing their social suffering.[56] On top of being formally excluded from membership and belonging in civil society, this legal violence and the fear such stories created informally kept them from civic engagement and other modes of social integration. The local media in particular contained reports of fugitive squads breaking into private homes in the middle of the night to detain parents in front of terrified children. This situation was experienced by a Haitian couple in 2006. The couple was arrested in their home, in front of their children, ages two and five. In spite of the mother's pleas to be allowed to stay with her children, and in contrast to Lourdes Sandivar's case, the agents detained both parents and took them to a Pompano Beach detention center.[57] The couple, who asked the reporter that they not be identified, left their US-born children behind with an aunt in South Florida and returned to Haiti alone.[58]

We highlight these cases because their outcomes led to fear and psychic insecurity among the immigrants we spoke to. These stories became part of a context in which immigrants felt persecuted. In the spring of 2006, as we continued with fieldwork, immigrants in our sample told of constant rumors that police were requesting documents in restaurants, shopping malls, and public transportation, which in some cases led to mass panic. In April of that year, for example, informants called our attention to a rumor that the Dadeland Mall in South Miami had been locked down while police requested proof of legal residency from shoppers. Even some graduate students at the University of Miami received text messages about these rumored raids. Although we could never substantiate the accuracy of this rumor, the fear it instilled was real. At the height of the rumors in 2006, the community became paralyzed. People were afraid to leave their homes, send their children to school, or even go to work. The rumors had an economic impact for the South Florida area and other large immigrant communities around the county when workers did not show up for work.[59]

The national US media quoted ICE officials stating that rumors of raids were completely unfounded.[60] Yet one month later, in May 2006, ICE launched a new national initiative, cynically named Operation Return to Sender. In Florida, this initiative led to at least 1,800 arrests in less than a year.[61] Other major fugitive team operations conducted around the country have included Operation City Lights in Las Vegas, Operation Phoenix in Miami, Operation Deep-Freeze in Chicago, and Operation FLASH in New England.[62]

Immigrants followed news about these programs through community newspapers and the Spanish-language publications *El Nuevo Herald* and *El Sentinel*. In particular, *El Sentinel*, a weekly newspaper for the Latino community in neighboring Broward County, reported regularly on immigration raids and deportation cases. These reports were the only available sources of reliable information for the undocumented community in Miami. ICE's denial that the operations were random was undermined when it surfaced that the hunt for "fugitives" led to "collateral arrests."[63] In the eyes of the immigrant community, even if they followed the law once they were in the

United States, they had no protections. They believed they had to be extra cautious any time they left their homes because a simple traffic infraction could land them in an immigration detention center and result in probable deportation.

The irony of some of the post-9/11 policies that have been enacted revealed itself in another one of our focus groups. In the course of trying to safeguard the US population from potential terrorist threats, these very policies themselves terrorized immigrants. The following statement from Gabriel, from Colombia, illustrates this fear, as well as its silencing effects in the community:

> Since 9/11 there has been persecution towards immigrants. They [the government] have utilized terrorism to justify the persecution of immigrants. They have confused the word immigrant with the word terrorist. They have tried to utilize the police as immigration agents. In fact, they do use them. I came across a case in Miami Beach where police were stopping people and asking them to show their driver's licenses. If the person showed a valid license, it was fine, but if the license had expired and had not been renewed, [it meant] it was an illegal immigrant. So what do you think they were looking for? Illegals! There is a persecution against them. And how many people could have prevented a crime but they are afraid to approach the police. I don't have papers. . . . I would not approach the police because perhaps they could ask me who I am, and I have no papers, and if they do, they will deport me. . . . I tried to send an article to *El Nuevo Herald* where I said what I just told you, that Bush has become the first terrorist in this country, but my wife was afraid because we had no papers at the time. I could have become a voice for other immigrants.

Research has shown how even if ICE raids occurred far from immigrants' own communities, rumors of raids and the perceived vulnerability that these rumors created contributed to a level of fear that drove immigrants to change around their routine activities to avoid being in public spaces where they feared apprehension.[64] But the quote above also reveals one of the consequences of living in a state of fear and insecurity. Gabriel wanted to express his opinion about the effects of these policies on the daily lives of immigrants such as himself, but as a subject with no rights, including free speech, he could not participate in Miami's public sphere for fear that he would be identified and deported. His structural position created for him and others a situation where they had no recourse if their civil rights (or human rights, for that matter) were violated. Gabriel's quote clearly articulates how legal violence, embodied in the figure of George W. Bush, created much harm to him and his family, and had ripple effects in the form of keeping his community from the benefits of his public voice. Legal violence, thus, perpetuates these structural conditions so that social suffering occurs in isolation from others who share the same experiences. This ultimate state of vulnerability is reminiscent of the Jim Crow era in the US South, in which separate was unequal and in which discriminatory practices were legally codified. The relegation of undocumented immigrants to the shadows or margins of social life not only legalizes inequalities of opportunity and discrimination but also rationalizes and even legitimizes the existence of both.

If Secure Communities and militarized deportation raids were meant to curb US residents' feelings of insecurity about the porosity of the border, for immigrants they only heightened their individual experiences of insecurity and fear. Paradoxically, terrorizing undocumented immigrants has spillover effects on US citizens when one considers that 53 percent of undocumented immigrants live in mixed-status families.[65] Here we see how particular legal statuses promote different experiences of psychic insecurity with the household being the mediating structure through which both immigrants and citizens felt vulnerable and insecure. For these families, migration ushered in new forms of insecurity rooted in policies that ramped up the post-9/11 anti-immigrant environment. Moreover, these policies, and our quantitative sample respondents' own negative experiences with immigration officials, made even more difficult the ability of immigrants to feel like they were part of US society.[66] Young immigrant children have the same challenge: in spite of feeling 100 percent "American" and having no recollection of their countries of origin, they are considered foreigners by the state and, as such, are also considered deportable. This quagmire leads us to examine how different immigration categories of admission, and the state of being in between statuses, are tied to various forms of psychic insecurity.

Categories of Admission and Psychic Insecurity

Immigration status influenced the extent to which immigrants felt secure in Miami. However, as we have shown, the bureaucracy of immigration services and the implementation of policies and programs after September 11, 2001, created a siege-like atmosphere that was perceived and experienced even for those with legal authority to reside and work in the city. In this section, we discuss how particular immigrant statuses shaped life chances and, in particular, feelings of psychic insecurity.

Unauthorized Immigrants

The terms *illegal* and *undocumented* are often associated with those who cross the border clandestinely and who do not have identity papers or documented proof of their authorization to be in the United States.[67] Although unauthorized immigrants have economic and social presence, they are not recognized legally by the state.[68] Paradoxically, although they are legally invisible, those without documentation nevertheless are subject to broad patterns of state scrutiny as we have seen thus far.

The number of unauthorized immigrants in the United States has exceeded the number of legal immigrants since 1995. Jeffrey S. Passel and D'Vera Cohn estimate that the unauthorized immigrant population in the United States reached its peak of 12 million in 2007, declining since then (to 11.1 million in 2011). An estimated 825,000 of those lived in Florida, giving it the third-largest population of undocumented immigrants after California (2.5 million) and Texas (1.6 million).[69]

The majority of unauthorized immigrants come from Latin America, with Mexico providing the largest number (59 percent).[70] Many of the Mexicans interviewed for our study crossed the border in Arizona, Texas, and California using smugglers known colloquially as *coyotes*. Maruja, who came in 1995, crossed the border in Nogales and was taken to Tucson, where she took a bus to her relatives' home in Los Angeles. After a few years of agricultural work, she decided to move to Miami to join her brother and look for a different kind of job. She found work in Miami in food service.

Being in the United States without legal status creates a level of insecurity that constrains agency and affects immigrants' emotional states. Immigrants have other ways, though, of becoming unauthorized in the United States, including migrating with a valid passport and visa but staying in the country after the visa has expired.[71] Estimates from 2006 place the number of visa overstayers at 4 to 5.5 million, compared to 6 to 7 million undocumented border crossers.[72]

Qualifying for a tourist visa is not an easy task. Regardless of the applicant's country of origin, the US State Department unambiguously states that US law assumes that anyone applying for a visitor visa is a prospective immigrant. As such, applicants for visitor visas must overcome this presumption by demonstrating that, among other things, they have compelling evidence of social and economic ties abroad.[73] The requirements for attaining a visa shape the profiles of those who overstay them. Esteban, a Colombian immigrant in our study, explained that "in the United States it would be almost impossible to find an immigrant who was a peasant back in Colombia." He continued, "The great majority of Colombian immigrants happen to be professionals because they have to come by plane, because they have to show their bank accounts, and just because it is plain impossible."

In addition, visa applicants from Latin America and the Caribbean must arrange for an interview at the US Embassy or consulate in the city where they live. Not all countries require interviews to receive a US visa, including many European and some Asian countries.[74] For those countries that do require them, the waiting time for an interview can be lengthy.[75] In addition, visa applicants must then wait several days for the visa to be processed and issued.

Many of our interviewees told us in unsolicited comments that they were visa overstayers. A focus group participant, Martin, came to the United States from Peru with his wife and two children. They had secured B-2 Tourist Visas at the US Consulate in Lima by stating that they intended to take their children on vacation to visit Disney World in Orlando, a popular destination for upper-middle-class families in Peru and other countries. Given economic uncertainties in Peru, Martin explained that their decision to overstay their visas had not been an easy one to make. Both he and his wife, Ana, knew that once the six-month authorization to visit the United States expired, their status would radically change. Without a valid visa, Martin, Ana, and their children could not return to Peru for visits, or even emergencies, because they would not be allowed to reenter the United States. This decision put great limits on their future mobility and took an enormous emotional toll.

Children and Teenagers Without Legal Status

If the Sandivars or the Haitian couple discussed above experienced distress from their encounters with fugitive operation teams, the situation of children and young adults who witness this process may be even more traumatizing, especially for those who were brought by their parents early in their lives to the United States. On a summer day in 2007, ICE raided the home of Juan Gómez, a graduating senior in a Miami high school. Right before the crack of dawn, ICE agents surrounded his family's house and rounded up Juan, his older brother Alex, and his parents, Liliana and Julio. His parents brought the two brothers as toddlers to the United States on tourist visas, which they overstayed. Julio and Liliana applied for political asylum because Julio had been threatened by a guerrilla group in Colombia that had already killed his brother.[76] Ten years passed before they ever saw an immigration judge.[77] During those years, the couple received work permits from the government, enrolled their children in school, and started a small business in Miami. But in 2003, their asylum petition was rejected and they were ordered to leave the country. Despite the order, the family remained in the country because Miami had become their home, and they had built successful lives with deep roots in the community. Four years and one raid later, the family was taken to a Broward County detention center to await deportation. Although they fought deportation, eventually the parents were returned to Colombia and the two teenage brothers were granted temporary stays. Juan got a scholarship and attended Georgetown University. After graduating in 2011, he went to work at a major financial institution in New York City. Alex did not fair so well. He attended Miami-Dade College for a while but withdrew because he could not afford tuition.[78] The separation from their parents had taken its toll. In 2013, Juan left the United States for Brazil because his application to renew his temporary work permit was backlogged and his legal status lapsed. As this case demonstrates, although US immigration policies ironically claim to prioritize family reunification, increasingly we are seeing families split apart by agents of the state, a problem affecting US citizens when we consider the prevalence of mixed-status families. Family separations have detrimental effects on members on both sides of the border, and in cases of reunification, which can sometimes take years, the road to family reconstitution can be rocky.[79]

In addition to the well-publicized case of the Colombian brothers who avoided deportation, Camila Hornung, a Florida State University honors student, was not so lucky. Camila was deported along with her parents to Peru in June 2008, after ICE agents arrested the family. Although they had lived in the United States for fourteen years, the family found themselves expelled from the country due to an outstanding deportation order. A year later, Camila, who found herself in Peru, was asked by a blogger to talk about the events that led to her family's arrest:

> It's something I think about everyday [sic], the worst day of my life aside from the day I got deported. It was just like any normal day, my parents and I were going to the library when an undercover cop pulled us over right near the corner of our house. There he handcuffed my dad as if he were a criminal (that was definitely the hardest part for me). From there the ICE police officers had no consideration towards us and took us to the Broward detention center. The conditions were that of criminals, words cannot describe what I went through. I did not do anything to deserve that treatment. At the detention center our personal belongings, cell phones and our human rights were taken from us. At that point we were viewed as criminals. My father was separated from my mother and I and taken to the men's side. My mother and I were forbidden to speak to my father if for some reason we crossed paths. My father was forced to wear an orange uniform and my mother and I were given used clothes to wear. It was definitely degrading and humiliating having to experience the life of a criminal.[80]

In Florida, as well as in the rest of the nation, many students are fighting for the right to receive an education and work in the United States. The Development Relief and Education for Alien Minors (DREAM) Act, which would provide "a path to legalization for eligible youth and young adults," was bipartisan legislation first introduced in 2001.[81] The DREAM Act would allow individuals under the age of thirty-five who arrived before they were sixteen years of age to apply for legal permanent resident status, provided they have lived at least five years in the United States and have attained a US high school diploma or its equivalent.[82] Since 2001, several versions have been introduced in Congress without success. If the legislation were passed, Florida would see the third-largest group of young immigrants change status, as 192,000 students (or 9 percent of the total number of eligible students nationwide) would benefit from the legislation.[83] The last attempt to pass the DREAM Act, however, failed in the Senate in 2010. In 2012, five months before election day, President Obama, relying on prosecutorial discretion, allowed for the DHS to defer orders of removal for young immigrants meeting certain criteria, resulting in the Deferred Action for Childhood Arrivals. This decision halted the deportation of undocumented students, although for Camila, this order came too late. Signed in June 2012, this temporary measure decriminalizes undocumented youth, protecting them from deportation— albeit, not necessarily offering them a path to citizenship.

Not being able to change the legal status of their children worried many of the parents we interviewed who had brought their children to the country under tourist visas. The same concern was present in the narratives of their adult children. Joaquín, the Peruvian immigrant discussed at the beginning of this chapter, came to the United States as a teenager with his parents. In addition to the financial penalties he paid by not having legal documentation regarding his immigration status, the worst part of living in this country for him was his inability to pursue higher education. His parents had helped him to apply for a student visa, which was denied. Instead, he came with a tourist visa and eventually started looking for a job to help his parents.

Joaquín always dreamed of being an architect. He applied to a regional art school but was told by a school official that he would have to provide documents to prove his immigration status. She told him that "it was bad to apply without them because they didn't know when immigration was going to show up to check papers. She said they could start searching for me and chase me, and once they located me, they could hold me and deport me."

At the time of this interview, Joaquín was twenty-five years old, had two jobs, and worked between eighty and eighty-five hours a week. Visibly stressed, Joaquín shared that he lived in constant fear of being detected by immigration authorities, and simply driving created angst because of the possibility of being pulled over. He had a friend who recently had been arrested for a traffic violation: "He was thrown in jail and has already been deported."

Joaquín's fears are not all that unusual; the closing of doors to unauthorized individuals, and in particular, to young adults, serves as a constant reminder of the exclusion and the lack of human rights undocumented people experience in the United States today. For these youths, Florida is their home. And yet they are rejected by a system that has labeled them as fugitives from justice. Although their status does not acknowledge their legal presence, the state's arm of enforcement heavily regulates their lives.

Asylees and Refugees

Other groups of immigrants in our study were either asylees or refugees, especially those from Colombia who had been threatened with physical violence. Asylum seekers differ from refugees in that they must already be in the United States at the time of the application.[84] The application to receive asylum must be made within one year from the date of arrival. One can seek asylum affirmatively or defensively. In the affirmative process, the person who seeks asylum submits an application to the US Citizenship and Immigration Services. Upon the paperwork being processed, the applicant is interviewed by an asylum officer, who quickly decides whether the applicant has a well-founded fear of persecution or not and, upon that determination, either to grant asylum or to refer the case to Immigration Court. In contrast, in the defensive asylum process, immigration judges with the Executive Office for Immigration Review of the Department of Justice oversee all cases and only hear defensive asylum requests in the context of halting deportation proceedings.[85]

These bureaucratic procedures take on central meanings in the lives of study participants, creating for them ambiguities; in spite of having legal status as an asylee, these statuses subjected immigrants' lives to substantial state regulation by restricting their ability to leave the country to see loved ones, sometimes causing frustration and sadness. The ambiguities appeared when they considered that the very same process that caused them pain allowed them to live in the United States, where they were physically safe and could pursue work and educational opportunities more openly than undocumented immigrants.

For Esteban, going back to Colombia was unthinkable. He arrived in 2003, initially with the idea of spending a holiday with his family and taking his daughter to Disney World. While in Florida, he received a call from his family back in Colombia telling him that the threats against him continued. Esteban was terrified to go back for fear of exposing himself and his family to kidnapping or even death. Friends recommended that he seek asylum; thus, seven months after arriving in the United States, he filed an asylum application. By that time, however, Esteban had used up most of his money and could only get a freelance job as a photographer, making $8 an hour, a big step down from his former position of national television producer. Despite this setback, he felt relieved because, unlike those for most

applicants, his asylum request was granted. However, the span of time leading up to being granted asylum represented a period of economic and social
vulnerability. We see this in the following case more clearly.

Many of our interviewees, including Ivan, a Colombian, requested and
were granted affirmative asylum after arriving in the United States. As discussed in the previous chapter, Ivan, a medical doctor, was threatened by a
guerrilla group while completing an obligatory year of service in a rural
area of Colombia. With no protection from the government, he was threatened with death if he refused to treat guerrilla members. Three months after
arriving in Miami, he applied for asylum, a process he found to be very
complicated because of the lack of help in place for applicants. While waiting for the asylum decision, he worked without legal authorization because
he had depleted his savings. He remembered this period as a time in which
he lacked any basic rights. His status made him vulnerable to unscrupulous
employers seeking to take advantage of immigrants because they realized
that undocumented immigrants have no legal recourse if they are abused or
exploited in the workplace. Indeed, Ivan felt he had been verbally abused
and unfairly treated in the places where he worked. He felt better and more
secure after he was granted asylum and received authorization to work in
the United States. However, his liminal legal status proved to be challenging to his social and economic livelihood. Liminal legality challenged immigrants like Ivan emotionally as well.

Rosa María, a former journalist, left Colombia because of physical insecurity but, in turn, experienced a demotion in social status and struggled
with the separation from her family. Rosa María arrived in Miami with a
tourist visa and made money to pay her bills by cleaning houses. Although
she missed working as a journalist, the most difficult issue for her in the
United States was her inability to see her parents, who remained in Colombia. Although asylees are permitted to go back to their countries of origin
(albeit, only with a special permit, otherwise their asylee status is revoked),
such visits are closely monitored to determine the specific circumstances
prompting their return.

Rosa María's parents planned a trip to visit their daughter and grandson
and were shocked when they were refused a tourist visa at the US Embassy
in Colombia. This situation was not uncommon. Rosa María stated that "not
allowing the parents of asylees to come to the United States for visits is an
injustice." She described asylees as "*prisioneros de la libertad*" (prisoners
of freedom), "escaping from countries where they were prisoners to continue to live as prisoners in a new place." Her inability to see her parents
given state regulations on the travel of asylees took a heavy emotional toll.
Moreover, Rosa María's father was an elderly man who, as a medical doctor, had a very good pension in Colombia, raising questions regarding why
he was not allowed to see his daughter when he could prove he had a

source of income abroad. The fact that he had worked for a US multinational company for over twenty-five years added insult to injury, as he felt horribly humiliated at the US Embassy.

Asylees could request asylum status for spouses or children under eighteen years of age, but under this provision, parents are not included.[86] Because of this regulation, Rosa María felt trapped. Because she could not go back to Colombia without fear of losing her status, Rosa María felt an affinity with undocumented immigrants: "In a way the asylee is in the same situation as an unauthorized person, because neither they nor we are able to go back to our countries. If we leave the United States we cannot come back. So in spite of the fact that an asylee is here legally and fortunately has papers to work, we do not have any other advantages over an unauthorized immigrant other than work because we also cannot go back to our countries. We are legal, we have social security numbers, while the undocumented are persecuted because they do not have papers."

Thus, state regulation of immigrants' lives affected those with legal status as well as those without it. In cases of defensive asylum, we see the convergence of both types of experiences. Immigration courts have a significant backlog of defensive asylum applications, paralyzing an applicant's life, often for years, until the court finally reaches its decision on the asylee's request. In Florida, overall asylum petitions of Colombian and Haitian immigrants peaked in 2002 and 2006, respectively.[87] Responses to asylum applications rely heavily on the particular judge in each case and can also vary widely, depending on the region of the country. Judges in Miami have a denial rate of 60 to 88 percent for all sorts of petitions to stay in the country legally.[88] Miami has one of the highest rates of asylum refusals in the country, with only 23 percent of asylum petitioners obtaining asylum, compared to an average of 40 percent nationally.[89]

In contrast to affirmative asylum, defensive asylum can be a long and complicated process. However, if an applicant receives a final denial letter, he or she must leave the country. By the time the court hands down its decision to the applicant and a deportation order arrives, many have already been waiting for years and thus have settled and built lives within their communities. When deportation orders are not obeyed, immigrants must adjust to a new status: that of "fugitive alien." This label imposes on them the stigma of illegality, which ultimately hovers over most immigrants (in spite of legal status) when we take into account that modern discourse often associates Latino/a immigrants, specifically, with "illegal" immigration statuses.

Legal Nonimmigrants: Dependency

Unlike for Joaquín and other vulnerable immigrants in our study, having legal status helped reduce psychic insecurity. Also important for many, immigrants with legal status had the flexibility to go back to visit their countries of origin. However, because these immigrants had permission to work and live in the United States only temporarily and had to rely on visa renewals, although their experience of psychic insecurity was less, it was still present.

Diego left Peru after closing his business and having trouble finding a job at age forty-four, even with experience and an MBA behind him. With the help of his brother, who owned a construction company in Miami, he secured both a job as a project manager and a sponsored visa that would allow him to work legally in the United States. Diego is one of few in our sample who claimed an H-1B Visa. These visas allow US companies to bring in university-educated foreigners for up to six years to fill jobs that require specialized skills and knowledge.[90]

Because the quotas for H-1B are so limited and difficult to obtain, many professionals feel vulnerable and insecure because, as temporary residents of the country, they are dependent on their employers' renewal of their nonimmigrant visas. This dependency reinforces their in-between status and introduces vulnerability into their lives. Catalina, another Peruvian H-1B Visa holder who was a top executive at a Miami corporation, spoke about her feelings and fears as an immigrant in a country she perceived to be unwelcoming: "The feelings you have, the fear you feel for being an immigrant, despite being legal. You feel discriminated against, marginalized. You feel you do not belong. I'll never be 100 percent American. I belong where I was. I am now in limbo." Among the many assumptions about immigrants is the idea that professional immigrants probably have the smoothest experiences when attaining legal permanent resident status and, eventually, US citizenship. However, Catalina reported feeling like she was in "limbo" because she did not feel part of the US nation. In spite of these feelings, she nevertheless recognized her privileged status when she compared herself to the undocumented: "One thing I wonder is what if I had decided to come here without work, because I got fired from my job in Peru, or because the company closed, etc. And I look for work and I cannot find any and I live with a friend until I find work here. You do not have papers, money, nothing. My case is different because I came to do the same job. I picked up my files and I moved from my country rather than from my work. My nine-to-six routine is very similar to the one I had in Lima. That made it very easy. The other situation is not."

Catalina's case makes it clear that levels of exclusion can be found even for those immigrants holding working permits. H1-B nonimmigrant visas are temporary, but they offer a path to seeking permanent residency in the United States,[91] which, in theory, gives one a greater sense of security. However, these visas also are tied to specific jobs, so if an immigrant loses the job, he or she also loses the ability to be in the country legally. This precarious situation raises questions about the degree of power that legal professional immigrants really have in the context of their occupations. If their legal status is tied to their employment, then they might feel unable to speak out against inequalities or abuses on the job. As such, even legal residents' basic rights are unprotected when they have temporary statuses. They are corporate or state subjects forced into compliance given the immigration policies that link legal existence to employability.

Fortunately, for both Diego and Catalina, their employment allowed them to become legal permanent residents a few years after the interviews took place, which untied them from their employers' goodwill. Although the United States had categorized both Diego and Catalina in the nonimmigrant category, they felt they had left their country for good and were in Miami to stay. In short, they achieved their dream of US settlement, even if they did not feel fully accepted in US society.

Temporary visas are pathways to obtaining residency and, for many, ultimately, to citizenship. But even this path implies a series of temporary and uncertain statuses. Fernando came to the United States from Mexico on a student visa after earning a scholarship. This transitory status translated into an occupational visa after graduation. At the time of his interview, he worked in Miami at a public relations office but was not unaware of the struggles of others who have not been as fortunate. He contrasted his experience with that of the lady who cleaned his house:

> My experience and that of my colleagues who work and develop as professionals is very different from the lady who cleans my house for example. I am here legally. And I have certain legal benefits. I have health insurance, life insurance. A job and benefits, that, the lady who cleans my house does not have. She comes here and works but cannot leave the United States. It has been ten years since she left Honduras, but she cannot go back because she is here illegally. Obviously the type of concerns and the type of life that she has is quite different to mine. If you go and ask her what is the trade-off of having come to the United States, she would probably tell you that here she has the possibility of a better life but it has been ten years since [she] saw [her] children. Her situation weighs a lot more; that's another world. I believe that not all immigrants are the same. You can't fit them all in the same category because their experiences are different. They live in very different worlds; they have different concerns and different worldviews.

Fernando clearly articulates how and why legal status matters. The choices available to someone without status are almost nonexistent. They include painful separations from family, lack of mobility, lack of access to education, and, by proxy, barriers to economic opportunities, all of which make the lives of undocumented immigrants and others with vulnerable statuses much more difficult than those of immigrants who are fortunate to live in the United States legally and on paths that, although rocky, can lead to citizenship.

Legal Permanent Residents and Naturalized Citizens: Theoretical Legality

The majority of immigrants who become legal permanent residents do so through the family reunification category. Altagracia came to the United States from the Dominican Republic through the family reunification policy. Her father sponsored her immigration to the country in 1993. Altagracia felt that very little is said about immigrants who came to this country legally, while much more attention is focused on people who come to the country through illegal channels. Her concerns indicated that the stigma of illegality is one that even legal immigrants confront. We saw this situation with Yvette, a Dominican immigrant, who also came through the family reunification category: "My dad did not want to bring us here [to the United States], but my aunt insisted. Then he started the process and brought us here. My brother and I spent about four and a half years waiting to emigrate. My dad took care of our papers so when I came here, I came with a permanent visa, permanent residency."

Yvette worked for a corporate janitorial service and stated during the interview that she had felt a lot of rejection since she arrived because many thought she was illegal: "One feels rejected because you are a person who comes from another country, and they think that one is illegal here. Even if you are not illegal in this country, even if you have all rights, they always see you as an intruder."

Altagracia and Yvette moved to the United States with legal status. Upon arrival, they did not experience the uncertainties of living in the United States without papers. But they could not escape discrimination. As such, they showed concern for being confused or compared to the undocumented. Working as a janitor, already a low-status position, perhaps increased Yvette's need to distance herself from the additional stigma of being undocumented.

In spite of the stigma and discrimination attached to being immigrants, both women became naturalized citizens a few years after arriving in the United States; thus, they were included as legal members of the nation-state. However, their experiences illustrate how the specter of illegality and stratification of immigrants through multiple immigration statuses creates contexts in which immigrant bonds of solidarity are more difficult to forge and sustain.

Naturalized citizens enjoy almost the same benefits as native-born citizens: "access to social services and the ability to enter and leave the United States at will."[92] The United States government tolerates (which is different from allowing) dual citizenship, and as a result, a newly naturalized citizen does not have to renounce his or her passport from the country of birth.[93] Maintaining dual-citizenship status allows for immigrants such as Yvette to maintain a sense of full membership to a collectivity (her home country) in spite of the mechanisms of exclusion in the United States that translate into the assumption that she is not a legal member of this country simply because she is an immigrant or "looks" foreign.

All nonlegal and legal permanent residents in our study aspired to become naturalized citizens. Many felt, though, that they were subject to increased scrutiny, given that a simple mistake could be enough to knock them out of status, so they were afraid to make any missteps that might impede their ability to gain legal recognition for their permanent presence in the United States. While waiting to get her residency approved, Catalina, from Peru, told us that she purposely overpaid her taxes every year. Her lawyer advised her not to claim her tax refund from the federal government, even though it was owed to her, to prove that she was not a burden on the state. This case illustrates how immigrants must go out of their way to show they do not fit into the stereotype of immigrants as dependent and burdens on the state.

Migrant Citizens

Among Latin Americans and Caribbeans, the case of Puerto Ricans is unique. In 1917, they were granted US citizenship through the Jones-Shafroth Act (commonly known as the Jones Act), a congressional decree. Puerto Rico is "neither a state of the federal union nor a sovereign nation."[94] As discussed in previous chapters, the peaks in migration of Puerto Ricans to the United States were during the Great Migration (1940s through 1960s), the 1980s, and in the first decade of the 2000s.[95]

In recent years, more Puerto Ricans have migrated to Florida, and many professionals have settled in the central and southern areas of the state. Paola, a veterinary technician from the island, explained that Puerto Ricans are often the object of resentment from other Latino/a immigrants. She perceived that others thought that "because we are American citizens, we believe we are the best because we can come and go without difficulty." She understood the resentment because, as she said, other Latin Americans "spend a lot of time and resources to immigrate, and I think that is what bothers them the most." Paola was not sure if this perceived resentment reflected "jealousy or anger [against Puerto Ricans]," but she was certain that other groups "talk negatively and even make jokes about us." Paola's interview suggests that Puerto Ricans' claims to citizenship come under question because of issues related to worthiness and work.[96] As Paola indicated, the first thing other Latin American immigrants point out upon meeting her "is the facility that we [Puerto Ricans] have to travel. . . . [They act] as if we have not *earned* the right to or we do not *deserve* to have" US citizenship (emphasis added by authors). Paola received questions such as "And why?" "Why you [Puerto Ricans]?" and "What did you [Puerto Ricans] do?" She also claimed that she had to contend with the belief that "Puerto Ricans are lazy." The ideas that Puerto Ricans have not had to work for their legal status, that they may be underserving of it, which is tied to the stereotype that they are lazy, stem from the stigmas attached to colonial subjects as racialized state actors. Although Paola attributed this perception to sociological data about Puerto Ricans in the United States, which, in her view, suggest that Puerto Ricans are "the poorest of immigrants, the laziest, and the ones who do not want to work," these perceptions could also be manifestations of cultural racism within the Latino population, in addition to ethnocentrism rooted in the idea that Puerto Ricans are somehow less because they do not have their own independent nation. We will explore these intra-Latino fissures in greater detail in Chapter 6.

As opposed to other groups, Puerto Ricans *can* move back and forth and have economic access to aid, social welfare programs, and other social rights afforded to US citizens. Many Puerto Ricans, however, have had to contend with the issue of ambiguity of status as they have been socialized in Puerto Rico into second-class citizenship (e.g., islanders cannot vote in federal elections, such as those for US president) and have faced discrimination in the mainland through their incorporation as racialized actors. Still, citizenship was a form of migration insurance for Puerto Ricans since it allowed them the possibility to go back to their place of origin, a decision not always available to other groups, particularly those out of status. Ultimately, if the costs of migration become too unmanageable, in the case of Puerto Ricans, they can return to their homeland without jeopardizing the option to remigrate to the United States in the future. Knowing this may give them a greater sense of security than those for whom return migration is not an option given their particular legal statuses.

Since the door to migration is a revolving one, settlement decisions are never really final, as seen in migration and settlement patterns in which Puerto Ricans spend periods of time alternating between living on the island and the mainland.[97] Puerto Ricans like Noelia and Paola believed that the difference between other immigrants and themselves was that the door to go back is always open. Noelia affirmed this notion: "We [Puerto Ricans] always have the opportunity to return. Some of us are here because of an economic situation, not because we were going to get killed, not because we are on drugs . . . or for other political reasons. We left because we wanted to, and we can go back anytime if we want to. I think also part of this relationship is that we live between two places. We don't have to cut our ties to Puerto Rico completely just to live here. We always have a plan."

Clear from Noelia's quote is that her formal citizenship has a positive impact in the way in which she evaluates her choices, recognizing the advantages of Puerto Ricans over other groups. The plan she refers to is really the option or opportunity to seek security elsewhere—the opportunity to be mobile. That option, in and of itself, can represent a source of security, a Plan B of sorts, which differentiates Puerto Ricans from groups that, lacking that option, feel more insecure and even trapped.

More and more Puerto Ricans have left the island in recent years due to the prolonged economic decline and US job recruiters who periodically visit the island, but others mention the increasing drug-related crime wave on the island as a reason for not returning. Thus, what is (perhaps was?) for some an always-open option to return or a plan to seek greater security elsewhere may no longer be an alternative. However, still clear is that, under conditions of fluid borders, immigrants have greater agency in making the choices that they think are best for their particular situations.

States of Belonging and Insecurity

Although the case of Puerto Ricans appears to be the one in which immigrant psychic insecurity in the United States is mitigated to the greatest extent by US citizenship status, we should acknowledge that Puerto Ricans were among the initial groups to be deployed as cheap, racialized labor for US nation-building projects in the twentieth century.[98] As we have shown, neoliberal economic policies, and earlier export-based production programs in the Caribbean, played active roles in restructuring the economies of countries and whole regions south of the United States. Moreover, the US economic structure, in which demand for labor exists both in high- and low-skilled work, is a magnet that pulls immigrants to the country. As Juan González has aptly summarized in his historical account of Latinos in this country, the roots of US intervention in the Americas have resulted in the harvest of empire—immigration to the United States.[99]

In spite of this structural pull, domestic policies in the United States have created new forms of insecurity for contemporary immigrants. The spike in anti-immigrant discourse and programs resulting from the securitization of immigration policy following the attacks of 9/11 have roots much deeper than the current context. For now, the maintenance of the status quo for people who remain in liminal legal statuses can be interpreted as benign neglect, political dysfunction, or a neoliberal racial project that

- Releases the United States from responsibility for investment in the

education and health of its citizenry (e.g., by using immigrant labor for productive and reproductive care work for natives, thereby absolving the United States from addressing the social and economic needs of its immigrant workforce);
  • Capitalizes on other countries' investments in human capital by absorbing their citizens as racialized labor, monitoring their comings and goings, and relegating them to temporary statuses that make them dependent on sponsoring stakeholders;
  • Further oppresses immigrants by politicizing their presence for political gain, including deploying discourse and tactics that rely on racial profiling in a broader effort to criminalize the undocumented population and use them as scapegoats for US social problems.

If viewed as a neoliberal racial project of the state, then the fear and emotional turmoil that result from immigrant psychic insecurity rooted in legal violence represent the human costs of increasing profits for US corporations that have a hand in framing and constructing the very policies they benefit from; they also limit immigrant labor migrants from full incorporation into US society by barring them from paths to citizenship and excluding them from conceptions of US nationhood. Framing undocumented migration as a process in which individual actors choose to ignore laws and commit criminal acts through their mere presence supports the structural processes and political discourse aimed at sustaining pools of flexible cheap labor to deploy according to the needs of government and private sector stakeholders. Thus, the criminalization of immigrants supports and even legitimizes institutional discrimination against them by segregating this group as a different class of people—separate and unequal.

Paradoxes abound at multiple scales of analysis when one attempts to understand Latin American and Caribbean immigrants' lives. As discussed in Chapter 1, the search for human security is often refracted, as through a prism, that at times shows signs of light (e.g., through perceptions of greater physical safety as we showed in Chapter 2), and at other times reveals new dimensions of oppression (e.g., psychic insecurity resulting from temporary and uncertain legal statuses). As immigrants embark on new journeys, their experiences often reveal the contradictions that characterize the lives of those who navigate through the web of global capitalism in the hopes of achieving some level of membership and belonging in an ever-changing world.

Conclusion

In this chapter, we have examined how the post-9/11 national security context redefined the forms and intensities of human insecurity immigrants faced upon settlement in Miami. Particularly, we focus on how Homeland Security efforts after 9/11 intensified and amounted to legal violence that has taken the form of xenophobic US racial projects embedded in state immigration and enforcement policies. These in turn exacerbated conditions in which immigrants became psychologically vulnerable to the insecurity of temporary and uncertain legal statuses and the state's power to acknowledge their existence and regulate their movement. Immigrants' ultimate fear was that they would remain in a state of legal limbo or complete nonexistence in which exclusions and restrictions erased personhood.[100] Or yet worse, they feared being apprehended and expelled from the country and, thereby, from the lives they had created in the United States with their families.

By examining the sociolegal dimensions of the context of reception that shaped immigrants' abilities to attain human security in Miami and in the country at large, we illustrate how immigrants confronted a new environment of insecurity that challenged their quests for sustainable lives by generating feelings of psychic insecurity related to the absence or temporariness of legal residency statuses. These policies further affected immigrants' livelihoods, particularly among those who were in between statuses, or who had temporary visas, expired statuses, or no legal status at all. Psychic vulnerability made life untenable for many immigrants. Also examined was the mitigation of such insecurities in the experiences of naturalized US citizens as well as migrant citizens by birth, such as Puerto Ricans. Although Puerto Ricans are full-fledged legal members of the nation-state, they are still subject to racialization through the construction of their foreignness.

In sum, the sociolegal context of reception is important for understanding experiences of immigrant incorporation, particularly when addressing perceptions of psychic insecurity. To understand other immigrant outcomes, such as the likelihood of material improvement in their lives, we must turn to immigrants' perceptions of social and economic security. In the next chapter, we will examine the economic context of reception of the global city and whether immigrants felt that migration led to material improvements in their lives.

Notes

1. Donato and Armenta 2011.
2. Menjívar and Abrego 2012, p. 1387.
3. Ibid., p. 1388. For discussion of social suffering and its cultural appropriations, see Kleinman and Kleinman 1996.
4. Menjívar and Abrego 2012.
5. Bonilla-Silva 1997.

6. Menjívar 2006, p. 1003.
7. *La migra* is a common term used for US immigration authorities.
8. Coutin 2003; Menjívar and Abrego 2012.
9. Portes and Rumbaut 2001.
10. Little and Klarreich 2005.
11. Donato and Armenta 2011.
12. Huysmans 2006.
13. Kinnvall and Lindén 2010.
14. Tirman 2006.
15. Ibrahim 2005; Tirman 2006.
16. Tirman 2006.
17. Little and Klarreich 2005.
18. García and Keyes 2012, p. 6.
19. Naples 2007, p. 21.
20. Aranda 2007; Marrow 2012; Naples 2007.
21. Little and Klarreich 2005.
22. Naples 2007; Menjívar and Abrego 2012.
23. The city's sociolegal context is perhaps one of the clearest examples of what Arjun Appadurai calls an "ethnoscape"—a shifting landscape of "tourists, immigrants, refugees, exiles, guest workers and other moving groups and individuals" (Appadurai 1996, p. 33).
24. Stasiulis and Bakan 1997, p. 117.
25. Ibid.
26. Ibid.
27. Rocco 2006.
28. Menjívar 2006.
29. Ngai 2004, p. 4.
30. Holston and Appadurai 1999, p. 4.
31. The Tri-County Commuter Rail Authority (Tri-Rail) is a commuter train that provides service between the counties of Miami-Dade, Broward, and Palm Beach.
32. Metrorail is a twenty-two-mile train system that operates within Miami-Dade County. It has a transfer Tri-Rail station that allows commuters to reach Broward and Palm Beach counties.
33. Navarrette 2010.
34. The growing emphasis on expediting deportations can be seen in the dramatic increase in the funds allocated to fugitive operations from $9 million in fiscal year 2003 to just over $110 million in fiscal year 2006 (US Department of Homeland Security 2007).
35. Around 349,000 were deported in fiscal year 2008 alone (American Civil Liberties Union of Massachusetts 2008), and almost 400,000 deportations transpired in fiscal year 2010, of which 73 percent involved Mexicans (García and Keyes 2012).
36. The American Civil Liberties Union of Massachusetts (2008) reports that the dramatic increase in arrests over the years has led to the creation of a network of about 400 jails and detention centers that hold around 30,000 immigrants on any given day.
37. Sánchez 2011.
38. Marrow 2012.
39. Little and Klarreich 2005, p. 2.
40. Ibid.
41. Ibid.
42. Ibid., p. 50.

43. Lacayo 2010.
44. See US Immigration and Customs Enforcement 2012.
45. Loewe 2011.
46. Francis 2011. These rates are quite high when compared with the 26 percent of noncriminal deportations reported in Maricopa County, Arizona, where Sheriff Joe Arpaio built a national reputation for having tough anti-immigration enforcement techniques (Francis 2011).
47. Little and Klarreich 2005.
48. Immigration and Customs Enforcement, Secure Communities, IDENT/IAFIS Interoperability, Monthly Statistics through February 28, 2011, quoted in García and Keyes 2012.
49. See US Immigration and Customs Enforcement 2011.
50. Ibid.
51. Mendelson, Strom, and Wishnie 2009.
52. García and Keyes 2012.
53. Sabogal 2005.
54. Eckland 2004.
55. Little and Klarreich 2005.
56. Menjívar and Abrego 2012.
57. Morris 2007.
58. Ibid.
59. Chardy 2006.
60. Wides-Munoz 2006.
61. "Return to Sender" 2007, p. 3B.
62. Mendelson, Strom, and Wishnie 2009, p. 12.
63. Ibid.
64. Jones-Correa and Fennelly 2009.
65. Passel and Cohn 2009, quoted in García and Keyes 2012.
66. Aranda and Vaquera 2011.
67. Sabogal and Núñez 2010. See Nevins (2002) for discussion of the rise of the "illegal alien" in the United States.
68. Coutin 2003; Menjívar 2006.
69. Passel and Cohn 2009, 2011, 2012.
70. Another 1.3 million (11 percent) come from Central America, 775,000 (7 percent) from South America, and 500,000 (4 percent) from the Caribbean (Passel and Cohn 2009).
71. The United States offers several types of visas to individuals wishing to come to the country as temporary visitors. The two most common ones are the B-1 Visa for business, and the B-2 Visa for pleasure, tourism, or medical treatment (US Department of State 2013c).
72. Pew Hispanic Center estimates based on the March 2005 Current Population Survey and Department of Homeland Security reports (Passel 2006).
73. The US State Department requires tourists to show (1) that the purpose of the trip is to enter the United States for business, pleasure, or medical treatment; (2) that they plan to remain for a specific, limited period; (3) that they have funds to cover expenses in the United States; (4) that they can provide compelling evidence of social and economic ties abroad; and (5) that they have a residence outside the United States as well as other binding ties that will insure their return abroad when the visa expires (see US Department of State 2013c).
74. There are visa waiver programs for thirty-seven countries. Citizens of those countries can come without a visa but cannot stay in the United States for more than ninety days. They also must register in advance, though not everyone is eligible (US

Department of State 2013c). The only Latin American countries to have waivers beyond the previous decade were Argentina and Uruguay, who lost their waivers in 2002 and 2003, respectively, due to economic turbulence that led to US concerns over possible visa overstayers (Sisken 2013).

75. As of November 6, 2010, in Mexico City, the wait was seven days; in Lima and Santo Domingo, three days; in Bogotá, thirty-nine days; in Port-au-Prince, twelve days; and in Havana, 999 days (US Department of State 2010).

76. Goodman 2007.

77. De La Cruz 2007.

78. Americans for Immigrant Justice 2011.

79. Menjívar and Abrego 2009.

80. See Life by Dream 2009.

81. Batalova and McHugh 2010, p. 109.

82. Ibid.

83. National Immigration Law Center 2010.

84. Martin and Hoefer 2009.

85. US Department of Justice, Executive Office for Immigration Review 2005.

86. US Department of Health and Human Services, Administration for Children and Families, Office of Refugee Resettlement 2012.

87. Wasem 2011.

88. Transactional Records Access Clearinghouse (TRAC Immigration) 2010.

89. Ramji-Nogales, Schoenholtz, and Schrag (2007) show that decisions made by immigration judges exhibit enormous variability, to such an extent that they use the metaphor of a roulette wheel to describe asylum outcomes. In Miami, for example, based on judges' individual histories of rulings, a Colombian asylum seeker could have either an 88 percent chance of attaining asylum or only a 5 percent chance, depending upon which judge heard the case.

90. In the 1980s, the annual quota for these visas was 195,000, but Congress cut this annual quota to only 65,000. In 2004, Congress approved an extra 20,000 H-1B Visas in addition to the 65,000 visas already given annually under the H-1B Visa Reform Act of 2004 (Hoag 2005). By 2010, the top three countries receiving H-1B Visas were India (53.3 percent), China (8.9 percent), and Canada (3.8 percent). In comparison, the top three Latin American countries receiving H-1B Visas were Mexico (1.4 percent), Colombia (0.8 percent), and Venezuela (0.8 percent) (US Department of Homeland Security 2012).

91. Wasem 2007.

92. Massey and Bartley 2005, p. 470.

93. US Department of State 2013a.

94. Acosta-Belen and Santiago 2006. For a complete history of the Constitution of the Estado Libre Asociado, or Commonwealth, of Puerto Rico, see Acosta-Belen and Santiago 2006.

95. Ibid.

96. De Genova and Ramos-Zayas 2003.

97. Aranda 2007.

98. González 2000.

99. Ibid.

100. Menjívar 2006; Coutin 2003, p. 28.

4

Inequalities and Perceptions of Social Mobility

When I came here, some people told me, "You have to start from zero, do whatever." . . . I had to start working at a Publix but life put in front of me a job in television. I had never attained that, and my life changed. . . . I have felt that this country has given me . . . the feeling of being proud of myself. Now, I am a television producer.

—Rafael, former writer for a theater group in Cuba

[In Miami] you have opportunities for work; you can do things here that in my country, you do not do. For example, I babysit here. In Colombia that is looked down upon; here it is not looked down on.

—Alejandra, former business executive in Colombia
who now works as a preschool teacher

In Florida I am a slave. . . . I don't have anything really. . . . Here I have been working for eight years and I don't even make $8 an hour. . . . I miss home, because when I was home I was not in such a bad state like this. . . . I did not think that Miami would be as bad as it is.

—Roland, former fisherman in Haiti
who now works in restaurants and in lawn care

Miami residents in the 2000s, half of whom were immigrants, faced an economy in which everyone except lawyers and managers lived "in misery." That is according to county wage data coupled with a 2012 *Forbes* magazine study that named Miami "America's most miserable city." The *Forbes* study considered a variety of indicators ranging from foreclosure rates to traffic, crime, and public corruption. "Life is good for the likes of LeBron James and Latin pop crooner Enrique Iglesias, who's building a $20 million compound on a private island with girlfriend Anna

Kournikova," wrote a *Forbes* senior editor. "But if you're among the 75 percent of households with an annual income under $75,000, it can be a hard place."[1]

Miami's pre-2008 housing price bubble was among the country's largest. The effects of the bubble's burst, compounded by Florida's political climate, were still felt years later. Miami's unemployment rate tripled between 2006 and 2010, home prices plummeted, and hundreds of thousands of properties entered foreclosure.[2] Compounding the "misery" is Florida's historical reliance on an inadequate revenue structure, its inelastic tax system, and the antitax political culture, all of which often result in state government revenue shortfalls.[3] These shortfalls tend to lead to drastic cuts in education and health services, as well as cost transfers to local governments, resulting in municipal shortfalls. Municipalities address shortfalls through workforce reductions (e.g., layoffs, furloughs, hiring freezes), postponing or canceling infrastructure projects, and cutting public safety services (e.g., police, fire, emergency personnel).[4]

In spite of eroding federal and state support for social infrastructure, in 2008 city and county commissioners agreed to fund 80 percent of the Miami Marlins' $634 million baseball stadium that opened in 2012. Yet the average family of four was unlikely to afford the $121 it would take to purchase the cheapest tickets, hot dogs and soft drinks, and parking to attend a ball game.[5] In short, the economic and occupational context of reception that immigrants to Miami encounter is one that caters to the rich and disadvantages the poor and middle classes.

In this chapter, we examine the context of reception and modes of immigrant incorporation in a regionally embedded global city and focus on how these shape perceptions of social class status and social mobility. We use a perspective that identifies "the global historical-structural processes"[6] that frame the receiving context and incorporation process. Beginning with an examination of the economic restructuring that swept the city in the last quarter of the twentieth century, we explain the origins of the economic bifurcation immigrants encounter as they claim places on the city's socioeconomic ladder. In the process we highlight how structural transformations immigrants sought to exit in Latin America also affected their experiences in the United States as residents of a neoliberal city. As Jason Hackworth argues, neoliberal restructuring is a global process that manifests itself differently across space and time yet has as its underlying driver a powerful philosophy of economics and government.[7]

We ground our analysis of perceptions of social class and mobility upon migration in an understanding of how social class has been conceptualized across borders. The social origins of immigrants are varied: Some come from a place of financial privilege, while others come from humble origins. Some are from urban areas in which higher education was accessible if one could afford it, yet others came from rural areas that only offered elementary levels of schooling. These backgrounds are important to understanding immigrants' patterns of social mobility in the global city, particularly the shifts in their perceived social status upon migration. We conclude by examining how trajectories of perceived social mobility shape immigrants' self-esteem and social security, and how a case study of unionization in Miami lifted wages for a sector of the working poor.

Neoliberal Context of Reception: Globalization and Economic Restructuring

Recall from previous chapters that Joaquín was a Peruvian young adult who immigrated with his parents after their company failed. His story is illustrative of how neoliberal restructuring links immigrant insecurities in the places of origin to those experienced in Miami. Although Joaquín said he had found economic security by working two low-skill jobs in Miami, he now experienced psychic insecurity, or anxieties due to uncertainty and vulnerability, associated with being undocumented and thus feeling like he was exploited: "I do not receive [in salary] what in reality I deserve to receive. . . . I am certain that this salary would never be paid to someone who has papers." In Miami, he said, "I do not feel at ease at all, but I feel better." Joaquín's story suggests how globalization, restrictive immigration policies, and neoliberalism become intertwined. Neoliberalism has spawned pools of undocumented laborers like Joaquín whose low-paid work supports the global city elite as they manage financial and trade flows across continents.

In contrast to the period before the 1960s, during which governments committed resources to building programs that would benefit the public good, including investing in infrastructure, public education, and housing, contemporary US neoliberal cities tend to "restructure government, deregulate business environments, and privatize collective assets" while they grant tax breaks to attract private investment.[8] Miami's ideal geographical location and the increasing and significant role of wealthy Latin American tourists in the local economy resulted in the Miami Chamber of Commerce's efforts to strengthen trade with Latin America in the postwar period.[9] To accomplish this neoliberal project, they had to "marketize the city and attract private capital for economic restructuring and downtown redevelopment." This process involved the concurrent Latinization and internationalization of the city, even if local policies were "increasingly determined externally."[10]

The business connection between Miami and Latin America was well cemented by the 1980s, when several multinational corporations moved their headquarters to Miami.[11] During this period, more financial institutions were established, facilitated by the liberalization of US international banking regulations, and converted the city into the second-largest international banking center in the country. Concurrently, a booming import-export business emerged, fueled by the free trade, foreign investment, and export-oriented production aspects of the emerging neoliberal policy hegemony, as well as by Miami's "Cuban Connection," in which networks and knowledge of language and culture were used by Cuban exiles to strengthen their business relations with Latin American and Caribbean markets.[12]

Miami's economic structure took on the form of a global city during a period in which the combination of its geography, intensification of capital concentration, and vulnerable pool of laborers enhanced its visibility as a hemispheric hub of neoliberalism, a combination made clearly evident in 2003 when city and state leaders promoted the area as the headquarters of the failed US-led attempt to economically integrate North and South America on a laissez-faire market model called the Free Trade Area of the Americas.[13] Regional internationalization also manifested itself in 116 Latin American companies that had offices in the Miami area by 2007. Many more European firms were headquartered in Miami to serve the Latin American market along with a large proportion of 420 regionally headquartered US companies.[14] *WorldCity*, a trade magazine targeting this rising industry, estimated these companies employed at least 180,000 people in Greater Miami, though the number of low-skilled workers servicing this emerging elite was even higher.[15]

Meanwhile, the headquarters and services of "Edge Banks"[16] diversified in the 1990s and 2000s. The first wave of international banks in Miami arrived in the 1970s and 1980s to coordinate capital transfers between the US Northeast and US multinationals operating in Latin America and the Caribbean. As a core city of the region, Miami saw a steady flow of capital, though the origins of such capital varied across the next two decades as sources of direct foreign investment in Latin America diversified. By early 2011, the eight Edge Banks operating in Miami included one from Spain, two from England, three from Latin America (Brazil, Ecuador, and Colombia), and only two from the United States (New York and Charlotte).[17] In addition to traditional export-import and other large-scale financial transactions, some promoted "private banking" for ultra-wealthy clients: "Wealth can present unique lifestyle situations. Whether you are buying new homes, investing in art or even relocating overseas, a relationship with HSBC Private Bank opens up a range of specialist services to you and your family."[18]

Solidifying Miami's promotional moniker as the Gateway to the Americas, these relationships directly and indirectly attracted immigrants. They came to direct the international linkage industries spawned by free trade or to fill jobs created to service the new international managerial class, lured at least on some level by the city's glitzy media image as it spread through a now transhemispheric Spanish-language media market.[19]

Indirectly, immigrants came via the deindustrializing US Northeast as well as from saturated labor markets in the US West. Neoliberalism, as experienced in the United States during the 1980s and 1990s, helped deliver immigrants to a broader swath of the country.[20] During this period, plants moved from the Midwest and Northeast to the US South and offshore to take advantage of lower costs and weaker labor and environmental regulations. Meanwhile, service-based enterprises, construction, and the financial services sectors of large southern cities attracted laborers from both within the country and abroad. Thus, many communities in the US South experienced a confluence of international migrants and secondary migrants from other areas in the United States.[21] The diversification of immigrant destinations is also linked to greater border enforcement.[22]

All of these factors contributed to the catapulting of immigration from a regional issue to a national "problem," as the discourse often presented it, that called for federal intervention and cast immigrants as burdens on state coffers. In short, the same processes that led to emigration from Latin America and the Caribbean contributed to the economic dislocations of many US natives, leading to rising anti-immigrant sentiment. As immigrants joined the labor force during this time, they too felt the income pressures affecting the US born since the early 1970s, in addition to the psychic insecurity from anti-immigrant discourses and policies.

Globalization, Income Inequality, and Poverty in Miami

Globalization transforms central city areas and ethnic places by rejuvenating warehouse districts, retail centers, and residential areas, transitions that often result in gentrification or the commodification of ethnic communities.[23] Similarly, Miami transformed from a southern US city housing a large Cuban enclave to a multiethnic, but still largely Cuban, metropolitan area. In marketing the city as a Latin American–*ized* version of a US city, appeals were made to global investment and to the new global elite based on Miami as a harbinger of multicultural cosmopolitanism. Miami followed a path similar to other neoliberal US cities in marketing itself as multiethnic and "conducive to transnational corporate capital," but Miami ultimately followed a different path because it was not just an ethnic central city,[24] but an entire metropolitan area.

Miami's internationalization along neoliberal lines meant that by the 2000s, the city had the distinction of being home to ultrawealthy elites while simultaneously being among the poorest cities in the country.[25] In spite of its consistent economic growth throughout the years, the majority of the city's population has been unable to secure better wages or improve their standards of living in part because US neoliberal policies disproportionately "impoverish and marginalize" inner-city dwellers.[26] By mid-decade, only Detroit and El Paso had higher poverty rates than the city of Miami. But income inequality and economic segmentation in the area were not always as drastic. Until 1979, per capita income was higher in Miami-Dade County than the national average, though, since then, local median household income has consistently lagged behind the rest of the nation.[27] In 1999, it was $35,966, "one of the lowest of the nation's 100 largest counties," and by 2005, it had only risen to $37,148, compared with the increase to $46,242 for the United States (see Figure 4.1).[28] As a result, higher proportions of the population in Miami-Dade County compared to the state and nation lived below the poverty level of $19,971 for a family of four in 2005 (with variations according to race and ethnicity). These patterns have remained unchanged since 1979, even though in the same time period, the area's economy exhibited solid growth.

Between 2001 and 2005 alone, Miami-Dade's economy grew at a steady rate of 3.5 percent, much higher than the 2.8 percent growth rate for the nation. Although income inequality has risen in the United States since 1968,[29] the polarization of income and wealth is more pronounced in Miami than in the United States as a whole. The richest quintile, or 20 percent of the population, in Miami makes twenty times more than the poorest quintile, while nationally, the top fifth makes 14.6 times more than the bottom one.[30] Figure 4.1, which illustrates the household income distribution for Miami compared to Florida and the United States, reveals these inequalities by showing larger proportions of Miami's population at the lowest income ranges, and lower proportions at the mid to upper ranges of the income distribution, with the exception of the highest income threshold (those making above $200,000). Important to keep in mind is that this income distribution comes from the "good times," before the economic collapse of 2008.

The link between neoliberalism and growth of bifurcated (low/high wage) trade-based employment, juxtaposed with shrinking compensation for public sector employment, becomes clear when local salaries are compared by category to averages from the state of Florida, which is less internationally dependent. Average salaries for business support and personal services jobs such as accountants, office and administrative support, health-care support, personal-care services, and food preparation are not significantly different between Miami and the rest of Florida. However, when we examine two upper-level occupations closely linked to finance and international trade, attorneys and managers, Miami's salaries are much higher than the state averages (e.g., attorneys in Miami make 133 percent of state attorneys' salaries). At the same time, the salaries for occupations affected by neoliberal government budget slashing, including teachers and protective

Figure 4.1 Distribution of Household Income for Miami, Florida, and the United States, 2005

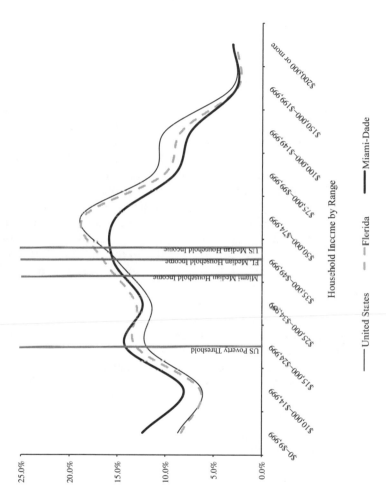

Sources: Miami-Dade County, Department of Planning and Zoning (2007); US Department of Health and Human Services (2005).

service workers, are lower than state averages (e.g., Miami's teachers, librarians, and teacher assistants make 75 percent of the state's average). Teachers' salaries in Miami are not much more than the city's police, fire, and other protective service workers (who make 72 percent of the state average). Thus, the county's income ladder is weighed in favor of the professional classes linked to internationalization, and against public sector employment that traditionally offered an urban economic niche to ethnic minorities and helped solidify the middle class in US cities.[31]

Added to this squeeze on the middle class were the effects of Miami's real estate boom and bust in the 2000s. Downtown "redevelopment," pushed by an alliance of elite developers and elected officials, drew immigrant labor to build glamorous condos for Miami's managerial class, second homes for Latin America's financial elite, and a taxpayer-funded sports arena for their entertainment, all staffed by minimum-wage workers. This redevelopment coincided with rising property taxes and insurance rates due to hurricanes affecting the state in 2004 and 2005.[32] Miami's cost of living rose, heightening the perception of a shrinking middle class. A 2006 *Time* magazine article noted "lots" of trouble in "paradise," claiming the city was the least affordable in the country with the highest median house prices and the lowest median incomes.[33] When the global financial markets collapsed in 2008, an economic meltdown caused in part by US real estate speculation similar to that in Miami, the boom stunningly collapsed. Table 4.1 compares incomes before and after the markets crashed, showing that the poor and middle classes bore a relatively larger burden due to the decline.

Miami immigrants began to witness scenes reminiscent of their former lives. The social movements that swept Latin America in the 1990s against economic liberalization replicated themselves in Miami, as protests emerged against the economic model and urban decline symbolized by the proposed Free Trade Area of the Americas.[34] While the county spent $1.5

Table 4.1 Median Household Income and Rate of Change by Quintile, Miami-Dade County (US$)

Income Quintile[a]	2007	2010	% Change
Top 5%	327,307	317,503	−3
Highest quintile	177,134	165,695	−6
Fourth	74,285	65,760	−11
Third	46,241	40,139	−13
Second	27,166	22,689	−16
Poorest quintile	10,535	8,348	−21

Source: Miami-Dade County, Department of Sustainability, Planning, and Economic Enhancement (2011).

Note: a. A quintile represents 20 percent of households.

million "getting the area red carpet ready" for the holders of $5,000 tickets for the 2007 Super Bowl, residents of Umoja Village, a makeshift shanty-town occupied by homeless women and men in Overtown, illustrated the paradox of a city that provided only bus benches for homeless individuals.[35] How did the city come to house such an economically polarized populace?

Occupational Segmentation and the Effects of Economic Restructuring

During the 1970s, when Miami still compared favorably to the national average in per capita income, Cubans increasingly worked for coethnics rather than for Anglos. Work in the Cuban enclave was thought to have yielded benefits comparable to jobs in the Anglo-dominated primary sector, brought higher returns by level of education and prior work experience, and paid overall better wages.[36] Although the enclave did not yield comparable outcomes to all classes of workers, it did facilitate women's entry into the labor force to maintain their families' middle-class status.[37] By the mid to late 1980s, Cuban women had higher rates of labor force participation than any other nationality.[38] Overall in the county, until 1988, opportunities in the professional and financial services increased, and high end service occupations employed just under one third of workers, most of whom were white Anglos with Cubans making modest inroads. At the same time, the proportion of clerical and low-end service workers increased in the 1960s and then stabilized, making up the largest percentage of workers by 1988. Latinos and blacks were overrepresented in these low-end occupations.[39]

Although Cubans integrated at both ends of the labor market, only 20 percent of Cubans in the late 1980s exhibited the "profile of success" that had been ascribed to this group in previous research.[40] Jimy Sanders and Victor Nee subsequently argue that the enclave hypothesis was only in part correct. Claiming that income returns on educational attainment were indeed comparable to the primary labor market, they believed this case was only true for entrepreneurs and not for Cuban laborers.[41] As the Cuban community began to polarize in the 1980s with the arrival of new cohorts from Cuba, elderly Cuban women in particular appeared to be overrepresented among the poor. Women in general were 58 percent of low-wage earners and held 70 percent of positions in service and clerical occupations during this time.[42]

In spite of economic growth from 1969 to 1999, the economic livelihoods of Miami households and families were deteriorating at a faster pace than in the rest of the state and country. Small-business owners were not immune; although blacks and Hispanics in Miami owned 64 percent of firms in the county (17.5 percent of private sector employment overall), most of these firms had no employees and were smaller in size compared to national minority-owned firms.[43]

Miami-Dade County workers are overrepresented in the category of lower-income earners in comparison to the nation. Just over 20 percent of county households made under $15,000 a year as of 2007, a picture that becomes bleaker when we consider the racial minority status of poor families; 28 percent of black households in the county make under $15,000 per year (see Figure 4.2). Although these structural imbalances are clearly endemic to a global city, according to Miami's Department of Planning and Zoning report, the identified culprits of high poverty and low income were Miamians' low levels of education and family structure.[44] This report indicated that 27 percent of the poor in Miami did not have a high school diploma and that another 17.5 percent had just a high school diploma. These low levels of education were overrepresented in the county compared to the nation. Moreover, 6.2 percent of the US population had less than a ninth-grade education, yet this number was nearly double for Miami-Dade County (for Florida, it was 5.5 percent). Part of this educational discrepancy was the surge in recent arrivals of immigrants, particularly immigrants originating in rural areas where access to secondary education is limited. Single-parent family structures exacerbate the likelihood of poverty. In Miami, 38 percent of female-headed households with children were poor (50 percent for blacks).[45] Although this report identified low education and female-headed households as two of the causes of increased poverty among Miami families, we should note that poverty rates at most levels of education were greater in Miami than in the rest of the nation.[46] What is typically not considered is that immigrants with high education credentials who were part of the professional and managerial sectors of their home countries were not always able to transfer their credentials across borders due to barriers to professional credentialing and what often amounts to discriminatory practices toward those with degrees from developing or underdeveloped countries.[47] Latin American and Caribbean immigrants are more likely to be disadvantaged than other immigrants regarding the devaluation of their home country educational backgrounds and work experiences upon arrival in the United States.[48] Two more barriers to consider when examining the structurally disadvantaged position of highly trained immigrant workers in the global city are that (1) language barriers impede the likelihood of passing licensing exams, and (2) status changes and the legal processes to acquire recredentialing are costly.

In sum, many obstacles can be found to the integration of skilled professionals into the US labor force, many of which stem from how the immigrants came into the country (e.g., whether through family reunification, international student visas, or occupational sponsorship), whether they have the proper legal status necessary to work in any kind of job (e.g., they may

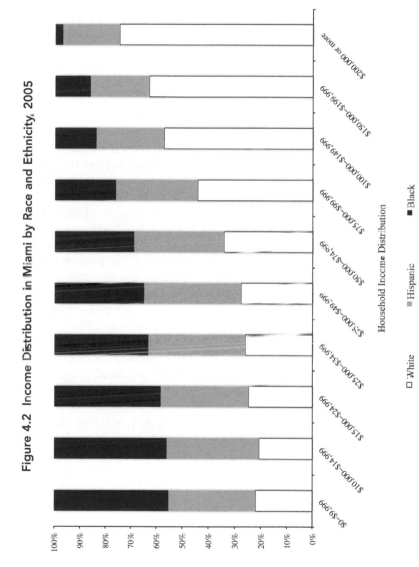

Figure 4.2 Income Distribution in Miami by Race and Ethnicity, 2005

Household Income Distribution

□ White   ▨ Hispanic   ■ Black

Source: Miami-Dade County, Department of Planning and Zoning (2007).

be here legally but not qualify for work permits), and the presence of barriers to recertification coupled with a lack of institutional support that facilitates the transferring of credentials across countries.

This highly educated segment of the immigrant workforce often gets lost in reports such as the ones we have cited in previous pages. Instead, policymakers often place the responsibility of being poor on human capital explanations and family structure arguments. While our intent is not to minimize the importance of these factors, the story that is told of low wages and high poverty in Miami is incomplete. If those with low levels of human capital were to increase their skills and education, the county would still have a need for unskilled, low-paid workers to fill the demand for these kinds of jobs. This bimodal economic structure relies on the premise that the lowest occupations in the global city, which are more often than not held by immigrant minority women and the elderly, are not intended to pay a living wage. Consequently, although one could argue that low wages are functions of the low education required for these jobs, the reliance on flexible sources of labor and the gender segregation of the labor force suggest that low wages are tied to the devaluation of jobs that require skills associated with femininity (e.g., care work occupations such as nannies or homecare workers for the elderly) and that have been a historical niche for the integration of minority workers, thereby devaluating the workers themselves, who hold positions in these segregated job sectors.[49]

In short, despite economic growth in real dollars for thirty of the past thirty-five years, and though Miami's economy grew at a higher rate than the country's due to high levels of labor productivity from 2001 to 2005, wages have not seen comparable growth, particularly among low-skill workers.[50] This resulted in a median hourly wage of $11.74 in Miami in 2006 (35 percent below the national mean hourly wage). Further, of the top twenty-five occupations in Miami, 44 percent paid a median hourly wage of $10 or less an hour (representing 17 percent of jobs in the county).[51]

Finally, to better understand the factors underlying high rates of poverty in the global city, we need to consider that housing prices in Miami skyrocketed in the past two decades before the market crashed, increasing the proportion of income used to pay for housing along with the housing affordability gap, which has grown since 2000. Moreover, the unusually high number of hurricanes that threatened South Florida in 2005 raised insurance premiums, increasing the squeeze on property owners and the middle class generally.[52]

A high cost of living intensifies levels of residential segregation among the poor, which also affects new immigrants who are trying to gain a foothold in the city's economy. The outcomes of this kind of segregation, which are overlaid with race and ethnic segmentation, are that "low income neighborhoods are often unable to develop their own internal dynamism as growth inducing resources are concentrated elsewhere. This has, in turn, led to the emergence of neighborhoods within the County that suffer from significant social and economic distress."[53] The situation for some communities is so dire that a county report warned that "unless actions taken by the County (hopefully in tandem with the private sector) lead to an increasing incorporation of those not benefiting from economic growth in the past, their income levels and living conditions will continue to experience relative deterioration over the long run."[54]

In sum, we find two dramatically different kinds of lived experiences in Miami. To state it in the language of *Forbes,* one Miami experience lives above the misery index, and another lives below it. In the rest of this chapter, we illustrate how immigrants will experience one or the other depending on their countries of origin, gender, legal status, class of origin, and trajectories of mobility in the global city. We examine how immigrants have fared in this context by analyzing perceived social mobility in our quantitative and qualitative samples.

Class Identities and Perceived Social Mobility

Historically, social scientists defined social class as a complex, ongoing, and essential part of understanding the social dimensions of one's economic and occupational statuses. Its subjective dimension involves the shared meanings ascribed to perceived economic conditions and the lifestyles that emerge from them, including understandings of how social class comingles with racial and gender self-positioning.[55] Subjective assessments of social class have been found to correlate well with empirical indicators of class position (e.g., education, occupation, income).[56] Thus, we examine changes in subjective class status upon migration.

Class Structure in Latin America

The Latin American and Caribbean societies from which our participants came were stratified traditionally in terms of upper, middle, and lower classes,[57] although defining the essential characteristics of each class has been a challenge since these rankings encompass both objective (income, occupation, education, wealth) and subjective criteria (lifestyle, manners, consumption habits, social relations, appearance, etc.). Coming from the most economically unequal region of the world, participants continued to regard subjective markers of class as very important as they adapted to their new lives in Miami.

Latin America's upper classes used to include landowning families who controlled political and economic power. When a new industrial class emerged in the 1950s, class boundaries became more fluid. The upper classes live isolated from others, establishing social distance through economic and racial hierarchies and spending their time in gated houses and communities, social clubs, and private schools.[58] Never as large as the US middle class, Latin America's middle class only emerged in the aftermath of World War II and was historically concerned with emulating the values and standards of the upper classes. Families employed domestic workers and emphasized private education to achieve social mobility, becoming a "quasi-elite."[59] Much heterogeneity, however, can be found within the Latin American middle class. It has traditionally included public sector employees, many of whom were hit hard by neoliberal privatizations and cuts in government bureaucracies, as well as professionals serving private enterprise.[60] Even though recent data reflect growth of the Latin American middle classes after the recent boom in commodity exports, they are still economically vulnerable, "subject to the risk of falling down the economic ladder."[61]

Traditionally, representatives of the Latin American urban lower class were unskilled workers, watchmen, street vendors, sweepers, porters, and domestics, most of whom worked in the informal sector of the economy without job security or benefits.[62] Since the 1950s, those who took part in internal mass migrations arrived in cities ill equipped for the influx of people displaced by agroindustries' transformation of rural areas and deflated food crop prices set to favor the expansion of industrialization under import substitution liberalization from the 1950s through the 1970s. With little access to public housing and formal employment, the majority of Latin America's poor now live in the shantytowns, which first encircled urban centers during these decades.[63]

The rise of closed neighborhoods and fear of crime has further fragmented urban space in recent decades, promoting isolation of the "haves" and social exclusion of the "have-nots."[64] A class-based apartheid thrives in which the middle and upper middle classes only come into contact with the poor if they employ them as household workers or as low-skilled laborers. As such, while the poor get to know the lifestyles of the well-to-do, the affluent rarely come to know the lived experience of poverty. As we will see later in this chapter, among the shocks that Latin American and Caribbean professionals experienced upon migration to Miami were economic struggles and poverty, two things they had never known.

Trajectories of Change upon Migration

Contrary to the beginning of the twentieth century, when immigrants integrated into an expanding US industrial economy with opportunities for upward mobility regardless of educational levels, migrating to a global city in the late twentieth and early twenty-first century is qualitatively different. Human capital and the ability of an immigrant to successfully transfer educational degrees and occupational experience largely determine whether one joins the ranks of the professional class. Yet transferal is difficult, and education and experience in the home country do not necessarily guarantee access to the US middle class, let alone the upper-end professions such as medicine or law. Many of the stories we heard suggested that although immigrants made more money than they did in their home countries, their occupational statuses declined and gains in income did not fully compensate for downward mobility.

Roland, who was quoted at the beginning of this chapter, felt he had nothing to show for his immigration in spite of eight years of living in Miami and working hard to hold down multiple jobs. He felt like a slave. Although Roland appeared no better or worse off financially compared to when he was in Haiti, he suggested that as a fisherman in Haiti, he had more control over his work schedule and how much he worked. Thus, he perceived that he was in worse shape in the United States, given what he considered to be a loss of control over his work life.

Understanding mobility is similarly complex in the case of Rafael, a professional playwright who left Cuba in 1995. Although initially he found employment packing groceries at the supermarket chain Publix, through hard work and a bit of luck, as he put it, he attained financial security after being hired for a job in Spanish-language television. Rafael's location in Cuba's class structure resembled what Erik Olin Wright has called a contradictory class location, or occupying a position in the class structure that has characteristics of two or more classes.[65] Having been a very successful playwright in Cuba, Rafael had control over his work and took pride in what he did. However, he said, "Personal triumphs in Cuba did not have any economic impact." Not making much money in Cuba placed him in a contradictory class location. This location changed when he came to Miami given the jobs he held, but it persisted in its contradictory nature. Even though Rafael felt gratified by the economic success he eventually achieved in Miami, success that would have been impossible in Cuba, and in spite of now having a house, a car, the ability to travel, and a better lifestyle, he found that the status and prestige he derived from his former occupation never waivered and possibly outweighed the prestige he seemed to derive from his current job, which inevitably entailed a degree of loss of control over his work. Objectively speaking, Rafael displays all of the signs of upward mobility if one takes a gradational view of social class (one that involves a hierarchy of positions, often determined by income or other factors).[66] What really changed upon migration was that Rafael's occupation was now well remunerated. Thus, from a relational perspective on social class (whereby classes are defined by the social relations in which they exist), Rafael lost full control over his work and was subject to relations of domination within a capitalist context. From this perspective, these societal contradictions make interpreting social mobility among Cubans more complex than for others.

The story of Angela, a Mexican, shows how gender played a constituting role in perceptions of social mobility. Angela worked for low wages throughout her time in the United States. Still, she felt that women in the United States had greater opportunities in comparison to Mexico. She felt that jobs that were open to women in Mexico were in low-paying gender-segregated fields (e.g., secretary or teacher) unless you became a professional. She perceived that she could now access the US occupational structure that was more open to women, enhancing feelings of progress. She viewed the US system as one in which social mobility for women was within reach.

As these examples show, we came across various trajectories of mobility that immigrants perceive they have followed based on subjective understandings of class status. When we examine the quantitative data regarding immigrants' perceived class status in their home country compared to Miami, we can track changes in their perceptions of social status and thus perceived mobility.[67] Using data we collected in 2008, we created Figure 4.3, which depicts subjective mobility by country/region of origin and gender. The prevalent trend was of immobility, although origin and gender mattered. Colombian, other South American, and Spanish Caribbean women seemed to have higher rates of immobility than their male counterparts, while Cuban, Haitian, and non-Spanish Caribbean women showed lower rates of immobility compared to their male counterparts. There appeared to be very little variation in immobility by gender among Mexicans and Central Americans and other non-Hispanics.

Haitian and non-Spanish Caribbean women and Cuban and Spanish Caribbean men had higher rates of perceived upward mobility than the total sample average. Regarding downward mobility, South American men, including Colombians, tended to experience the highest rates, particularly in comparison to their female counterparts. Cuban, Mexican, and Central American women, however, showed higher likelihoods of perceived downward mobility compared to their male counterparts. Important to note is that these patterns of mobility reflect not only immigrants' experiences in Miami's labor market but also the class positions they came from. Additionally, the category of immobility may be masking ambiguities in the perceived shifts in social status upon immigrants' arrival to the United States, especially if they occupied contradictory class locations in their home countries or in Miami. Thus, as in Rafael's case, if income has gone up but perceived status has gone down upon migration, respondents may interpret this shift as immobility.

Figure 4.3 Perceived Social Mobility by Country/Region of Origin and Gender (percentage)

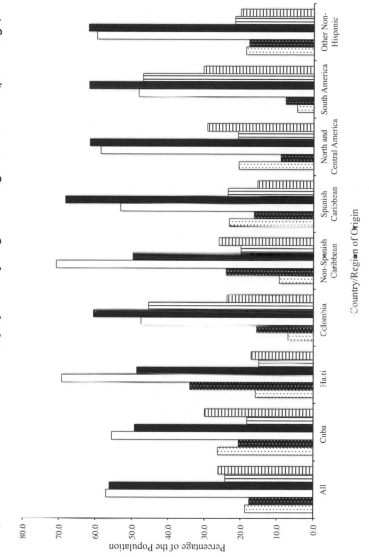

☐ Male Upward ■ Female Upward ☐ Male Immobility ■ Female Immobility ▥ Male Downward ▤ Female Downward

Source: ITMI Quantitative Survey.

Explaining Perceived Social Mobility Among Immigrants

In addition to describing the shifts in subjective social status among immigrants, we seek to further understand those factors associated with perceived social mobility. We calculate statistically the differences by country/region of origin in the odds of upward mobility before and after controlling for key demographic and social factors such as gender, age, marital status, years in the United States, educational attainment, US citizenship, English fluency, perceived racial discrimination, and perceived class status in the country of origin. Table 4.2 presents the results of this analysis. Model 1 examines only the differences by country of origin on the likelihood of reporting perceived upward mobility (we only discuss relationships that showed statistical significance). The odds for perceived upward mobility are higher for Colombians, other South Americans, and North (Mexico) and Central Americans in comparison to Cubans, the reference group.[68] The odds for upward mobility for the rest of the groups in Model 1 are no different than those of Cubans. When controlling for other important factors, the results in Model 2 indicate that among origin groups, North and Central Americans in fact have 8 percent *lower* odds than Cubans of perceiving themselves as upwardly mobile, while South Americans (excluding Colombians) have 6 percent *lower* odds of perceiving upward mobility (again, compared to Cubans). When we examine the relationship between the control measures and mobility, we find that women have 3 percent lower odds of perceiving upwardly mobile compared to men and age is not related to the odds for upwardly mobile. For every year of education attained, the odds for perceiving mobility increase by 1 percent. Not speaking English or not speaking it well lowers the odds for upward mobility by 7 percent when compared to those who speak English very well. Regarding perceptions of racial discrimination, perceiving this to be a small problem or a major problem decreases the odds of upward mobility by 4 percent and 12 percent, respectively, when compared to those for whom it is no problem at all.

We need to consider immigrants' class of origin to understand the odds for mobility in the United States. Compared to those who identified as upper class in the home country, identifying as poor before migration increased the odds of perceiving upward mobility by almost 2.5 times; identifying oneself as working class raised the odds for upward mobility by 30 percent; and those who considered themselves middle class in the country of origin showed 9 percent higher odds for upward mobility compared to those who were upper class. Thus, the chances for upward mobility were highest when coming from poorer backgrounds, but at the same time, these findings may reflect the inability of those from upper-class origins to state they had moved up if they identified as upper class before and after migration. The next section expands this analysis and examines how immigrants discuss perceived changes in their social status upon migration.

Table 4.2 Perceived Upward Social Mobility by Country/Region of Origin (odds ratio)

	Model 1			Model 2		
	Odds	SE		Odds	SE	
Country/region of origin						
Cuba[a]						
Haiti	—	—		—	—	
Colombia	2.20	0.33	*	—	—	
Non-Spanish Caribbean	—	—		—	—	
Spanish Caribbean	—	—		—	—	
North and Central America	1.86	0.25	**	0.92	0.03	**
South America	3.78	0.32	***	0.94	0.03	*
Other non-Hispanic	—	—		—		
Control variables						
Female				0.97	0.02	†
Age				1.00	0.0007	**
Married				—	—	
Years in the United States				—	—	
Years of education				1.01	0.003	***
Citizen				—	—	
Perceived English fluency						
Does not speak English well/at all				0.93	0.03	**
Speaks English well				—	—	
Speaks English very well[a]						
Receiving differential treatment because of phenotype is						
No problem[a]						
A small problem				0.96	0.03	†
Somewhat of a problem				—	—	
A major problem				0.88	0.05	**
Social class in country/region of origin						
Poor				2.46	0.04	***
Working				1.38	0.03	***
Middle				1.09	0.03	**
Upper[a]						

Source: ITMI Quantitative Survey.
Notes: a. Reference group.
Predictors lacking any significant effect are excluded from the table, even though they were included in the models.
Dependent Variable Upward Mobility = 1.
† = p ≤ 0.10; * = p ≤ 0.05; ** = p ≤ 0.010; *** = p ≤ 0.001.

Upward Social Mobility

When immigrants come from low socioeconomic backgrounds, if they can avoid destitution, then the only mobility available is upward mobility. Alternatively, they could remain in a low socioeconomic status or return to the home country if they fail to make ends meet. Although we have no information regarding rates of return, we do know that many immigrants who came from low socioeconomic backgrounds and who identified as members of the lower class in their home countries stated that, in Miami, they felt like part of the middle class. This feeling was particularly the case for those who migrated from rural areas, and it generally supports the findings illustrated in the regression analysis that shows that those from poor social class backgrounds perceived the highest odds for upward mobility.

Even though the quantitative data showed that Mexicans and Central Americans have lower chances of experiencing upward mobility in comparison to Cubans when controls are taken into account, the rural migrants we interviewed qualitatively perceived upward mobility as a result of economic improvement, even if by US standards their levels of improvement did not reach normative middle-class standards (which are elusive themselves). Additionally, rural participants from Mexico were highly motivated by the possibility of accessing education once in the United States. The mean education among those in the poorest fifth of the Mexican population is 3.5 years in comparison to the average years (11.6) of education among the richest fifth. Thus, even by Latin American standards, Mexico has one of the largest education inequality gaps in the region.[69] This gap explains why access to education in the United States often becomes synonymous with upward mobility.

Migration to Pursue Education as a Means of Achieving Upward Mobility

The literature on immigrant social mobility often emphasizes the returns on education for immigrants. The assumption is that each subsequent generation will attain greater levels of education than their parents, and the differential between immigrants' and natives' incomes will lessen.[70] When we examine the context of reception and the patterns of social mobility that immigrants exhibit, what we find is that although higher education does enhance the odds of perceived upward social mobility, the returns on education are relatively small, as seen in our quantitative analysis. Other factors are possibly at work in terms of mediating mobility outcomes, such as legal status, as seen in the previous chapter. Nevertheless, access to education seemed to increase perceived upward mobility.

Ignacio grew up in a small town in Mexico in which children only had access to a third-grade education. The only hope of improving his chances of becoming educated was to leave his town: "It was not my intention to stay there, in my town, but to keep studying. . . . I came for the first time to the United States. I did not have money, or a future in my country." Ignacio arrived in the United States without speaking any English but with the intention of studying here. As he told us, "I always tried to study a little bit of English. Always, while I had the opportunity to study." Ignacio worked at several jobs and was trained in carpentry. He stated that carpentry was the job he truly enjoyed: "This job is one of the jobs I have liked. When I came from Mexico, I was very frustrated because I did not know what I was going to do, or what I would like in my life. I see . . . a lot of people that don't know how to educate themselves. . . . In my case, I consider that I am trained for this. To me, this is my profession."

Ignacio appears to have done much better in the United States than he would have if he had stayed in his Mexican hometown. He talked with pride about his educational achievements and training. Similarly, Estella, a participant in one of our focus groups, came to the United States because she did not have access to education in Puebla, the town where she was born: "Well, right now I am studying English. I am giving English my all. I have been two years and three months in schools. I took a course in child care, day care. I just finished it [and] I am about to receive my diploma, thanks to God. Now, next month, I finish school for English and I will start a course for computers. I already registered. I am counting the money because it costs me. And I am taking steps and achieving them."

The interviews and focus groups strongly suggested that many of our participants came to this country not only to find a job but also to have access to education. These findings confirm the argument that lack of educational, economic, and political opportunities in rural areas of Latin America have contributed to the social exclusion of marginalized groups and perpetuated inequalities in the region.[71] If Ignacio and Estella had not migrated to the United States, they would have found improving their educational and economic prospects almost impossible.

The narratives above speak to the origins of some of our Mexican participants, mainly small farmers that migrated from rural and very poor areas in Mexico. Most of them were secondary migrants, arriving first in California and other states and then moving to Miami through family connections. Generally, the first agricultural jobs they secured in California were physically draining and gave them no future opportunities for financial improvement. In contrast to the lack of opportunities in the small towns and rural areas where they came from, or the marginal jobs they attained upon arriving at their original US destination, Miami instantly provided them with jobs, the possibility to study to get a technical degree, and a much brighter future for their children. Not surprisingly, these immigrants perceived that they had experienced upward mobility, even those who found themselves in low-wage jobs.

The story of Tobias is emblematic of the path followed by many rural Latin Americans. When he was a child, his grandfather taught him to work in the fields. By the time he turned fourteen, he secured an agricultural job in Mexico to help his parents. His parents built their house on land his grandfather had given them, but the area had no electricity or clean water and money was tight. When Tobias was asked about his social class in

Mexico, he did not hesitate when he responded: *"clase baja"* (lower class). When he turned eighteen, Tobias came to the United States to get the education that his parents could not afford (he was interested in earning an engineering degree in Mexico). He left home carrying with him a cousin's phone number, crossed the border in El Paso, and found his first job in New Mexico pulling weeds and cleaning harvested grapes. By the time Hurricane Andrew descended upon South Florida in 1992, he was told there was ample demand for labor. Thus, he relocated to the region.[72]

During his first years in Florida, Tobias found employment only in nonskilled positions and worked hard every day of the week, even though he had begun school in New Mexico and attended every night after work. Although he did not reveal to us how he attained legal documents or became eligible for citizenship, by the time he became a US citizen, he was ready to find a less physically demanding job. In Florida, he enjoyed a lifestyle he never thought would have been possible to achieve in Mexico: "To have your own house, a car, and all the material things that one dreams of and to have the time to be with family too, to take a walk, to have the opportunity of knowing more, of traveling, and living well." Although a long way from a degree in engineering, at the time of the interview, he worked as a maintenance supervisor for three day-care centers and felt strongly that he had finally achieved the economic security he dreamed of. When we asked him about his social class in the United States, he replied without any hesitation: "I am middle class." Tobias strongly felt that he had attained economic security because of the combination of his education, citizenship, and experience. His is the profile of someone who has become upwardly mobile through migration.

Experiencing Upward Mobility by Overcoming Rigid Gender Roles

For rural women and men in Latin America, migration opened up not only the possibility of studying and gaining economic independence, but also a level of freedom that they perceived they would not have experienced back in their hometowns. For women, particularly from the urban middle sectors, immigration also opened up new avenues to making money that might have been looked down upon in the home country (e.g., taking an extra job or earning money on the side) in addition to expanding opportunities to broaden their social networks. Estella, the Mexican immigrant introduced earlier, argued that work and education facilitated upward mobility, but additionally, migration opened up other possibilities such as meeting new friends in different places without any restrictions: "I have lots of friends . . . for example in the schools, from different jobs. I have changed jobs a lot and I have met many friends, in different places, and I like it. I like to be in that type [of situation] of meeting people." Friends were important for Estella because "we spend 99 percent of our time at work and only 1 percent with our family." When comparing her present situation with her experiences in Mexico, she stated, "Yes, it is different because my town does not have that opportunity of meeting up with other people from work because in the first place, I was in my town, inside my house. I did not go out. It was too small, where we knew everybody but it didn't have . . . what is here. Here, you have to work. You need to work to live. It is different." From Eduardo Lora and Johanna Fajardo's research we know that class status in Latin America is partly defined by the social relationships one has.[73] Having networks of friends and more options regarding getting out of the house (e.g., for work and social activities) made Estella feel like she had moved up in the world.

Fredeline, from rural Haiti, also believed that more options were available to women in this country: "In the United States you have a lot of opportunities even if you are an immigrant. If you have papers here, you can look for employment and you are not dependent on anybody else. You can help yourself as opposed to [in] Haiti. [In Haiti it] is difficult to find work and to find independence. You are always dependent on someone else."

We need to emphasize not just that legal status, but the kind of legal status, has an effect on the kinds of opportunities available to women and men. When women enter the country legally but as spousal dependents of another wage earner, not having authorization to work can be demoralizing, particularly if they have career experience and high skill sets that make them otherwise employable in the United States. This legal status sets them up for dependence on those sponsoring their immigrations.[74] Men suffer too in the labor market if their visas do not give them work authorization, even if they have the skills to be in high-caliber positions. Not being able to work emasculates men and relegates both genders to a status of dependency. Thus, regardless of gender, legal status determines to a great extent one's ability to contribute to the productive workforce. The nature of this participation affects perceptions of upward mobility, particularly as they relate to overcoming traditional gender roles—efforts that themselves are constrained by certain legal statuses.

In Fredeline's case, since arriving in the United States, she felt empowered, and more importantly, she found herself "in a position where I can help my children and myself. If I were in Haiti, I would not be able to do that." Fredeline attributed her inability to get ahead in Haiti to the structure of gender relations in that country: "In Haiti it is the man that has all of the control. I mean, the woman is submissive, because it is the man that controls everything. What the man says, that is what goes, that is how I see it in Haiti. It is not like it is a team. The man is the chief and the woman is the one that listens." This newfound sense of independence due to migration is possibly what explains the gender variations in perceptions of upward mobility found in the quantitative results presented earlier. Although the regression results showed that women's odds for upward mobility were somewhat lower than men's, the bivariate analysis revealed a large discrepancy between Haitian women (who had the largest proportion of any group who reported experiencing upward mobility) in comparison to other women across groups and, in particular, to Haitian men.

Fredeline attained a bachelor's degree in health-care management and felt that earning this degree would not have been possible had she stayed in Haiti. She praised the US education system, particularly the idea that education was a public good that was funded through property taxes. This access was important to her because it allowed her the opportunity to, in her view, properly raise her children and for them to go "farther than I was able to go." She fully embraced the notion that the United States was the land of opportunity and her children's access to these opportunities through education itself embodied the experience of social mobility in her life.

Women now make up a larger segment of the international migration stream.[75] Traditionally, women migrate with their male partners or follow male family members.[76] Variations in gendered patterns of migration from other Latin American countries, however, exist, and they are shaped by legal status.[77] In our sample, women from different class backgrounds and legal statuses came in with different levels of education, and some made the decision to migrate on their own to seek better prospects. Women were seeking to escape environments of both a general economic insecurity and a more specific social insecurity that stemmed from traditional gendered patterns in their villages of origin that maintained normative structures for women and kept them from fully developing their potential and from doing what they needed to attain greater security in their lives.

Another case to consider is Maruja, a young woman who had lived her life in extreme poverty in a Mexican village. As a child, she helped her parents and grandmother cultivate the fields; money was hard to come by. They rarely had the basic necessities, and the possibility of getting an education was slim. At age sixteen, Maruja left the village with her brother: "We came here to look for a better life, try to work and to have money to eat and live a little better than how we lived in my town. In my town, you could not find food to eat, there was no money to buy [food], so we decided to travel, work, and make money to be able to eat." Maruja also "wanted to keep active, make my money, have things . . . you know a car, clothes, shoes, jewelry, things. . . . I had the idea in my head and I told my grandmother, 'I want to go to the United States,' because I saw a lot of people migrating." Maruja was unsure about how to describe her desire to migrate to seek a better future, stating that "I don't know if I should call it ambition or . . . I

wanted to study. I wanted to be somebody. I wanted to be different, a prepared person. At first I wanted to study English; I wanted to speak English."
She tried to put it more simply: "I wanted to stop having to ride on a donkey
or to have to wait for a car to go by." What comes through in Maruja's narrative is her desire to not just leave a context of economic deprivation but
also to leave behind the traditional roles of women in her village. She
wanted to be "independent" and seek out a different sort of life from the one
for which she was slated. Had she not embarked on her journey, her life
would have been "cleaning the house and making lunch and dinner and that
would be the day." In contrast, migration meant the possibility of working
outside the home, studying, and acquiring a new lifestyle. This goal was a
departure from the gendered life course ingrained in village norms.

When examining Maruja's case, we must point out that people from her
village commonly immigrated to the United States. The transnational cir-
cuit connecting her village to this country facilitated the two-way flow of
ideas and values, or, as Peggy Levitt calls them, social remittances.[78] When
emigrants returned to their home countries for visits and brought with them
new ideas, perspectives, and ideologies to share with those who had never
migrated, the possibility of attaining new and different kinds of lifestyles
emerged for all. This exchange of ideas, in part, explains Maruja's desire
for something more than what she had, even if she could not articulate
clearly what that "something" was. However, clearly, her desire for something more in life and her curiosity about the opportunities that migration
could offer led her to cross the border into Arizona and settle temporarily in
California, eventually making her way to Miami. While still undocumented
at the time of the interview, Maruja felt she had achieved a comfortable, although not perfect, level of economic security working as a cook in an ethnic restaurant. This new job represented a drastic change from her prior
work in agriculture.

Similar to the New York Mexicans in Robert Smith's research, work in
food services has created a niche that is being used as a stabilizing step, on
a rickety ladder of social mobility.[79] By gaining a foothold in the formal, albeit secondary, sector of the workforce, Maruja felt more mature and had a
greater sense of pride: "I feel I have a great responsibility . . . so it would
succeed, in a restaurant where people from different nationalities go with
different tastes. And it is me who is in charge of preparing their plates . . .
prepare the food for them to eat, enjoy, and feel good. And that they can
come back. It is a great responsibility."

Even with these gains, Maruja still did not consider herself middle
class. Nonetheless, she made clear that since migrating, she had experienced upward mobility. Miami increased her sense of economic security
and also, like other women in our study, her social security. The idea that
gender would, in theory, no longer limit her life chances gave her comfort.

In US society, gender continues to be a source of many inequalities and discrimination; however, Maruja's bifocality—her conscious comparison of two distinct social contexts—for the present time blinded her to these conditions.

Gender emancipation through migration was just as much a product of rigid gender roles in immigrants' countries of origin as it was of their class statuses and village upbringing. Smith's research has shown that gender roles are not static, and just as they shift in the US context, they are also moving targets in Mexican and other Latin American and Caribbean societies. The emancipation that many women felt, though, was real in its consequences. As Smith notes, there are a variety of ways in which women and men perform masculinity and femininity, and these variations are very much a product of class. Thus, women from more urban, middle-class backgrounds did not feel the kind of liberatory effects of migration as immigrants from rural origins did (although they did feel that as older women, age would not work against them as much in the US context), perhaps because they already partook in the flexibility of gender that increased access to resources in their countries of origin. Thus, the opportunity to earn a wage may be a departure for women from rural and modest backgrounds, but it was not as remarkable an experience of mobility for middle- and upper-class Latin American and Caribbean women, for whom education and work outside the home may have been already a standard expectation.[80]

Social mobility stemming from the ability to depart from their prescribed gender roles applied to men just as much as it did to women. For men such as Tobias, after years of hard work, achieving economic security opened up new opportunities, particularly regarding increased leisure time to spend with his family. Social mobility for men also afforded them a newfound ability to establish closer bonds with children as well as develop companionate relationships with partners, efforts that were enhanced by not being so overworked and having jobs that offered them downtime. In this regard, perceptions of social mobility are also about the creation of opportunities to explore other forms of masculinity that differ from the often-taken-for-granted machismo used to describe Latin American men.

Confounding Effects of Legal Status for Perceptions of Mobility

The story of perceived upward mobility is not without costs. Even though migration served as a vehicle for social mobility for many in our sample, we should not forget, as *Forbes* has reminded us, that Miami still ranks high on the magazine's misery index. For those who have felt their lives are better, we should understand that even if they are in unskilled positions, they are likely better paid in the United States than if they had a comparable job in Latin America. However, better compensation for similar work does not change the reality that some low-level jobs, particularly those in sectors that are not regulated by the government and that employ undocumented workers, are exploitative. Take Angela, a Mexican mentioned earlier, who could only find work in a horticultural nursery when she arrived to Miami: "I did not want to be one more of all the people working in the field. You see all the people: Mexicans, Guatemalans, and Nicaraguans, all muddy, full of sweat. It is hard work and badly paid. So I did not want to see myself in this kind of situation." Her lack of papers at that time, however, limited her options and made her vulnerable to exploitation. Even though she tried to avoid backbreaking work, she took a job at a nursery and described the conditions there:

> I worked with the orchids they have, and it is not heavy, the orchid because you have to put a stick, tie it up, and fertilize it and that was not very difficult. What was more difficult were all the big plants and those hours on the floor and they exploited you. They want you to work more than the eight hours, sometimes ten to twelve hours. They do not care if it is raining; they do not care if it is thundering. And you had to walk around with scissors cutting, cutting the trees' dry leaves, fertilizing while bending over, and if they saw you straighten up, they would be upset because you had to be bent over fertilizing and under a horrible sun, and then came the rain. Imagine it: you are hot, sweating, and then it rains as it happens here. When it is hot it rains. They don't care about any of that.

Oftentimes, immigrants' undocumented status left them more vulnerable to exploitation, as if they were a separate social class with no rights or recourse. In addition, the need to constantly work to earn enough to sustain the basics of daily existence meant that they led lives that left them little room for anything else, in some cases, even family, as Angela recounted: "On one occasion, I had one of my daughters that was sick and I told them [employer], 'I have to go because my daughter is sick. They called from day care.' And they said, 'You can't leave because if you go, you are fired because it means you don't care about the job.' And I said, 'Look, I have needs and the job does matter to me but my daughter matters more.' Then, I took things off, I left their things, I came, the manager was upset, but I didn't care because my daughter comes first before any job."

Angela was not the sole breadwinner in her family so perhaps the extra income allowed her to walk away from the job. Her husband was a permanent legal resident, which meant that she eventually became a legal resident. Once she had legal status, she went back to school. As a result of her bad experience in the nursery, "That's when I decided that I had to get ahead. I had to study. I studied English at the Adult Center, and I finished high school." At the time of the interview, Angela was working in a day-care center and continuing her education to obtain a better job and a better salary. During the interview, she asked, "If you do not have your residence, how do you work? They may have a Ph.D. in something but if they do not have residence, they cannot work. I know people who come from there, who are licensed or are doctors or who are secretaries but do not have papers and they cannot work here. Sometimes they do not know the language. As a result, they then end up in poorly paid jobs." As we will see next, Angela's assessment of the importance of legal status for social mobility in the United States was right on target; education and work experience alone were not enough to get ahead in Miami.

Perceptions of Downward Mobility Among the Highly Educated

In Alejandro Portes and Rubén G. Rumbaut's conceptualization of immigrant incorporation, immigrants' human and social capital, in combination with elements of the contexts of reception, shape their modes of incorporation into the receiving society, particularly among the second generation.[81] Following this logic, an immigrant arriving with high levels of education and work experience will face a smoother process of incorporation than an equally positioned immigrant with the same characteristics but with a lower level of education and fewer skills. However, in the case of many of our interviewees, despite high levels of education, specialized skills, and work experience, they were working in jobs that were outside of their professional fields or in positions for which they were overqualified. The modes-of-incorporation framework assumes human capital can be appropriately transferred in the United States. But, in fact, other factors are at work that must be accounted for if we are to fully understand immigrants' experiences of integration and their ensuing outcomes.

For some professional immigrants in our study, high levels of training and experience did not translate into upward social mobility, or even immobility (e.g., lateral mobility). The lack of legal status often accompanied downward mobility. Other factors such as the inability to obtain degree equivalencies or lack of English fluency further delayed immigrants' upward mobility in Miami. These findings are consistent with research on Filipino, Colombian, and Russian immigrants, who occupy jobs for which they are overqualified.[82] This was the case for Cristobal, a Colombian journalist who left his country because of threats against his life: "The first thing a lot of people who have immigrated from the middle or upper classes want to do is to become citizens. They know they are nobodies. Instead, in Colombia, they were somebodies. Here no one knows us. We do not have a club. When I was on the way here with every intention of staying, I remembered that song by John Lennon, 'Life Starting Over,' on the airplane. That's how I felt, as if I had to begin all over again. The precise moment we all understand that we are starting over again is when we're delivering pizza, for example."

"Delivering pizza," Cristobal's poignant symbol for "life starting over," illustrates that immigrant professionals are acutely aware of their declining social status.[83] Their insertion into the unskilled sectors of Miami's economy was a constant reminder of who they used to be—"somebodies" who now found themselves as "nobodies." Their self-esteem waned as a result. As Cristobal put it, "no one knows us." This statement illustrates that those in Cristobal's situation become disembedded from their networks and sources of social capital. Unless their home society social networks were transnational in nature, the potential of activating this capital was of little utility in the receiving country.

The participants that identified themselves as members of the upper middle class in their home countries who were downwardly mobile had completed high levels of education and worked hard to position themselves competitively in their national economies, yet in the global economy where the exchange and investment of capital know no bounds, their high levels of training did. It was difficult to transfer credentials as a result of three factors: undocumented status, lack of degree equivalency, and lack of fluency in English.

Downward Mobility and Undocumented Status

Lola, the Peruvian immigrant we discussed at the beginning of Chapter 2, arrived in Miami with her husband and two children on tourist visas after the failure of her husband's business. Once in the United States, Lola and her husband secured jobs in a telemarketing company making $8 an hour. A year later, they found themselves unhappy with these jobs because of increased pressure to sell more services, the difficulties of working the night shift, low salaries, and her family's inability to keep up with the rising cost of living. Someone in the condominium where Lola lived offered her a cleaning job that she took to supplement her low-paying telemarketing position. Shortly after, she found other cleaning jobs through her client's recommendations, which led her to resign from her position. At the time of the interview, Lola cleaned houses from Monday to Friday while her husband worked six days a week and had two jobs. Between the two of them, they met all of their financial expenses: "We live well. There is no extra money but we eat well and we do not have debts." Although her family was doing better financially in Miami than back in Lima, her experience of downward mobility distressed her. Before migration, Lola was a stay-at-home mom. As the daughter of two lawyers, she graduated with a degree from what she called the best university in Lima. Although she told us, "There is no such thing as undignified work," her disbelief about her new status emerged when she shared the following: "Me, a Catholic University graduate, cleaning bathrooms!" Lola's experience was similar to other participants in our study who, despite having professional backgrounds, lacked legal status and found themselves taking jobs that in their former lives would have been unthinkable.

Pedro, another Peruvian and a former sales manager for a pharmaceutical company in Lima, arrived in Miami with what was left of his life savings after enduring two consecutive years of unemployment. Lacking legal status, the only job Pedro found was laying tiles for $7 an hour. In the absence of other alternatives, he took the job even though he had never laid a tile before. To make ends meet during weekends, he took odd jobs repairing and painting houses. His wife, Camila, a former educator, usually went along with him to assist and get materials for him when needed. During the week, she worked at a cafeteria preparing food and serving lunch. Camila assured us that this experience had been enriching but also said that she hoped she would soon be able to stop working at the cafeteria and get back to teaching, her original profession.

These cases exemplify downward mobility as a result of undocumented status. Lola, Pedro, and their spouses were not able to receive the financial returns on their educations even though they had knowledge, skills, and professional backgrounds. The lack of legal status increased their vulnerability and led to experiences akin to those of undocumented labor migrants, who must accept work wherever and whenever they can find it. Thus, Angela's analysis, stated earlier in this chapter, could not be more accurate: education alone is not enough to get ahead. In the United States, legal status is a key factor to achieve upward mobility.

Downward Mobility and Degree Equivalency

Ivan, the Colombian doctor introduced in the previous chapter, left Bogotá seeking greater physical security. As a child, Ivan had lived in the United States but returned to Colombia while still in school after his parents divorced. Unlike many of the professionals in our study, he was fluent in English when he arrived in the United States. Ivan, his wife, and his brother, who immigrated with them, arrived in the United States seeking asylum. At the time of his application, he faced up to a fifteen-year wait for his permanent residency documents, and to practice medicine, he

needed to pass US exams. The problem was that he needed time to study
for them, but he also needed to earn a steady income to support his household: "As a doctor . . . I don't have a license to practice medicine, so the
exams are to validate the license; but in the meantime, there is nothing that
could help you. So if you can get it [employment in your area of exper-
tise], you can be a medical assistant, I think that pays $8 an hour, and it's
simply like being a receptionist. So actually the law really is not broad
enough for professionals."

In this quote, Ivan referred to the legal hurdles faced by doctors trained
in foreign countries to receive licenses to practice medicine in the United
States. Ivan felt that the United States should take advantage of professionals' high levels of education rather than relegate them to positions that required little training. Ivan was not alone. As Mirta Ojito highlighted in an
article published by the *New York Times* in 2009, "while the rest of the
country is suffering from a shortage of primary physicians, Miami is awash
with Cuban doctors." Some had obtained licenses, but many more faced obstacles and challenges as a result of not knowing the language or, similar to
Ivan, lacked time to study as they had to work to support their families.[84]

While he waited for his asylum papers, Ivan was hired at a gas station
in one of Miami's poor neighborhoods. He stated that he constantly felt uncomfortable knowing that as a professional with a formal education, he felt
he was being exploited. Here, he belonged to "the working class," he said,
without hesitation. But then again, he needed to specify what this category
meant to him, and thus, he laughingly added, "Well, actually, that depends
on where you find me." He articulated that his social class "depends [on]
who you work with." For a man who was part of a family firmly entrenched
in his country's dominant class and clearly recognized in Colombian society, his own self-esteem required that the people he worked with acknowledged his education. To feel like a professional he needed others to know
he was one and treat him accordingly. Describing his current work environment, he told us that he had found doctors who listened to him and re-
spected him and what he told them. Thus, for professionals like Ivan, perhaps even more than income and material symbols of success, being
recognized as a professional became essential to mitigate the loss of status
and the sense of devaluation of his hard work that accompanied his perceptions of downward mobility.

Downward Mobility and Language

In the Dominican Republic, Altagracia had worked in her parents' family
business selling electrical equipment, when she decided to move to the
United States with her husband, a Bronx-born Dominican whom she met in
high school in the Dominican Republic. As we indicated in the previous

chapter, Altagracia's father, who often traveled back and forth to the United States on business, was a US resident and got his daughter her US residency. Thus, when Altagracia and her husband moved to the United States, they both had legal status and their reasons for immigration were clear: "You can make great sacrifices and achieve things that you could never have in Santo Domingo, so that was why we stayed here [Miami]. To create a better life for ourselves." But Altagracia's lived experience of being an immigrant to Miami came as a surprise to her:

> It was very difficult. The change to a different culture, the change in language, to find a job in a different place and with different schedules entirely different to the ones I was used to in Santo Domingo. . . . For me it was a very hard process because first I was not used to work in restaurants. Second, it was a complete change in language. I did not understand anything. I went through a lot of trouble [working as a cashier] in McDonald's. I did not understand what they were asking me, and a lady almost threw me a coffee in the face one day because I did not understand. She was asking me to put cream in her coffee and I did not understand. That for me was a tough process of adaptation of one language to another.

While she believed that they had achieved their dream of a "better life," Altagracia also felt that she had become downwardly mobile: "I have had to follow a time schedule for coming and leaving work, wear a uniform, work [at a fast-food restaurant] directly with people who don't speak the same language that I do. I mean the change is difficult. . . . In Santo Domingo, I belonged to the middle upper class, and here you could say I belong to the working class."

Although life was harder in Miami, she consoled herself knowing she could enjoy an economic status that would have been impossible in Santo Domingo. "To know that in Santo Domingo, as much as you worked, with the exchange rate it would be really difficult to acquire what you want. Here there is financing for things and in Santo Domingo no. . . . I was setting up my household, buying things for my house. It gave me a lot of hope. It gave me a desire to stay here and keep working here, to say, 'Okay, I work a lot, but I can buy what I like.' In Santo Domingo I couldn't because of the economic situation then." Altagracia missed, however, one key symbol of status from her country of origin: someone to help with household chores. She stated, "In Santo Domingo, many people have maids, the person in charge of cleaning and cooking. Here it is not like that. Here you have to do everything. You have to clean, you have to cook, [and] you have to wash clothes. . . . [T]o go from Santo Domingo where everything was done for me to having to do it all for myself was a change; I had to get used to a different kind of life." In Miami, a perceived sense of financial stability had come at the expense of her status. Rather than being catered to, she was now in the position to have to cater to others. But the US consumerist lifestyle seemed to provide her with some satisfaction.

Contradictory Class Location

Thus far we have seen cases in which immigrants who identified with their home countries' upper or middle classes found themselves carefully negotiating the shifts in their perceptions of status. These shifts came as immigrants faced a new reality of integrating into a society that was often reluctant to acknowledge their past accomplishments and the attainment of credentials in foreign countries. In this sense, immigrants were left to cope with the psychological consequences of occupying contradicting class locations, or positions in the occupational structure with characteristics of more than one class (within the context of downward mobility). We see a somewhat similar trend with Cuban immigrants, however, in reverse. Cuban society experienced drastic economic changes as a result of the revolution of 1959. For Cubans, the transition from one economic system to another entailed a "re-ordering of the social structure," and in the years that followed the Cuban Revolution, the stated goal was to build class homogeneity.[85]

Class homogeneity, however, was never attained. In recent years, the application of reforms and the impact of globalization on Cuban society brought even more diversification to an already heterogeneous social structure. As a result, Mayra Paula Espina Prieto argues that Cuban society has moved toward restratification involving a "whole process of quantitative and qualitative change in social relations, bringing in new strata, transforming the situation of others, and changing the rankings among them."[86]

Susan Eckstein draws comparisons among the socioeconomic situations of the varying waves of migration from Cuba to Miami. The self-defined exiles arrived between 1959 and 1980 and belonged to the upper and middle classes; in contrast, the *Marielitos* (Cubans who arrived in Miami in 1980 as part of the Mariel Boatlift), were essentially working class. In contrast, the backgrounds of the rafters who arrived in 1994 were very diverse, but their high levels of education most closely resembled those of the first Cuban arrivals.[87] Thus, although Cubans are coming from a society that claims to be "classless," their society comprises workers whose past experiences embody the essence of contradicting class locations. Espina Prieto invokes discussions of "the inverted pyramid," or "a rupture of the link between professional training and income-level [*sic*] that had been one of the capstones of the Cuban salary system." High skill levels did not transfer into high income, "which depends on access to dollars and on links with emerging sectors."[88]

Newly arrived Cuban immigrants, having experienced scarcity for much of their lives, were shocked with the economic abundance they saw in Miami. This context is important when considering the class ideologies that Cubans, particularly long-established immigrants, held, for they applied these ideologies to more recent migrants. Initial waves of Cubans brought with them high levels of human capital and integrated into an enclave system that gave them access to character loans, which were indicators of coethnic solidarity and social capital. Their household structures were conducive to productive work (work done outside the home for pay) to which all members of the household contributed (e.g., particularly women). And like other groups, upon arriving in the United States, they embraced the ideology of meritocracy. However, in contrast to others, initial waves of Cuban migrants also received generous assistance from the federal government to set up businesses, recredential themselves, and learn English. Later Cuban arrivals did not receive the same economic benefits, but in contrast with other Latin Americans, they could still adjust their status and have a path to citizenship set upon arrival in the United States by physically touching dry land. However, even with the combination of the human capital of initial waves, the household strategies of pooling income, and the structural conditions that have facilitated greater access to opportunities, the Cuban population has also bifurcated in recent decades with pre-Mariel immigrants displaying much better social outcomes than post-Mariel immigrants.[89] These recent immigrants occupy a class position where they can identify the prejudices of old-time Cubans against them, and at the same time, they expressed appreciation for the struggles that non-Cuban immigrants went through. They have a unique vantage point on the social divisions in Miami, as we will see in Chapter 6.

Although the stable Cuban community in Miami paved the way for other immigrants to follow, the integration of Cuban professionals since the 1990s has taken a very different path, particularly in terms of their understanding of social mobility. In spite of the changes in class structure in recent decades, many of our respondents characterized Cuban society as a "society divided into two sides"—those who were affiliated with the government and had government-sponsored education and jobs, and those who did not. They largely came from an economically oppressive society despite its classless claims, which meant they held contradictory class locations in Cuba. For example, Yumara, who came from a family of professionals in Cuba and arrived in the United States as a young girl, had difficulty placing herself within a "class" structure in her homeland: "As was the case of the majority of Cubans . . . I was not doing badly, but we were not doing well either." Similarly, asked whether she believed Cuban society was divided into "social classes" and whether she belonged to any particular one, Yu-mara, who worked as a receptionist at the time of the interview, responded, "Cuban society is divided into two sides: people who work for the govern-ment or who are tourists who have money, and the rest of the Cuban people, who do not have money."

Thus, many of the Cubans in the study discussed their homeland class positions in terms of the social sectors to which they perceived they had be-longed in Cuba: "[I belonged] to the poor, not to the rich" (Rodolfo, a liter-ary editor). "We weren't rich, but as poor people we lived well, we ate every day, and things like that" (Jazmin, homemaker). Even so, their class positions embodied contradictions. Rafael explained, "It is very difficult to describe what social class you belonged to in Cuba. I don't know—I don't have an answer to that. You can't say middle class, you can't say anything, [because] maybe someone who is a famous intellectual abroad lived in a shed. There is no way to define how one lived. However, I lived in a house that was in good shape. I had a motorcycle that I bought with royalties from my books when authors began to be paid royalties; in other words, I think that given the conditions in Cuba, I lived very well."

Still, regardless of their social position in Cuba, and like others we in-terviewed, Cubans talked about coming to Miami in search of a better life, for themselves and their children, as well as to help those they left behind. Barbara, a former educator and accountant, stated, "I wanted my daughter to live more independently, to have a greater chance of choosing her future, since my dream career had been psychology as well as art history, and I had never been able to achieve either, since politically, I was not well placed in that system."

Barbara's hopes for her daughter suggest that the move to Miami was particularly significant in view of the fact that, in Cuba, the connection be-tween education and expanded economic opportunities would not necessar-ily have been self-evident to them because that was not the way the Cuban system operated. Thus, Yumara explains, "I always thought about getting a university degree in Cuba. I think that here, I was hit with the reality of what it means to work and aspire to get a better job." In spite of her will-ingness to study to increase her financial opportunities, the financial returns on her education would not have been known to her, nor could she have feasibly advanced herself through education within Cuba's society, because, as Yumara concludes, "even though I may have gone on to college once I graduated [from high school], I wouldn't have had many opportunities for advancing my career." Paradoxically, although the US meritocracy implies that education results in greater financial gains, the quantitative analysis earlier in the chapter suggests that every year of education increases the likelihood of perceived upward mobility by only 1 percent. Thus, questions remain regarding the extent to which immigrants and natives can fully translate their educational backgrounds into financial rewards in a global city structure.

The consequences of class distinctions and social inequality in the United States affected immigrants' sense of self and the esteem they had for what they did. However, these feelings depended on one's perceived social status trajectory. Our qualitative analysis, supported by the regression analysis, generates a number of propositions that deserve further study. First, those who perceived their statuses as upwardly mobile because of increased access to education, consumer goods, better working conditions, or positive lifestyle changes associated with better work schedules or release from gender restrictions in the place of origin, seemed to express positive feelings associated with increased social security. On the other hand, for those who experienced downward social mobility upon migration or who experienced working conditions of exploitation, emotional or psychological discomforts enhanced social and psychic insecurity.

Another finding is that holding a contradictory class position creates ambiguity surrounding how to identify oneself along class lines. However, these ambiguities may be the same ones that scholars have struggled with when defining social class in US society. Like Altagracia, who struggled to make sense of these contradictions involving reconciliation of her class of origin with the class in which she found herself at the time of her interview, many US-born natives are also finding that in spite of high levels of education, returns in the form of earnings have not kept up. The same economic context that is squeezing the native born is also increasing economic insecurity for immigrants. For example, Domingo, a Puerto Rican migrant with a master's degree who worked as a consultant, stated, "I would not have been able to imagine what I would be doing here [in Miami] fifteen years later. . . . I would say I am not doing better or worse." Domingo sees no room for mobility: "[Here] you are limited. . . . I don't know if it is something short . . . or long term, but housing is very expensive, and for many professionals it is more and more difficult because salaries are not high, and there is a huge gap between what we make and housing prices."

Although we have laid out in this chapter several paths of social mobility that immigrants followed in the global city, the status of having a contradictory class location and the idea that immobility prevails are part of a trend that may represent a new "normal." As Domingo notes, if professionals are having a hard time keeping up with the cost of living, most residents in Miami may truly become miserable due to the city's economic placement in the landscape of global capitalism. We conclude this chapter with a brief case study that describes how some of the lowest-wage-earning immigrants in the city have increased their standard of living in recent years, largely due to rare unionization efforts in the South at Miami-Dade County's largest private employer, the University of Miami (UM).

Increasing the Standard of Living Through Unionization

Previously the home institution of all three authors, UM's main campus lies in the posh city of Coral Gables, home to affluent Anglos, Cubans who for the most part arrived soon after the revolution, and, thanks to the university, students paying around $38,000 a year for undergraduate tuition, room, and board in 2006.[90] Like many private US universities, UM subcontracts its custodial work, as well as its food services (catering and cafeteria work), to outside firms that bid on contracts.

On an afternoon in 2006, one of UM's subcontracted workers, Reinaldo Hernández, lay immobilized by hunger under a tent on a grassy public space in front of the university's main entrance on US Highway 1, the county's principal north-south artery. Hernández had left his home country, Cuba, in hope of a more secure life in Miami, similar to janitors we talked to in our own office buildings, who included Cuban, Peruvian, Honduran, and Nicaraguan women, as well as male groundskeepers we came to know who were Cuban, Peruvian, and Dominican. The fifty-two-year-old Hernández had immigrated fourteen years earlier from rural Villa Clara with his wife and infant son. He worked at UM for Massachusetts-based UNICCO, one of the largest cleaning service companies in the United States.

That April day he joined nine other subcontracted workers, all immigrants from Latin America and the Spanish Caribbean, who had gone on a hunger strike to protest practices Hernández equated with human rights abuse—his poverty-level wages, lack of health care, and inability to vote for unionization through a method he believed would be fair. Hernández earned $6.40 per hour cleaning at UM and told the *National Catholic Reporter* that after forty hours a week at the university, he worked another thirty hours washing cars at Alamo and cleaning dishes at Denny's. He said his wife, who also worked, had become mentally ill from the stress. "Florida is poor with high rent and it is very hard to get by," he said on day 15 of the hunger strike, after having lost thirty pounds. "I live in a very humble house and still have to pay $1,300-a-month rent. . . . I am fifty-two-years-old but cannot see a doctor because I have no health insurance. I wanted to give my son a better life, but could not with the wages I earned."[91]

The idea to take the drastic step of going on a hunger strike was familiar to some of the workers, who had engaged in political protest under communism in Cuba.[92] While the Cuban workers on strike were part of the politically dominant Cuban community in Miami, they exemplified its increasing heterogeneity. The workers were among later Cuban arrivals and were not experienced professionals or entrepreneurs like the first waves of exiles in the 1960s and 1970s, nor were they met with the level of US government support or ethnic community solidarity that the first waves experienced.[93] Research has confirmed they are also not reaching the highest levels of economic success at the same rate as the early waves.[94]

Other subcontracted university workers came from all over Latin America and the Caribbean, some with less human capital and others highly skilled but facing the disadvantages in transferring occupational credentials and experience we identified previously. Many of the workers at the time of the hunger strike, which itself was part of a wider labor strike, were in their fifties and sixties and in poor health; some were single mothers. The overrepresentation of elderly workers was something that struck union organizer Eric Brakken when we interviewed him in 2013. "This is something that we have found in Miami that is different from other cities where we do organizing. . . . I don't know why they are older, other than [that] there are not great opportunities in the city for work."[95]

For the university, the controversy over its subcontracted workforce had started five years before the strike. In 2001, the *Chronicle of Higher Education* reported results from a survey of wages at 195 institutions. It found that most of the institutions that paid the lowest wages to janitors and groundskeepers were in the US South, among them, UM's contractor, UNICCO, placing UM as the second-lowest-paying institution for custodial workers, after public Tennessee State University.[96] The average custodial worker at UM was paid $13,120 per year, which equated to about $6.30 an hour for full-time workers.[97] In short, workers like Hernández were among the worst paid university maintenance workers in the country.

At the time, the UM administration defended the wages with a market efficiency argument that provided ideological cover not only for poverty-level wages but also for the inequalities of the wider global city economic structure. David A. Lieberman, then senior vice president for business and finance at the university, was quoted in the article as saying, "The trustees (who oversee the university, which has non-profit status) have taken a very strong position that we conduct our business on a marketplace basis." Referring to subcontractor UNICCO's human resource decisions, he continued, "We don't raise any questions about their business. We allow them to pay whatever they want to pay as long as they can recruit and retain workers, and still make a buck at the end of the day. . . . The biggest factor is 'what is the market for a given type of work?' . . . Miami, in this century, and in centuries before, is a city where a lot of immigrants are coming in. These are their first jobs in the United States."[98]

The administrator's statements located the university's philosophy squarely in the unregulated marketplace and away from any alternative value system based on dignity or solidarity. It also belied knowledge of workers who had spent many years on the campus, could not transfer their homeland educational and experiential credentials, or were well into their fifties and even sixties, or faced any combination of these obstacles. Instead, the statements tapped into uninspected ideas of immigrants starting on the bottom but moving up as they integrate into the US labor market.

The *Chronicle* article prompted faculty involvement. A faculty senate committee issued a recommendation to increase janitors' pay by instituting a living wage policy for all UM employees and contract workers.[99] Such a policy would commit employers to paying the wages necessary to afford the basics in a given community, which in Miami at that time was $11.23 per hour.[100] The university refused, instead offering them computer and English-as-a-second-language classes, classes to prepare for their General Education Development (GED) tests, two floating personal days, and a screening clinic.[101] Instead of paying a living wage, perhaps the university had the rationale that with better English and more computer skills, the workers would find better jobs and leave UM, just as the finance administrator had predicted. Yet this line of thinking makes a lot of assumptions, among them that those working more than one job along with potentially raising children or approaching old age, or both, could somehow find the time and energy to take these classes. It further assumed what our economic data and historical analysis had already disproven, that global Miami had a growing middle class.

The article also caught the attention of the Service Employees International Union (SEIU), which was organizing service workers across the country whose jobs could not be sent offshore, as had manufacturing jobs during the acceleration of neoliberal free trade policies decades prior. SEIU had been successful in "Justice for Janitors" campaigns in Los Angeles and other cities around the country when it approached UM's UNICCO janitors in August 2005.[102] Over the course of that academic year, from our many conversations with workers, we learned that they were requesting more than higher wages and health care; they also were not given proper materials to do their jobs (e.g., gloves for mixing cleaning chemicals). Additionally, some were harassed by supervisors and demeaned by management, among other grievances. The workers were seeking protections they believed a union would afford them. Their struggle for unionization reflected one approach to achieving upward social mobility for the low-wage workforce in Miami, even though unionization rates have been falling nationally for decades because of deindustrialization, outsourcing, subcontracting, and, some argue, election regulations disfavoring unionization.[103]

One hundred and fifty of the 400-plus janitors working at UM went on strike on February 28, 2006. UM's president, Donna Shalala, who was President Bill Clinton's secretary of health and human services for eight years prior to taking her university position, called for a working group to study the compensation of contracted workers on campus, akin to one she had called for in 2001. By this time though, the workers wanted a union, not just higher wages. Nelson Hernández, a former Cuban political prisoner who had worked at UM for twenty-five years and earned $6.80 an hour, said, "I was here the first time the university formed a committee to talk about our wages. I was making barely over minimum wage then, and I still am now."[104]

In late April of that year, as UM's commencement was fast approaching, commencement speaker Madeleine Albright, former secretary of state in the Clinton administration (and a child immigrant herself), made clear that she would not attend graduation if the strike was not resolved. Albright followed a parade of activist politicians and clergy who had given the strike national prominence. On May 1, UNICCO and SEIU announced they had agreed to a union election via a "card check" process in which workers sign union cards to cast their votes. Janitors went back to work on May 3, 2006, after 70 percent voted to unionize.[105]

Gains Associated with Unionization

Among the relatively immediate outcomes that UNICCO workers attained were (1) an increase in housekeeper wages from $6.40 to $8.00 an hour; (2) an increase in groundskeeper wages from $6.40 to $9.30; (3) a newly instituted system of recognition of pay scale and years of service; and (4) access to affordable health care, with the employer paying $250 per month per employee and the employee contributing $13 per month.[106] Seven years after the strike, in 2013, UNICCO workers were making on average $11.58 per hour.[107] While this rate was about 50 cents per hour less than county workers' living wage minimum for 2012–2013, university janitors were eligible for more pay if they worked the night shift, had opportunities for job advancement since they were the first in line to see job vacancies that opened up in the company, and had contracts with job protections in place in case workers' immigration work permits lapsed or their government paperwork was delayed. Brakken, who started out as a union organizer and later became SEIU's Florida organizing director, told us,

> The janitors' lives are a lot better than they were back then. . . . [I]n the intervening seven years what happened was UNICCO workers' wages continued to go up. They got into a health-care plan, which was high quality and much lower cost. They were making on average, from our estimates, $2 an hour more than Chartwells workers. That was a difference of seven years of having a union versus not having a union.

Brakken made reference to Chartwells workers, who were those who worked for the food subcontracting company for the university. In 2013 they wanted to join SEIU and began their own struggle for unionization. Different from the UNICCO workers, they were a predominantly African American female workforce and had benefited in 2006 when Shalala unilaterally included a higher wage requirement for subcontracted UM workers after UNICCO workers had been on strike for two weeks. However, compared to their unionized peers at UNICCO, their wages had not kept up with UNICCO workers' wages over time. Among Chartwells workers' grievances was that they were often furloughed when the university was not in session, making it very difficult to work full-time, and they were afforded little to no opportunities for job advancement. Unbeknownst to many, Chartwells also employed a small group of Hispanic men who, rather than work as cashiers and food service workers in the main cafeteria, were part of the catering workforce as higher paid waiters and chefs, often working faculty and staff functions. These positions did not appear to be open to the lower-wage, black workforce.[108] Although Chartwells workers never actually went on strike, the threat of the strike, and in particular, the negative press that it would bring to the university, which appeared to allow unionization options to Hispanics and not to their African American peers, facilitated their unionization drive. However, the effort to unionize Chartwells workers was not easy.

Brakken said that in addition to widespread fear among the workers, they also had a deep sense of cynicism that what had worked for Hispanic workers would not work for them:

> We always go to workers in every fight and say, "You are not alone. The community is going to support you." But with the Chartwells workers we had to demonstrate that before people were really willing to put their necks on the line. That was a slight difference and I don't fully know how to account for it. I do think that it has something to do with . . . the perception amongst the African American workers [that] "we are lowest on the totem pole in the campus, in the city. There are not a lot of reasons for us to expect that that is going to change."[109]

On May 3, 2013, a majority of Chartwells workers voted to join the SEIU. Contract negotiations were to follow.

Support for Living Wages: Unlikely Alliances and Foes

A large part of the support generated for UNICCO workers grew from students involved in the group Students Toward a New Democracy. Once the strike began, workers also had the support of some faculty who later became known as Faculty for Workplace Justice.[110] Since all three book authors were on the faculty network listserv and were among a handful who could speak Spanish with the workers, we provided some context to a discussion that at one point centered on perceptions that workers were not supporting the strike given the small numbers who were observed picketing. We jointly wrote an e-mail to the listserv that read,

> We have been researching the immigrant/Latino communities here for a couple of years now. In the course of our research, we have spoken to UNICCO

workers on campus. One of the things we have learned is that many are part of a vulnerable population—more than earning poverty wages, these workers share an immigrant background that places them at an additional level of disadvantage. . . . One thing we have consistently heard in our interviews is that life as an immigrant has become harder to endure since 9/11 due to increasing fears of deportation in spite of being in the country legally. . . . Even though some who we have spoken to do not plan to picket, rather than interpret this as a sign of ambivalence or non-support, in our view, it is part of their strategies for survival that involve remaining "invisible."[111]

Faculty brainstormed about ways in which they could hold their classes off campus so as to not cross the picket line, which was considered to be the boundary surrounding the Coral Gables campus. In an effort to make faculty support more visible to the university's administration, these outdoor classes were soon moved to the area quad in front of the main administration building. In the weeks that ensued, there were sit-ins, marches, and broad support for the workers coming from diverse constituencies in the city. Among them, members of the Coral Gables clergy became involved, including the Catholic auxiliary bishop of Miami, Felipe Estevez, who expressed a willingness to mediate the labor dispute during a Sunday mass at a Coral Gables church. Striking workers often brought their families to marches as we saw many of them with not just their children but also grandchildren. Broad constituencies that ordinarily would have no reason to come together united in collective action for a common cause.

Although many thought that Shalala's work in the Clinton administration would have made her amenable to the workers' movement, she refused to speak with the janitors and maintained that UNICCO was a subcontractor of the university and therefore the janitors were not UM's employees. When two weeks into the strike she instructed all companies with UM contracts to abide by the new university wage standard, she wrote to students in a letter dated March 20, "We are very satisfied that this new university program establishes a wage and benefit level that is near the top of the market." The workers rejected the offer. They wanted a union.

To attain this goal, they wanted UNICCO to agree to hold a card-check election. UNICCO argued that if the workers wanted a union, then the National Labor Relations Board should hold an election. At that time, the organization had already accused UNICCO of interrogating workers about their union support and threatening retaliation if they continued. Given that elections organized by the National Labor Relations Board can take months to unfold, and witnessing management's efforts to quash the union drive, the workers were steadfast in their goal to have an election whereby in one day they could simply sign union cards as a way to cast their vote to join the union. That said, it was difficult to maintain a strike and community support when the sticking point was a question of process.

During this time, ten UNICCO workers, seven of them Cuban, one Nicaraguan, and two Peruvians, initiated the hunger strike. They were joined one week later by several students from Students Toward a New Democracy. This tactic was interpreted very differently by the different groups we examined. For the workers, the tactic was a logical next step in their fight for rights. Some of the Cuban immigrants were already familiar with hunger strikes when they were political prisoners in Cuba.[112] Miami's Catholic clergy supported the hunger strikers, washing strikers' feet to commemorate Jesus Christ's Last Supper and saying the protest took on a larger meaning given the increasing number of impoverished workers in Miami.[113] For others, it was seen as a radical tactic incommensurate with the cause and falling in line with right-wing reactionary Cuban politics. These different vantage points were intricately related to the kinds of support workers received throughout the hunger strike.

Anticommunist Cuban activist Ramón Saúl Sánchez supported the workers in their cause. Leader of a group called Movimiento Democracia (Movement for Democracy), a few months earlier Sánchez had gone on a hunger strike to halt a US Coast Guard decision to return fifteen Cuban rafters who had made it to a bridge piling in the Florida Keys, but not, in the Coast Guard's opinion, to "dry" land as policy required. Sánchez also had become known in the late 1990s in the Cuban community for his devotion to local workers' causes and his organization of street protests, contrasting sharply with the second-generation, well-heeled leadership of the Cuban American National Foundation, which preferred to lobby through its congressional allies behind closed doors in Washington.[114]

Besides Sánchez, Brakken told us of letters received by the SEIU from Cuban trade unions in exile expressing their support. Miami-Dade County mayor Carlos Álvarez and Miami city commissioner Tomás Regalado, who later was elected mayor of Miami, both Cuban, showed their support for workers as well. The politicians visited "Freedom Village," the makeshift tent city that housed the hunger strikers, located under the Metrorail across the street from the university's main entrance. Congressional representative Kendrick Meek (D-FL), who is African American, also supported the strikers. Paradoxically, to our knowledge, none of the area's three Cuban-born Miami congressional representatives showed support for the mostly Cuban workers. Likewise, the Cuban and Cuban American elites who were on the university's board of trustees remained publicly silent throughout the ordeal.

The hunger strikers continued for eighteen days until the national president of the SEIU, Andy Stern, convinced them to allow him and sympathetic local clergy to replace them in symbolic fasting. National Latino labor leaders Eliseo Medina and Dolores Huerta, who led the farmworkers movement with César Chávez, were among those who fasted for twenty-four hours, passing the torch to other supporters who would come to Freedom Village, spend the night, and fast with the workers in solidarity. Among the supporters who would join in fasting were members from a Puerto Rican chapter of the SEIU who had flown up to Miami to support the workers, revealing the transnationalization of the movement.

Although the surrounding community of faculty, students, and clergy were supportive of the workers' movement, some backlash came from the broader community in Miami, particularly regarding the hunger strike. The *Miami Herald* editorialized against the card-check method and supported the university administration's positions editorially. The editorial page editor blocked some of the faculty's submissions to the opinion pages, saying they were written by partisans.[115] News coverage hit only big moments in the strike, with a neutral tone, although in coverage years later the newspaper emphasized the university administration's support for the workers. An editorial columnist, Cuban American Ana Menéndez, often reported workers' perspectives with an empathetic ear. Yet the strike also met derision and brought to the surface ugly anti-immigrant sentiment on the broadcast airwaves.[116]

Perceived Social Mobility Through Personal Empowerment

Ultimately, the strike was not just about pay and benefits; it was about becoming empowered to make one's presence and right to be heard known to all. One example stands out for what it reveals about how the strike represented a form of resistance to intersecting forms of oppression. Some of the striking workers made themselves available to faculty to come to their classes to explain to students the reasons they were fighting to form a union. On one of these occasions, one of the authors of this book, Elizabeth Aranda, had mentioned to workers in passing that the course they were visiting was about families. One of the workers, Veronica, began to tell her story of growing up in Honduras in a household where she faced much physical abuse. She spoke about how she came to the United States fleeing years of violence.

Veronica spoke in Spanish as the author translated for the class. At one point in her story, her peers interrupted her in Spanish and began to instruct her to stay on topic, which was to explain the reasons for the strike. Immediately, Veronica explained to the class that joining a union represented to her a chance to finally speak out against the people who had abused her in her life. This abuse was not limited to those who hurt her in Honduras but also included her UNICCO supervisors. Veronica saw the strike as her chance to fight back for all of the times when she could not. The students in the class, Veronica's peers, and the author herself were left stunned. For

Veronica, this new sense of personal empowerment and the idea that she could fight back enhanced her sense of self-worth and esteem.

One Miami?

At the beginning of this chapter, we talked about "miserable Miami" and the income threshold separating the haves from the have-lesses. The question that remains is how this gap could be narrowed. In the case of the unionization efforts at UM, although workers who could join the union appeared to be better off than those who did not (and are joining as this book goes to print), their better wages and health care have not erased precariousness, and we cannot fully speak to the immigrant workers' own perceptions of how the union has improved their lives because we do not have data on this. However, seeing that UNICCO workers reached out to Chartwells workers to motivate them to join the union, the strike apparently accomplished at least some of the goals that workers sought, including to fight against oppression and for dignity.

As part of a new program called "One Miami," in part based on the university-organizing experience, Brakken said the service workers union has decided to reach across ethnic boundaries that divide Miami in the formal political system and target for organizing all neighborhoods where the average household incomes are less than $35,000 a year. He stated,

> That takes you to Liberty City, Little Haiti, Little Havana, Allapattah, Hialeah. And at the time some people were like, "Why are you going to go to Hialeah? There are all Republicans there." And our thing was . . . "they are poor and are suffering the same thing everyone else is. We think they will have very similar perspectives." . . . I think the name One Miami had two ideas. One is that we have two Miamis in the city: one for the rich and one for the poor. We need to create one for all of us. But the other thing is across all these racial lines, we all have one fight.[117]

Conclusion

Economic inequality in Miami is linked to global and regional trends through flows of capital, traded goods, and labor—both highly skilled and unskilled. The neoliberal economic policies shaping immigrants' contexts of departure were also partly responsible for the hollowing out of Miami's economy, a deterioration that increased toward the latter part of the twentieth century and played a central role in the experiences of immigrants. Miami's reliance on tourism for economic production has always contributed to the area's weak middle-income sector, but the expansion of interregional trade and financial services coupled with low pay for public sector employees produced an hourglass income structure typical of global cities, where low-wage workers provide personal services to higher-income financial workers and ancillary professionals, and the middle sector is comparatively small.

This context was the one that immigrants in our study entered. Migration to Miami often was accompanied by changes in immigrants' perceived social class statuses. Factors such as country of origin, legal status, gender, class of origin, and education were associated with varying perceptions of social mobility. Although women were significantly less likely to perceive upward mobility in comparison to men (albeit at a marginally significant level in the survey data), our qualitative data shed light on some of the pathways for upward mobility for immigrant women arriving in Miami. The United States offered opportunities including the possibility to pursue advanced degrees, make extra money through nontraditional forms of work that perhaps in their home countries only men took on (e.g., double shifts and side jobs), and mitigate the kind of age and gender discrimination they had faced in their places of origin, where, as women advanced in age, they were perceived as less productive members of society.

Among those who were professionals in their countries of origin, some faced English-language credentialing barriers and lack of degree equivalencies, which lowered their career prospects. This challenge was particularly pronounced for undocumented professionals who were the most likely to share stories of how they were downwardly mobile upon migration. Professionals from various countries with legal status did not face the same dislocations of undocumented professionals; however, they did experience changes in relative deprivation in Miami because incomes were not keeping up with the rise in costs of living. Cubans, the group most likely to report upward social mobility, also identified the ambiguities of their class identities given the contradictory class locations that they occupied in Cuba. In some cases, the ambiguities persisted in Miami due to their insertion into a capitalist economy. Overall, as one might expect, upward social mobility contributed to stronger feelings of social security among immigrants, while downward mobility resulted in social as well as psychic insecurity. Last, grounded in unionization efforts in Miami in the past seven years, union support, as we illustrate, can enhance the life chances of low-wage workers, and cross-ethnic and cross-racial alliances can be effective in overcoming the city's socioeconomic divide.

Immigrant security was reshaped in other ways through immigration, however. Among these ways, we find the notion that immigrants lack not just presence but voice and representation. In the next chapter, we will examine more closely the ethnic politics in the city that shed light on the ethnic/racial dynamics in Miami that we have touched on briefly in this chapter.

Notes

1. Badenhausen 2012; Miami-Dade County, Economic Development and International Trade 2011.

2. US Department of Labor statistics show Miami-Dade County's open unemployment went from 4.1 percent in 2007 to 12.4 percent in 2010, ranking that county's unemployment forty-second of the fifty largest US counties. By 2012 unemployment had declined to 9.3 percent, as construction cranes reappeared (US Bureau of Labor Statistics 2013). Zillow, a real estate data firm, said Miami-Dade was in the worst 10 percent of US counties for "negative equity," or homeowners who owed more on their mortgages than their properties' market value. By early 2013, 30 percent of mortgagees remained in arrears, 42 percent had negative equity, and prices were down 49 percent since 2007 (Zillow 2013).

3. Grizzle and Trogen 1994.

4. Hoene 2009.

5. Based on the median hourly wage in Miami-Dade in 2005, a head of household would have to work ten and a half hours to afford to take his or her family to see the Marlins (T. Wright 2010).

6. Grosfoguel 2004, p. 317; see also Petras 1981.

7. Hackworth 2007; see also Lin 2011.

8. Lin 2011, p. 45.

9. Rose 2012, p. 739.

10. Lin 2011, p. 45.

11. Grosfoguel 2003.

12. Grosfoguel 2003; Sassen 2011.

13. For some of the Free Trade Area of the Americas' promotional discourse, review *South Florida CEO* (2004) and *WorldCity* (2003).

14. *WorldCity* 2008.

15. Ibid.

16. Edge Banks are named for the Edge Act of 1919, which amended the Federal Reserve Act to allow for nationally chartered financial organizations, generally subsidiaries of national banks, to offer banking services to international clients, but all the services had to be related to foreign or international investment. In 1979, the guidelines were changed to allow US Edge Banks to offer services domestically and foreign banks to establish Edge Banks themselves on US soil.

17. Data were compiled from the Federal Reserve System National Information Center database, available at http://www.ffiec.gov/nicpubweb/nicweb/SearchForm .aspx (accessed October 15, 2011).

18. See HSBC Private Banking 2011.

19. Sinclair 2003; Yúdice 2003.

20. Massey and Capoferro 2008.

21. Baker 2002; Massey and Capoferro 2008.

22. Massey, Durand, and Malone 2002.

23. Lin 2011.

24. Ibid., p. 32.

25. City Mayors Foundation 2009; Cohen 2001.

26. Lin 2011, p. 45.

27. Miami-Dade County, Department of Planning and Zoning 2007.

28. Brookings Institution 2004, p. 9; see also Miami-Dade County, Department of Planning and Zoning 2007.

29. Miami-Dade County, Department of Planning and Zoning 2007.

30. Brookings Institution 2004.

31. See Stowers and Vogel (1994) on Hispanic and African American employment in Miami area police and other public services in the 1980s.

32. Kofman 2007; Lin 2011.

33. Padgett 2006.

34. In response, city officials sent police to suppress protests against the agreement, injuring hundreds of people. Later dubbed "The Miami Model," the suppression plan cost the city and county governments $23 million to implement (Lush 2007).

35. Kennedy 2007.

36. Pérez-Stable and Uriarte 1997; Portes and Bach 1985.

37. Grenier and Pérez 2003.

38. Prieto 1987.

39. When we discuss Latinos versus Cubans specifically, we do so often because county data are not disaggregated by country of origin.

40. Pérez-Stable and Uriarte 1997, p. 153.

41. Sanders and Nee 1987.

42. Pérez-Stable and Uriarte 1997.

43. Whether the firms were owned by Cubans versus other Latino groups is unknown (Miami-Dade County, Department of Planning and Zoning 2007).

44. Ibid.

45. Ibid.

46. Comparisons between Miami-Dade and the rest of the country show that poverty rates are high for individuals holding a bachelor's degree or higher in Miami-Dade, as opposed to individuals with the same educational attainment in the rest of Florida and the nation (6.4 percent versus 3.5 percent). Moreover, poverty rates for people with only a high school diploma were much higher in Miami-Dade County than for people with equal education across the nation (17.5 percent versus 11.2 percent) (ibid.).

47. Purkayastha 2005.

48. Ibid.

49. Glenn 1992.

50. Miami-Dade County, Department of Planning and Zoning 2007. Another reason cited for high poverty rates in Miami is the city's "inability . . . to adequately absorb workers at low education and skill levels" (p. iv). However, even when employment rates and labor productivity are high, wages are so low that immigrants find themselves holding down one or more jobs to make ends meet. This situation does not change even when the economy is in an expansionary cycle, revealing the structural nature of income and occupational factors that disadvantage workers. Individual and group-level characteristics (e.g., education, race, family structure) only exacerbate these inequalities, which are rooted in the intersection of race, class, and gender and are endemic to the modern system of global capitalism (Miami-Dade County, Department of Planning and Zoning 2007).

51. Ibid.

52. Ibid.

53. Ibid., p. 79.

54. Ibid., p. 80.

55. Portocarrero 1998; Wright Austin 2008.

56. Hout 2008.

57. Portocarrero 1998.

58. Lipset 1967; Portocarrero 1998.

59. Gilbert 2007, p. 15; see also Lipset 1967; Portocarrero 1998.

60. Lora and Fajardo 2011.
61. Organisation for Economic Co-operation and Development 2010, p. 58.
62. Williamson 1997.
63. Cerrutti and Bertoncello 2003.
64. Janoschka and Borsdorf 2006.
65. E. O. Wright 1979.
66. See ibid. for discussion of gradational and relational perspectives on social class.
67. The question we used to measure perceived status was "Back in [home country] what was your or your family's class or economic level? Would you say it was poor, working class, middle class, or upper class?" We asked the same question of their status in Miami. Based on these answers, we created a measure of mobility that combined the answers into three categories: upward social mobility, downward mobility, or immobility. Although we only used a subjective measure of mobility, scholars such as Michael Hout believe that if the task is to describe a social pattern, "any notion that captures how people differentiate themselves into 'haves' and 'have-lesses' will serve that purpose" (Hout 2008, p. 27).
68. Cubans were used as the reference group because they are the largest immigrant group in the county and have undeniably established the strongest presence in the county's economic, political, and cultural life. They would be, then, the immigrant group that is most likely to be socially and culturally integrated in Miami.
69. McKenzie and Rapoport 2006.
70. Borjas 2006.
71. Reygadas 2010.
72. Homestead was one of the areas located directly on the path of Hurricane Andrew, which hit South Florida on August 24, 1992. In 1990 the census reported that Homestead, a town south of Miami, had a population of around 27,000, mostly non-Hispanics (Dash, Peacock, and Morrow 2000). Twenty years later, Homestead had doubled in size to almost 61,000 and its population is mostly Hispanic, with large concentrations of Mexicans (US Census Bureau 2013).
73. Lora and Fajardo 2011.
74. Purkayastha 2005.
75. Donato et al. 2006.
76. Donato 1993; Reichert and Massey 1980.
77. Donato 2010.
78. Levitt 2001.
79. Smith 2006.
80. Aranda 2007.
81. Portes and Rumbaut 1996, 2001.
82. Dumont and Monso 2007.
83. See Sabogal 2012 for a discussion of social class identities in the context of migration.
84. Ojito 2009.
85. Espina Prieto 2001, p. 23.
86. Ibid., pp. 31–32.
87. Eckstein 2009.
88. Espina Prieto 2001, p. 33.
89. Portes 2013.
90. Coral Gables's mean and median household income levels are more than double those for Miami-Dade County, and the city residents' occupations skew toward the managerial positions that help direct Miami's global economic functions. Demographically, the city is 40 percent white non-Hispanic, 34 percent Cuban and

Cuban American, 21 percent other Hispanic, and only 2 percent black or African American (US Census Bureau 2009–2011a, 2009–2011b).

91. Newall 2006.

92. Albright 2008.

93. Alberts 2005.

94. Eckstein 2009.

95. Interview with Service Employees International Union (SEIU) Florida director, Eric Brakken, May 23, 2013.

96. Although universities are not the formal employer for janitors and other contract workers, they do have the power to establish wage rates for the contractors to pay the workers they employ.

97. UM was one of twelve colleges and universities that year that paid salaries that were less than $14,150, the federal poverty level in 2000 for a family of three (Van der Werf 2001).

98. Ibid., p. A27–A28. Miami's endowment at that time was valued at about $465 million, but Lieberman said that the endowment was not taken into consideration in setting pay rates.

99. Casebeer 2008.

100. Swartz 2007.

101. Albright 2008.

102. Fischl 2007.

103. Fisk, Mitchell, and Erickson 2000; Milkman 2000.

104. Casebeer 2008, p. 1063.

105. Albright 2008.

106. Ibid.

107. Interview with SEIU Florida director, Eric Brakken, May 23, 2013.

108. Ibid.

109. Ibid.

110. Giovanna Pompele and Simon Evnine, UM faculty members, created the website Picketline (picketline.blogspot.com).

111. E-mail communication on listserv and posting of Faculty for Workplace Justice to Picketline, "Why Are All the Workers Not on Strike?," http://picketline .blogspot.com/2006/04/why-are-all-workers-not-on-strike.html (April 7, 2006). Although some in the academic community believe that researchers should not become activists, in the course of our research up to that point we had learned enough about the community to know that immigrants had tremendous fear of ICE and any law enforcement officials. Although we did not intend to become activists, we felt we had an obligation to be a mouthpiece for members of communities who opened their doors to us and shared with us many of their deeply personal struggles. For this reason, we felt compelled to provide our insights on this discussion, especially since they were grounded in empirical observations over the course of three years.

112. Interview with SEIU Florida director, Eric Brakken, May 23, 2013.

113. Newall 2006.

114. De Fede 1999.

115. The faculty blog Picketline documents many of these communications. For the *Herald*'s editorial page editor's position, see "Our Goal Is to Publish Thoughtful Commentary" at http://picketline.blogspot.com/2006_04_01_archive.html.

116. For example, CBS's WFOR-Channel 4 news anchor Elliot Rodriguez said the students were more on a diet than a hunger strike. Watch the broadcast at http:// www.youtube.com/watch?v=n1VkS5C8ATI (accessed July 29, 2013).

117. Interview with SEIU Florida director, Eric Brakken, May 23, 2013.

5

Politics, Membership, and Representation

The success of this [Dominican] community will come when the authorities of this city are diversified into different communities. The success of this community will come when each community has representation in local government. Because at this moment all of the state agencies, and city agencies, are controlled by only one community. When this community begins to have a city council member, a mayor, a police representative, a fire official, this city is going to change.
—Pablo, a retired exporter from the Dominican Republic

Diversity in Miami's Latino and Caribbean population has grown enormously since the first cohorts of Cuban immigrants consolidated a powerful ethnic political block in the 1980s and 1990s. However, the diversity in national origins that drives Miami's pan-Latino discourse is not reflected in the county's electoral politics or the elite arena of political communication. Nicaraguans, Colombians, Puerto Ricans, and other non-Cuban Latino groups, as well as immigrants from the English-speaking Caribbean, have been unable to incorporate politically. Only Haitians, after a thirty-year struggle for formal citizenship rights, have begun to see community members elected regularly to local office.

In this chapter, we explore how formal legal citizenship associated with territorially bound conceptions of belonging and exclusion are perceived, and how they sort immigrants' opportunities for formal political voice, rights, and representation. Claims for membership based on national policies for naturalization and political citizenship contrast with claims to membership based on "on the ground" vernacular practices of social participation and contributions, but legal citizenship has powerful consequences.[1] Political rights conferred by formal legal citizenship shape access to employment opportunities, social welfare benefits, public employment patron-

161

age, and public policy on issues such as education, economic development, and, importantly, possible reform of exclusionary immigration policies. As we will show, an analysis of formal political representation in global Miami also highlights how contested US projects of racial formation, both white supremacist and the pluralist project of the civil rights movement, were adapted when emplaced in a transnational setting such as Miami.

Although culturally diverse, Miami is politically stratified as the result of unequal contexts of immigrant arrival, including opportunities for legalization and naturalization, national-origin community dispersal geographically, and local political boundaries that are drawn to represent certain ethnic groups. These conditions politically advantage older cohorts of Cuban immigrants the most.[2] They disadvantage newer non-Cuban immigrant cohorts. As a result, one group of naturalized immigrants and their US-born offspring predominate in Miami politics. Left without voice, vote, or representation from someone of their community, many of Miami's newer immigrant residents perceive formal political exclusion as a long-term condition.

Monochromatic Politics in a Multiethnic City

Politics in Miami are structured along three interrelated dimensions of political power: pluralism in electoral politics, agenda setting for debate and deliberation about policy and politics, and, perhaps the most important of all, definitional power.[3] The first and most visible dimension of political power stems from pluralistic approaches to local *electoral* politics that conceive of US democracy as an open system of contesting interest groups. Minority or marginalized groups have the opportunity to organize, send members to office in free and fair elections, and, through them, obtain address for demands, grievances, and deprivations.[4] Through a process of political incorporation, immigrant groups gain power over time to affect public policy and increase their share of government services and employment.[5] In Miami, electoral power opened for Cubans and African Americans in the 1980s and 1990s when legislative redistricting and civil rights court decisions prompted new political boundaries and electoral formulas for the county commission, school board, the Miami City Commission, and Congress. However, Miami's non-Cuban immigrant residents are largely excluded from electoral office.

A second dimension of power involves *agenda setting*. *Agenda setting* in this chapter refers to the ability of elites in a restricted political system to control the agenda of public discussion and debate prior to policymaking or other political action. Political agenda setting allows privileged groups "to predetermine the agenda of struggle—to determine whether certain questions ever reach the competition stage."[6] Setting the agenda means not only controlling the topics of public discussion and possible action but also limiting who gets to participate in the discussion and on what terms. Based on an analysis of Miami's primary political reference, the *Miami Herald*, the public agenda in multiethnic Miami is set by those who have already obtained formal political power, especially those in government and in advocacy organizations that conform to established rules and values of political contestation. This system gives a clear advantage to maintenance of the current arrangements of power, which exclude many non-Cuban immigrants.

A third dimension of power is *definitional*. Definitional power originates in configurations of values and assumptions that underlie the established hierarchy of social power in the metropolis. Often tacit or unacknowledged, these assumptions sustain social conditions that are absorbed as natural and legitimate or simply accepted as inevitable. This attitude may result from socialization, insurmountable obstacles, accumulated defeats, and disappointments, or some combination of all four. In its strongest form, definitional power resembles Antonio Gramsci's concept of hegemony[7]— systemic solutions for grievances or demands of the marginalized remain unformed and unvoiced because they are never recognized as legitimate. For example, the absence of political equality or social justice for immigrants from countries deemed politically unimportant to the United States is naturalized when national security defines equality as a secondary value.

To understand how political power works in Miami, we start with an analysis of how pluralism fares in elections and then analyze how definitional power and agenda control prevent consideration of solutions that would enfranchise more Miamians. Strictly speaking, electoral pluralism does not exist in Miami. At least one-fourth of the population cannot participate in electoral politics because they are noncitizens.[8] In other words, they are disenfranchised based on their citizenship status rather than residency, payment of taxes, the ability to purchase a home, or even the possibility of offering military service to the United States. Similarly, about one-fourth of the population is underrepresented based on shared national origin or ethnicity. Sixty-one percent of the county's population is Cuban, Anglo, or African American,[9] but as we show below, these three groups controlled 90 percent of elected offices as of 2010. Residents of non-Cuban immigrant origin make up 35 percent of the population, but in 2010 controlled 10 percent of elected offices, based on our analysis of elected offices in that year as described below.

Agenda-setting power and definitional power reinforce the unequal distribution of electoral power in Greater Miami because those who have already achieved elected office or lead advocacy organizations that follow established rules and routines are also the ones who have the most power to

determine whether, and on what terms, the question of who gets to participate in electoral politics is publicly discussed in the media. Because of jour-
nalistic conventions regarding news agendas and source legitimacy, those
who are already powerful in politics have preferential power to determine
the agenda of publicly debated issues, as well as who speaks about them
most clearly. Definitional power, which is related, stems from dominant
values and worldviews embedded in public communication. We explored
two possible systemic reforms found nationally or internationally: allowing
noncitizens to vote in local elections and proportional representation of ethnic groups as an alternative to, or in addition to, representation based on
ethnic residential geographies as is the current practice. We found that allowing noncitizen residents of Miami to vote in local elections and in-
stalling some form of proportional representation to guarantee ethnic representation on governing boards are largely not discussed in elite public
communication. When they are mentioned, noncitizen voting and proportional representation are framed in ways that maintain the current system of
disenfranchisement.

In the remainder of the chapter, we examine how our non-Cuban participants perceived political power in Miami. We turn to each form of political power in Miami in more detail, explaining how each has helped create
and reinforce the current political status quo. We conclude with an exploration of what would be required for non-Cuban immigrant groups to politically incorporate under the current system.

Political Power in the Immigrant Mind

Our participants clearly perceive and describe an ethnically based political
hierarchy in Miami, which they link to their own prospects for economic
advancement. Cubans, the political reference group for participants from
every country of origin in our study, are perceived as having reached the
peak of the political pyramid because of their numbers, automatic legal immigration status, and group solidarity. All other national-origin groups fall
below Cubans in the political constructions of study participants. On the
other hand, our participants rarely discuss Puerto Ricans, who also are citizens, nor do they dwell upon the local political power of Anglos or African
Americans. This omission may be because the size of these groups is too
small to dominate local politics, and interaction among groups was restricted by dispersed living patterns, intragroup hiring, and, often, language.

Jorge, a Colombian lawyer working as a kitchen cabinet maker, believed that the political disenfranchisement of his national-origin group
made his quest for legalized immigration status, educational attainment,
and professional ascension all the more difficult. Like Pablo, the Dominican merchant quoted at the opening of the chapter, Jorge linked his

predicament to the intragroup political solidarity of Miami's Cubans and Cuban Americans, who he believed "monopolize" political and economic positions.

> The Cuban is identified with something, a political line. Even though they come from Cuba, within three months they are identifying themselves with this political group here fighting the system in Cuba. So because of this solidarity, they have achieved the majority that they have. They have achieved all of the positions in the City of Miami. So as I see it, it is a little harder struggle for me to penetrate this society, where the Cubans have the majority of the possibilities. With the other [nationality] groups, I've had all sorts of experiences. With all of the national-origin groups, there are different ways of behaving, different types of people. I have even had bad experiences with educated people, with *gente de bien*.[10] And it makes my struggle difficult, but not impossible, but yes a little more difficult for me to penetrate this society because of the monopolization that there is . . . to advance in both economic and political positions, to enter a school.

To Jorge and other participants, the key to political success in Miami is obtaining legalized immigration status. Legalization is both a political resource (it allows group members to naturalize as citizens and vote) and a political outcome (politicians presumably pay attention to voters who want immigration eased for their family and friends). Being Colombian and a relatively new arrival, Jorge benefited from neither previous US geopolitical interests that helped Puerto Ricans become citizens in 1917 and Cubans immigrate legally after 1959, nor the 1986 amnesty law that legalized 2 million Mexicans. Of the largest Latino-origin groups in the United States—Mexicans, Puerto Ricans, and Cubans—only Cubans have a critical mass to achieve political power in Miami, their homeland in exile.

Cubans who arrive in Miami today benefit from the legacy of the Cold War context of the first waves of Cuban exiles, although not as much as the early exiles. They legally enter the United States as soon as they touch its soil; after a year they can apply for citizenship. Though government support for newer Cuban cadres has diminished over the years, Cubans' ability to legally immigrate distances them from other immigrants in the eyes of our participants. Says Jorge, "They have rights. They are above everyone else. What do you do to move this Cuban group so that they show solidarity with the rest of us?"

Some participants believed that the presence of an immigrant community dominating local politics inhibited pan-immigrant solidarity, even among the disadvantaged groups. Some also believed that immigrants compete with one another rather than forge pan-ethnic strategies in the workplace or support immigrant political rights. Hector, a Puerto Rican accountant, compared Miami's fractured Latino/a identity to wider ethnic solidarity he experienced in the US Northeast, blaming rivalry on Latino/a majority status and a single group's dominance.

> When you go to the Northeast United States, Massachusetts and
> New York, where I have lived the most, when you see the
> Hispanic culture, it is Hispanic culture because the Anglos are on
> top and after them comes everybody else. Well, the Anglos and
> the Asians and then everybody else. And when you see a
> Colombian, Guatemalan, Salvadoran, everything is good, cool.
> But here in Miami, since the majority are Hispanics, then the
> pyramid is first the Cubans and then everybody else. There is
> more competition and more cultural collision even though they
> are polite. And with the clients that I have worked with and in my
> auditing group—we were all Hispanic—there were always
> Cubans there, I was the Puerto Rican, we had people from
> Mexico and Argentina and Venezuela, and so on. And so there
> was a debate about what was better. It was like a competition
> because we thought the circumstances in each of our countries
> was better even though we are all here for the same thing, more
> or less, some more political than others, but we are all here for
> better opportunities, for jobs, or to raise our families in better
> conditions. . . . I find less unity here in the Hispanic culture than
> in other places where Anglos are the majority.

Electoral Power and Restricted Pluralism

Cubans' ascendancy to the pinnacle of local political power within one generation makes Cuban Miami's story both similar and different from other US cities where immigrant groups eventually came to dominate urban politics. The rise of Cubans in Miami is similar in that Cubans, like other immigrant groups, turned away from old-land politics to focus on dominating political power in the new setting when faced with native prejudice and a prolonged struggle against the regime at home. It is also similar in that immigrant groups incorporating politically into the United States have done so—and continue to do so—by voting coethnic candidates into urban office, whether they are Irish or Italian in Boston, Mexican in Los Angeles or San Antonio, or Cuban in Miami.[11]

But the Cuban rise to political dominance in Miami is also different. Most obviously, the pace of their ascension was quicker than earlier examples of dominant immigrant incorporation. Miami's Cubans took power across the county within thirty years of arrival en masse. Cubans elected the first Cuban mayor of Miami, Xavier Suarez, in 1985, only twenty years after the start of the "Freedom Flights" airlifts from Cuba. Irish arrivals in Boston in the 1830s took fifty years to elect their first mayor, Hugh O'Brien, in 1884. Italians who began arriving en masse in Boston in the late 1880s did not elect a coethnic mayor until 1993. While Los Angeles had Mexican American mayors in its early days, the last one finished his term in 1872, and Mexicans would not have another coethnic mayor until the election of Antonio Villaraigosa in 2005, more than 130 years later. The Cuban rate of ascension is more similar to the Vietnamese in Orange County, who elected their first coethnic member to the board of supervisors in 2007, twenty-eight years after the United States began to accept about 850,000 Vietnamese refugees, but the Vietnamese are not nearly as dominant in Orange County politics, which leads to a second difference. Miami politics also are different because an exiled immigrant group that came with an automatic path to citizenship politically dominates the elected and administrative offices of a metropolitan area primarily composed of economic immigrants and sojourners, many of whom lack access to citizenship or to formal sector employment. This imbalance of power creates a set of obstacles to immigrant incorporation that may be particularly hard to overcome for the less powerful groups.

Scholars define political incorporation as the ability of immigrant and ethnic communities to obtain elected office for members of their group. Political incorporation is considered "strong" when ethnic groups elect members of their community over a number of years and in the process obtain substantive government response to their particular group's needs. Weaker incorporation, on the other hand, implies that communities help to elect coethnic officials who are only symbolically responsive to community needs once in office.[12]

Empirical studies of ethnic political incorporation in US cities have found that descriptive representation increases levels of political trust and belonging among the members of the group that sends coethnics to office, increases their representation in civil service employment such as public school administration and police, and often mobilizes further political participation. They disagree about whether coethnic representation substantively helps the group receive better public services or reorients policy to address their concerns.[13]

Miami has seemed to follow this general pattern. The numbers of Cubans and African Americans in public administration and police posts increased after group members gained elected office in the 1980s and 1990s, and the city and county took strong anticommunist stands such as prohibiting the use of public money for performances of artists from communist

Cuba and repealing an "antibilingual" ordinance in the county charter. Cuban congressional members successfully pressured the Social Security Administration to reinstate benefits for noncitizen Cubans and Haitians who overstayed visas before getting legal permanent residency in the United States after Cuban immigration attorneys alerted the legislators to a rule change that hurt elderly Cubans. However, no wholesale reorientation of policies has taken place to aid newer immigrant cohorts' economic incorporation or diminish the degree of poverty or economic inequality in Greater Miami.[14]

As a basic indicator of political incorporation in Miami, in Table 5.1 we present the national origin or ethnicity of a sample of 110 elected officials in Miami-Dade County as of October 2010, twenty-five years after the first Cuban became mayor of the city of Miami.[15] The sample includes elected officials in the county's thirteen largest municipalities, the county government, the school board, and the county's five congressional representatives as of 2010.[16] Additionally, we tabulated the total number of constituents represented in the sample (constituents can be counted more than once since they are represented by more than one officeholder) and then calculated percentages of the total constituency represented by candidates of each ethnic or national-origin group.

Table 5.1 also presents two measures assessing over- or underrepresentation of ethnic or national-origin groups. The first measure of representation is the difference between the percentage of ethnic elected officials in the sample and the percentage of ethnic residents of the same community in the county. The weighted measure takes into account the size of the constituency represented by a public official as an imperfect proxy for level of political authority, since a small-town council member does not have the same level of authority or symbolic power as the county mayor or a congressional representative. This measure reports the number of percentage points difference in representation—overrepresentation or a representation gap—between the ethnic or national-origin group in elected office and the group's numbers in the wider county population. The two measures thus provide a comparison of differences in representation calculated as one-to-one representation and representation weighted by size as a proxy for the level of authority of the office.

Table 5.2 and the county maps below add further clarity to differences in representation by showing the distribution of ethnic political representation according to type of government and size of constituency. Congressional districts represent the largest constituencies, followed by school board and county commission districts. After that follow municipalities. Large municipal constituencies include the cities of Miami and Hialeah; middle-range districts are in the cities of Miami Gardens, North Miami, Miami Beach, and Coral Gables; and smaller municipal constituencies are

Table 5.1 National Origin/Ethnicity of Elected Officials in Greater Miami, 2010

	Number in County		% of Total			Gap in Representation	
	Number of Elected Officials	Number of Constituents Represented	% Elected Officials	% Constituents Represented	% County Population	Gap, % Officials to % County Population	Weighted Representation Gap, % of Constituents to % County Population
Cuban or Cuban American	45.0	5,832,127	41.0	67.0	35.0	5.0	32.0
African American	16.0	1,695,707	15.0	19.5	10.3	4.7	9.2
White non-Hispanic	38.0	990,558	35.0	11.4	16.0	19.0	-4.6
Non-Cuban of immigrant origin	11.0	177,970	10.0	2.1	37.1	-27.0	-34.9
Haitian	6.0	110,213	5.0	1.3	5.0	0.0	-3.7
Other West Indian	0.0	0	0.0	0.0	2.1	-2.1	-2.1
Non-Cuban Hispanic	5.0	67,758	5.0	0.8	30.0	-29.2	-29.2
Total	110.0	—[a]	100.0[b]	100.0	—	—	—

Sources: Percent County Population data from US Census Bureau (2011). Other data based on 2006–2010 or 2008–2010 terms in office and size of cities and electoral districts at 2000 census.

Notes: a. Represented constituents add up to more than the county population since constituents are represented by multiple elected officials.
b. Total may not add to 100 percent due to rounding.

Table 5.2 Size of Represented Constituency

	Cuban or Cuban American		White Non-Hispanic		African American		Haitian or Haitian American		Non-Cuban Hispanic		Total in Public Office	
	N	%	N	%	N	%	N	%	N	%	N	%
Congress	3	6.7	1	2.6	1	6.3	0	0.0	0	0.0	5	4.5
School board and county commission	13	28.9	4	10.5	6	37.5	0	0.0	0	0.0	23	20.9
Biggest cities	12	26.7	1	2.6	1	6.3	0	0.0	0	0.0	14	12.7
Medium-size cities	5	11.1	9	23.7	7	43.8	3	50.0	0	0.0	24	21.8
Smallest cities	12	26.7	23	60.5	1	6.3	3	50.0	5	100.0	44	40.0
Total[a]	45	100.0	38	100.0	16	100.0	6	100.0	5	100.0	110	100.0

Source: Primary source data collected by authors using public information or e-mail queries.
Note: a. Totals for percentages may not equal 100 due to rounding.

found in Miami Lakes, Homestead, Palmetto Bay, Aventura, Doral, and Hialeah Gardens.

A number of patterns are notable in the tables and maps. First, although in terms of raw numbers Cubans share power with white non-Hispanic Miami residents, "Anglos" as they are called in Miami, non-Hispanic whites held public office primarily in smaller residential communities. Considering the most powerful elected positions in Greater Miami, Cubans no longer share power with Anglos as they did when the seminal *City on the Edge* was researched in the late 1980s and early 1990s.[17] Cubans politically dominate other ethnic and national-origin groups in offices representing the largest constituencies.

Three of the area's five congressional districts are held by two Cubans and a Cuban American. The fourth is held by an African American, coming from a seat that was drawn in 1992 by court order to ensure an African American representative. The fifth district, which begins in Broward County to the north and runs along affluent communities with predominately Jewish and Anglo populations in the eastern part of Miami-Dade County, is held by a Jewish American politician from Broward County.

Cubans dominate the county commission, the most powerful local governmental body. The county mayor's post, considered by many to be Greater Miami's most powerful local elected position, was held by Cuban Carlos Álvarez. Of eight school board members, four were Cuban or Cuban American, two were African American, and two were non-Hispanic whites. Of the three largest cities, two, Miami and Hialeah, are dominated by Cubans and Cuban Americans. In the city of Miami, where districts were drawn in anticipation of a civil rights court order, the mayor was Cuban and three of six commission districts were held by a Cuban and two Cuban Americans, two districts were held by African Americans, and one commissioner was a non-Hispanic white. All of Hialeah's commissioners were Cuban or Cuban American, and the mayor was Cuban. The third-largest city in the county, Miami Gardens, was incorporated from an African American section of the unincorporated county in 2003. All commissioners and the mayor were African American.

A second trend is that no official of non-Cuban immigrant origin held a powerful elected post in the county. Indeed, with the partial exception of Haitians, non-Cuban immigrant groups remain essentially voiceless. Although the 2011 American Community Survey estimated that 37 percent of the county is of non-Cuban immigrant origin, only 10 of 110 politicians in the sample were non-Cuban Hispanics or of Caribbean origin, and all were elected in smaller cities.[18] A Colombian American and a Guatemalan sat on the city council of Homestead, a city of 31,909. A Mexican-origin politician was elected to the city commission in Doral, population 21,000, and a Puerto Rican was elected in Aventura, population 25,267.[19] Of non-

Hispanic immigrants, only Haitians are beginning to be incorporated polit-ically at the local level, holding majority positions in the North Miami City Commission, that city's mayoral post, and a minority of positions on the North Miami Beach commission. Other Caribbean-origin groups do not have a community member in an elected post within our sample.

The reason Haitians are incorporating in smaller cities in the north county points to a third pattern in Miami's mode of political incorporation that is illustrated in the political maps of Miami-Dade County (see Figure 5.1). Most local government bodies are dominated by politicians of one or two national-origin groups, due to the fact that ethnic and national-origin groups not only vote for coethnics but tend to live near them as well. Haitians are the only non-Cuban immigrant group to reach a critical mass of voting members within the boundaries of a municipality or electoral dis-trict. Haitians are beginning to overcome the obstacles slowing political in-corporation of other groups, including numbers, the lack of a path to citi-zenship, or a mismatch with the boundaries of established political units. Cubans' successful political incorporation involves numbers, automatic cit-izenship, spatial concentration, and more.

Cuban Model of Political Incorporation

Exiled singer Celia Cruz said it well when the first of three Miami Cuban congressional representatives was elected in 1989 following an ethnically divisive election—"*¡Los cubanos han ganado!*" ("The Cubans have won!").[20] And then they won even more, as Table 5.1 shows. Starting out as coequals with the traditional Anglo establishment, Cubans have become the predominant ethnic group in Miami's political circles. Cuban political suc-cess in Miami can be explained by a coalescence of interrelated factors that would be difficult for any of Miami's other ethnic groups to replicate in to-tality, but that help us to explore Miami's political future. The keys to the Cuban model, that overlap and reinforce each other, include

- Automatic legal status and government financial support for reset-tlement.
- Ethnic solidarity and issue intensity, which increase electoral salience and turnout.
- Spatial concentration and the formation of an enclave economy with human capital and financial backing for campaign management as well as media outlets, all of which fostered numeric majorities and aided community mobilization.
- Changing political incentives such as small-business ownership and instances of native discrimination that reoriented exile politic efforts toward domestic elections.

Figure 5.1 Ethnic Political Representation, 2010

County Commission District Boundaries

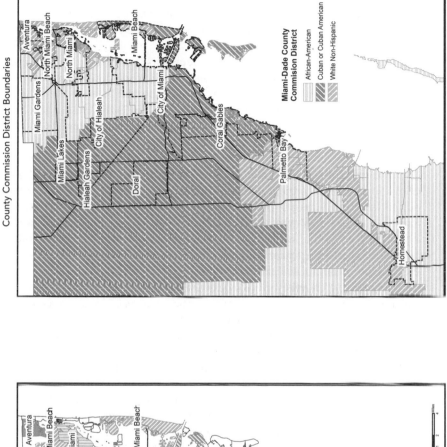

Municipal Commissions and Councils

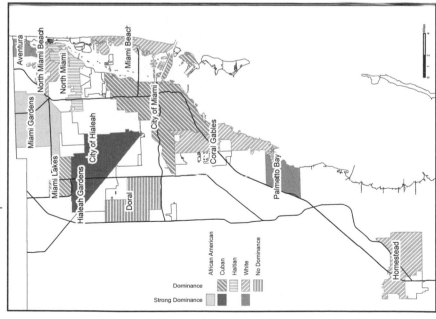

- An underdeveloped state Republican Party to use as an organizational vehicle since old guard practices blocked entry into the Democratic Party.
- Civil rights legislation and court decisions that created new political boundaries and single-member districts that helped Cubans elect co-ethnics to office.
- Cuban possession of key positions in the state's legislature since the 1980s, assuring that Miami's congressional and state legislative districts would remain drawn to support Cuban Republicans.[21]

The first Cuban immigrants, or the Golden Exiles, reached Miami with education and entrepreneurial experience. Their success in exile was also supported by US geopolitical strategies during the Cold War. As part of these strategies, documented in Chapter 1, Cubans received unprecedented support for economic success in the United States. The experience and ideology of exile formed strong bonds among the first cohorts of arrivals. The exile ideology dominated the campaign discourse of Cuban elected officials well into the 2000s, even while mass opinion about relations with Cuba diversified within the Cuban community as new waves of immigrants arrived with different politically formative experiences and other traits that distinguished them from the first arrivals. Bonded solidarity based on shared values and experiences weakened over the years, although initial help for Cuban newcomers and rhetorical support for immigrants fleeing leftist governments remained strong.

Silvia Pedraza and others classify waves of Cuban migration since 1959, identifying the differing socioeconomic traits, racial characteristics, and political experiences characterizing each wave.[22] The original exiles, about 250,000, who left between 1959 and 1965 in response to incremental nationalizations, closure of private schools, and the collapse of elections, essentially shared social class origins in Cuba and fled for the same reasons. A second wave of immigrants arrived via the Freedom Flights, which brought another 340,000 refugees to Miami from December 1965 through April 1973. Of largely middle-class origin, later arrivals were more flexible on return visits and contacts between the United States and Cuba, but group solidarity remained strong based on the experience of exile that bound the community in the 1960s and 1970s.[23]

Cubans during these decades built the entrepreneurial enclave by raising capital through ethnic channels, hiring Cubans as employees, and using conationals as suppliers, distributors, and manufacturers. The small community provided each other character loans based on business experience in Cuba, apprenticeships, and networks of social capital. Lisandro Pérez called the enclave "institutionally complete,"[24] meaning Cubans could live, work, pray, and do business all within their community, and usually in Spanish.

Enclave isolation was facilitated by predeparture social networks, use of a minority language, and in-group solidarity based on the exile experience, but also because, even with US support, Cubans faced hurdles within the then-Anglo-dominant community. Most arrived without tangible assets such as collateral for bank loans or knowledge of how the wider society operated. In politics, the county's monolithic Democratic Party made few efforts to incorporate Cubans in the 1960s and 1970s.[25]

Enclave politics focused on the homeland. As Castro dug in, however, Miami's economically successful exiles realized they could be in Florida for a long time. As business owners, immigrants saw issues, such as ordinances, taxes, and zoning, grow in priority.[26] And though partially sheltered from labor market discrimination, Cubans faced political discrimination. The peak was a countywide vote banning expenditure of public funds "for the purpose of utilizing any language other than English or any culture other than that of the United States."[27] The ballot initiative passed in 1980 as a wave of Nicaraguan and Haitian immigrants was arriving in Miami, along with a new wave of Cubans from the port of Mariel. Cubans in Miami had achieved a great deal of economic success by the late 1970s and had even created the first bilingual situation comedy, critically acclaimed *¿Qué Pasa U.S.A.?*, which aired on national television and explained Cuban exile family life to Anglos.[28] So older immigrants were surprised by the English only initiative and negative reaction to Mariel Cubans. They formed civic organizations to fight misperceptions and discrimination and turned politically to the Republican Party as a vehicle for Cuban candidacies for local office. Also at this time, they formed what would become the most powerful national lobby on US-Cuban affairs, the Cuban American National Foundation. These efforts did not erase the difficult reception for the newer arrivals. For the first time since 1958, a Cuban immigrant wave was not granted automatic legal residency. Legal status arrangements took four years and creation of a special immigrant category under the Cuban Adjustment Act. Public assistance benefits had also been greatly reduced. Included in a onetime amnesty under the adjustment act were 25,000 Haitians when African American politicians and civil rights lawyers drew contrasts in treatment.[29]

Heike Alberts's interviews, echoed by others, found that many previously established Cubans in Miami resented Mariel refugees for what they believed to be poor work ethics, demands for support from relatives, false expectations, and the negative impact they had on Cubans' model minority image in the United States.[30] Indeed, press accounts in Miami's Anglo-dominated media and replicated nationally disproportionately highlighted the minority of "Marielitos" who got into trouble with the law. Susan Eckstein and Lorena Barberia report that while the negative sentiments have softened, the older Cuban and Mariel cohorts rarely live near or socialize with each other.[31] The powerful first waves of immigrants had more respect for immigrants who arrived by raft in the mid-1990s, known as *balseros*. Escaping Cuba at great personal risk, they were highly educated and motivated to succeed. Further, they were easier to absorb than the larger Mariel wave.[32]

Despite these differences, the first waves of Cuban immigrants and their offspring hold political power in Miami, speaking for all, even though their interests diverge from later arrivals, and imposing social controls on public expression that diverges from hard-line approaches to Cuba.[33] Discussions in our focus groups support the findings of other scholars in this area. In animated discussions, later Cuban arrivals among our participants spoke of being "underestimated" or insulted by first-wave Cubans or their US-born children. While they also acknowledged forms of group solidarity that included help to newcomers, the negative sentiments were expressed more strongly.

Sandra, a nurse in Cuba who learned English and worked in a mental health clinic, spoke about how the Cuban American son of her boss at the restaurant where she found her first job underestimated her nursing skills because she had learned them in Cuba and then refused to believe she was learning English. She said "even my own uncle," a first-wave immigrant, advised her not to date or marry a newly arrived Cuban: "And I looked at him like, 'How can my uncle tell me that when I have not even spent twenty-four hours yet in this country, tell me that I should not marry a recently arrived Cuban?' But this is the mentality, that the person who has just arrived comes with all of the affectations of that government, comes with all of the ideas of that government also, and so it is someone who comes with different criteria than those who have been here longer."

Cubans more easily unite as a community on issues involving refugees or general anti-Castroism. Protests erupt when Cuban rafters are to be returned to Cuba after nearly reaching Florida's shores and thus qualifying for residency under current "wet foot, dry foot" policies. Polls found that most Cubans opposed the Clinton administration decision to return Elian González, the boy rafter whose mother died on the journey, to his father in Cuba instead of leaving him in Miami with his more distant relatives. However, even on the issue of Elian's return, our participants mentioned an imposed homogeneity in public expression; one participant said she could not even tell her friends that she would want her daughter's father to care for the girl should she die because the father lived in Cuba. Writing of a semiannual poll of Miami Cubans, sociologist Guillermo Grenier argues that the political, economic, and media dominance of older, more conservative Cuban cohorts is creating a "cultural friction that [is] slowing down the process of change."[34]

Other conditions that aided the political success of Miami's earliest

Cuban arrivals were numbers and spatial concentration. While large federal programs tried to settle Cubans across the country, most came back to Miami, where they initially concentrated in just two areas. Low-income housing and working-class employment or commercial opportunities initially attracted Cubans to the area due west of downtown Miami, later known as Little Havana, and to the city just north, called Hialeah. Little Havana became the entrepreneurial center of the Cuban enclave while Hialeah was the home of manufacturing plants, which Cuban blue-collar employees quickly populated. Miami's Cuban community forged a broad and diverse entrepreneurial class in fairly short order, with numbers, spatial concentration, ethnic solidarity, and entrepreneurial skills that would soon be turned toward politics.[35] The basis of the Miami Cuban enclave was highly differentiated entrepreneurial activity that initially served the Cuban ethnic market of Miami and then dispersed into the wider county market, eventually (though more slowly) penetrating downtown development, law offices, and banking.

From the core settlements Little Havana and Hialeah, Cuban settlement patterns in the county branched east and west as numbers grew and economic possibilities advanced. Between the 1990 and 2000 censuses, the expansion of a Cuban beltway was noticeable, running from Miami Beach to unincorporated West Miami and Sweetwater. In the 1980s, professionals who advanced economically left Little Havana and Hialeah for the growing southwestern suburb of Kendall. Later in the 1990s, they penetrated wealthier Anglo bastions in affluent Coral Gables and the Pinecrest/Old Cutler area. Cubans mixed very little with African Americans and Haitians, a fact that remains today. Census maps show Cuban presence in the northeast county dropping in the 1990s as wealthier Haitians moved to Miami from the Northeast United States or moved upward economically from the Little Haiti neighborhood into cities such as Miami Lakes and North Miami. However, successive replacement of outgoing Cubans with newer exiles has kept Little Havana and Hialeah the heart of Cuban settlement in Miami-Dade County. Even as Little Havana came to house low-income immigrants from other Latin American nations in the 1990s, the area remained 62 percent Cuban in 2000.[36]

The initial concentration of the Cuban community in the cities of Miami and Hialeah aided political incorporation in a number of ways. It meant that political boundaries could coincide with electoral districts and made community mobilization easier. Further, the enclave's sources of capitalization and high rates of business ownership enhanced political fundraising. Concentrated living and successful fund-raising meant increasingly professional Cuban political electioneers could target and get out the vote in percentages that aided Cuban candidates.[37]

Analysts identify the first election of a Cuban to the US Congress as a turning point. Longtime representative Claude Pepper, a Democrat, had sat-isfied his growing Cuban constituency for two decades with a hard line on communism. When a special election was called in 1989 after his death, na-tional Republican Party leadership called the seat "a Cuban seat" because of demographic change bringing Cubans and Republicans to close to 50 percent of the district's voters. Cubans originally had tried to obtain Demo-cratic nominations for local office, since the Democratic Party in Florida was nearly unchallenged. When this approach failed, Cuban politicians turned to the underdeveloped Republican Party of Florida, which embraced them.

In 1989, the national Republican leadership supported the nomination of Ileana Ros-Lehtinen, then a state senator. The Democratic candidate was a Jewish American, who responded to the "Cuban seat" statement by call-ing the post an "American seat." Ros-Lehtinen's election strategists dubbed the "American seat" phrase a code to enhance anti-immigrant sentiments, an interpretation Cuban Spanish-language radio station hosts amplified. Ros-Lehtinen won thanks to almost monolithic Cuban support and high Cuban turnout, reaching 70 percent, becoming the first Cuban elected to Congress and the first of three Miami-area Cuban representatives.[38]

By 1980, 25 percent of Greater Miami was of Cuban origin, equal to 52 percent of all Cubans in the United States,[39] but Cubans had done little in local politics. Three sets of events changed that. The first was national US politics, where the candidacy of Ronald Reagan in 1980 meant that support-ing a Republican would replace Jimmy Carter's attempted rapprochement with Castro with what Miami Cubans saw as a hard-line anticommunist in Reagan. The second had to do with domestic conditions in Miami-Dade County. The arrival of the Mariel immigrants augmented Anglo fears of a growing Spanish-speaking population. Unfavorable press coverage and the successful attempt to make English the only language used in county poli-tics ensued. However, contrary to dominant accounts of Miami Cuban po-litical ascendency,[40] neither of these can alone explain the extraordinary rise of Cubans to local political power. Rather, court-ordered redistricting in re-sponse to civil rights claims led mostly by African Americans assured Cubans' rapid and wide ascension to elected office.

Reform of county electoral districts to ensure minority representation had a tremendous impact on Cuban empowerment. Ros-Lehtinen was joined in Congress by Cuban Lincoln Diaz-Balart in a district created by court order after the 1990 census and then by Lincoln Diaz-Balart's US-born brother Mario Diaz-Balart in a district created by the legislature and approved by the court after the 2000 census. From 1957 to 1992, only two Hispanics had ever been elected to the county commission. When at-large elections, which favored Anglos, gave way to single-member districts in 1992, Cuban and Cuban American county commissioners increased to six seats from one.[41] The shift in Miami city government was similar. City government representation became predominately Cuban. African Americans also were elected in greater numbers following the court-ordered changes, but in terms of volume, Cuban politicians were the clear winners.

If Cubans' rise of political dominance in Miami has been relatively fast and easy by historical standards, Haitian political incorporation has been more slow and arduous. Haitians are just beginning to emerge as a local political force.

Haitian Model of Political Incorporation

Modern migration from Haiti to the United States started in the 1950s with professional and middle-class exiles fleeing the dictatorship of François "Papa Doc" Duvalier. A turn to export-oriented commercial agriculture and attempts to industrialize in the 1970s uprooted the Haitian peasantry, creating pressures for urbanization and immigration. At the same time, state brutality against the black urban middle class pushed more to leave for the established Haitian community in the US Northeast.

The South Florida Haitian community remained small until the late 1970s and 1980s when the regime destabilized, sending thousands fleeing both poverty and political violence by whatever means possible. Jean-Claude "Baby Doc" Duvalier finally left for exile in 1986, but the Duvalier dynasty was followed by a series of short elected presidencies interrupted by coups until 2006. When the January 2010 earthquake occurred, the country was set to complete a full presidential term and was just beginning to experience the economic fruits of political stability.

Whether Haitian immigrants to the United States are considered economic or political migrants has depended upon whether the federal government at the time wanted to legally bar them from refugee status. But whatever their official classification, Haitians have had the misfortune, from an immigration standpoint, to be dramatically poor and black and fleeing a noncommunist authoritarian regime. Haitian asylum seekers lacked a US Cold War nemesis of the likes of Fidel Castro in Cuba or Daniel Ortega in Nicaragua to support their claims. The poverty of the most disadvantaged arrivals was generalized to the entire Haitian community in dramatic boat landings broadcast nationally by Miami television stations. For advocates in the 1980s, they became known as the "black boat people" to contrast them with Cuban balseros and strengthen appeals for equal treatment. Moreover, US public health officials publicly associated them with acquired immune deficiency syndrome (AIDS) in the 1980s, feeding into media stereotypes about all Haitians that depicted them as poor, black, and stigmatized. As such, Haitian immigrants did not experience the same context of reception as the first Cuban waves fleeing communism. Local Democratic Party leaders, as well as some Cubans, convinced the federal government to unleash "an unprecedented" campaign to discourage and deport Haitians from South Florida.[42]

The campaign included imprisonment, denial of work permits if allowed out of jail, generalized rejection of political asylum, and, for the first time, Coast Guard interdiction of immigrants at sea.[43] Public health authorities quarantined these immigrants in hospitals, citing the three Hs that officials associated with HIV—hepatitis, homosexuality, and Haitian.[44] More than two decades later, federal officials implied that terrorists might pose as Haitian refugees in order to sneak into the country by boat. Even though they were fleeing political violence, of the 22,940 Haitians interdicted at sea between 1981 and 1990, only eleven were considered qualified to apply for asylum by US immigration.[45] Haitians who pass the standard "credible fear threshold" for political asylum are still held in detention until their court hearings, rather than being paroled into the community as typically occurs with other nationalities.[46]

Even with such severe anti-immigration measures, by the 2000s, Haitians had begun to incorporate politically in South Florida by winning municipal elections in the northern Miami-Dade County cities of North Miami, North Miami Beach, and El Portal. In November 2010, a Haitian American candidate became a Miami-Dade County commissioner for the first time. How did Miami's Haitian community in the 2000s begin to overcome obstacles to political incorporation? First, their numbers grew despite strong federal government discouragement of immigration. Second, Haitians who arrived in the 1980s naturalized as quickly as possible and mobilized in local elections. Third, middle-class Haitians concentrated geographically in clusters that aligned with the North Miami and North Miami Beach municipalities, which created critical voting mass within defined electoral boundaries and also helped dilute problematic class divisions carried over from Haiti.

Despite gains, Haitian political incorporation remains limited by the difficulties in forging pan-racial coalitions. No formal alliance of Haitian and African American candidates has occurred. The only Haitian candidate to defeat an African American in a county-level race did so because of a set of circumstances particular to that election, including a door-to-door campaign by the Haitian candidate in African American neighborhoods and an incumbent who was so unpopular with some of his coethnics that candidate ethnicity did not matter.

The number of Haitians in the United States grew exponentially in the late twentieth century. The US Census, while likely undercounting Haitians, found that Haitian-born US residents more than quadrupled between 1980 and 2000. From the 92,395 Haitian-born residents counted nationally in the 1980 US Census, there were 419,317 counted in 2000, and 592,260 estimated in Census Bureau surveys in 2011. About half of US Haitians are naturalized US citizens, and about 230,000 more had gained lawful permanent residency status by 2008.[47]

The Haitian community in South Florida grew in numbers through family reunification, step migration from the older communities in New York and Boston, and political advocacy that used comparisons with treatment of Cold War refugees to embarrass US politicians into granting legal permanent residency to Haitian refugees. Generally less educated as a group than the first northeastern US arrivals, some of the so-called Haitian boat people that made it to Miami reunited with relatives in the North, but most stayed in South Florida, initially congregating in the Little River/Edison area of the city that came to be known as Little Haiti.[48] By the twenty-first century, the Miami metropolitan area had become the primary destination for Haitian immigrants heading to the United States. The 2011 American Community Survey from the US Census Bureau estimates that 49 percent of all foreign-born residents from Haiti live in Florida (264,224), and most of those in the Miami–Fort Lauderdale–Pompano Beach metropolitan area (187,521). Florida now well surpasses New York as the destination for Haitian immigrants.[49]

The largest single increase for the South Florida Haitian community came in 1980, when about 25,000 Haitians arriving by sea were admitted with the same rights as 150,000 Cubans who had mostly been ferried across the Florida straits by Miami Cubans desperate to retrieve relatives. The arrival of Haitians and Cubans at the same time made it politically impossible for the Carter administration to treat the two groups so differently. Known as "Cuban-Haitian Entrants," these Haitians received a onetime humanitarian parole and later were allowed to adjust their immigration status to lawful permanent residency under the Immigration Reform and Control Act of 1986.[50] Another jump in the number of legal Haitian residents came in 1998, also through comparison with anticommunist asylum petitioners, when Congress passed the 1998 Haitian Refugee Immigration Fairness Act one year after Congress eased residency requirements for about 66,000 Nicaraguans, 3,500 Cubans not covered by earlier status adjustments, and other Central American and Eastern European asylum petitioners.[51]

Each time the door was opened to Haitian asylum petitioners, however, it was quickly shut for those who followed. After the Carter era "Cuban-Haitian Entrants" program, the Reagan administration, at the behest of local Democratic Party leaders and incumbent Miami-Dade politicians,[52] entered an agreement with then-dictator Jean-Claude Duvalier allowing the US Coast Guard to inspect private vessels in Haitian waters. In practice, officers on board rejected claims for political asylum wholesale and returned almost all to Haiti.[53] Since 1992, Haitians claiming a "credible fear" of political retribution have been prescreened for asylum in Haiti or the Guan-

tanamo Bay Naval Base. All but a handful have been denied parole awaiting hearings. In 2005, only 9 of 1,850 interdicted Haitians received a "credible fear" hearing, and only one man was granted status as a political
refugee.[54]

Even with such stringent measures, federal authorities could not stop
all of the boats, deny all of the asylum applications, or catch all of the
tourists who overstayed visas. While most probably failed, many Haitians
managed to reach the United States and eventually gain lawful residency
with the aid of church-funded immigration lawyers and African Americans
motivated by shared perceptions of discrimination.[55] Once Haitians secured
legal residency, they obtained US immigrant visas for family members. Of
26,000 Haitians who received permanent US residency in 2008, 72 percent
qualified as immediate relatives of US citizens or through sponsorship of
family members who were lawful permanent residents.[56]

Over the years, Haitian immigrants in New York, Boston, and elsewhere in the North, seeking a warmer climate after years working in exile,
joined other first-generation Haitians and their Haitian American offspring
in Florida. The Census Bureau's American Community Survey estimates
that 35 percent of Haitian-origin residents in the United States lived in
Miami-Dade and Broward counties as of 2011.[57] Along with Haitians from
the island who moved economically up and out of Little Haiti, Haitians
from the US Northeast tended to settle in the cities of North Miami and
North Miami Beach, the Golden Glades area of Miami-Dade County, and
the smaller village of El Portal, as well as in southern Broward County. By
the time the first Haitian mayor was elected in North Miami in 2001, about
one-third of the population was of Haitian origin. The latest American
Community Survey and US Census estimates available suggest that people
of Haitian origin make up 37 percent of the population of North Miami, 24
percent of North Miami Beach, and 13 percent of small El Portal.[58]

The number of Haitian immigrants in Florida who became naturalized
citizens also grew. By the 2000 census, 47 percent of Haitians in Florida
who had arrived between 1980 and 1989 had naturalized, and 64 percent of
those arriving before 1980 had naturalized. This rate is slower than some of
the other major national-origin groups in Greater Miami, such as Colombians, Dominicans, and of course Cubans, but still by 2011, 83,030 Haitian
immigrants, or 44.5 percent of those in Miami-Dade and Broward counties,
had naturalized.[59]

Like Cubans and other immigrants in Miami, Haitians live in a context
in which local political boundaries were purposefully drawn to increase the
importance of candidate ethnicity and where, in many elections, voters see
candidate ethnicity, national origin, and race as the most important factors
when deciding how to cast their ballot.[60] Immigrant community political incorporation depends upon these structural and social dimensions of politics

in combination with the particular characteristics of each national-origin group, particularly the size of its citizenry, their residential concentration, and the degree of community solidarity. Haitians have faced difficulty securing pan-racial coalitions necessary to achieve countywide office but have seen success in cities with higher concentrations of Haitians, including North Miami, El Portal, and North Miami Beach.

To gain political representation, Miami's Haitian community also has had to struggle against internal divisions originating in Haiti's politics and class structure. Haitians lost their first majority on the North Miami City Council in 2005 because differences over the coup against populist Haitian president Jean-Bertrand Aristide, who was loved by the poor, kept many at home rather than vote for a Haitian candidate deemed anti-Aristide.[61] In 2006, paid Creole-language talk show hosts hurt the chances of Haitian candidates for county commission and the school board when they accused the candidates of being anti-Aristide elitists. Both candidates lost to African Americans.[62] When postcoup political divisiveness waned, Haitian candidates retook the North Miami mayor's post and two of the four posts on the city council. Calls to unity appear often, but the homeland's strident politics and class differences could reassert themselves.

Beyond homeland differences that fracture community solidarity, Haitian candidates in Miami have had difficulties attracting African Americans to the pan-racial coalitions necessary for them to win in Miami's larger political districts. The African American community, like other ethnic and national-origin groups in Greater Miami, is more likely to vote for candidates from their own group. Cultural differences emerge between Haitian and African American youth, and political support has its limits at election time. An unusually public example of differences with African American politicians occurred when retiring Miami-Dade county commissioner Barbara Carey-Shuler stated in 2005 that her commission district position had been "carved out for an African American." She then endorsed an African American over a Haitian protégé to replace her in District 3, which encompassed historically African American portions of the central county, as well as Haitian enclaves. Carey-Shuler was referring to the court-ordered redrawing of districts in 1992, replacing a system of electing county commissioners at large with single-member districts drawn to guarantee black and Hispanic representation on the Anglo-monopolized county commission. Carey-Shuler's African American protégé was elected and remains in office. The Haitian instead ran for school board and lost.[63]

Electoral competition between Haitians and African Americans is not a coincidence. Since Haitians settled in or near traditionally African American areas of Miami, which the courts purposefully grouped as political units, Haitian candidates usually compete against African American candidates in elections for county commission, school board, and Congress. In these elections, when a Haitian runs against an African American, ethnicity usually trumps other qualities and outnumbered Haitians lose. The school board and county commission districts in which most North Miami and North Miami Beach residents vote were represented by African Americans from the creation of the districts in the early 1990s until 2010, the first time a Haitian politician in Miami won a county-level office. This exception to the general rule highlights that other candidate qualities can be significant under the right circumstances. The candidate Jean Monestime created a winning coalition by making his incumbent opponent's perceived incompetence and corruption more salient than his African American ethnicity.

Monestime is a former North Miami councilman who came from Haiti by boat in 1981. He unseated Commissioner Dorrin D. Rolle with the help of disgruntled African American voters. Running a door-to-door campaign in Haitian and African American neighborhoods, Monestime forced a runoff with an incumbent hampered by ethical breaches and strong anti-incumbent sentiment. Monestime took 26 percent of the vote in the general election to Rolle's 40 percent. The rest was split among three African American candidates and a Haitian candidate. All of the African American candidates endorsed Monestime in the runoff, and he won 53 percent to 47 percent. For the first time in sixteen years, a member of the county's most powerful political body had been unseated, and for the first time, a Haitian candidate at the county level had beaten an African American with the help of African American voters.[64]

Monestime won by dividing his African American opponents in the general election and creating a pan-ethnic coalition against the incumbent in the runoff, a turn of events that has yet to happen in other large elections. The same year, an African American candidate beat a divided field of Haitian candidates for the Democratic nomination in the Seventeenth Congressional District of Florida, which includes North Miami, North Miami Beach, and El Portal. An African American Democrat has held the district since its boundaries were changed in 1993, part of a deal between the legislature's black caucus and the rising Cuban power bloc in the state Republican Party.[65]

At the municipal level, competition with African Americans has not been as problematic because Haitians outnumber African Americans and other blacks from the Caribbean, who tend to unite with them against Anglo and Hispanic candidates.[66] In a review of North Miami elections since 2005, a pattern emerges in which Haitians either win the first round of voting outright with 50 percent plus one vote, or win in a runoff election when the large majority of Haitian residents vote behind a single coethnic candidate. In these cases, based on precinct-level analysis, Haitian candidate victories depend on at least some African American support. Blacks of all national origins make up about 50 percent of the North Miami electorate.

The election and reelection of the second Haitian American mayor of North Miami, Andre Pierre, is illustrative of the candidate distributions and voter coalitions necessary for Haitian candidate victories there. In the 2009 North Miami mayoral race, Pierre came in second behind Anglo Frank Wolland, 29.5 percent to 36.7 percent, in a candidate field that included three Haitians, a Jamaican, an Anglo, and a Cuban. In the runoff between only the top two candidates, Pierre and Wolland, Pierre gained 24 percentage points and won 53.2 percent to 46.8 percent. In 2011, Pierre was reelected without a runoff when he ran against a single Anglo candidate and a weak Haitian candidate. This pattern of pan-racial coalition building supports what Sharon D. Wright Austin found in her analysis of predominantly Haitian and African American precincts in Miami-Dade County elections: when the ballot features no candidate with shared ethnicity, black voters will form pan-racial coalitions against Anglo and Hispanic candidates.[67] However, the Rolle defeat suggests that black voters will sometimes form a pan-racial coalition when the coethnic candidate is judged poorly enough and the coracial candidate's appeal is strong.

One other aspect of Haitian political incorporation bears mention, especially when compared to the Cuban model. While Haitians usually vote Democrat, they have not traditionally viewed one party as more sympathetic to their community than another. Candidates win by addressing the needs of individuals and families.[68] Unlike Cubans, who helped move the Florida Republican Party to its leadership position in the state, and through the Republican Party asserted power over electoral district boundaries, Haitians do not have a strong voice in the leadership of the state Democratic Party or its black caucus, which is headed by African Americans.

As Haitians win formal political office, a pluralist vision of political power suggests their community will gain greater responsiveness to its needs, and some indication can be found that this has happened. The state's first Haitian legislator convinced fellow legislators in 2002 to allow immigrants who are applying for or appealing their immigration status to be allowed to get a driver's license. North Miami government printed city materials in Creole, and many candidates began to speak on Creole-language radio talk shows in the late 1990s. The city commission appointed Haitians as the police chief and assistant city manager. However, complaints from the less-affluent west side of the city, where many Haitian and other black residents live, resurfaced against incumbent Haitian council members in 2011. Further, the denial of fast-track family reunification after the devastating 2010 earthquake suggests Haitian political influence remains limited. The community does not have a strong voice in Congress, nor are Haitians yet considered a key to Florida's votes in the Electoral College.

Political Incorporation Model for Other Groups

Viewed functionally through a pluralist lens on power, Cuban incorporation and eventual dominance in local politics depended on large and concentrated numbers, an automatic citizenship path with high levels of naturalization, ethnic solidarity and strong turnout in the earlier immigration cohorts, civil rights court decisions and then state party political leaders who drew favorable district boundaries, and, finally, the ability to win office without ethnic or racial electoral coalitions. Haitians are beginning to politically incorporate on the local level because even though their struggle has been more difficult, they have reached a sufficient number of citizens within three municipalities and a county commission district and can elect coethnics to office when they are unified and form pan-racial coalitions.

Table 5.3 presents summary data on each of these variables for the four largest immigrant communities in Miami-Dade County as of the 2005–2009 American Community Surveys—Cubans, Haitians, Nicaraguans, and Colombians. Using the variables we identified as important for immigrant community political incorporation in Miami through a comparison of Cubans and Haitians, we see more clearly why other national-origin groups have not politically incorporated in multiethnic Miami and what obstructs the incorporation of other communities in the future. When judged by numbers alone, Nicaraguans would seem to have a possibility of gaining political representation in Greater Miami. Moreover, the largest immigrant wave in the 1980s consisted of politically bonded exiles fleeing the Sandinista Revolution. However, Nicaraguan political incorporation has been blocked by low rates of naturalization and geographic dispersion throughout the county. Consider the city of Sweetwater, which has 17,966 residents, according to estimates from the 2011 American Community Survey three-year estimate, 75 percent of whom were born outside of the United States. Forty-four percent of Sweetwater residents are not US citizens and so are disenfranchised in local elections.[69]

Sweetwater has the largest concentration of Nicaraguans in the United States, earning it the nickname of "Little Managua." Even so, Nicaraguans only make up about 22 percent of Sweetwater's population, and Cubans make up 44 percent. Another 18 percent of the population is spread between sixteen other Latin American groups, and almost no Anglos or blacks of non-Hispanic origin live here, so a Nicaraguan candidate has no potential ethnicity-based coalition partner in Sweetwater large enough to overcome a Cuban majority.[70] The mayor of Sweetwater in 2011 was Manuel M. Maroño, a Cuban American who highlights in his official biography sketch that he was born and raised in Sweetwater. The biographies of the vice mayor and six other city commissioners all tout their Cuban origins; five were born there.

Table 5.3 Immigrant Community Political Incorporation

Ethnic/National Origin Group	Population Miami-Dade County	Number Naturalized in Miami-Dade County	Voter Bloc Potential	Solidarity	Voter Coalition
Cuban	893,628	611,786	At all levels	Divisions surface based on homeland and US politics	Not needed
Haitian	125,146	84,855	County Commission District 2, North Miami, North Miami Beach, El Portal	Divisions surface based on homeland politics	Needed
Nicaraguan	109,433	71,703	No	No candidates	Needed
Colombian	113,995	73,117	No	Divisions surface based on homeland politics	Needed

Source: US Census Bureau (2011h).

When Maroño was first elected to the city commission in 1995, eleven candidates were running for five at-large seats, and only one candidate was Nicaraguan. "There are only 40 registered Nicaraguans in Sweetwater," the single Nicaraguan candidate told the *Miami Herald*. "I guess I'm the one with the most interest in running."[71] She lost. More recently, in 2011, Deborah Centeno, a Nicaraguan, came in third against incumbent Prisca Barreto and Elsa Thompson, both born in Cuba. Centeno received only 17 percent of the vote.[72] Miami's Nicaraguans in the early 2000s could claim only a member of the community zoning board in Kendall as an elected official; they lost that representative when she resigned to make a failed bid for the state house in 2010.

Colombians are equally numerous in Miami-Dade County, and they naturalize at the rate of Cubans and twice the rate of Nicaraguans, but they are geographically dispersed or concentrated in political districts where they do not reach critical voting mass. With at least thirty community organizations in South Florida, their political divisions have surfaced when coethnic candidates run against each other and unity organizations rise and fall in popularity. They explain the divisions as related to personal ambitions in Miami and contentious partisan politics in the homeland. Some argue that they have also been more interested in homeland politics than politics in Miami.[73] Colombians in Miami have a better track record in electing coethnics to office than Nicaraguans, but only slightly. They claimed as elected representatives in the first decade of the century a member of the Florida House of Representatives, the Homestead town council, the Miami Lakes City Commission, and the county zoning council in Kendall.

To win elected office, Colombians require Cuban support and strong candidate appeal, which has happened for only one large elected position. Republican Juan Carlos Zapata won reelection three times to his post as state representative from southwest Miami-Dade County with Cuban support. Zapata won for the first time in the 2002 Republican primary by barely beating a Cuban contender whose showing was weakened by another, weaker Cuban candidate. Zapata won again in the 2004 Republican primary against a Cuban by a large margin. He drew no Republican competition in 2006. In 2008 he had to beat only a weak non-Hispanic Democrat, which he did by a large margin, helped by shared ideology and the electioneering skill of Miami's Cuban Republicans.

Zapata, born in Peru to Colombian parents, was a popular figure with many Latin American immigrants because of his work with the Colombian American Service Association, better known by the more ethnically neutral name CASA. Zapata founded the popular organization in 1994 and worked with it until 2005, as Colombians fled their violence-prone country and their numbers grew rapidly in Miami. CASA provides immigration, educational, and legal assistance to not only Colombians but recent immigrants from many countries.

Zapata said early in his career that part of the reason why he was running was to diversify the national origin of Miami's elected officials, but he soon stopped making that sort of statement and thanked Cuban voters. In his first bid for wider elected office, to the county commission in 2000, Zapata, former head of the county's zoning board in West Kendall, told a reporter that "when you talk about Hispanics, it's all dominated by one group."[74] He was easily defeated in that race, when he competed against a Cuban and another Colombian candidate diluted his support. Elected as a state representative two years later, Zapata was embraced symbolically by Cuban Republican legislators who changed their name from the "Cuban Caucus" to the "Miami-Dade Hispanic Caucus."[75] Zapata drew no formidable Cuban challengers after 2004. "I wasn't elected by the Colombians, I was elected by the Cubans," he said in 2007. "Physically, the Colombians are here, but their hearts and minds are still in Colombia."[76]

As a state legislator, Zapata pushed a symbolic agenda for his community, including the public dressing down of a Cuban mayor of Miami Beach who had equated Colombians to drug dealers. His legislative effectiveness on Colombian issues was mixed, however. He never received fellow Republicans' support for a signature proposal to grant in-state tuition to undocumented students, failing despite repeated attempts, but a resolution in favor of a Colombian free trade agreement passed the state house with help from Miami's Cuban legislators, including the speaker of the Florida house, now US senator Marco Rubio (R-FL). The resolution was only token, however, since trade agreements are a federal issue.[77]

Summarized in Table 5.3, we see that Cuban political incorporation is supported by community numbers, rate of naturalization, and favorable districting, diminishing the importance of immigrant community solidarity and ethnic electoral coalitions except in smaller municipalities with Anglo or black majorities. For Haitians, geographic concentration and pan-racial coalitions at the municipal level helped win offices in a few cities. Internal divisions based on class and homeland politics, as well as competition with African Americans in higher-level elections, obstruct incorporation. However, these challenges have been overcome under optimal conditions, and Haitians have incorporated with greater success than any other non-Cuban immigrant group.

Colombians' numbers, naturalization rate, and ability to form coalitions with Cubans helped them win a few offices, but geographic dispersion and internal political divisions have weakened incorporation. Nicaraguans are hurt by everything except their numbers. These structural and community characteristics explain Cuban domination of major offices and the triadic patchwork of municipal Cuban, African American, and

Anglo or Jewish officials that we see across Greater Miami's smaller governments. Without structural reforms such as more open paths to citizenship, local immigrant voting, or alternatives such as proportional representation, these variables foretell what immigrant groups, including newly arriving Venezuelans, must do to incorporate in multiethnic Miami. Numbers alone will not suffice.

Controlling the Agenda and Defining the Possible

Since the bracero guest worker program ended in 1964, the national debate on immigration reform has mostly been a cat-and-mouse game that partisan and economic interests renew cyclically before election periods, most recently by President Barack Obama before the 2012 election. Over the years, Cubans have benefited most from immigration law modifications by appealing to the federal government's Cold War strategic aims. In 1986, historic and wide-scale amnesty for undocumented entrants, visa overstayers, and agricultural workers under the Immigration Reform and Control Act was approved, leading to 2.7 million new permanent residents by 2001, 27 percent of whom were Mexican.[78] Congress granted Nicaraguans, Haitians, Salvadorans, and other asylum seekers sporadic reprieves when the political and economic stars aligned, such as the Nicaraguan Adjustment and Central American Relief Act of 1997. Local Miami politicians have played a role in these battles, leading the way to pass reforms based on anticommunism benefiting Cubans and Nicaraguans but still playing more ambiguous roles in the treatment of Haitians who came by sea. Ultimately, the success of their efforts has always been dependent upon wider US considerations.[79]

Political reform at the local level could support wider political incorporation in Miami's non-Cuban immigrant communities, but these reforms face powerful obstacles. The possibility of opening local voting rights to all residents of Miami, or seeking alternatives to geographically drawn electoral districts so that they better reflect the ethnic diversity of Greater Miami, must become part of the local public sphere in conditions that allow for full and honest consideration before a meaningful reform proposal stands a chance of reaching the arena of formal political decisionmaking. That, however, has not been the case. Instead, the only way that the estimated 650,000 foreign-born noncitizens residing in Miami as of 2011 can participate in formal politics is by becoming naturalized citizens.

We looked to coverage in the *Miami Herald* to empirically answer the questions of which issues surrounding immigrants and political participation reached the public agenda in Miami and under what conditions, as well as who were the parties considered to be legitimate interlocutors. While its circulation has declined in recent years, the *Miami Herald* remains the media outlet of reference for local politics. Local Miami politicians respond to the

Herald with leaks against rivals or outrage in response to negative coverage and pay close attention to candidate endorsements on its editorial page. In 1993, 1999, and 2007, the newspaper won Pulitzer Prizes for investigative coverage of local politics and government. Electronic news outlets—in Spanish, English, or Creole—reach portions of the fragmented media audience in Greater Miami, but none cover local politics as regularly or deeply as the *Herald,* nor do any of the county's diverse ethnic media outlets reach a cross-ethnic audience similar to the *Herald* in English. Many of our recipients said they read homeland papers on the Internet or sometimes *El Nuevo Herald* for news about politics at home or in Latin America, but referenced the *Miami Herald* as their source for local news if they read English.

Based on our review of the *Herald*'s news coverage and opinion pages, we argue that control over the agenda of public communication prolongs unequal access to the electoral arena in Miami by shutting down all but federal immigration reform as a route to political incorporation of Miami's large diverse immigrant communities. This power imbalance need not necessarily be the case. While representation based on ethnic group status is rarely heard of in the United States, many examples can be found of ethnic power sharing or consociational democratic arrangements in ethnically divided countries around the world, and the academic discussion on their features and advantages is vibrant. In some countries in Latin America and Europe, ethnic minorities and women are guaranteed representation in national ruling bodies. As for local voting by noncitizen residents, a number of US cities or school boards have enacted or have honestly debated local electoral rights for noncitizen residents in recent years, including Chicago, San Francisco, New York City, Washington, DC, and others. The argument in favor is that as city residents, taxpayers, and public service recipients, immigrants need to participate and have a voice in local government even if they are not political citizens of the country.[80]

In a review of the *Miami Herald* since 1982, we found that discussion of local alternatives such as proportional representation based on national origin or local voting rights for noncitizen Miamians are absent from the agenda. A search of all *Miami Herald* articles with the keywords *noncitizen* and *voting* between May 19, 1982, and June 17, 2011, using the NewsBank "Access World News" database, identified only twelve articles that in some way referred to the idea. A search for articles mentioning *proportional representation* or *proportional election* during the same twenty-nine-year span turned up only three mentions.[81] When one further considers how these issues are framed within the public communicative sphere—in other words, how they are defined by those with power to shape mediated communication—the use of definitional power becomes more obvious. Frames of media content reflect the underlying interpretation of reality that guides the selection and salience of certain information in a news story. Robert M.

Entman writes, "To frame is to select some aspects of a perceived reality and make them more salient in a communicating text, in such a way as to promote a particular problem definition, causal interpretation, moral evaluation, and/or treatment recommendation for the item described."[82]

Frames can be identified by close reading of sources, stock phrases, and keywords describing the issue of interest. In Miami's main source of public communication, proportional representation is defined as creating geographically based political districts that rely upon segregated residential settlement patterns to guarantee Anglo, African American, and Cuban representation. No discussion of other formulas for proportionality occurred. As for noncitizen voting, none of the stories frame local voting as a legitimate proposition for local electoral reform. Eight articles link noncitizen voting with voter fraud, never mentioning its legality or debates about its implementation in other cities. One suggests that noncitizens only need to become educated about the benefits of citizenship in order to become citizens and vote. Another argues against noncitizens serving in the military by saying that without their relatives being able to vote, politicians might use the military recklessly.

The remaining two articles provide an interesting contrast and identify questions about the modifying condition of class status. The first article is a column by staff writer Glenn Garvin, who lambasts a legislative proposal in Maine that would give local voting rights to noncitizens. Garvin writes, "In effect, they seek to abolish the concept of American citizenship—the US government would be turned into a matter of geographical whimsy, under the control of whoever happened to be physically present at a given moment." To Garvin, citizenship requires adoption of English and knowledge of (presumably the class, gender, and racially dominant version of) US history and political culture. "Immigrants, legal and otherwise, play an important role in the US economy. But if they're interested in voting, they need to learn the language, the history and the political culture—that is, they need to become citizens."[83]

The contrasting article is written by then political editor Tom Fiedler. Fiedler's story is about noncitizen donations to political campaigns and the effect in South Florida of proposed federal changes after foreigners' donations to President Bill Clinton's reelection campaign caused Republicans to claim a conflict of interest for the Democratic president. While noncitizen voting was never presented as legitimate in the *Herald*, political donations from wealthy noncitizens were supported in the article. The wealthy donors are referred to as "unintended victims" and the proposed reform in a subheadline as carrying a "message of exclusion." The patriarchs of a multimillionaire Cuban sugar family exiled in Palm Beach County, big donors to Republican candidates, were held up as the primary example. Voting is mentioned at the end of the story, when the writer neatly ties up the piece by saying the family's problems will soon be finished because the Cuban brothers have decided to nationalize after thirty-seven years in the United States. In the article, Fiedler directly quotes Al Cardenas Jr., the Cuban-born vice chairman of the Florida Republican Party: "What you're basically doing by passing that law is saying that more than a half-million people in this community will not have the right to participate [in politics] in the only way they can. Is that fair?"[84]

According to those with definitional power, to participate in politics in Miami, noncitizens must first become naturalized citizens. Otherwise, they are lawbreakers. However, the requirement of citizenship creates a difficult dilemma for noncitizen immigrants. To get citizenship, disenfranchised residents must convince officials elected by other constituencies to pass a reform that includes a path to citizenship for the 650,000 noncitizens estimated to be living in Miami in 2011.[85] They need the solidarity of the native-born and naturalized groups, which in Miami are mostly native whites, African Americans, and Cubans. This dilemma, as we have shown, is one only Haitians have been partially able to overcome using racial solidarity and moral shaming of politicians through contrasts with Cubans over three decades.

Who sets the agenda and frames the news about political power in Miami? Newsroom studies find that mainstream professional journalists in the United States typically interact with government officials and a small sector of established elites when deciding legitimate news topics and sources of information. While the most professional news organizations independently monitor government on issues that involve widely shared values, such as honesty in government, they share similar frames of reference and interpretations of society with the officials, experts, and established community advocates with which they interact regularly, especially in cities without wide diversity of opinion among elected officials.[86]

The *Herald* seems to follow general patterns in professional US journalism. Officials, ex-officials, and the advocates and experts who interact closely with officialdom set the agenda of public discussion. In our review of text-based content on the printed newspaper front page, local section front page, editorial page, and opinion page, on five dates selected in a composite week format, 37 percent of the people directly quoted and 47 percent of paraphrased sources were elected officials, government workers, party politicians, or candidates for office. In local section stories where local political events are usually placed, such individuals made up 69.5 percent of all directly quoted sources and 63 of all paraphrased sources.[87]

Conclusion: The Limits of Symbolic Representation

Scholars argue that representation has symbolic and substantive dimensions, and that both are important. Symbolic representation—simple political inclusion of a group through election of a group member to office—should not be underestimated, Mala Htun argues. "The presence in power of some members of a group confers status and dignity on all its members. Political presence changes the social meanings attached to certain ascriptive characteristics (gender, skin color, ethnic origin), particularly those that have been stigmatized or devalued in the past."[88] On the other hand, symbolic representation should not be overestimated. The substantive activity of representing goes beyond mere symbolic presence, ideally leading to policy outcomes that improve the situation and life chances of excluded or less powerful groups.

Christopher Warren and Dario Moreno note that symbolic representation of African Americans and Cubans has not changed the orientation of public policy in Miami-Dade County, which has one of the most economically divided populations in the United States.[89] The rise of a middle- and upper-class Cuban cohort to a dominant position in local politics did not significantly redirect economic resources on behalf of poorer neighborhoods. Class trumped other interests:

> In effect, the ethnic makeup of the political and business leadership of the community has changed dramatically, but the broader socioeconomic and political tone of local public policy has not. Thus, the proposition that minority empowerment might lead to a redirection in the flow of resources through local public policy programs, or that issues rooted in the conditions of poorer and working-class neighborhoods might achieve greater attention, has not yet received any significant validation in the Miami experience.[90]

Symbolic representation does not mean that all segments of a national-origin group will feel the benefits equally of the election of a coethnic. As Warren and Moreno suggest, class interests still predominate in Miami. Class, however, is just one of the statuses that structures significant political representation in multiethnic Miami. Class and other statuses interact to produce (and reproduce) an opportunity structure for immigrant success in Miami, an intersection of global, regional, and national forces. Most notably, political incorporation overlaps with and reinforces differences due to not only national origin but also race, class, and gender. In other words, axes of political power, economic power, national origin, gender, and race are overlaid. We see a glimmer of the overlay of class and political power in the articles favorably describing wealthy Cuban foreigners who contribute to presidential campaigns while other immigrant voters are labeled criminals. We saw another glimmer in the comparisons of support for more professional and lighter-skinned Cuban immigrant cohorts to later Afro-Cuban arrivals from Mariel, and especially the comparison of treatment of Cubans to treatment of Haitians. In combination, class, gender, race, and political incorporation form an opportunity structure for successful immigrant incorporation. We turn to those dimensions of multiethnic Miami's hierarchy in the next chapter.

Notes

1. Reed-Danahay and Brettell 2008.
2. We use *Cuban American* only to distinguish people of Cuban origin who were born in the United States from Cubans who were born in Cuba, not to refer to citizenship or self-expressed identity. Following local vernacular, we refer to the various generations as the *Cuban community*. We apply the same rule to other national groups discussed in this chapter.
3. Lukes 2005.
4. Dahl 1971.
5. Portes and Rumbaut 2006.
6. Parenti 1970, pp. 521; see also Gaventa 1982.
7. Gramsci 1992.
8. US Census Bureau 2011a.
9. The calculation for African Americans is an estimate. It was created by subtracting numbers of those identifying as being of Haitian or Jamaican ancestry from the African American and non-Hispanic Black category of the 2011 American Community Survey (US Census Bureau 2011b). The result leaves the following percentages for Miami-Dade County: non-Hispanic whites, 16 percent; African Americans, 10.9 percent; and Cubans, 35 percent
10. This phrase is translated as "people from good stock" or "well bred," usually referring latently to class status mixed with race.
11. Portes and Rumbaut 2006; Warren and Moreno 2003.
12. Browning, Marshall, and Tabb 2003; Wright Austin 2008.
13. Marschall and Ruhil 2007; Pelissero, Holian, and Tomaka 2000.
14. Stowers and Vogel 1994; Warren and Moreno 2003.
15. Except for congressional representatives who serve two-year terms, most of the local electoral posts were four-year terms elected in 2006. Cities included were the largest in the 2000 US Census, plus municipalities that incorporated between 2000 and 2010: City of Miami, Hialeah, Miami Gardens, North Miami, Miami Beach, Coral Gables, North Miami Beach, Homestead, Palmetto Bay, Aventura, Miami Lakes, Doral, and Hialeah Gardens (Miami-Dade County, Department of Planning and Zoning 2010).
16. A number of explanations of the data are necessary. First, the number of constituents is higher than the number of people in the county population because people are represented by more than one public official (e.g., a city commissioner, a school board member, and a congressional representative) and therefore are counted in more than one public official's constituency. Second, the percent of the total constituency represented by a group of ethnic politicians is the sum of all of the constituents represented by the ethnic group officials as a percentage of the sum of all constituencies considered in the sample. The weighted representation gap takes into account the size of the public offices held by an ethnic group while the unweighted representation gap measure only considered the number of officeholders, not the importance of the office. Third, constituencies were figured based on the 2000 census population for each city or district. The national average of 647,000 constituents was used for congressional districts.

17. Portes and Stepick 1993.

18. US Census Bureau 2011a.

19. The first Venezuelan mayor in Miami-Dade County, Caracas-born Luigi Boria, was elected to office in November 2010, after our sampling period. The city's Mexican commissioner, Tijuana-born Sandra Ruiz, left in 2010 for a failed bid to become a state representative, returning in 2012. Doral's population of Venezuelans has boomed in recent years.

20. Cited in Stepick 1992, p. 39.

21. This strategy was successful until 2012 when Cuban American Democrat Joe García was elected to represent District 26, which covers southwest Miami-Dade County and the Florida Keys.

22. Pedraza 1996.

23. Alberts 2005; Eckstein and Barberia 2002; Pedraza 1996; Stepick and Stepick 2009.

24. Pérez 1990, p. 93.

25. Moreno 1997; Moreno and Rae 1992.

26. García Bedolla 2009.

27. Cited in Portes and Stepick 1993, p. 161.

28. Rivero 2011.

29. C. Charles 2007; Grenier and Castro 1999; Nackerud et al. 1999; Stepick et al. 2003.

30. Alberts 2005.

31. Eckstein and Barberia 2002.

32. Alberts 2005.

33. Eckstein and Barberia 2002; see also García Bedolla 2009 and Moreno 1997.

34. Grenier 2006, p. 211.

35. Pérez 1990.

36. US Census Bureau 1990, 2000.

37. Moreno 1997.

38. Moreno and Rae 1992.

39. Pérez 1990.

40. See Portes and Stepick 1993 and Portes and Rumbaut 2006.

41. *Martinez v. Bush* 2003; Warren and Moreno 2003.

42. Marcelin 2005; Stepick 1992.

43. C. Charles 2007; Marcelin 2005; Stepick 1992.

44. Marcelin 2005.

45. Wasem 2007.

46. Wasem 2010.

47. US Census Bureau 2011c; US Census of 2000; and legal, permanent residency figures, as cited in Terrazas (2010).

48. Metellus et al. 2004; Rhodes 2001.

49. US Census Bureau 2011c, 2011d, and 2011e.

50. Wasem 2010.

51. Ibid.

52. Stepick 1992.

53. Wasem 2010.

54. Ibid.

55. Stepick 1992.

56. Terrazas 2010.

57. Ibid.

58. US Census Bureau 2011e, 2011f, and 2011g.
59. US Census Bureau 2011h.
60. Warren and Moreno 2003; Wright Austin 2008.
61. Teproff 2009.
62. Charles and Figueras Negrete 2006; Figueras Negrete and Charles 2006.
63. Charles and Figueras Negrete 2006.
64. Brannigan 2010a, 2010b; Brannigan and Haggman 2010; Haggman and Figueroa 2010; Monestime 2010.
65. Fiedler 1992.
66. Jamaicans in Florida naturalize at a similar rate to Cubans, and they have won multiple elected offices in nearby Broward County, but their overall numbers in Miami-Dade are much lower than in Broward. They cluster in north Miami-Dade but have not reached a critical mass as a voting bloc. A Jamaica-born councilwoman in tiny South Miami won two terms in the 2000s with the support of the African American and Bahamian communities there.
67. Wright Austin 2008.
68. Simon 2006; Stepick, Stepick, and Kretsedemas 2001.
69. The latest data available for a small city. US Census Bureau 2011i and 2011j.
70. This information is based on data from the 2011 American Community Survey five-year estimate (US Census Bureau 2011k). Because it is a small place, the data were not large enough to use the three-year estimates as we do for others.
71. Menendez 1995.
72. Cassola 2011a, 2011b.
73. Woods 2007.
74. Ross 2000.
75. Charles, Salazar, and Martinez 2002; J. Charles 2002.
76. Woods 2007.
77. Mazzei 2011.
78. Rytina 2002. See Chapter 3 for a detailed explanation on the stratification of legal statuses in multiethnic Miami, and Wasem (2007, 2010, 2011) for histories of immigration reform for Haitians, Cubans, and Central Americans. See Massey, Durand, and Malone (2002) on the "smoke and mirrors" deception guiding US-Mexican immigration policy.
79. Portes and Stepick 1993; Stepick 1992.
80. Bogaards 1998; Dominguez and Shifter 2003; Lijphart 1977; Renshon 2008.
81. *Martinez v. Bush* (2003, p. 11) and a review of all issue-relevant *Miami Herald* articles identified with the keywords *Miami-Dade County* and *proportional representation* or *proportional election* or with the keywords *proportional representation* or *proportional election* (May 19, 1982–June 17, 2011, NewsBank "Access World News" database).
82. Entman 1993, pp. 52–53.
83. Garvin 2009, p. 13A.
84. Fiedler 1997, p. 1A.
85. US Census Bureau 2011l.
86. Bennett 2007; Berkowitz and TerKeurst 1999; Reese, Grant, and Danielian 1994.
87. There were 141 directly quoted sources and ninety-two paraphrased sources coded. The dates coded were Wednesday, April 27; Thursday, May 5; Friday, May 13; Saturday, May 21; and Sunday, May 29, all in 2011. PDF files of the entire newspaper were downloaded. All text was coded, including stories, columns, letters

to the editor, editorials, editorial page blog excerpts, daily polls and quotes, and opinion articles. Picture captions and graphics were not coded. Only the portion of the items on the front page, local section front page, editorial page, and "op-ed" opinion page were coded.

88. Htun 2008, p. 73.
89. Warren and Moreno 2003.
90. Ibid., p. 302.

6

Race, Discrimination, and Ethnic Rivalries

Dark skin is worthless to many who come here from other countries. And people make judgments about you before you even open your mouth and they treat you in that way. . . . It comes to a point where enough is enough.
—Amanda, Puerto Rican migrant

Sometimes intolerance comes from ourselves. It's not the US against Latin America. It is Cuba against Colombia. We are all Latinos; we are all Hispanics. It is Cuba against Nicaragua. Nicaragua against Panama. So it is not just like, the gringo against the South American. It is not the black against the white. . . . If we ourselves cannot stand each other, how are we going to form a united group so that the rest of the world will respect us?
—Damian, Colombian immigrant

Racialization in global Miami is not just the triangular dynamic involving whites, blacks, and "Latins" as dominant accounts of the area have suggested.[1] As white and African American populations decline,[2] Cuban and non-Cuban immigrants, who are contributing to the diversification of the area's Latino and black populations, are taking up new positions in the system of racial and ethnic stratification in the city. Along with the influx of new immigrants come the racial meanings that they carry with them from their own countries of origin. The growing polarization between the rich and poor, the squeeze on the middle class, the growing segregation of immigrant Miami from the rest of the country, and the increase in xenophobic immigration policies that favor some groups over others, all have complicated processes of racialization in Miami, often resulting in fragmented communities and ethnic hostilities.

In this chapter, we seek to understand Miami's changing racial and ethnic landscape. We examine racial meanings brought from Latin America and the Caribbean and how they blend with US racial frames. We illustrate how the merging of racial understandings contours the ethnic and racial discourses that emerge in Miami. We also examine patterns of perceived discrimination and the ethnic rivalries that have taken shape in this global city. We pay particular attention to the roles of cultural racism and legal status in the racialization of groups that fall between white and black categories.

Racialization and Racial Meanings

Racialization occurs through the social construction and reconstruction of the definitions and meanings attached to a racial category. Racial formations take shape within particular social and historical contexts and are given meaning through interactions.[3] Contained within each racial category are expectations of behaviors attached to it, resulting in impressions, often stereotypes, that are adopted as societal ideologies. Racialization creates a system of oppression that gives rise to myths regarding the inferiority and superiority of particular racial groups.

When immigrants move to a new country, their previously understood conceptions of race fuse with new racial meanings to create new understandings of how race and racism operate at a societal level to shape individual experiences in the country of destination.[4] We begin with a brief examination of race in Latin America and the Caribbean to illustrate the interpretations of race that immigrants in our sample carry with them to the United States.[5]

Race in Latin America and the Caribbean

The defining racial characteristic of Latin America's population is *mestizaje*, defined as the mixing of Indian, Spanish, and African populations. Ideologically, it has been deployed as "proof" that Latin American societies are not racist given the assumption that racial distinctions are insignificant because of the high degree of intermixing and the resulting fluidity among categories.[6] This ideology, often used for nation-building purposes, neglects the reality of racial inequality in Latin American and Caribbean societies created by years of social, economic, and political exclusion of indigenous, black, and mixed-race populations.[7]

Mestizaje has resulted in complicated hierarchies in which whites are at the top and Indians and blacks are at the bottom. Peter Wade argues that mestizaje is in fact a "key mechanism for reiterating and recreating [*sic*] racial hierarchies in both public and intimate spheres."[8] The resulting continuum of racial gradations that mestizaje yields has been overlaid with conceptions of social class resulting in a broad spectrum of terms associated with mixed-race peoples that are positioned in between black and white. Thus, miscegenation has coexisted with racial hierarchies and social exclusion in regions south of the United States; however, Latin Americans' emphasis on class over race has long ignored these racial hierarchies.

Ideologically, mestizaje has fueled beliefs that Latin American race relations and racism are superficial based on phenotype and social class, vis-à-vis US racism that is considered more "real."[9] This ideology has prevailed, in spite of patterns of exclusion found in Latin American countries, or as Mark Q. Sawyer calls it, inclusionary discrimination (whereby ideologies of racial inclusion mask racial exclusion).[10] Erroneously equating mestizaje with the absence of racism travels with immigrants and is superimposed on the new local racial hierarchies that they encounter in the United States. Thus, conceptions of race among immigrants involve relational hierarchies that have become transnationalized.[11]

Three themes emerged from our interviews with immigrants regarding questions of race in their countries of origin, including (1) the denial of racism as a problem, (2) negative racial discourse masked as class ideologies, and (3) use of mestizaje to draw attention to the constructions of their countries as white.

Illustrating the denial of racism as a societal feature, one of our interviewees, Liliana, affirmed, "In Mexico, there is racism through social class, but not through skin color." As a professional, Liliana views social class as the dividing line in her country of origin. This ideology represents how many Latin Americans, particularly in the upper echelons, distance themselves from people with darker skin or indigenous features. Social class is used as a proxy for race, thereby maintaining colorblind discourses. When the issue of race and the experiences of racial minorities are addressed, they reveal contradictions and, sometimes as in the following case, a sense of paternalism: Discrimination in Colombia "is social," affirmed Fabio, who was an accountant in his country of origin. "We all coexist there, and 40 percent of the Colombian population is black. And they are '*los negritos Colombianos*' (the little Colombian blacks). And they are very much loved." In addition to infantilizing the Afro-Colombian population, the exaggerated perception of their presence in the population reveals paranoia of being overwhelmed by people perceived to be occupying a lower position in the country's social hierarchy.[12]

Regardless of national origin and in many different ways, our interviewees repeated different versions of Liliana and Fabio's views concerning race and class, often contradicting themselves as they talked in circles about race and social class. Altagracia, who was a salesperson in her family business in the Dominican Republic, first defined discrimination in her country in terms of the social class differences that existed: "There is no racism in terms of people of color, but there is racism in terms of social classes, because, in Santo Domingo, there are different social classes. In other words . . . there's the economic level of the poor, of the well-to-do middle class . . . and then there's the rich, so from the rich to the poor there is a lot of discrimination and racism." Only after she was specifically asked about skin color, did Altagracia explain the racial issues on the island, doing so not in terms of social class, but rather in terms of geographic propinquity with a black nation—Haiti. Altagracia contradicted herself and disassociated racism from the issue of social class altogether, focusing instead on how national origin determined racial status in the Dominican Republic.

Wendy Roth has called this approach to race in the Caribbean a "nationality schema" in which race is cognitively understood along the lines of national origin.[13] Once Altagracia acknowledged the presence of Haitians in the Dominican Republic, she conceded that the country was in fact a multiracial society composed of different ethnicities: "Sometimes, because we are neighbors of Haiti, and there are a lot of people who tend to be racist toward other people of color in Santo Domingo, not all of us are white and blonde with blue eyes; there are a lot of people of color here too." Thus, although, at first, Altagracia racialized classism, she then associated racism with nationality, indicating that racism was mainly an issue affecting Haitians in the Dominican Republic. Consciously or not, Altagracia conveyed a white conception of her country and projected blackness onto Haitians, whom she saw as "the other."

Even though Dominicans' racial roots, like Puerto Ricans', lie at the intersection of African, Spanish, and indigenous (Taíno) backgrounds combined through conquest and miscegenation, Dominican society, like other Latin American and Caribbean societies, ignores the legacy of blackness in contemporary patterns of identification, illustrating the hefty stigma that is deeply ingrained in the island's racial ideology. Instead, indigenous roots are thought to dilute black bloodlines.

This case does not necessarily apply in other parts of Latin America that have larger indigenous populations and where indigenous ancestry is heavily stigmatized. Ambiguous labels, such as *cholo*[14] in Peru, have negative racial connotations that also refer to indigenous phenotype and socioeconomic factors associated with these categories. Other racial markers may include indigenous languages and clothing.

In some countries, the acknowledgment of racial identities has been undermined through the creation of the label *campesino* (peasant), a generic term that emphasizes the poor and working-class roots of rural peoples.[15] For example, labels such as *guajiro* in Cuba and *jíbaro* in Puerto Rico are used pejoratively at times to insinuate peasant backgrounds implying not just low levels of education but a kind of cultural racism, suggesting ignorance and other deficits due to a lack of modernization within this segment of the population. Cultural racist discourse is a form of colorblind racism in which race is removed:

> Yet cultural racism is always related to the notion of naturalizing racism to the extent that a group's culture is reified in terms of some absolutizing notion of inferiority contrasted with the judging group's self-proclaimed superiority. Cultural racism is articulated in relation to poverty, labor market opportunities, or marginalization, but also cultural habits, moral attitudes, or behaviors. The problem with this is that the poverty or unemployment of minoritized people is construed as a predicament of habits or beliefs, that is, a cultural problem, implying cultural inferiority and naturalizing/fixing/essentializing culture.[16]

The elements of racial ideologies that relegate people with indigenous roots and low social class or education to inferiority can be seen in the following quote from Agustin, a Peruvian who distanced himself from his own country's indigenous roots. He talked about his embarrassment about the portrayal of all Peruvians as rural and indigenous in the newspaper, the *Miami Herald*: "When there is an election in Peru, the *Miami Herald* publishes a photo of our campesinos voting. And I say, 'Why do they sell that idea? Why don't they print a photo of a voting center in Lima, for example, of people who dress like us [middle-class Peruvians]?' Obviously the campesinos dress differently, the women in their *polleras* [indigenous skirt], the men chewing coca leaves. The caption says, 'Peruvians went to vote,' and that is not Peru either."

These examples illustrate that throughout Latin America, commonalities can be found in racial understandings, although the specifics of racialization vary from country to country. Although *indio* in the Dominican Republic is used to avoid classifying someone as black, the same term in countries with large indigenous populations is considered an insult. Sofía, a Peruvian immigrant who worked as a data coordinator, said, "Well, in my country, there is classism more than racism." She added, "You're either white, or you are cholo. Either you have the [prestigious] last name, or you are Mr. Nobody." In the Peruvian stratification system, indigenous and Afro-descendent populations continue to be marginalized and embody persistent social and economic inequalities in the region.

Rafael, a Cuban immigrant, first relied on differences in country of origin to discuss racism and why he thought it occurred in the United States but not in Cuba: "In Cuba everyone is Cuban. White, black, and everything, everyone is Cuban. There are more differences here [in the United States] because here you can find people who are white, and they are from different countries, and to a certain extent I have noticed it in the population since I arrived that there is a certain hierarchy that is no longer woven together by race, but by country of origin."

In the case of Cuban study participants, racial narratives were tinged with political party principles given that the official national ideology is that Cuba harbors no racism, and that, in efforts to support antiracist and anticolonial struggles, communism has redistributed resources to all groups alike.[17] However, "the view from the ground in Cuba," states Sawyer, "indicates that the race situation on the island nation is much more complex," made evident by the fact that blacks in Cuba have less education and income than whites.[18] In spite of this fact, our participants gave more importance to national identity ("we are all Cubans") than race, revealing contradicting descriptions of Cuban society. Rafael, in particular, utilized a nationality-based racial schema,[19] homogenizing the Cuban population through its ethnicization and acknowledging US hierarchies based on nationality. But as he continued, his discourse revealed how race became conflated with nationality (or world region) by focusing on those of indigenous descent: "There are persons who refer to Indians as those who come from Central America, and they call them Indians contemptuously. So then it does not matter if those people are totally Indianized."

Rafael's discussion of prejudice against Central Americans reverts back to the discourse of racialization as the category of "Indian" is often used as a derogatory term.[20] His shift to a racial discourse led him to reassess the case of race in Cuba: "In Cuba everyone has black friends and everything, but in Cuba too racism exists there, and I feel that the Cubans have transferred it here. It is a racism that is only between whites and blacks because there were no Indians there."

Thus, initially, Rafael did not see race in Cuba, conceptualizing racism as a system that relied on nationality and regional differences that created boundaries between US immigrant groups but not between island Cubans themselves. Once he began speaking about blacks and whites in Cuba, he revised his original statement that racism did not exist in Cuba. He acknowledged racism on the island and its social distancing functions—indicating that having black friends was acceptable but implying that intermarriage would not be. He believed that Cubans brought this ideology with them to the United States. In this country, however, he also saw a hierarchy of nationalities. This hierarchy could be rooted in Latin American styles of racialization (whereby national origin is used as a proxy for race). In this regard, Central Americans are singled out for their indigenousness, itself a racial construct that conjures up images of primitiveness and a lack of civility.[21] Alternatively, ethnicizing race could reflect the ethnic landscape that Rafael lives in whereby Latinos of different nationalities come into most contact with each other.

In sum, Latin American immigrants represent an embodiment of the legacies of colonization and the ensuing racial projects of their home societies. Racial projects, in which "human bodies and social structures are represented and organized," are linked to the ways in which societies are organized and ruled.[22] As we will demonstrate shortly, immigrants bear the brunt of each others' home countries' racial projects.

Confronting US Racial Structures and White Racial Framing

In contrast to Latin America and the Caribbean, race in the United States often has been understood as a black-white system in which other groups are typically considered in relation to their ethnic identities.[23] In his work on systemic racism and the "white racial frame," Joe Feagin argues that the dominant perspective guiding the interpretation of racial issues in the United States is one rooted in a centuries-old ideology that ascribes a "positive orientation to whites and whiteness and a negative orientation to those racial 'others' who are exploited and oppressed."[24] A collection of racial stereotypes, interpretations, images, emotions, and inclinations to discriminate, the white racial frame is hegemonic and embodies the structural foundation in which discrimination is embedded. At the individual level, "it both guides and rationalizes discriminatory behavior," thus reinforcing racial stratification.[25]

Latino/a immigrants in the United States have been racialized and incorporated into this white racial frame.[26] When they confront US racial structures, what might have been a hierarchy of race with three or four racial categories based on phenotype and other physical and social characteristics in the Caribbean or Latin America crashes into a two-tiered system in which divisions are based on white and black categories rooted in hypodescendence.[27] How do immigrants construct racial meanings when they enter different racial social systems[28]—in particular, the US system, in which the white racial frame is entrenched?

The immigrants in our study shared experiences that illustrate their insertion into the US white racial frame through migration. Monica discussed how her perceived social status changed with migration. A Dominican immigrant, she compared how she was perceived in the United States with how she was perceived in the Dominican Republic:

> I was used to being in a family in which the situation was that I was part of the upper class, and I was white and that is a Dominican thing. . . . So people [in the United States] are racist no matter what. If you are 15 percent black here, you are black, and over there if you are 15 percent white, then you are white. So I have been very influenced in that regard and here I am a person of color. And to me, I say of "color," but that did not mean anything to me. I saw it more in terms of people who had money and their situation, whether people knew the family, or how

known was one's family in the country. And we were very well known and with everyone and we had respect in my country and here I am a nobody. And so it has been strange. It has been difficult for me to feel like I am no longer important.

Monica felt that her racial and social statuses had declined in the United States. Considered a high-class white in Dominican society, in the United States, she was considered black, afforded little advantage by her previous social class background. Her elevated racial status in the Dominican Republic may have been due to her family name, and the resulting social capital that came from her networks. In their home countries, immigrants perceived room for those of lower classes to elevate their social status regardless of skin color. This idea was challenged once they faced perceptions of their race in the receiving country.[29] Monica struggled with the idea that she was no longer important and deserving of respect due to her newfound minority status.

Peggy Levitt and others similarly have found that immigrants perceive a drop in their status when confronted with US racial structures upon migration.[30] Their former self-understandings of whiteness, or of being members of the dominant group in their countries of origin, conflict with their US status as members of a racial minority group. This change shocks them and makes them more vulnerable to the stings of racism and discrimination.[31] A Colombian, Rosa María, described these sentiments in her interactions with her US landlord: "In the last building in which I lived, the manager was American, and he did not want us, the Hispanics who were living there. And my lawyer would say, 'And could not you report him?' Because you could really notice the persecution. . . . 'Why am I going to fight with that man?' Those of us who spoke Spanish, I would try to talk to him in English, and he would tell me, 'I do not want to talk to you. Talk to a secretary,' one who he had there. And he rejected various persons. I preferred to get out of there."

Even though Rosa María made efforts to communicate with her landlord in English, his disinterest in her concerns and his preference for his secretary to address her needs resulted in feelings of rejection and a perception of disrespect and anti-Hispanic bias. Rosa María's reaction led her to seek out a more ethnically concentrated area of Miami to live—Little Havana. Her experience and those that her friends and clients had shared with her resulted in a preference to stay within an ethnic neighborhood rather than move north, where she reasoned that she would likely have more encounters with white US residents and be vulnerable to increased racism: "I don't want to move to the north of this country because I don't want to feel that racism that is there against us, because I have clients and friends who have perceived this up there. Because of that I want to live here, in Little Havana."

Although moving to the United States marked their entry into the US racial social system, for some, immigrants found that living in Miami buffered this process. Yanira, a Puerto Rican, believed being Latina in Miami was easier than in the rest of the country. Yanira grew up in Puerto Rico and moved to Miami for the first time to attend college. She moved back and forth a couple of times, but by the late 1990s, she had moved to Texas for three years, only to return to Miami once again. Discussing her adjustment to Texas, she stated, "A Latino in Texas is not considered the same as a Latino in Miami; you have to prove yourself a lot. For example my kids talked with their hands a lot and that was considered a lack of respect. . . . One time they asked me where my dark skin came from. My . . . skin complexion is a bit dark, and [they asked] if I was Latina because it looked like my skin complexion was different. I mean I would hear comments like that. That was a bit, sometimes annoying, and later it made me laugh, but at the beginning it was a bit shocking."

Yanira indicated that her children stood out in Texas for their mannerisms, which she associated with Latino/Caribbean culture, implying that these cultural forms of expression did not racially mark her in Miami. Her observation regarding reactions to her complexion reveals that aspects of culture, and perhaps even her Spanish accent, relegated her to the bottom of the racial hierarchy, since her complexion appeared to be white. Moreover, the stigma of being Hispanic perhaps was greater in that particular part of Texas than in South Florida, where Hispanics tend to hold positions of power.

In short, confronting US racial structures can be shocking experiences for immigrants with various implications. In Rosa María's case, it fomented greater solidarity with other Spanish-speaking populations, seen in her desire to live in a part of Miami with the highest Latino density. We also saw this rather prevalent sentiment in Yanira; however, living in Greater Miami, demographically a Latino metropolis, exposed her to enough diversity that she did not feel like she or her children were part of a minority group.

Not all immigrants were insulated from white or Latino racism in Miami. Stephane, a Haitian immigrant, related the following story regarding his experience at a job site: "There was a job that I was doing for him [his boss], and after he called me a nigger." Black immigrants like Stephane find themselves in a precarious position upon migration to the United States, particularly if they are coming from societies in which they formed part of the majority group. In this case Stephane's ethnicity was irrelevant as he was seen for only what his skin color represented to his boss, who evidently still used racial epithets to refer to black individuals.

Research has shown how black immigrants try to distance themselves from black native groups by playing up their ethnicities with the hopes of deflecting racism.[32] Whether knowledge of Stephane's nationality would have changed the outcome of this interaction is unclear. In fact, as Alex Stepick and his colleagues illustrate, in certain social arenas where different groups might hold cultural power, ethnicity may be a stigmatized identity. They show that in the Miami context, being Haitian can have worse results than being mistaken for African American.[33] If we consider distantiation from blacks overall as a strategy of incorporation, it is a counterproductive one at best, for it fractures solidarity and ultimately reinforces segregation and marginalization given that it buys into the relegation of blackness to an inferior social position. In this regard, multiethnicity in Miami does not necessarily mean that all kinds of diversity are equally valued. The racial legacies of US slavery and Jim Crow laws have led to the historical positioning of Miami as similar to any other southern US city.[34]

Segregation and the Color Line in Miami

Whether immigrants arrived in Greater Miami or another part of the United States, they were still exposed to some degree to US white racial framing. The incorporation of Latinos into the city from 1950s to the 1970s followed a pattern of ethnic succession and segregation in which Latinos dispersed into white neighborhoods, and whites relocated to other areas of the city, contributing to the segregation of Latinos and the further isolation of other subgroups.[35] Thus, white neighborhoods shrank as Latinos and blacks took up their place, although Hispanics dispersed into white neighborhoods more than blacks, who moved into ones adjacent to historically black neighborhoods. Hispanic dispersion was due in large part to the greater economic well-being of the group—particularly Cuban families from the earliest migration waves that hailed from higher prerevolutionary class backgrounds. Additionally, blacks feared further violence in response to court-ordered desegregation of schools and the end of legally bounded neighborhoods.

By the 1980s, the pockets of white neighborhoods in the city were characterized by expensive housing that Hispanics and blacks could not afford (e.g., Miami Beach). These patterns continue today, as Figures 6.1, 6.2, and 6.3 show. The northeast and central part of the county just west of downtown grew from historic black districts. The central district was the only area where blacks could buy property when Miami was incorporated, but the district was later devastated when Interstate 95 was constructed through its heart. The northern section originated in segregated public housing built in the 1930s. Cubans initially settled around the black central city in what became Little Havana, as well as in blue-collar Hialeah, and then spread into predominantly white areas. Today only pockets of whiteness exist, many in municipalities that have incorporated in only the last thirty years, as an attempt to remove them politically from the diversifying

Figure 6.1 Residential Clustering of White Non-Hispanics in Miami, 2010

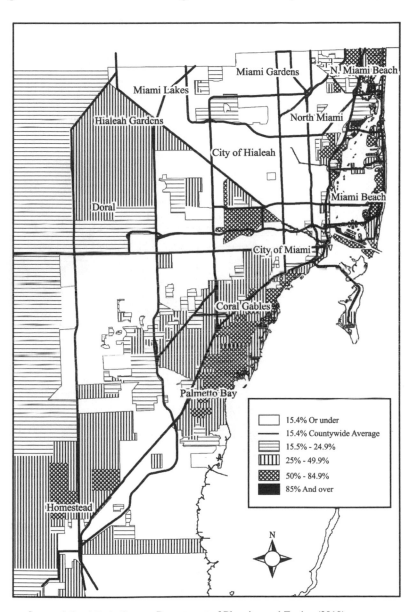

Source: Miami-Dade County, Department of Planning and Zoning (2010).

Figure 6.2 Residential Clustering of Black Non-Hispanics in Miami, 2010

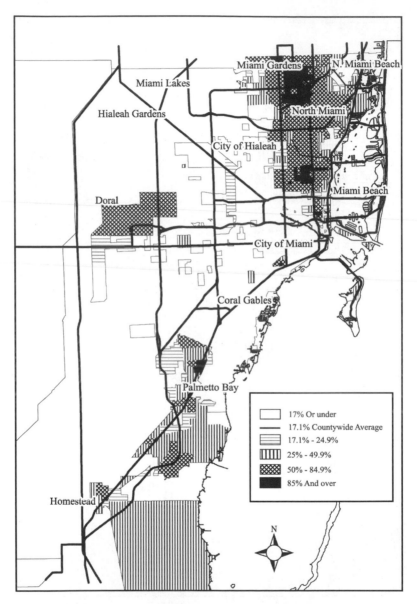

Source: Miami-Dade County, Department of Planning and Zoning (2010).

Figure 6.3 Residential Clustering of Hispanics in Miami, 2010

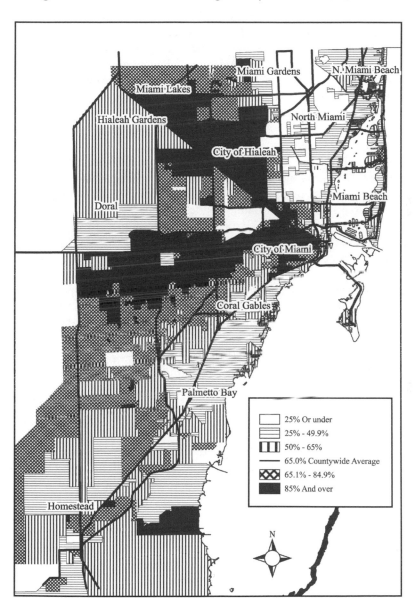

Legend:
- 25% Or under
- 25% - 49.9%
- 50% - 65%
- 65.0% Countywide Average
- 65.1% - 84.9%
- 85% And over

Source: Miami-Dade County, Department of Planning and Zoning (2010).

county. These maps show that Miami as of 2010 was a Hispanic metropolis, with pockets of whiteness and blackness, but where in the majority of the territory, Hispanics predominated.[36]

Contrary to other southern cities, in which blacks became empowered by the civil rights movement, the confluence of the Cuban Revolution and the civil rights movement "moved Miami onto an alternative path in race relations."[37] As we have shown, Miami's Cuban community is the predominant group politically in the city, surpassing native-born white Americans and African Americans; therefore, they have, to a large extent, thwarted the traditional white-black binary.[38] Although Cubans, particularly those who came before the 1980s, have been able to cross the color line historically entrenched in Miami, post-1980 arrivals and other Latinos have encountered more difficulties integrating, and Haitians, as a group, have only moderate success in crossing the city's racial divide.[39] The reasons for this difference in success, though, go beyond the hybrid set of ideologies based upon how race is treated in Latin America and the Caribbean and US racial constructions. A product of a racial social system,[40] the placement of Haitians in particular at the bottom of Miami's social hierarchy and the increasing status of long-established Cubans are outcomes of state racial projects that emerge in the form of immigration policies. Thus, Latin American forms of racialization, coupled with US immigration laws as state racial projects, result in racial formations conflating nationality, race, and, as we will show, legal status. These racial formations work in combination to construct minority subjects and place them in a hierarchy that encapsulates the legacy of segregation and modern-day forms of racialization through color-blind strategies that have resulted in emerging variations of the traditional color line.

Emerging Color Lines

In light of the historic US black-white color line, scholars have asked, where do the various Latino and Asian subgroups, both immigrants and US born, fall along this line? Moreover, what are the implications of their particular placements? One approach is that whiteness will expand to include nonblack groups leading to a bimodal racial structure in which the divide will be between black and non-black populations. From this perspective, race is viewed as declining in importance for mostly non-black groups, leading to largely optional or symbolic ethnic and racial identities for Asians, some Latinos, and Native Americans.[41]

Others have illustrated how "in-between" groups, such as Latinos, see themselves as a separate group from whites and blacks.[42] Recently, scholars have found that integrated Latinos are more likely to remove themselves entirely from the racial categorization system while lighter-skinned Latinos identify with whiteness in spite of some discrimination. Their darker-skinned counterparts are more likely to experience discrimination (e.g., in income) and show lower levels of education. This body of research suggests that the boundaries surrounding some Latino immigrants, mainly those with darker skin and those opting out of the racial system, remain.[43]

Another perspective is found in the work of Eduardo Bonilla-Silva and colleagues, who argue that the United States is coming to resemble a pigmentocracy that mimics race relations in Latin America.[44] Rather than a bimodal racial structure, a triracial stratification system has emerged in which class has the potential to racialize groups. This shift has led to the transformation of the white-black divide into a series of groups in which each ethnic subgroup can be placed in one of the following categories: whites, honorary whites, and the collective black group.[45]

We address these debates in this section; however, we argue that several other factors should be considered when formulating these debates in the context of South Florida: place, policies, and power. As discussed previously, the demography of an area (place) shapes the contours of the ethnic and racial boundaries between groups, but which groups have power is also of consequence.[46] Even in cities with high immigrant concentrations and where various ethnic groups hold or share political power, racism has been institutionalized by larger structural entities. Although Latinos and Haitians can create spaces of belonging in Miami more easily than they report they can in other areas of the country (see Chapter 8), the paradox we identify is that Miami immigrants are still subject to US racial projects at many levels, particularly regarding US domestic and foreign policies.

As part of the US racial social system, black immigrants from poor countries are disfavored groups in immigration policy and among the general public. As Mae M. Ngai states, "law not only reflects society but constitutes it as well . . . [and] law normalizes and naturalizes social relations and helps to 'structure the most routine practices of social life.'"[47] Whiteness is entrenched in US racial projects that affect immigrants in Miami and support the white racial frame, reinforcing institutional racism. Although in Chapter 3 we discussed the construction of illegality as a racial project of the state, and in Chapter 5 we contrasted Cubans' and Haitians' political modes of incorporation, here we identify the immigration policies that have produced a Cuban-Haitian divide in the community as another outcome of US racial projects. This divide has crisscrossed the white-black divide that lays at the foundation of Miami's development and that still permeates relations among native white and black Miamians.[48] It also frames the nature of ethnic rivalries and discrimination that immigrants in Miami perceive.

The Cuban-Haitian divide is a racial formation in which the status of "honorary white" has been given to wealthy, long-established Cubans who fled communism through policies that aided their migrations and incorporation processes. Although some of these immigrant policies have been scaled back over the years, entry policies still favor Cubans by letting them remain in the United States if they reach dry land, yet this status has not been afforded to Haitians, who have among the lowest rates of being granted asylum and for whom policies reinforce their feelings of exclusion from the US nation-state.[49] Even if these policies are not intended to be racist, they are identified as such by immigrants because they are racial in their consequences. From a structural approach to race relations, regardless of intent, these policies reinforce the contemporary racial order in which Haitians face disadvantages that Cubans as a group do not.

Positioning on the Color Line Through US Racial Projects

On October 29, 2002, about 200 Haitian migrants jumped from a freighter after it ran aground off of Key Biscayne. The migrants swam ashore, reaching the Rickenbacker Causeway connecting Key Biscayne to Miami, and tried to persuade motorists to help them evade capture by the Border Patrol. Among the Haitian migrants were five pregnant women and ten unaccompanied minors. Once the bridge was closed and the Haitians were rounded up, they were taken to an immigration detention center for deportation hearings.[50]

When Representative Carrie P. Meek (D-FL) was asked about this incident, she indicated that the policy "reflected racial discrimination against Haitians, most of whom were black."[51] However, quoting the State Department and the US Coast Guard, an immigration service court brief stated that the rationale behind holding Haitian asylum seekers in detention was that releasing them would "encourage more Haitians to come and could prompt terrorists to try to enter the United States from Haiti."[52] These concerns do not appear, however, in regard to the "wet foot, dry foot" policy applied toward Cubans, in which they are allowed to stay in the country if they reach dry land and are released to the community within hours of their apprehension.[53] This double standard of treatment has divided South Florida's immigrant community, and many, such as Haitian Emmanuel, perceived race to be at its core:

> The main thing I find difficult here is the immigration system. . . .
> There are a lot of people who would have left Haiti already
> because of repression . . . for political reasons. There are people
> that if they return they will kill them. Now, when that person
> comes here, immigration, the laws that they apply to other
> nationalities, it's not applicable to Haitians. . . . [They] are still
> deporting the Haitian right now, which is totally wrong. That's
> the worst that I see right now in this world. That shows how the

Haitian is a bunch, like I say they treat the Haitian like garbage.
. . . [T]hat [immigration] is the thing that is the most racist. . . .
[T]his shows you according to history, this color has no
importance.

Like many in the immigrant and advocacy communities, Emmanuel
compared the government's treatment of other groups in similar situations as
Haitians, revealing discrepancies. He mentioned the impact of one of the recent hurricanes to hit Haiti and the fact that the US government did not extend temporary protective status to Haitians in the United States, while such
status was extended to Central Americans fleeing the devastation caused by
Hurricane Mitch in the late 1990s.[54] A similar situation unfolded when the
US government refused to grant temporary protective status to Haitians who
were fleeing the devastation caused by Hurricanes Fay, Gustav, Hanna, and
Ike in September of 2008.[55] Not until an earthquake hit Haiti in 2010 did the
US government grant temporary protective status to Haitians already in the
United States. This status for Haitians meeting the government's criteria was
in place until January 2012, and extended into 2014.[56]

Our Haitian informants were acutely aware of the differences in how
US policies treated immigrants: "They treat the Cuban better than us, the
Haitians. Because when they are giving the Cubans residency, they do not
give the Haitian residency," said Stephane. Emmanuel argued that the
right to remain legally in the United States was a human right that
Haitians were being deprived of, which resulted in perceptions of Haitian
dehumanization:

I mean all the rules that apply to like, not everybody, to human
beings, it seems like Haitians are not human beings. I don't know,
what kind of beings are we? . . . So what applies to other people
does not apply to us. And I feel like that is totally wrong by
immigration. . . . How you gonna show favor for this Cuban man
and not show favor for the Haitian? You tell the Cuban as long as
he touch land he safe, like a game of baseball. . . . The Haitian
man, he come in, he touch the land . . . he touch the land so hard
that he somewhere living . . . got his own business, and he still
got problem with that person. . . . I feel like the biggest racism
that [is] right now in America is dealing with immigration. . . . I
would like to ask the chiefs of immigration what beef they got
with my country, with the Haitian people, because this is
something that makes me very sick.

Emmanuel viewed immigration policy as a game in which, even in situations where Haitians established their own businesses and contributed to

the community's vitality, their lack of legal status meant they could be whimsically ejected from the game. Fredeline, also Haitian, believed this system unfairly favored Spanish-speaking countries: "They do not care for Haiti. I don't think they like Haiti. If it were a Spanish country . . . like, when you look in the laws that are here if a Cuban reaches here and their feet [touch] the soil, they can stay; if it is a Haitian they have to go. You know, that is not fair. . . . How is it that one can and the other can't?"

These policy inconsistencies shape the boundaries separating the various racial and ethnic groups in South Florida and frame the dynamics between immigrant communities, fracturing potential alliances that might otherwise be formed, and maintaining the present racial order by pitting groups against each other. These community dynamics seep into the realm of interpersonal relations among immigrants. The results are racial tensions and ethnic rivalries that fragment immigrant solidarity and reinforce patterns of white-on-black discrimination that also frame intra-Latino racism. As we will demonstrate, we find the most support for Bonilla-Silva's triracial stratification thesis in that skin color and class shape placement in the groups he proposes. We add, though, that institutional racism embodied in government policies that have been influenced by the white racial frame and represent racial projects of the state dictate the template according to which racial hierarchies in Miami develop. In what remains of this chapter, we discuss the patterns of perceived discrimination that our data revealed and the nature of the ethnic rivalries that have played out "on the ground."

Ethnic and Racial Discrimination in Miami

How does race complicate Latin American and Caribbean immigrants' patterns of living in Miami? How are they perceived and treated by others? What are some of the implications of this treatment? We examine immigrants' experiences with discrimination in Miami by first analyzing data from the quantitative sample of our project. In this survey, immigrants were asked about various dimensions of perceived racism and discrimination. The first of these variables is *perceived racial discrimination*, which measures whether immigrants attribute their perceptions of discrimination specifically to their race.[57]

Model 1 of Table 6.1 compares how immigrants of the various countries and regions of origin perceive and experience racial discrimination in comparison to Cubans.[58] Findings reveal that members of non-Spanish Caribbean countries and Haitians perceive more discrimination due to race. Immigrants from the Spanish Caribbean, Mexico, and Central America also reported marginally greater racial discrimination than Cubans. When control variables are accounted for (see Model 2), Haitians and non-Spanish

Table 6.1 Perceived Racial Discrimination by Country/Region of Origin (OLS regression)

	Model 1			Model 2		
	Estimate	SE		Estimate	SE	
Country/region of origin						
Cuba[a]						
Haiti	0.54	0.09	***	0.47	0.1	***
Colombia	—	—		—	—	
Non-Spanish Caribbean	0.57	0.08	***	0.5	0.09	***
Spanish Caribbean	0.15	0.08	†	—	—	
North and Central America	0.13	0.07	†	—	—	
South America	—	—		—	—	
Other non-Hispanic	—	—		—	—	
Control variables						
Female				—	—	
Age				—	—	
Married				—	—	
Years in the United States				—	—	
Years of education				—	—	
Citizen				—	—	
Perceived English fluency						
Does not speak English well/at all				—	—	
Speaks English well				—	—	
Speaks English very well[a]						
Yearly income (US$)						
Less than 19,999				—	—	
20,000–39,999				0.15	0.09	†
40,000–59,999				0.19	0.09	*
60,000–79,999				0.37	0.13	**
80,000 + [a]						
Intercept	1.26	0.04	***	1.34	0.17	***

Source: ITMI Quantitative Survey.
Notes: a. Reference group.
Predictors lacking any significant effect are excluded from the table, even though they were included in the models.
† = p ≤ 0.10; * = p ≤ 0.05; ** = p ≤ 0.010; *** = p ≤ 0.001.

Caribbean immigrants still report significantly more racial discrimination, suggesting that some of the differences in perceived discrimination among the other groups are explained away by other factors incorporated into the model. More specifically, we observe that income is the main factor in reducing the differences in perceptions of racial discrimination for these other groups. Compared to those in the highest income bracket ($80,000 or more), individuals who make between $20,000 and $80,000 per year perceive more discrimination due to race, though no difference can be found in perceptions of discrimination between those at the highest and at the lowest income levels (less than $20,000). This trend can be partially explained by drawing from Philip Kasinitz and colleagues' study on second-generation immigrants.[59] As their social statuses increased and placed them in positions in which they came into greater contact with whites, so did their reports of discrimination. This same process may be at work in the case of Miami immigrants as well, in that those who are in working- or middle-class jobs, and who may encounter more diverse, integrated workplaces, may be more likely to be in situations where they perceive they are discriminated against based on their race.[60]

We also consider another dimension of discrimination—a compound measure of perceived everyday discrimination that combines answers from seven related questions that have to do with immigrants' perceptions of their social interactions with others.[61] Table 6.2 presents the results of the factors related to everyday perceived discrimination. Model 1 reveals that, in comparison to Cubans, all other groups perceive more discrimination in their everyday encounters. When controls are added (see Model 2), differences by country/region of origin remain significant and several factors also emerge as important predictors of perceived everyday discrimination. In other words, while the control measures considered are related to differences in perceived discrimination, they are not sufficient to account for differences between immigrants of different origins and Cuban respondents.

According to Model 2 in Table 6.2, women and older immigrants perceive significantly less everyday discrimination. The longer an immigrant has been in the United States and the greater his or her linguistic abilities in English, the more likely he or she is to report everyday discrimination. Finally, those whose earnings place them in the second-highest income bracket (making between $60,000 and $80,000) report greater everyday discrimination than those at the very top. These last two findings suggest similar results as the analysis of perceived *racial* discrimination (see Table 6.1). As immigrants come to occupy middle-income jobs, they may be more likely to encounter greater diversity in the workplace and perhaps more likely to feel discriminated against.

As we have seen, Miami's context for race relations combines racial ideologies from many countries, including the United States, into a framework in which whites and long-established Cubans are the dominant groups, blacks (e.g., Haitians and Jamaicans) are at the bottom of the hierarchy, and other Latinos as well as more recent Cuban immigrants are in the middle. The results regarding perceived racial discrimination support the prevalence of much of this hierarchy (although only the qualitative data speak to the status of recent Cuban arrivals), with the added condition that as income levels grow (up to a certain extent), so do perceptions of racial discrimination. But with regards to everyday discrimination, while the previous patterns largely hold true, an interesting change is that the non-Hispanic immigrants, who are mostly from European, African, Asian, and Middle Eastern countries, also reported significant levels of everyday discrimination. Possibly, the Cuban and Latino cultures that are prevalent in the city cause everyday

Table 6.2 Perceived Everyday Discrimination by Country/Region of Origin (OLS regression)

	Model 1			Model 2		
	Estimate	SE		Estimate	SE	
Country/region of origin						
Cuba[a]						
Haiti	0.84	0.13	***	0.7	0.12	***
Colombia	0.42	0.11	***	0.35	0.12	**
Non-Spanish Caribbean	0.59	0.1	***	0.58	0.12	***
Spanish Caribbean	0.32	0.1	**	0.23	0.11	*
North and Central America	0.32	0.09	***	0.25	0.09	**
South America	0.36	0.09	***	0.3	0.1	**
Other non-Hispanic	0.49	0.12	***	0.45	0.13	***
Control variables						
Female				−0.18	0.06	***
Age				−0.01	0.002	***
Married				—	—	
Years in the United States				0.007	0.003	*
Years of education				—	—	
Citizen				—	—	
Perceived English fluency						
Does not speak English well/at all				—	—	
Speaks English well				0.15	0.08	*
Speaks English very well[a]						
Yearly income (US$)						
Less than 20,000				—	—	
20,000–39,999				—	—	
40,000–59,999				—	—	
60,000–79,999				0.32	0.15	*
80,000 + [a]						
Intercept	−0.3	0.05	***	−0.007	0.22	

Source: HMI Quantitative Survey.
Notes: a. Reference group.
Predictors lacking any significant effect are excluded from the table, even though they were included in the models.
† = p ≤ 0.10; * = p < 0.05; ** = p ≤ 0.010; *** = p ≤ 0.001.

interactions between non-Hispanic and non-Caribbean immigrants to be strained when groups intermingle. Although our qualitative data support and add nuance to how racial hierarchies are socially constructed in the city and the nature of interpersonal interactions within this context, they do not provide additional information on the case of non-Hispanic or non-Caribbean immigrants, aside from what the quantitative data reveal.

Last, we also examine determinants of perceived employment discrimination based on one's immigrant status.[62] Table 6.3 presents the results.[63] According to Model 1, Haitians, Mexicans, Central Americans, non-Spanish Caribbeans and South Americans (excluding Colombians) are more likely than Cubans to report experiencing discrimination based on immigrant status. However, Model 2 shows that when controls are added, no significant

Table 6.3 Perceived Employment Discrimination by Country/Region of Origin (OLS regression)

	Model 1			Model 2		
	Estimate	SE		Estimate	SE	
Country/region of origin						
Cuba[a]						
Haiti	0.29	0.09	***	—	—	
Colombia	—	—		—	—	
Non-Spanish Caribbean	0.15	0.08	†	—	—	
Spanish Caribbean	—	—		—	—	
North and Central America	0.17	0.07	*	—	—	
South America	0.11	0.08	†	—	—	
Other non-Hispanic	—	—		—	—	
Control variables						
Female				—	—	
Age				−0.004	0.001	**
Married				—	—	
Years in the United States				—	—	
Years of education				—	—	
Citizen				−0.13	0.06	*
Perceived English fluency						
Does not speak English well/at all				—	—	
Speaks English well				0.13	0.07	†
Speaks English very well[a]						
Receiving differential treatment because of phenotype is						
No problem[a]						
A small problem				0.29	0.06	***
Somewhat of a problem				0.39	0.08	***
A major problem				0.88	0.11	***
Yearly income (US$)						
Less than 20,000				—	—	
20,000–39,999				—	—	
40,000–59,999				−0.24	0.1	**
60,000–79,999				−0.22	0.13	†
80,000 + [a]						
Intercept	1.3	0.03	***	1.46	0.17	***

Source: ITMI Quantitative Survey.

Notes: a. Reference group.

Predictors lacking any significant effect are excluded from the table, even though they were included in the models.

† = p ≤ 0.10; * = p ≤ 0.05; ** = p ≤ 0.010; *** = p ≤ 0.001.

differences can be found by country or region of origin, though other measures appear important in predicting reports on perceived employment discrimination. For example, older immigrants report perceived discrimination happens less frequently than their younger counterparts. In addition, immigrants with US citizenship reported less discrimination. Compared to those who speak English very well, speaking it only "well" increased reports of perceived employment discrimination based on immigrant status. Interestingly, not speaking English well or not speaking it at all did not seem to be different in reports on discrimination compared to those who speak English very well, suggesting that perhaps those who do not speak English may be employed in the ethnic economy.

Compared to those who reported racism was no problem, those who reported it was either a small, moderate, or major problem also reported experiencing more employment discrimination based of immigrant status. Finally, compared to those with the highest income, those who made between $40,000 and $80,000 perceived less discrimination based on immigrant status. Interestingly, no difference could be found in perceptions of discrimination between those in the lowest and highest income brackets. This former finding may speak to markers of foreignness cast on those who are most successful as they come to interact with whites or natives, thereby increasing the likelihood of discrimination in employment. Thus, when examining discrimination based on immigrant status, once control measures are accounted for, age, citizenship, language (more specifically, knowing English but not having perfect command of it), being in a high-paying occupation, and perceptions of racism seem to increase the risk of discrimination. In the sections that follow, we explore patterns of perceived discrimination reported from the qualitative sample and the ethnic rivalries emerging from these experiences to illustrate the contours of Miami's socioracial hierarchy. While the quantitative data show widespread discrimination, discerning the source of discrimination is important for understanding the nature of its impact on immigrants' lives.[64] We employ findings from our qualitative interviews and focus groups to elaborate on these findings.

Discrimination from Whites

Many of the experiences of immigrants with the US white racial frame occurred in parts of the country outside of Greater Miami, a subject that will be discussed further in Chapter 8. This fact does not mean, however, that they did not encounter white racism in the city. For example, Angela, a Mexican, discussed the discrimination that she and her husband faced when they tried to rent an apartment in Miami. She explained her perceptions of why this happened: "On one occasion we were looking for an apartment and we were discriminated against because they told my husband, it was an American who said he had no places, that there were no available apartments. And then we realized that he did have some but that they saw our status as immigrants and so they turned us down. So they think that you come here, I don't know what kind of ideas they have that you're not going to pay them rent or that we want to live off of the government . . . when you are a hardworking person who comes here to work and to get ahead."

Angela attributed the difficulties in renting an apartment to bias due to the perception that Mexican immigrants come to the United States to live off of the government, and the assumption that they would not be financially capable of paying the rent. The stereotype of the immigrant that needs to subsist by depending on government services reinforces notions of inferiority and assumptions that they cannot make it on their own because they are lacking in character, work ethic, or some other positive individual attribute. The stereotype fuels anti-Mexican prejudice and also reifies their liminal status, which is by itself the cause of many of the blocked opportunities for integration Mexicans and other immigrants face. This kind of discrimination combined with the labor demand in the niches of agriculture and horticultural nurseries in the southern part of the county may be among the reasons why Mexicans have mostly settled in Homestead, where many of these jobs are located.[65]

Although others in our sample discussed experiences with white racism, widespread consensus existed among the respondents in our qualitative sample that Hispanics discriminated against other Hispanics in Miami. Irene, a Colombian, stated, "I think there is racism, and not so much on behalf of the Americans, but on behalf of Latinos themselves." Fernando, a Mexican, also stated that Latinos discriminated against blacks: "I have come to experience this racism but not from Americans toward Latin Americans, but from Latin Americans towards, for example, blacks (immigrants and nonimmigrants). And it is very curious, no? Because Latinos always complain about racism, but certainly Latinos perhaps have not engaged in the exercise of reflecting on how racist we are."

Upon closer examination, the data reveal that when Latinos talked about discrimination on behalf of other Latinos, they often meant that Cubans discriminated against them. As our quantitative data illustrate, Cubans were less likely to perceive varying types of discrimination. Our qualitative data generally support this trend and suggest that some Latinos felt that Cubans have reproduced patterns of white racism and discrimination toward other immigrant groups, including more recently arrived co-ethnics.

Cuban Privilege, Intraethnic Animosity, and Discrimination

Cubans appear to be the most privileged immigrant group in Miami, although important to keep in mind is that not all Cubans are equally privileged—some Cuban immigrants, particularly recent arrivals, experienced social disadvantages akin to other nationalities at an interpersonal level. Our data illustrate that, overall, immigrants perceived discrimination from Cubans in both public spaces and other institutional settings, and they felt that a hierarchy of nations represented a locally constructed ethno/racial queue. This queue was contoured by transnational racial formations and US racial projects resulting in the emergence of Cubans as "honorary whites." Ramona, a Dominican immigrant, was very specific to label this discrimination "Cubanismo." She described Cubanismo as a pattern whereby Cubans were favored by US social policies and were in positions of power as "owners" of the city: "What we have here is like Cubanism [laughter]. That's where you see the difference . . . [and] you notice the difference in how, for example . . . mostly immigration, how they treat Cubans, and how they treat those of us who come from other countries is very different. . . . Also in politics, everything Cuban . . . those who have the best positions in the . . . city, most of them are Cubans. Here [laughter] we would all say that this all belongs to Cubans and we arrived [to what is theirs]."

Ramona believed that Cubanismo reflects the privileging of Cubans over other groups, from national policies favoring Cubans to Cuban domination of local politics, and she used laughter to diffuse her biases. Possibly, much of the anti-Cuban rhetoric that some immigrants exhibited stemmed from resentment felt toward the privileged position that US racial projects afforded Cubans.

Because Cubans were viewed as the dominant group in South Florida, any kind of unfair treatment involving members of this group appeared to be viewed as discrimination. Thus, the discourse of Hispanic-on-Hispanic discrimination often translated into Cuban-on-non-Cuban discrimination, although sometimes, it involved Cubans against more recently arrived co-ethnics. Odalys, a Cuban herself, explained how Latinos were biased against other Latinos, although she did not agree with this prejudice: "Sometimes we, Latinos, sometimes establish differences among one another. For example, these are things that we talk about. Many of the Latino groups, some of the Latinos from other nationalities, Cubans do not like them much. They have their reasons. Maybe they have them, maybe not. Everyone is not the same, but they sometimes tend to generalize, and when one, any one of us, generalizes about another group of another nationality, you tend to make mistakes."

Odalys believed that generalizing led to stereotypes of other Latino groups. Others such as Emilia, from Peru, perceived social distance between Cubans and immigrants like herself: "You might not notice so much, but I have noticed that there are certain differences among Latinos themselves. There are many differences, let's say, between Cubans, who are a portion of the population who consider themselves different. That's how I see them, that they consider themselves different from the rest of immigrants. . . . I've conversed on two or three occasions with Cubans and I have noticed that they feel superior."

Recent Cuban immigrants felt discriminated against by established Cubans too. They felt like established Cubans judged them as inferior due to their class backgrounds, as economic migrants, not exiles, and as originating from a lesser "stock." Odalys shared that she had experienced this bias:

> Sometimes the Cuban community that arrived at the beginning of the revolution, sometimes they make a series of allusions regarding the persons [like me] who have arrived later. Sometimes some of them even attack us saying that we have come to this country because of economic problems, that we have no principles of any kind and I, I do not like to generalize, but I do not think that this is right. . . . Because in reality, there is something that they say in political economy, they say that politics is a concentrated expression of the economy, and if the economy is upside down, politics will be bad and if you leave because of an economic problem, it is obviously a political problem because the government does not work.

Odalys made reference to the ways in which older Cubans perceived recent arrivals as having bought into the communist ideology. The assumption was that they did not migrate earlier because they accepted communism as a way of life, therefore rejecting the values of Western capitalism and what the Golden Exiles stood for. Odalys tried to explain the interconnectedness of Cuba's economic and political arenas and argued that she obviously migrated for political reasons, since both the economic and political were interwoven. Like the immigrants discussed in Chapter 2, Odalys comingled political and economic factors when explaining her departure from Cuba.

As a result of perceived Cuban ethnocentrism, or because of non-Cubans' own prejudicial attitudes, some non-Cubans in our sample held contempt for Cuban immigrants in general. For example, Liliana, a Mexican, wanted to relocate somewhere without so many Cuban immigrants. She explained the reasons why she wanted to move: "I have encountered many Cuban immigrants that, well, that, you cannot expect much from their attitudes, from their education, from their behavior. That, even though Miami is precious, but with those people it turns a bit ugly [laughter]."

This prejudice and backlash against Cubans may not just be a product of their immigration status or their political power. Liliana's discourse reveals a form of cultural racism in which she denigrates "those people" for their perceived lack of education and lack of cultural capital. She used laughter to soften the harshness of her words, perhaps because, at some level, she realized that she was stereotyping Cubans and might have felt the need to "save face." This kind of talk amounts to discourse resembling culture-of-poverty arguments of the past.[66]

Cubans were not unaware of these prejudices or the ethnic rivalries that existed in Miami. If anything, some Cubans, like Rocio, empathized with why other immigrants felt resentful of them, even if she did not condone it:

> Maybe the majority feels a bit jealous of Cubans. We have the possibility of arriving to this country with residency, a visa. And other people from other countries have to come in illegally, and it takes a lot of work to legalize their papers. And basically it is a bit . . . not envy but a discomfort that it is so much easier to enter this country and we have the doors a bit more open than them. And maybe in South Florida, in Miami . . . even though there are Latinos from all over the world, the majority are Cuban. It is like they feel we may dominate more, and that makes them feel less. But basically I feel that it is that. . . . [I think] that most people have a negative vision of Cubans and I think we are heavily criticized.

Rocio understood the difficulties that non-Cubans faced when trying to legalize their status or even come into the country. She also believed that the local power that Cubans had also caused others to view Cubans in a negative light. Rocio's ideas lend some support to the notion that, as racial projects of the state, immigration policies lay the foundation for ethnic rivalries to develop. Rodolfo, also Cuban, articulated the link between the double standards in immigration policies and the resentment among the various groups. He also implied that the local concentration of power in the Cuban community might be viewed by others as hoarding resources.[67] Rodolfo pointed out, "When a raft of Cubans gets here . . . they treat them with a certain exclusivity that for example, they do not treat a Haitian or a Dominican or a Salvadoran or a Mexican, and that starts creating resentment. . . . The other element is the power issue. Because of the information and the history of immigration to South Florida, they have led to Cubans having a certain political power in South Florida that allows other Cubans to benefit from that and that also creates resentment in the communities."

At this juncture, we must consider that patterns of residential and occupational segregation in the city are shaping ethnic rivalries, in that the immigrants who originated from the countries represented in our qualitative data seem to share proximity with Cubans rather than whites, perhaps leading to a greater likelihood that these specific ethnic rivalries would emerge. In fact, during one of our focus groups, as the participants engaged in a lively discussion of intra-Latino discrimination in Miami, the moderator interrupted with the statement, "You have not mentioned Anglos. . . . The question was, how do people get along? You have talked about other Hispanics. Do you not relate to them [Anglos]?" In response to this question, one of the participants, Duanys, a Colombian immigrant, answered, "Well, in general, here there is little opportunity to have contact with the gringos. Because in our particular case we live in an area that is Latino, we work in a Latino area, and so the contact that you might have with Americans might be at the post office or in government places but the rest, in reality we have limited opportunities [to come into contact]."

This segregation of life across various social arenas explains why discussions of racism centered mostly around white racism in other parts of the country or Cuban discrimination in Miami. Thus, US racial projects and patterns of segregation in Miami conditioned the ethnic rivalries that emerged. While much intraethnic hostility can be found among Latinos, so can widespread antiblack prejudice toward Afro-Latinos as well as black Caribbeans.

Black Disadvantage

The quantitative data in our study reveal that groups such as Haitians and other black immigrants from the non-Spanish Caribbean perceived various forms of discrimination to a larger extent than Cubans. Our qualitative data show that they also experience more discrimination than other non-Cuban Hispanics. This discrimination is indicative of the prevalence of antiblack prejudices in Miami, which Amanda, a black Puerto Rican, who was quoted at the beginning of this chapter, alluded to when she said that "dark skin is worthless" among those who come from other countries. The denigration of blackness, however, could be mitigated to some extent among those who were Latino. But overall, our qualitative data show that Latin American racialization blended with US white racism so that blacks in general were relegated to the bottom of the racial hierarchy.

Odette, a Haitian immigrant, argued that her own name often led to discrimination in South Florida, not so much because she was black, but because she was black and Haitian: "My name is easily discriminated. . . . Let's just say my name is Toussaint, you already know I am a Haitian. . . . I won't get the job because my last name is Toussaint. . . . [If] [y]ou don't want any Haitians in your workplace, you're not going to hire anyone with the last name Toussaint." Odette also felt that discrimination was related to skin color: "Because you are a darker complexion, you automatically have to work a little bit harder. Smile a little bit brighter. You know you have to do a little bit more things because no matter what, you are in competition with the other person that's lighter than you. And that person, although you are more qualified, they are gonna get the job because they look better than you."

The racialization of black immigrants occurs in many areas of the country, but depending on the place, ethnicity can elevate or detract from one's racial status. Patrick referred to anti-Haitian prejudice in Miami in the following quote: "A lot of people believe that people who come from Haiti for example are animals . . . meaning that they are not people." Patrick's comparison between treatment of Haitians and treatment of animals was sobering as it uncovered how he perceived the deep extent of Haitian dehumanization. Fredeline, in turn, discussed why she saw a need for programs such as affirmative action; however, toward the end of her quote, she expressed that certain groups had advantages because of their backgrounds—mainly whites and people from Spanish-speaking countries: "If you look at history, you would like to believe that this [racism] is not a problem, but in everything [it is]. If it weren't so, then we would not need measures like affirmative action to make sure that blacks are able to go to school. If you are white you will not have any problems. If you are Spanish you won't have a problem."

Fredeline suggests that in spite of skin color, Spanish-speaking people can deflect race to a greater extent than non-Spanish speakers (with the exception of whites). However, as our qualitative data suggest, ethnic backgrounds, while contributing to the in-betweenness of certain groups (between white and black), does not deliver the same returns for all.

We believe these disparities in the degrees of racial disadvantage are due to the ethnic origins of varying groups and that the places in which they tend to settle have different social consequences. Being Haitian in New York or in Boston might serve the purpose of deracializing, or even socially whitening, the group by distinguishing them from African Americans, but in Greater Miami their depictions in the media in the 1980s and the association of Haitians with "boat people" and disease explains why they have been subjected to extreme forms of stigmatization that only worsen their experiences of racialization in the region.[68] Thus, ethnic capital is moderated by place and, as Alex Stepick and colleagues argue, power.[69] For Odette, South Florida's context did not afford her ethnic privileges at all. Antiblack and anti-Haitian prejudices emerged as significant sources of constraint among Haitians, who, in Miami, perceived that they were seen as unwanted boat people, not just by whites but also by Latinos.[70]

This point takes us back to mestizaje and the racial understandings that immigrants come with to the United States. Although Latin America's racial dynamics allow for social class to have social whitening effects, some Latinos do not allow blacks—particularly African Americans and Haitians in Miami and, as we will show, those with indigenous roots—to claim class privilege or to experience social whitening that stems from a high class standing. Thus, blackness and indigenous roots trump class privilege. This emphasis on phenotypical characteristics above social acheivement may partly explain the quantitative results that suggest that as the different groups move up the socioeconomic ladder, the more likely they are to experience discrimination, and how even controlling for various social factors does not explain away the significance of race for Haitians and other black immigrants. Thus, when it comes to patterns of racial discrimination, class works in contradictory ways, depending on the group that is referenced.

In sum, a perception exists that Cubans experience greater privilege compared to other Hispanic groups, and that blackness is denigrated indiscriminately. Constructions of race, class, gender, and also legal status play into the racial formation process among Latinos and Caribbean populations in the US context. We further expand on how these in-between groups are racialized in order to better understand where the color line falls in Miami.

Racialization of In-Between Groups

When we examined the midsection of Miami's racial hierarchy, the qualitative data suggested that class and indigeneity have racializing effects, and legal status shapes the construction of race in a variety of ways. In particular, we found evidence that groups associated with undocumented legal status are categorized near the bottom of the social-racial hierarchy.

As we have shown, the various groups in South Florida harbor resentment against each other, with country of origin and race being the central statuses that organize social stratification. We have also shown how even within a particular nationality, Latin American patterns of racialization emerge as social class can have racializing effects, a situation that is especially true for groups that fall between black and white categories.

Social class and cultural racism. Recall Odalys, who was quoted earlier discussing how long-established Cuban immigrants looked down on the more recent Cuban arrivals. While recognizing how this kind of treatment was unjust, Odalys, a recent arrival herself, revealed her own classist ideology that, in effect, allowed her to distance herself from the populations that were objects of long-established immigrant Cubans' scrutiny. After discussing why someone such as herself should be considered a political exile, she stated,

> I think that above all, because of the problem of the people who
> have arrived, many of the Cubans who have arrived lately do not
> express themselves in a way that they do not have the same
> education that perhaps the people who came here in the 1960s had,
> who were either middle or upper class in Cuba, many of them.
> There were some from the lower class, but the large majority were
> from a social extraction that was pretty . . . good . . . [so] many of
> the people who come here . . . you don't view them the same as
> you do them [older Cuban immigrant groups]. . . . [Recent
> arrivals] are products of the same disorder that exists in Cuba, so

there are people like that. If you yourself are saying that in Cuba everything is bad, how can you then expect the product generated by that society to be an elaborate and refined product?

While Odalys recognized that earlier generations of Cubans looked down on the more recent immigrants because of differing class backgrounds, she also seemed to ascribe to the notion that today's Cuban immigrants were of an inferior stock, seen when she asked how one could expect the "product" of contemporary Cuban society to be refined? This judgment could be considered a form of cultural racism, perhaps to separate herself from the stigmatized group. In doing so, she validated why other Cubans see the newest arrivals as inferior—in other words, she pointed to lower levels of education and class as contributing to that inferiority, although she was careful to tie this inferiority to Cuba's social structure.

Cultural racism also reared its head in other contexts. José, a Colombian immigrant, best captured the existence of this type of racism when he discussed intraethnic animosity in the context of one of our focus groups:

You feel the rivalry among the many nationalities [in Miami]. It feels like . . . sometimes we generalize about others. . . . For instance, that "the Nicaraguans are too complicated," that "Cubans are this and that." So there's always this rivalry just to end up saying that our own country is the best. The Cubans say that everything from Cuba is the best, [and] the Nicaraguans say [the same]. . . . It's like a rivalry. . . . So there are conflicts. So, in general terms, no, people do not get along very well when they are from different countries. For instance, if you and I work together and I am not from Peru, and you ask me if I am Colombian, this interaction already starts something. This is just an example, a hypothetical story. Because if I am also from Peru, you will respond differently and say that you will put in a good word for me with the boss. But also it could be that you are from a different region in Peru. . . . Sometimes the rivalries get to the point in which, without any doubts the Cubans are the majority, they have most of the benefits and those from other nationalities, it is a little bit more difficult to obtain things because they have less influence.

Even though José lamented the lack of intergroup solidarity, he illustrated how the racialization of ethnicity results in ethnic rivalries that can affect access to opportunities, such as jobs. Making reference to what he perceived as the ethnic hierarchy in Miami, he used a nationality "schema" to describe the nature of race relations. Thus, as much thought as he seemed to give the subject in the previous quote, he proceeded to engage in cultural racism: "I also agree, sorry if there's anyone from Central America here, I apologize (laughs) but I think that people . . . and I say it literally . . . they are from the lower class, in my opinion. . . . I don't know if I am offending anyone here . . . [but] they come from the segment that is less educated, they don't know how to express themselves correctly, they are not respectful, [and] they don't ask for permission."

Although José did not go as far as using the term *indio,* as others did, he associated Central Americans with those of a lower class, which in Latin America embodied the discourse of racialization. Besides resentment toward Cuban gatekeeping practices, José discussed resentment among the different immigrant groups in Miami but then scapegoated Central Americans. So what initially appeared as a hierarchy of nationalities quickly turned into a Latin Americanized discourse of race in which those with indigenous roots were seen as an inferior category of people. References to Central Americans were placeholders for this racism.

Noah Lewin-Epstein and Asaf Levanon argue that although new immigrants represent an economic threat to the dominant ethnic group of a locality, they also pose "an economic and cultural threat to subordinate ethnic groups."[71] José is aware of his positioning in Miami's racial queue. Not sharing in Cuban privileges, he bemoans the presence of Central Americans, perhaps to distance himself from immigrant identities that threaten his status as an educated South American. As much as he criticizes ethnic rivalries, his own derision toward other "classes" of immigrants reinforces cultural racism among Latinos and further fuels ethnic animosities.

Others used this approach as well, particularly those who worked side by side with Central Americans. For instance, in one of our focus groups, Walter, a Peruvian, explained that in the course of his work in construction, he worked alongside Hondurans, Salvadorans, Guatemalans, and Nicaraguans. He stated, "With all due respect to Central Americans, it is through Central Americans where we get all the chaos . . . [because] there are many of them . . . and like I say, they are not very educated." Guadalupe, a Dominican, acknowledged the existence of the anti–Central American bias: "I have seen the rejection sometimes from Americans with Latinos, and Latinos themselves with other Latinos." Guadalupe followed up with an example: "Sometimes . . . the Central Americans will be called Indians. Because maybe they do not have that much culture, and so people reject them."

In spite of a common Latino culture often characterized as having more similarities than dissimilarities, Latin American categories of racialization, in this case against Central Americans, override the potential for a pan-ethnic consciousness, so that Central Americans are seen as originating from an inferior cultural stock—as uneducated "Indians"—which lessens their position within the racial hierarchy in Miami. Thus, in spite of the commonalities involved when one takes into account Miami's immigrant origins, cultural racism permeates ethnic relations among the groups that fall between black and white.

Legal status and citizenship as markers of racial otherness. The issue of legalization and citizenship also has become a marker of racial formation in contemporary society as discussed in Chapter 3. Indeed, the ability to become a legal immigrant and, ultimately, a US citizen, is a divisive issue. This mode of legal stratification pits groups against each other, as we have seen in the case of the Cuban-Haitian divide. On a larger scale it casts suspicion over many immigrants and US minorities that are at times stereotypically assumed to be foreign. In this regard, who can claim or, more importantly, "earn" citizenship is a racial project with implications for intra- and interethnic group cohesion.

Paola, a Puerto Rican, is a US citizen by birth. Her issue, however, is that perceptions by others that she was simply *granted* citizenship, rather than having to *work* for it, tapped into stereotypes of Puerto Ricans as entitled, lazy, and undeserving of having this status because others did not perceive them as having earned it: "The first thing they say, and pardon my language, is that we are snobs. [They think that] because we are American citizens we think we are a big deal because we can come and go without difficulties. And since they go through a lot of work to be able to immigrate, I think that this is what upsets them the most. . . , Yes, I do believe that there is a negative perception of Puerto Ricans for this very reason, because of the conflict that comes from being able to come and go because we are American citizens."

Other immigrants have the perception that Puerto Ricans have it easy when it comes to migrating to the country and living without the hassles of having their lives subject to intense state regulation. Citizenship does in fact confer many advantages, both material and psychic, on Puerto Ricans, who can come and go at will. However, the assumption that Puerto Ricans have not *worked* for what they have received seems to cause resentment among members of various ethnic groups. Nicholas De Genova and Ana Y. Ramos-Zayas argue that the politics of citizenship, as seen in this instance, shape the "ideologies of work and worth" among Latinos.[72] Similar to the privileges bestowed upon Cubans, immigration policies and the politics of citizenship appear to have the effect of creating beneficiaries and victims, which in turn impedes the creation of ethnic alliances and exacerbates ethnic animosity among all newcomers.

Similar forms of racialization can also be seen in the case of Mexicans, who have come to occupy an inferior racial status in the United States due to the stereotype that they are in the country illegally.[73] Tobias, a Mexican, believed that stereotypes of Mexicans reinforced their subordinate status in Miami. Since Tobias believed he did not fit the stereotype, he expressed that, oftentimes, people did not believe he was Mexican at all:

> People think that all Mexicans drink tequila and eat hot sauce and know how to sing, and I do not even drink tequila, nor do I eat hot sauce and I cannot sing. Here people get confused a lot. Here they might think that I am Peruvian, or that I am Nicaraguan. I think because the Mexicans who come here are often coming from Southern Mexico so [people] imagine that all Mexicans are short, and they see me and do not believe that I am Mexican. Mexicans are the minority here. We are a minority and even my accent disappears and people do not believe I am Mexican. . . . They think that Mexicans drink too much (laughter) and I do not drink. That we are violent and [I am not that] either. It is like they judge based on the movies that they see from Mexico.

The notions that Mexicans drink a lot and that they are violent reinforce culture-of-poverty explanations for why certain groups cannot get ahead, thereby claiming to explain Mexicans' subordinate position in the United States. These racializations are also gendered and involve notions of machismo and hypermasculinity among Mexican men. Tobias emphasized over and over again that he did not fit the stereotype, but he knew the intricacies of the perceptions that he felt others had of Mexicans. Angela echoed what she perceived others thought of Mexicans. She expressed anger over these stereotypes:

> It makes me mad because I have noticed that many people, let's just say that many people, without naming names, simply nationalities, many Cubans, Puerto Ricans, Americans believe that we Mexicans come to the United States to work in the fields. They view us as persons with little brains, with little intelligence. They believe that we are not capable people, that we are people who are little studied or that we cannot excel. Because if you start to look, maybe the situations of the Puerto Ricans and Cubans makes it easier for them to get involved in this country and they believe that the Mexicans are dumb and they are very wrong because they do not know.

Angela discussed the stereotypes of Mexicans and pointed to certain groups as responsible for propagating these views. These groups happened to be those with legal status (Cubans, Puerto Ricans, and other US citizens). She wanted to challenge the notion that Mexicans were "undeserving" because of their lack of human capital, while pointing out that perhaps those groups that looked down on Mexicans had advantages, such as the ability to become involved in their communities because they had the legal status that some Mexicans did not have access to. Angela believed that having legal status was the mechanism that would open up the opportunity structure for her coethnics.

Legal status, thus, has become a symbolic boundary separating various immigrant populations. Illegality has emerged as a factor increasingly used to turn low-wage laborers into a suspicious class of people as we saw in Chapter 3. As De Genova and Ramos-Zayas have shown, the image of the illegal Mexican worker is a racialized construct.[74] This construct contributes to a racial hierarchy where undocumented immigrants cannot clamor for rights because, for fear of deportation, they need to remain in the shadows of their employers and the public at large. Moreover, being labeled as "illegal" by government officials and in the mainstream press sends the message that some immigrants are criminals. When we consider what some respondents had to say about undocumented migrants, that many immigrants themselves have come to subscribe to these misconceptions is clear, as in the following from Luis, a Puerto Rican:

> I tell you, these people who cross the border, those people are very bad. They are quite needy and we [the country] is full. . . . Another thing too is that there are too many of them and they want to keep coming. When we realize what is happening, what? We do not fit. There are more of them than us. In Puerto Rico it is the same with the Dominicans. The Dominicans are practically keeping Puerto Rico. You see them in bus stops and you can tell, "That one is Dominican." What are they doing? They are taking us out so they can stay here. There are no jobs because what I do for $14, Dominicans do it for $8. This is what is happening. And to get to Puerto Rico many drown but they keep trying. It is not easy, but if you go to their country, you will see that the situation is so inhumane.

Luis's narrative is packed with prejudice, as he engages in racial profiling of Dominicans in Puerto Rico, complains of overpopulation due to undocumented immigrants to the United States and the island, and uses the discourse of minorities as exaggerated threats to the interests of the majority groups, singling out Dominicans specifically. The contradiction lies in his last statement, in which he expresses a hint of understanding or empathy for why Dominicans would embark on life-or-death water crossings in *yolas* that either arrive at the western shores of Puerto Rico or sink at sea, leaving many dead. While at the individual level, he fears economic competition and scapegoats the group he is most threatened by (racializing them in the process), he also shows an understanding for people experiencing difficult economic or "inhumane" circumstances in their countries of origin. Unfortunately, this empathy does not necessarily improve the disadvantaged statuses of the undocumented, as border crossers as well as those arriving by sea are relegated to the lower rungs of Miami's—as well as Puerto Rico's—social hierarchies. The following quote by Mateo, a Peruvian, illustrates this emerging form of stratification: "I believe that the Hispanic is underneath the Mexicans and even underneath the people who are black. In the United States there's still a lot of ill treatment toward the Hispanics. It should've changed already. . . . Maybe to receive the same help as other immigrants, other people who have legal status in this country. And I think that sometimes they block you just because you are Hispanic. Well, I believe that I have . . . that I need to improve [my situation] in this country."

How Mateo characterizes Miami's racial hierarchy is interesting, especially his implication that those without "papers" (whom he refers to as Hispanics such as himself) are beneath the historically marginalized groups of Mexicans and African Americans. In this sense, the invisibility of being an undocumented immigrant could just as well be a racial marker that renders a group at the bottom without the access to rights or resources to help improve the group members' conditions. Moreover, he believes that his status as a "Hispanic" makes acquiring a legal immigration status more difficult, illustrating how ethnicity and legal status combine to form new layers of stratification among immigrants and within the Latino population.

The figure of the illegal immigrant, which has become the object of great scorn, becomes a threat to the status of legal immigrants, some who expressed a desire to disassociate from them, perhaps to deflect possible stigmas. Marita, a Mexican, discussed this social distancing based on perceptions of illegality. She even commented on how these distancing techniques literally are found among Latinos themselves: "I have seen this where you are walking down the street and you see someone who clearly you can tell that they arrived to work in the fields with no papers, and you say, 'Oh, that one better not come near me.' I mean, or you might see people who say, 'Those are . . . the worst, [and] those are among the worst,' and you don't even get close."

The anti-immigrant climate that has surged in the United States, particularly since September 11, 2001, has cast suspicion on nonwhite immigrants, US-born minorities (among them, Latinos), and those from certain countries that are typically associated with the stereotype of the illegal immigrant (e.g., Mexico). This increased tension has led to the creation of an environment where even immigrants who enjoy legal status might not identify with conationals out of fear that they, too, may be perceived as undoc-

umented, in spite of their shared immigrant background. Rather than forming bonds of solidarity with others confronting similar experiences, some
immigrants themselves reproduce the anti-immigrant hostility they bemoan.
Thus, in a city with a high concentration of foreign-born people, social distance prevails, a situation seen clearly in the following quote by Pilar, a
Colombian professional, who discussed what she perceived to be the worst
aspects of living in Miami: "Well, the negative aspects, let's say the idea of
the American Dream, which for me there never really has been an American
Dream. . . . So many persons have come chasing the American Dream that
there are not as many opportunities as there were before. It is so overpopulated, so many immigrants."

According to Pilar, the American Dream is increasingly unattainable
because of declining opportunities, which she attributes to overpopulation
and increasing immigration. Immigration, thus, is seen as the key culprit
behind those issues that keep Miamians from getting ahead. The immigrant
presence in the city is perceived as having an overpopulating effect, and the
presumable solution is greater immigration control. The irony is that Pilar
is an immigrant herself. Her views of other immigrants reify the hierarchical positioning of native and immigrant groups and reinforce the negative
stigmas that immigrants such as herself are trying to deflect.[76]

In sum, regarding patterns of racialization among the "in-between"
groups, cultural racism, increasingly joined by racial ideologies that rely on
perceptions of legal status, is woven into the process of racialization in the
United States. The end results are new variants of old patterns of racialization in which even those who bear the brunt of them reproduce the current
racial order through their own attitudes toward other immigrant groups and
their efforts to distance themselves from stigmatized immigrant identities.

Immigrant Disidentification and Counterframing

Efforts at disidentification from those who share immigrant backgrounds
may reflect the internalization of the white racial frame in the lexicon of
immigrants, as well as the class-based disdain that is endemic to Latin
American racialization, so that in some cases, immigrants reject and cast in
a negative light characteristics that they associate with their own cultural
and immigrant backgrounds, although they paint themselves as individual
exceptions. Liliana, a Mexican immigrant quoted earlier in this chapter, illustrated this process:

> In every place, I mean, since there is not 100 percent, here in
> Miami, the population is not 100 percent American [laughter],
> there is a high percentage of Latinos. So Latinos in some cases do

not have manners . . . [and] those are the occasions that I have
[experienced]. . . . [Those] I have found. I omit myself, I exclude
myself there, because, even in my country, you encounter
unpleasant people, poorly educated. So here, well the same.
Maybe even a bit more, because a lot of people come with
extreme need . . . [because] they had no education, they were
hungry, they had to immigrate, so people who are rude, poorly
educated, dirty, that is what I have encountered that has been
uncomfortable.

In accordance with this statement, Liliana used social class to racialize
other Latinos she considered inferior to her. In her interview she had mentioned that she wanted to move to San Francisco to be around more "Americans," thereby equating "American" with whiteness. She had disdain for
Latino culture in general and Cuban culture in particular. In sum, she de-
plored those who shared a Latino culture with her and actively worked to
set herself apart from them.

While the US racial social system as well as racial ideologies brought
from home countries heightened immigrants' awareness of the salience of
racial and ethnic divisions in Miami, in some cases, these hybrid ideologies
also exposed immigrants to civil rights counterframing, which involved co-
opting the ideology of equal opportunity and social justice to challenge US
racism,[76] thus offering tools to immigrants to confront the racism. In the
following quote, Amanda from Puerto Rico recognized that many immigrants have not yet incorporated US antiracist discourse into their own
identities and practices, but she acknowledged the potential for civil rights
ideologies to challenge Latin American patterns of racialization. She stated,
"I think it [racism] is worse here [in Miami compared to Puerto Rico] because you are dealing with a lot of people who come from different parts of
the world with no American influence. When you are born with that American influence, you know that there are persons from different races, and it
is like, 'We shall overcome.' . . . You have that teaching that even though
you are different, it does not matter. We are just as intelligent or . . . equal.
And in Mexico they are not celebrating Black History Month."

Amanda's experience suggests that, even in Puerto Rico, she felt marginalized, as her race was perceived by others to be incompatible with her
Puerto Rican upbringing and culture. Her experiences on the island included people thinking she was from St. Thomas, one of the US Virgin Islands, when she spoke English and people thinking she was Dominican
when she spoke Spanish. Amanda's experience of racialization in Puerto
Rico suggests that blackness was incompatible with membership in Puerto
Rican conceptions of nationhood and belonging. However, she felt like
Miami was worse, not because of US white racism, but because of the

transnationalization of Latin American race relations and antiblack prejudices that others in the immigrant community brought with them. While her interview suggests that she had indeed experienced US white racism, exposure to counterframing and antiracist projects influenced her racial consciousness so that the impact of the civil rights movement (to which Amanda alludes) shapes the contours of her own racial identity, leading her to reject and challenge antiblack prejudices rather than internalize them. Thus, Amanda illustrates the hybrid racial ideology that absorbs her perceptions of US antiracist ideas.

In the case of Fernando, a Mexican, his exposure to racism heightened his racial consciousness, so that he not only identified his own experiences with racism but also identified the racism against blacks and those of indigenous origins prevalent in the United States, as well as in his home country: "In Mexico we create a very strong social problem that we have not wanted to acknowledge. It is very easy for us to complain about the US and how badly they treat blacks, but we also don't realize how racist we Latin Americans are too. And I believe that in general it is a Latin American problem. Against the indigenous and against blacks. And Cubans in particular. If you go and ask Cuban people, and they talk to you a bit about what their relationship is with blacks, including Cubans or Afro Cubans, they are highly racist, and the Mexicans too."

The development of a transnational racial ideology involves making linkages between systems of race relations in referent countries. By making such connections and adopting counterframing strategies, immigrants are more likely to identify with those who are marginalized and are better positioned to bring about social change. Karla, a Puerto Rican, summarizes the consequences of racialization patterns and disidentification succinctly in the quote below. She insightfully points to intersecting categories of group membership that serve as divisions within Miami's immigrant community: "The bad thing about Miami is that even though the language is beautiful, the food is good, [and] the people are good, the groups are also polarizing themselves. It's sad to see how some are mistreated based on income, or where they live, etc. And others have privileges for political reasons . . . and issues regarding who they know and where they come from, and it is not fair."

Conclusion

In sum, when we think about race relations in Miami, rather than viewing the issue as a three-part puzzle of relations involving whites, blacks, and Latinos, we need to consider how ethnic rivalries and discrimination play out within a context in which the white racial frame is entrenched in institutions, including US immigration policies that take on the form of racial projects of the state, and how these mediate relationships among the different constituencies of the city. At the same time, Latin American and Caribbean immigrants bring with them their own racial baggage that, with time, merges with US racial formations constructed within the white racial frame; together, they serve as a means to interpret what they see on the ground in their everyday lives. These patterns of racialization among immigrants in global Miami involve complexities that have been glossed over in previous accounts of race relations in the city.

The structures of global capitalism that have given rise to inequalities around the world are reproducing themselves locally; just as colonial racial subjects were constructed through US imperialism in the form of military intervention in Latin American and Caribbean countries, these racialized subjects are reconstructed in the US collective imagination regionally and on a larger scale within the United States. In the context of Miami,[77] US neoliberal racial projects that take form in immigration policies have positioned established Cubans as "honorary whites" and Haitians as part of the "collective black" in a system of stratification that not only supports the white racial frame, but assigns in-between categories based on social class, cultural racism, and perceptions of worth attached to legal status, reflecting a hemispheric approach to understanding race and ethnicity in the twenty-first century.

For those groups who fall "in between" US notions of white and black, various social statuses combine to form patterns of racialization in a social context in which being an immigrant invokes anxieties about being perceived in suspicious ways. The patterns of disidentification that some—presumably those who share in white privilege—develop run the danger of fracturing ethnic and immigrant alliances. However, acculturating to the ideology at the core of the civil rights movement can position immigrants to be agents of social change regarding fractured race relations. This kind of immigrant solidarity is needed now, more than ever, as the country attempts to pass meaningful immigration reform.

Notes

1. Grenier and Castro 1999; Portes and Stepick 1993; Stepick et al. 2003.
2. Frey 1996.
3. Omi and Winant 1994.
4. Duany 1998; Levitt 2001; Roth 2012.
5. Although beyond the scope of this chapter, we should consider that perceptions of race and racism in Latin America and the Caribbean have also been shaped by social remittances of immigrants who convey US racial meanings to kin remaining in Latin America (Roth 2012).

6. Telles 2007.

7. Ibid.

8. Wade 2010, p. 95.

9. Ibid.

10. Sawyer 2004.

11. Roth 2012; Wade 2010.

12. According to the 2005 Colombian Census, Afro-Colombians are 10.62 percent of the population (Departamento Administrativo Nacional de Estadística 2007).

13. Roth 2012.

14. Although the term *cholo* is used in various countries, including Ecuador, Bolivia, Peru, and even the United States, it has a range of meanings. Bourricaud (1975) argues that the term *cholo* encompasses most of the ambiguities that can surround an individual's status, although Laurie and Bonnett (2002) argue that in the Peruvian context, it is a term used to label people who live in poverty and are affected by racism.

15. Safa 1998, quoted in Hoffman and Centeno 2003.

16. Goldberg, Grosfoguel, and Mielants 2006, p. 261.

17. Sawyer 2004.

18. Ibid., p. xvii.

19. Roth 2012.

20. Wade 2010.

21. Ibid.

22. Omi and Winant 1994, p. 56.

23. Gómez 2007; Telles and Ortiz 2009.

24. Feagin 2009, p. 11; see also Feagin 2006.

25. Feagin 2009, p. 16.

26. Cobas, Duany, and Feagin 2009.

27. Omi and Winant 1994; Telles 2004.

28. Bonilla-Silva 1999.

29. Duany 1998.

30. Levitt 2001; see also Basch, Glick Schiller, and Szanton Blanc 1994.

31. Greenbaum 2002.

32. In Haiti, the first independent black nation in the world, the urban elites associated more closely with their French roots reinforcing the ideology that "equates civilization with whiteness" (Marcelin 2005, p. 212). See also Waters 1999.

33. Stepick et al. 2003.

34. Winsberg 1979.

35. Ibid.

36. Mohl 1995, 2001; Pérez 1990.

37. Mohl 1990, p. 55.

38. Marcelin 2005, p. 211.

39. Ibid.

40. Bonilla-Silva 1999.

41. Gans 1999; Lee and Bean 2004.

42. Frank, Akresh, and Lu 2010; O'Brien 2008.

43. Frank, Akresh, and Lu 2010; Murguia and Telles 1996.

44. Bonilla-Silva 2002, 2004; Forman, Goar, and Lewis 2002.

45. Whites include "traditional whites," new "white" immigrants, assimilated Latinos, and light-skinned multiracials; honorary whites include most light-skinned Latinos, some Asian groups, and Middle Easterners; and the collective black group

includes blacks, dark-skinned Latinos, and a few Asian groups (Bonilla-Silva 2002, 2004).

46. Stepick et al. 2003.

47. Ngai 2004, p. 12.

48. Mohl 1990.

49. A 2005 US Commission on International Religious Freedom reported that asylum seekers' release rates correlate to their countries of origin. This study compared the rates for the period of 2000 to 2004 of Cubans (80 percent were allowed to stay), Iraqis (60 percent), Haitians (a little over 10 percent), and Salvadorans (fewer than 5 percent). The study also found that foreign asylum seekers were treated like criminals and deterred from asking for protection. Additionally, it stated that asylum seekers were held in horrid conditions, often in solitary confinement (Little and Klarreich 2005).

50. Sutton 2002.

51. Ibid.

52. Chardy 2002.

53. Stepick 1998.

54. "Haitians in America" 2006.

55. Ramdin 2008.

56. See US Citizenship and Immigration Services 2014.

57. This measure came from the following question: "Has people treating you unfairly because of your skin color been no problem at all, a small problem, somewhat of a problem, or a major problem?"

58. We present results from ordinary least squares (OLS) regressions as this type of analysis provides the most easily interpretable coefficients. Preliminary analyses confirmed that the dependent variable behaved normally. Further, alternative models (e.g., probit) were quantitatively and qualitatively comparable, leading to the same conclusions reported.

59. Kasinitz et al. 2008.

60. See also Roth 2012.

61. Most questions were adapted from Williams and colleagues (1997). The respondents could answer "never," "rarely," "sometimes," or "always" to the following questions: "How often were you treated with less respect?" "How often do people act as if they are afraid of you?" "How often do people act as if they think you are dishonest?" "How often do people act like they think they are better than you?" "How often are people unfriendly to you?" "How often are you called names and insulted?" and "How often are you threatened or harassed?" The answers to these questions were recoded in the form of four-point Likert scales, taking values from 1 to 4. These questions were reduced to one factor—*everyday perceived discrimination*—using principal component analysis. The measure was centered (mean = 0 and SD = 1). The internal reliability of the component was deemed as good (Cronbach's alpha = 0.79).

62. The dependent variable, perceived employment discrimination, is based on a question from the ITMI Quantitative Survey that asks, "How often have you not been given a job because you are an immigrant? Always, sometimes, rarely, or never?"

63. We present results from OLS regressions as this type of analysis provides the most easily interpretable coefficients. Preliminary analyses confirm that the dependent variable behaves normally. Further, alternative models (e.g., probit) were quantitatively and qualitatively comparable, leading to the same conclusions reported.

64. Kasinitz et al. 2008.

65. Over the past couple of decades, Mexican migration flows have diversified and redirected themselves to nonmetropolitan areas (Massey 2008). In some counties, immigrants are replacing the native population, counteracting population loss and contributing to communities' livelihoods. Also, as a result of high costs of living in some metropolitan areas, immigrants are branching out into small towns adjacent to expanding metropolitan areas known as "exurbs." These areas are known for their labor demand in manufacturing, construction, and services (Massey 2008). In Homestead, Hurricane Andrew, which struck in 1992, accelerated these processes. Homestead took years to recover from this natural disaster, which ushered new immigrants into an already immigrant-dense area. Even though in the 1990 census, Homestead had 4,116 Mexicans (15 percent of the population) and 17,388 non-Hispanic whites, in 2000, 7,279 Mexicans (23 percent of the population) and 15,372 non-Hispanic whites lived in Homestead—for Mexicans, a 76.8 percent increase in population and for whites, a 13.1 percent decline (US Census Bureau 1990, 2000). By 2010, the Mexican population grew again, this time at the rate of 28 percent (to 9,311), though the white population declined to 9,684 (a 37 percent loss). Mexicans are overrepresented in Homestead when one considers that in 2000 they only made up 1.7 percent of the population of Miami-Dade County and by the 2010 census, they were 2.1 percent of the county's population (US Census Bureau 2010).

66. Goldberg, Grosfoguel, and Mielants 2006.

67. For a discussion on opportunity hoarding, see Tilly 1999.

68. Stepick 1998.

69. Stepick et al. 2003.

70. Stepick 1998.

71. Lewin-Epstein and Levanon 2005, p. 93.

72. De Genova and Ramos-Zayas 2003, p. 57.

73. Ibid.

74. Ibid.

75. Killian and Johnson 2006.

76. Feagin 2009.

77. The context of Miami, not necessarily because of the city, but because of the transnational social space that it represents, is important in this racialization process.

7

Immigrant Emotions and Strategies of Co-Presence

When you arrive, there are no experiences that connect you to this place. You are thinking all the time about your place of origin, the fact of being in complete contact by phone, by mail, by television, with your place of origin. I don't think I did it consciously to fill a void. Simply it was because I was still emotionally attached and with activities still there. When I arrived, I was still part of a research project in Mexico and so was still sending results and things, and little by little that has changed. I have not lost the emotional ties, though, because I keep them very clearly present. But also now there are things that connect me to this place.

—José, Mexican immigrant

Many immigrants experience disruptions in their social relationships and sense of place when they migrate. They lose the embodied experiences of being with the important people, such as family and friends, and participating in groups, who inscribed their natal homes with comfort, a sense of being nurtured, and positive affect. These changes can challenge feelings of security associated with continuities in the understanding of one's place in the world, or what is more properly known as ontological security. Ontological security usually results from having stable personal relationships, identities, and connections to larger collectivities that promote feelings of acceptance and belonging. Such feelings and relationships are associated with particular places and inscribed in the culture of the country of origin as well as tangible embodiments of home such as built and natural landscapes.[1] According to sociologist Anthony Giddens, the bedrock of ontological security is trust, and this type of security is experienced emotionally, rather than cognitively, as it is "rooted in the unconscious."[2]

In this chapter we show that immigrants who feel ontologically insecure, to varying extents, seek to lessen those feelings by maintaining their relationships with loved ones abroad and trying to re-create the positive emotions associated with the places they left behind. We argue that immigrants' search for continuity in their "social and material environments of action"[3] is a strategy employed to minimize conflicts that sometimes arise between their emotional well-being and their prior decisions to relocate to the United States. We show that Miami is particularly conducive to Latin American and Caribbean immigrants' strategies to reconcile conflicting emotions as they relate to migration and settlement. The area is perceived as materially developed and orderly compared to immigrants' places of origin, while at the same time the city reminds immigrants of home in other, more positive ways. They thus choose to live in Miami, at least in part, because it facilitates strategies to keep them present and active in the lives of those left behind. At the same time, these strategies inscribe elements of home society cultures into the spaces of Miami. By settling in Miami, immigrants attempt to combine the physical, psychic, and economic security they associate with a more economically developed country with the security that comes from relationships formed in the home and hearth. More broadly, we will show how the strategies that help them to remain embedded in their communities of origin can result in a translocal form of social citizenship, or a collection of practices and participation in collectivities that amount to the equivalent of citizenship among individuals whose everyday activities contribute to civic life across borders. These practices are conducive to greater levels of happiness among immigrants.

José's quote at the opening of the chapter suggests he is following just such a strategy. As he told us, he keeps his emotional ties intact "and clearly present" while he engages in activities and forges new relationships that "connect me to this place." To explain how immigrants such as José participate in life translocally—by which we mean that their everyday activities involve some sort of presence in places that are anchored in two distinct geographical locales—we begin by examining the emotions associated with life as an immigrant. We illustrate how these emotions turn into strategies of maintaining their presence in a translocal place constructed through citizenship practices that span borders.

Immigration, Emotions, and Ontological Security

Emotions have been integrated into much of the social sciences,[4] but they are not frequently explicitly considered in dominant accounts of international migration.[5] This seeming omission may be because, as historian Susan Matt documents, homesickness, and what later came to be known as nostalgia, went from being openly discussed, legitimate sources of pain and struggle for migrants, to taboo subjects.[6] Nineteenth-century internal migrants in the United States faced pressures to cut ties with old communities and adapt to new ones, while experiencing minimal distress throughout the process. Matt demonstrates how, by the twentieth century, ideas of adaptability grounded in Darwinian philosophy and psychological theories on maturation came to associate "failure to separate from home" with "failure more generally." She continues, "Those who were homesick were considered premodern, unsophisticated, ill-equipped for the shifting and individualistic conditions of modern society."[7] Feeling homesick, or admitting to having such feelings, was considered a sign of emotional immaturity that was perceived to be incongruent with the demands of a capitalistic society. Thus, throughout much of the twentieth century, normative assumptions underlying mobility hinged on the expectation that emotions of loss—whether related to families, friends, communities, or nations—should be suppressed and fade over time.[8]

This denial of attachment is not necessarily the case in modern times. In the following quote, Adrian discloses persistent feelings of loss rooted in his exit from Mexico and the circumstances underlying his relocation to the United States: "It is very hard to leave the things you have . . . your family above all, to leave your country, to leave the only animals you've been able to acquire. . . . You get sad for the absence that's about to occur. . . . That is the burden that everyone carries. . . . Nobody congratulates oneself for being an immigrant, for being an outsider. No matter how much money you have, in your heart you will always carry with you that you are a man without a country."

Adrian was fifty-four years old and had lived in the United States for twenty-two years at the time of this interview. Yet his nostalgia, and the resulting emotions of loss, persisted. Adrian reflects what Pauline Boss has termed "ambiguous loss," an enduring loss one experiences when closure is elusive, if not impossible.[9] Ambiguous loss may be experienced when a family member goes missing, or when one cares for a loved one with Alzheimer's; in this case, ambiguous loss resulted from the separation from loved ones through migration. Adrian no longer thinks of returning to Mexico and has reluctantly accepted that he will likely live out the rest of his years in the United States. But like many cases that will be documented in this chapter, his story shows that migration and settlement can be marked over the long term by emotions such as ambiguous loss and, more generally, nostalgia. We argue that nostalgia as a concept and a condition should be problematized to a greater extent than what it has been in the scholarly literature, particularly as it relates to other emotions that appear to be endemic to the experience of migration.

In the process of identifying patterns of emotions found in immigrants' narratives, another one of the emerging themes in our data pertains to the prevalence of ambivalence toward migration. Although many in our study expressed gratitude for the opportunities gained by moving to the United States, because of the experiences of ambiguous loss, they often generally expressed mixed emotions about migration. For example, despite financial or educational gains attained in the course of US settlement, greater peace of mind attained by exiting environments of greater physical insecurity, or positive emotions regarding gains in self-esteem when mastering a new language, many immigrants in our study had to manage the disjunctures between what they had attained and what they had lost. The simultaneous experience of accomplishment and pride in tandem with ambiguous loss and sadness led to conflicting emotions. These internal conflicts took work, specifically emotion work (the active management of emotions), to resolve, or at least attempt to resolve.[10]

Experiencing mixed emotions about immigration raises the question of whether immigrants are engaging in strategies to manage their emotions. Neil Smelser argues the importance of ambivalence: "Ambivalence is such a *powerful, persistent, unresolvable, volatile, generalizable,* and *anxiety-provoking* feature of the human condition, people defend against experiencing it in many ways."[11] He continues, "When we bond with people deeply, or even superficially, we become to some degree less emotionally free as a result. These relations invariably become fused with some ambivalence, and when we lose or separate from others, dealing with that ambivalence becomes a necessity."[12]

As past research has shown, when migrants cannot resolve ambivalence or overcome feelings of ambiguous loss, this tension may open the door to return migration or resettlement elsewhere (secondary migration), or alternatively, their conflicting emotions may remain unresolved and manifest themselves as poor emotional well-being.[13] In our quantitative sample, when immigrants were asked if and how often they had thought of moving back to their home countries, 53 percent of the men and 46 percent of the women said they had thought about returning to their home countries some or all of the time. Among the most common reasons why they wanted to return were that they desired to reconnect with kin (46 percent of men, 54 percent of women) or felt drawn by emotional attachments (38 percent of men, 44 percent of women). At the same time, almost all immigrants (92 percent) expressed being satisfied or very satisfied with their lives in the United States, and 80 percent of immigrants agreed or strongly agreed with the statement, "Living in the US has made me happier." No gender differences could be seen in either of these two subjective assessments of life in the United States. Our qualitative data support the presence of ambivalent emotions toward migration and settlement and illustrate how sadness is associated with loss of connection with loved ones and abandoned life projects, just as positive affect results from opportunities for self-realization and greater human security as Fernando, a Mexican, described:

They are mixed feelings. On the one hand, when you live in a
place and you grow up in a place and you have your family and
friendship ties—it could be Mexico, it could be Alabama, [or] it
could be Dallas—you are obviously very close to that place. And
you very much love that place for what it represents and what it
represents in your life. But, on the other hand, without ceasing to
recognize or ceasing to be sad, the majority of people . . . leave
their country and have to leave these things behind, to look for
better opportunities for their children and themselves. Then that
too creates mixed feelings. Much sadness for what Mexico could
not give you. . . . But with that affection that you have toward the
place where you grew up, where you have your friends, your
family.

Fernando illustrated a deep connection to the place where his personal
and collective identities were formed and nurtured and to the people associated with this place. But also, part of his experience involved sadness toward his country and the perception that political failings have made life
there unsustainable.

Fernando's narrative illustrates how emotions toward migration are
shaped by the conditions of exit in the country of origin; other migration
stories, such as those documented in Chapter 3, show how the context of
reception also shapes emotions through the experiences of psychic insecurity. Overall, the type of migration will condition how immigrants experience the emotions of migration as seen with those fleeing physical insecurity. Asylees and refugees faced constraints on their abilities to return to
visit. This limitation made worse the emotional struggles associated with
US settlement.

Rosa María, a Colombian political asylee, lived with this quandary. She
could not return home to visit because of her immigration status as an
asylee, as she feared persecution upon her return. At the same time, her parents were denied a US visa to travel to the United States to visit her. Rosa
María described the ambivalence she felt after trading the ability to share
her life with her aging parents for safety in the United States. After bitterly
describing her parents' inability to get a visa to travel, she stated that the
one thing that would make her happy would be to see them:

Because the truth is that the United States is the best country in
the world, where there is more economic stability, where one
feels better, where I can start over again economically, where one
can study, get training, where there is a lot of police, a lot of
security. Whenever you call the police, they arrive right away. In
my country they arrive in an hour or two hours or they never

arrive. One even likes to pay taxes. It is a pleasure, and it doesn't
bother me to pay my taxes, and I pay them just as I should. . . .
They have given me education. . . . This country has given me
more than my own gave me. The only difficulty is the sadness.
The loneliness at not being able to see one's family. That is the
only difficulty I have. If I could see my dad and mom, I think I
would be complete. I would not have any more difficulty and
would be here only to work hard and progress.

Although Rosa María's return is blocked by her asylee status, other immigrants who lacked legal status also expressed sadness at not being able to
go home for visits out of fear of not being able to return to the United
States. The emotional fallout from restricted mobility worsened during
major life events such as weddings, births, religious rituals, and funerals, as
Emilia's account illustrates. Emilia came to the United States with her husband after he lost his job in Peru. Having both overstayed their tourist
visas, they found work and settled in the area. Emilia experienced a double
trauma when a young niece died in Peru. For one, the loss of her niece was
devastating. On top of that, she was not allowed to travel to share in expressions of communal grief or to mourn in person. Emilia's inability to return
illustrates how ambiguous loss is a "definitive" and "fundamental" part of
her migration experience:

The emotional impact [of migration] is definitive because in my
case I had a little niece who was very gravely ill and I could not
see her, I could not accompany her, and, yes, God decided to take
her. . . . But I could not be with my cousin[14] or with the rest of
my family, to accompany them in a moment like that, which is
when you most need your family. So this was a horrible thing
because those there suffer because of what is happening and also
knowing one is here impatiently desperate, suffering alone,
because you don't have anyone to share this pain with. More than
that, you feel like you are drowning in a glass of water, that you
cannot do anything.

Cubans' context of reception and arrival often meant reuniting with
family in Miami who had previously immigrated. Yet like other immigrants
in our study, a sizable number of Cubans also experienced emotional ambivalence about migration because of the loved ones they had to leave behind. Rocio, a Cuban, described a situation where she felt good about accomplishing her goal of reaching US shores yet sad because of the
ambiguous loss she felt for those in her family who could not come. She
also felt guilt that some in her family had not been granted the opportunity

to emigrate: "Those of us who are here . . . that we feel good. We feel like we've accomplished what we wanted. But at the same time, we miss those we left behind." Cubans with family members on the island expressed feelings of displacement common to other groups that could not return home for visits. For much of the previous decade and during the time in which these interviews were conducted, US law limited the visits that Cuban nationals could make to the island. Odalys, also Cuban, described the feeling as "being torn apart."

Numerous immigrants conveyed loss not only of loved ones but of life projects that "did not work out." Isidro, who had lived in the United States for five years, illustrated the depth of the emotions associated with the experience of leaving a life project in Colombia. Although slightly more than half of Colombians thought about returning to their country some or all of the time, in their case, violence and a lack of physical security in Colombia led them to perceive limited return options, as Isidro explained: "It hit me hard. It is sad to abandon the place where you were really educated, where you grew up, where you worked as a professional, where you've already struggled all that you thought you had to struggle in life. It is sad to see that you struggled, but it did not work out. That you struggled but the country does not offer security to its people so that they can continue to produce money for that country. It is painful to leave your family, your mother, your brothers and sisters, basically your family."

Like Fernando discussed earlier, Isidro's emotional ties are not only to family but also to ways of living that have been abandoned. Loss was also expressed as love toward a country. Haitian musician Emmanuel described feelings of belonging when physically present in Haiti, although like Fernando, he also recognized the country's hardships, which had driven his parents to migrate and then send for him as a child: "Haiti is a country that I love a lot. It could be as black as charcoal, garbage everywhere, but all of my heart is [in] Haiti. I do not see any other country in the world that I would choose over Haiti. In Haiti I feel like that is where I was made to be. It is hard to say what I most like. It is something that is indeed mystical. When I am in the country I feel that is where I should be forever."

Like Emmanuel, many Haitians desired to return to their country, even though, similar to Colombians, most believed that migration had made them happier. Happiness, though, did not erase the "mystical" connection Emmanuel felt when he was there. His discourse reflects ambiguous loss not necessarily toward individuals but toward his natal home. This quote is reminiscent of Robert C. Smith's use of the concept of socioproprioception to describe the feelings that Mexican second-generation youth felt when they participated in religious ceremonies in Mexico.[15] These are feelings of awareness of one's body in space. Emmanuel's reaction to being in Haiti is akin to being in a place that elicits exuberance, satisfaction, and well-being. Being present in the country of origin puts immigrants in touch with the sensorial and embodied experiences of being "home." Even though Emmanuel had lived in the United States for twenty years, he still longed to experience that mystical feeling of being embedded in the physical spaces, cultural community, and nurturing structures that he experienced in his formative years in Haiti. Contrary to assumptions that nostalgia wanes with time, Emmanuel's story illustrated that two decades in the United States did not dull the longing. If anything, immigrants were faced with the task of managing feelings of longing and loss throughout their lives. Not only do such feelings persist, but they are also affected by the structural constraints on mobility rooted in immigration policies and by lack of access to financial resources that often keeps immigrants from being able to carry out the practices that would help to alleviate their nostalgia.

The pattern of ambivalence observed among immigrants emerges from a reality in which immigrants' lives and senses of self are split across borders. As Jorge Duany has argued, in spite of legal boundaries demarcating the geographic limits of the nation-state, bifocality best describes how immigrants experience life across borders that are blurred.[16] This bifocality entails "aspects of life 'here' and life 'there'" that are "constantly monitored and perceived as complementary aspects of a single space of experience."[17] Reflecting this bifocal perspective, immigrants are pulled in both directions, as old and new members of multiple communities wrapped in a single experience.

Building on work done in the areas of immigration, transnational caregiving, and media reception,[18] we argue that, like visiting the country of origin, the way that immigrants cope with ambivalence is by engaging in translocal practices. These practices establish the feeling of social co-presence—of being in the same place with loved ones or being in meaningful places left behind. Establishing feelings of social co-presence is a strategy to reconcile the conflicting emotions resulting from migration and US settlement in addition to managing the homesickness or displacement that immigrants feel. Thus, emotions that characterize the immigrant experience, including ambivalence, ambiguous loss, and nostalgia, can lead to immigrant agency in the form of devising strategies to mitigate their negative effects.

In the following section we examine these practices, including *physical co-presence* and *physically absent co-presence,* as attempts to alleviate ambivalence, ambiguous loss, and nostalgia. Co-presence strategies can lead to translocal participation in more than one society by nurturing relationships in the places of origin, which, at a broader level, can result in feelings of greater ontological security that might have been lost through the process of migration.

Co-Presence as a Strategy

How do immigrants manage ambiguity and loss and, at a greater level, the ontological insecurity that may result from disruption of relationships that anchor personal and collective identities? What sort of implications do emotional strategies have for adaptation in the country of destination? We analyze how immigrants seek to resolve emotional conflicts within themselves by engaging in practices that maintain relationships and other linkages to the country of origin. We create a typology of the different ways of maintaining feelings of co-presence that draws from sociological and anthropological studies of care work and mobility,[19] reception of transnational or diasporic media,[20] and ethnographic studies of media culture and literature on the social richness of media technologies.[21] Although our quantitative data do not measure every way in which immigrants may embed themselves in homeland relationships, we employ both quantitative and qualitative data to illustrate the range of practices immigrants use to maintain relations with family, friends, groups, and places from the country of origin.

Embodied Co-Presence

Embodied co-presence is face-to-face or face-to-place physical co-presence with homeland loved ones or meaningful places. This type of co-presence may occur by way of travel to the home country, visits of family and friends to Miami, migration of family members together, the reconstitution of families, or the reunification of longtime friendship networks. Embodied co-presence facilitated the reaffirmation of emotional bonds with significant others. It allowed group members to share the emotional richness of verbal and, especially, nonverbal communication, including physical ways of expressing affection such as touching, embracing, and overall body language and eye contact. Additionally, travel for embodied co-presence gave both immigrants and those who received them the opportunity to engage in reciprocal expressions of affect and care.

In addition to face-to-face encounters, the desire to be physically present in country-of-origin spaces, particularly the hometown, was an emotional need documented across many migration experiences.[22] As David Conradson and Deirdre McKay write, place plays "a major role in the ongoing constitution of identity."[23] Family relations, friendships, and work activities would be hard to imagine without placing them in identifiable locations, whether they are geographically close or distant. Further, tastes in music, food, or style of dress, even everyday mannerisms such as an ironic sense of humor or formality in speech, are linked to particular local or regional spaces, sometimes much more than a national territory. Reaffirmation of immigrant identities and the relationships that constitute them thus include strategies of embodied co-presence with important places, just as much as with people from the original home.

The large majority of immigrants in our study (88 percent) told us that being able to visit the country of origin was important or very important, with no difference apparent between men and women. Almost two-thirds in the quantitative sample (64 percent) had visited their place of origin since immigrating. Women returned more than men (68 percent compared to 59 percent), even though, as mentioned earlier, men contemplated returning to live in the country of origin more than women (53 percent and 46 percent, respectively). Strong national-origin differences could be found in who went back for a visit, most notably between Cubans and other groups. Table 7.1 illustrates the frequency with which men and women from different countries/regions visited their home countries.

Due to immigration policies, embodied co-presence was not an option equally open to all immigrants alike. Cubans rarely visited the homeland compared to other groups, most likely because of government travel restrictions in previous decades. However, they were more likely to have their whole families and lifelong friendships in Miami. In this case we have a clear example of how historical US immigration policy, by facilitating the emplacement in Miami of a dense network of familial relations and friendships formed in Cuba, has shaped Cubans' abilities to re-create embodied co-presence in the country of destination.

Our qualitative data support the importance of embodied co-presence for immigrants. Javier, a Colombian, said his parents' visits to him filled the void he felt from not being with them after his decision to remain in the United States upon completing his education. The visits also alleviated the guilt he sometimes felt as a result of this decision: "It was very difficult for my parents, at first, I think, but now they have a lot more opportunities. Now they can visit here when they want. They have me and [my work] helps the family advance."

Several studies suggest that embodied co-presence is the most important form of co-presence for conducting care work in geographically separated families,[24] but visits to and from the familial home are just one of multiple overlapping forms of connectivity immigrants use to keep intimate relationships alive. Various forms exist of absent co-presence—or the ways in which immigrants try to re-create feelings that come from experiences of embodied co-presence, but from a distance. We begin with a discussion of virtual co-presence.

Virtual Co-Presence

Virtual co-presence is a commonly employed compensatory form of co-presence that relies on technology and mediated forms of communication.

Table 7.1 Frequency of Visits to the Home Country (percentage)

Country/Region of Origin	Never Visited			Visited but Not in Past 12 Months			Visited Once in Past 12 Months			Visited Twice in Past 12 Months			Visited Three or More Times in Past 12 Months		
	Men	Women	Total Pop.	Men	Women	Total Pop.	Men	Women	Total Pop.	Men	Women	Total Pop.	Men	Women	Total Pop.
Cuba	68.4	55.4	62.0	25.7	38.0	31.7	3.2	5.9	4.5	1.9	0.0	1.0	1.0	0.4	0.6
Haiti	24.9	35.4	29.8	28.4	35.7	31.8	31.3	11.5	22.0	4.8	13.1	8.7	10.6	4.4	7.7
Colombia	25.5	18.7	21.6	43.6	41.5	42.4	23.3	20.0	21.4	2.8	16.5	10.6	4.8	2.7	3.6
Non-Spanish Caribbean	8.2	15.3	12.2	34.4	41.0	38.2	38.3	26.0	31.2	9.3	7.3	8.1	9.9	10.5	10.2
Spanish Caribbean	4.2	19.5	12.9	40.8	38.6	39.5	49.1	31.3	38.9	3.4	8.5	6.4	2.6	1.0	1.7
North and Central America	41.9	24.9	32.3	26.1	35.3	31.3	24.4	28.7	26.9	6.3	5.7	5.9	1.2	5.4	3.6
South America	30.7	15.2	22.3	32.6	40.1	36.7	13.4	30.9	22.9	8.9	9.6	9.3	14.1	4.2	8.8
Other non-Hispanic	21.1	16.4	18.9	26.2	47.4	36.3	39.7	21.2	30.9	9.2	0.0	4.8	3.8	15.0	9.2
All countries	40.9	32.1	36.3	29.9	38.9	34.6	19.7	19.1	19.4	4.8	5.7	5.3	4.6	4.0	4.3

Source: ITMI Quantitative Survey.
Note: N = 1,264.

Virtual co-presence is invoked through synchronous communication technologies, or interaction in real time, especially over the telephone. Other forms of virtual co-presence involve instant messaging and Internet video chat, to participate in simultaneous, interactive communication with family or friends.

Researchers using "media capacity theories" place technologies on a continuum from the richest types of media that mimick the fullness of face-to-face social interaction, to less rich, less interactive media such as written communication technologies such as e-mail or text messaging. Media that provide a richer sense of co-presence are usually audiovisual. They transmit nonverbal communicative cues such as a shrug, smile, or blown kiss that researchers describe as "primarily affective and connected to personal relationships."[25]

Frank Biocca and Chad Harms define mediated social presence as a "sense of being with another in a mediated environment . . . the moment-to-moment awareness of co-presence of a mediated body and the sense of accessibility of the other being's psychological, emotional, and intentional states."[26] The researchers distinguish a range of social richness, ranging from awareness of the other's mediated body to awareness of the other's attentional engagement, emotional state, comprehension, and behavioral interaction, and finally to a dynamic, intersubjective level of a mutual sense of presence by both communicators. In other words, the richest mediated experiences of co-presence involve both communicators interacting dynamically while being mutually aware of each other's physical and emotional states. Studies of intimate communication suggest a mutual sense of co-presence can be evoked by visual communication technologies such as Skype and other Internet-based video-conferencing tools. The telephone can also evoke a sense of mutual co-presence when participants engage in richness-enhancing verbal interactions such as interruptions, turn taking, use of tone of voice, or expressions acknowledging the communication partner.

Ethnographies of families split across international borders show how virtual co-presence allows members of these groups to express care and manage emotions of longing and loneliness. For Loretta Baldassar's geographically distributed families in Italy and Australia, telephone calls provided the preferred form of virtual co-presence because they allowed parents, who were usually uncomfortable with computer-mediated communication, to hear their distant children. Hearing their children made parents feel closer and more connected. Parents reported arranging routines around these calls, as they reacted physically and emotionally to their children's voices.[27]

Our qualitative data show that virtual co-presence alleviated ambiguous loss because it provided an experience similar to being physically together. "Chatting has been marvelous because I can see her, [and] I can hear them. I call by telephone too. We chat every day, even for just five minutes. I know that my grandmother is okay, that my sister is fine. I find out a bit about what's going on in their lives," said Cecilia, a Peruvian who left a close-knit family after her unemployed husband got a job abroad. Diego, also a Peruvian, attributed his preference for emotionally richer communication technologies to the nostalgia that he felt: "I communicate by phone every other day, one day yes, one day no. It is because I have nostalgia. I also have e-mail, but I prefer to talk on the phone."

Virtual forms of co-presence were the most frequent among immigrants in our sample, and the telephone was the preferred means of communication. About 92 percent of all immigrants in our quantitative sample communicated with family and friends in the hometown through telephone calls while just 28 percent used e-mail and 16 percent used Internet-based chat or video communication. The large majority in every national-origin group thought keeping in touch was important or very important. While a majority of Cubans also believed in the necessity of staying in touch, about one-third disagreed, much more than any other national group. Immigrants sought out family members followed by friends. Table 7.2 shows the frequency of communication across country/region of origin groups and gender.

The South Americans in our sample tended to come from urban centers with higher levels of technological development and report more frequent contact with home. Like all the immigrants in our study, they utilize the telephone to create the basic infrastructure for virtual co-presence with family and friends, but they also report using instant messaging and e-mail more than immigrants from the other countries and regions in the study. Unlike Cubans, they rarely discussed reunifying their extended families in Miami during the qualitative interviews. More likely, they received visits from friends and family, or visited them (except for some political asylees), and used frequent phone calls, video chat, and e-mail to keep in touch with homeland social networks.

The transnational embeddedness of most Cubans was different from that of South Americans. Like everyone, Cubans relied heavily on telephone calls for virtual co-presence, but they called less often and tended to call only close relatives, mostly due to the high cost of phone calls. E-mail was restricted to people who had Internet access in universities and other government agencies; thus, participation in instant messaging and chatting was very rare given Cubans' relatives' irregular access to e-mail. Such constraints reflect the Cuban government's foreign exchange strategies and attempts to control dissent, especially given the conflictive relationship between political elites in Miami and on the island. Thus, political and economic conditions in Cuba and relations between the United States and Cuba restricted Cuban immigrants' abilities to manage ambiguous loss through virtual co-presence, while urban South Americans' technological

Table 7.2 Frequency of Communication with People in the Country of Origin (percentage)

Country/Region of Origin	Always Communicates			Sometimes Communicates			Rarely Communicates			Never Communicates		
	Men	Women	Total Pop.	Men	Women	Total Pop.	Men	Women	Total Pop.	Men	Women	Total Pop.
Cuba	21.3	17.6	19.5	24.4	33.3	28.8	25.0	22.1	23.6	29.3	27.0	28.2
Haiti	50.9	52.2	51.5	25.8	26.9	26.3	17.1	16.6	16.9	6.1	4.3	5.3
Colombia	63.0	62.5	62.7	35.7	23.9	28.9	1.3	11.2	7.0	0.0	2.4	1.4
Non-Spanish Caribbean	56.1	59.6	58.1	27.6	20.9	23.7	16.4	11.6	13.6	0.0	7.9	4.6
Spanish Caribbean	73.3	71.6	72.4	5.0	19.6	13.3	6.3	7.1	6.8	15.4	1.7	7.6
North and Central America	51.4	49.3	50.2	35.4	31.2	33.0	6.0	10.8	8.7	7.2	8.7	8.0
South America	60.9	67.8	64.6	20.6	15.0	17.6	17.3	13.4	15.2	1.2	3.7	2.6
Other non-Hispanic	65.5	64.4	65.0	14.8	12.1	13.5	12.8	13.3	13.1	6.9	10.1	8.5
All countries	44.9	46.4	45.7	24.0	25.7	24.9	16.6	15.2	15.9	14.4	12.7	13.5

Source: ITMI Quantitative Survey.
Note: $N = 1,262$.

know-how and wider homeland access to communications infrastructure
encouraged a variety of strategies for virtual co-presence.

Imaginative Co-Presence

Another strategy for maintaining translocal relationships is imaginative co-
presence. Imaginative co-presence involves consumption of homeland
media and other cultural artifacts to prompt imagination about significant
others, meaningful places, and what it would be like to be again in their
presence or in these places. Ethnographer of television Paddy Scannell describes the "doubling of space" that live national television created for
viewers in the intimacy of their living spaces.[28] What we suggest here is a
doubling of space that is binational, and that linked immigrants to intimate
spaces and persons left behind.

Consumption of transnational television and other objects does not
work the same way for all immigrants,[29] yet substantial evidence has revealed that most immigrants do use certain media content to prompt experiences of imaginative co-presence that are meaningful.[30] Victor Sampedro
describes how foreign students in the United States engaged in daily or regular rituals of reading homeland newspapers in the university library that
placed them in the imagined presence of intimate others such as family and
friends, as well as broader cultural collectives such as homeland youth
groups or consumers back home.[31] Another study of media reception among
adolescent immigrants in the US South argues that teens used imaginative
co-presence to create "spaces of complete belonging" where they felt relaxed and secure. Media consumption prompted "not only imaginary visits
to past times and places, but also resources" to help the teens navigate
racialization and stigmatization.[32]

Roger Silverstone and others have argued that consumption of national broadcasting helps sustain familiarity and predictability because
consumption becomes regularized in routines and content carries culturally familiar and predictable symbols of everyday life.[33] What we argue is
that consumption of media content from an immigrant's country of origin
or content produced in an immigrant's ethnic community increases ontological security in similar ways, but for audiences that cross borders or
form a national-origin community abroad. Consumption of these media
incorporates into the routines of daily life the culturally familiar symbols,
rhetorical styles, and rituals of media consumption such as watching telenovelas or discussing political programs that were common to group
memberships.[34] Thus, consumption of homeland and ethnic community
media re-embeds immigrants in nationally based familiarity and predictability, as well as the intimate landscapes of home. At the same time,
immigrants integrate media consumption and the notions of "home"

media carry into their everyday routines and lifestyles while living in the country of destination.

Questions about media use in our study suggest that immigrants regularly access country-of-origin media or media produced in their coethnic community in Miami to learn what is happening back home. Most immigrants, regardless of their national origin, told us that getting news about the country of origin was important to them (82 percent of the overall sample). More respondents reported using television to get news about the country of origin (49 percent) than any other medium, including Internet (35 percent), radio (27 percent), or newspapers (25 percent). Television ranked higher than interpersonal forms of communication such as getting news from family (45 percent) or friends (27 percent).

Qualitative analysis found that consuming news from home or from their own immigrant community helped participants continue to locate themselves within homeland collectives.[35] Luis, a fifty-five-year-old Dominican doctor, imagined himself as a leader in a larger national family by combining both virtual and imaginative forms of co-presence: "I call three times a month and read the news every day. I watch the Dominican satellite channel every day. I listen to the Dominican programs on Sundays. I am in contact with the Dominicans 100 percent. I'm like the father leading the chicks (*el papá de los pollitos*). Sometimes I get bored and I go to the beach and take my radio with me, and I find out what's happening in the DR, the daily happenings, politics. The Dominican likes politics a lot. He likes to know what is happening and so here we all talk about all of it."

Mayra, a Puerto Rican who moved to the US mainland fifteen years prior, watched cable news in English to learn what was happening in the United States and read the website of the San Juan newspaper *El Nuevo Día* every day to keep up with what was happening with her family. "I love to know what's going on in San Juan, with my sister, you know. Also to know what is happening in politics. I love to be up to date with what is going on." Similarly, Santa used the news she heard from Internet-based Dominican newspapers and transnational television in mundane conversations with her family over the phone, allowing more fluid participation in daily relationships. As she explained, "Just today I told my sister, 'Wow, we will be able to call you with a new area code.' I heard it on the Dominican channel. . . . She said she had just heard commentaries. Sometimes we get the news confirmed here more than the rumors they hear there."

Haitians in our quantitative survey had a distinctively strong preference for and use of radio to obtain news about their country of origin compared to other groups. Qualitative interviews suggest that Haitians seek out Creole-language radio for information about Haiti as well as the positive emotional effects of immersing themselves in their own language and cultural references. Haitian participants explained that hearing Creole on the radio made them "happy," or "feel good." Haitian Creole is marginalized in comparison to both Spanish and English in Miami. It is the primary language of most Haitians. The most easily accessible Creole-language media in Miami is AM radio, which carries dozens of informational, cultural, and musical programs targeting the Haitian community audience. Immigrants' homeland and ethnic community media consumption supports Silverstone's argument that consumption of national news reinforces the social embeddedness of national audience members.[36] Although his cases were geographically bound, the patterns we find in our study are transnational.

Co-Presence Through Embodied Proxies

As a final strategy of evoking feelings of co-presence, embodied proxies also involved imagining, but further implied that people who shared the same physical space with immigrants in Miami were embodied representations of absent loved ones. Proxies for country-of-origin family members and friends shared cultural markers and references with the immigrant, including religious practices, distinct uses of humor and language, or references to people, places, and things. Similar to the use of cultural objects to stimulate imagination, embodied proxies for loved ones and groups promoted experiences that made immigrants feel as if they were physically co-present with people they knew and cared about back home.

Some of our survey questions captured aspects of co-presence by embodied proxies, such as questions about friendships and participation in activities with people of the same national origin. Almost half of those in our quantitative sample, 45 percent, said their closest friends in Florida were of the same national origin, though variation occurred by national origin. Haitians (66 percent), Cubans (53 percent), and Colombians (50 percent) were more likely than the average respondent to have friends from the same country of origin, which could reflect their higher numbers in the city. About one-third of the overall sample (34 percent) participated in religious services in Miami with conationals. About 44 percent at least sometimes participated in national festivals, but only about 10 percent participated at least sometimes in organizations and associations related to the home country. The *outlier* group in almost all of these categories was Haitians. Haitians were more likely to have a best friend from the country of origin, especially women (72 percent compared to 61 percent for men), and much more likely to attend religious services with people from the country of origin (79 percent compared to 34 percent for the entire sample).

Ivan, a Jewish Colombian doctor discussed in earlier chapters, engaged in practices that illustrated this mode of co-presence. It was important to him to create support networks of friends in Miami after he moved from Colombia:

My Colombian friends [in Miami] are Colombians I met here or
that I knew in my country. As professionals and as friends we
grew up together. Or friends that I met here and that really are
friends—not the type who will invite you for a drink once in a
while—but friends who when you need it, they may not be able to
help you economically, but they will give you support, which is
what one needs in this country because it can be very lonely. The
only customs that I maintain here are from my family home
(*hogar*), from my house, typical Colombian food that I make
kosher but is still typically Colombian. *Ajiaco, sancochos,*[37]
empanadas, all of that. Because it is part of the legacy of my
family home, just like in my house in Colombia. The rest of it,
not really, because I do not go around with the Colombian flag on
July 20 [Colombian independence day] in the park that would
present me as one of them. I don't do it, no, no.

Ivan explained he did not attend national Colombian festivals in
Miami because he felt they were held only to create constituencies for
politicians and had heard that many non-Colombians went to them to get
drunk and fight. He and his friends believed politics was a waste of time
and did not want to mix with the entire community of Colombians or the
non-Colombians who attended the rowdy festivals.

Ivan told us that many of his friends in Miami shared his Jewish culture and faith, and he would turn to his rabbi or the wider Jewish community in a crisis. Thus, in addition to proxies for hometown friends, he
sought members of a transnational religious community for support. The
customs Ivan maintained were those that most closely resembled his life in
Colombia, including the particular food of his sentimental home, interacting with the friends he grew up with, and engaging proxies for friends and
members of his religious community from Colombia. Ivan believed they
gave him the security of social support in what, for him, could be a lonely
place. But despite his bouts with loneliness, Ivan was not interested in connecting to the wider group of Colombians in Miami who participated in national politics or festivals. This reluctance on Ivan's part suggests that proxies more likely involved close relationships. Moreover, preparing and
consuming food just like in his home country were a cultural practice he
engaged in, in tandem with cultivating his friendships with hometown coethnics as well as other proxies. As we discuss below, overlaying strategies
of co-presence are common and create richer experiences of social co-
presence generally, thereby enhancing emotional well-being.

Finally, finding cultural stand-ins for friends and family back home
was part of the transition many immigrants made from remaining active
only in personal relationships with those in the place of origin to being em-

bedded socially in both poles of translocal space at the same time. Like José, the Mexican immigrant who opened this chapter, Ivan retained memberships in hometown relationships through co-presence at the same time that he sought proxies for his hometown friends and loved ones in Miami. Although co-presence was about remaining socially embedded in the place of origin, it allowed for a seamless lifestyle that drew on and wove together life in two geographically distinct places into one experience of social life, thereby compressing the time and space separating homes located in the country of origin and the homes created in the country of destination. Thus, co-presence using embodied proxies was a strategy, like imaginative co-presence, to feel as if one was socially embedded in the relations of the original home, while at the same time, it was part of a strategy of creating new but familiar social memberships in Miami. In the next chapter, we will describe how creating social memberships in Miami based on cultural similarities was also part of a strategy of translocal placemaking. Together these strategies were meant to produce and reproduce a translocal home.

More than any other group, Haitians evoked absent co-presence with homeland places and loved ones using proxies. Haitians simulated homeland embeddedness through coethnic friendships, participation with coethnics in religious ceremonies, and residence in coethnic neighborhoods. Haitians exhibited some other patterns of co-presence that were common to immigrants from the less-developed countries in the sample, such as slightly less frequent telephone communication or the near absence of Internet chat and instant messaging.

While friends and others at church or in other activities represented, or stood in, for loved ones back home, at the same time, many immigrants sent proxies of themselves back home that embodied their participation in the household from far away. This proxying involved immigrants' sending loved ones gifts, money, and possibly photos or handwritten cards. Although some migrants sent remittances for family survival, justifying their presence abroad and reminding them of why they endure the ambiguous losses caused by migration, just as many told us in interviews that they sent mementos or "tokens" for special days such as birthdays and weddings. Such gifts made their presence felt back home and allowed them to participate by proxy in family events. Similarly, friends of Joaquín, a Peruvian, asked for handwritten correspondence rather than disembodied e-mails because his handwritten letters enhanced his friends' emotional connections to him: "I maintain a constant connection with my family and friends in Lima, by phone and through the Internet. Every now and then I write letters because I have friends that ask me to write to them because they have not seen my handwriting in a long time. So you take your time and you write to them by hand."

That his friends have not seen his handwriting in some time is indicative of the void often left upon immigrants' departures and that handwriting embodies a physical presence—something to hold on to that is more personal than an e-mail printout. Wanting a handwritten letter from Joaquín is a way to establish a link to him—in other words, co-presence by proxy, in spite of how far away he was.

As Loretta Baldassar along with Sean McKenzie and Cecilia Menjívar argue, the emotions undergirding remittances, gifts, and handwritten correspondence mean that money and goods sent back home are important for more than the monetary value of the remittance itself.[38] They were reassurances that immigrants had not forgotten about those in the sending country and provided a means of participating in the reciprocal obligations of an intimate relationship.

In our quantitative sample, more men (54 percent) sent economic remittances than women (50 percent). This percentage included those who sent remittances frequently and rarely. More specifically, about one-fifth of men and women sent money at least once a month. Haitians (47 percent) and Central Americans and Mexicans together (38 percent) sent more money on a regular basis than those from other countries. These larger and more frequent monetary remittances could reflect that those who are on the receiving end of the remittances faced greater need or had less of a safety net, therefore higher amounts were needed and, thus, sent.

Overlapping Strategies of Co-Presence

Although we have examined various measures of embodied and absent co-presence, most immigrants in Miami incorporated several modes of absent co-presence in their daily routines and supplemented those with embodied co-presence if they could travel or had others visit them in Miami. Camila, a Peruvian who migrated when her husband lost his job, said that "the emotional part is the hard part." Camila took steps to remain embedded in the daily life of her family and friendship network in Lima. Multiple strategies of co-presence allowed her to participate in these relationships as part of her daily life in Miami, feeling as if she were there in Lima:

CAMILA: Well, they [family] come to visit. Everyone comes. I've had friends, relatives, constantly I have visitors. Or by telephone, or by e-mail.

RESEARCHER: So, for example, when your mom is in Lima, how often do you communicate with her?

CAMILA: I think three times a week.

RESEARCHER: And, for example, your friends from high school?

CAMILA: I chat with them almost every day. I call them by phone, and I call them and I participate as if I was at a get-together with them.

Camila, like many others in our study, used multiple forms of co-presence to embed important home country relationships in her daily life in Miami. Some groups, however, were constrained when enacting certain strategies of co-presence, particularly embodied co-presence as we have seen (e.g., through visits) but also Internet-based communications. Immigrants from different countries faced different kinds and levels of constraints in their attempts to experience and remain active in cross-border relationships.

Despite national-origin differences in how individuals from particular groups sought to establish co-presence, the large majority of our participants sought to regularly establish some mode of co-presence with significant people and places from the country of origin no matter what constraints they confronted. However, what do the efforts to maintain these strategies represent to those left in the countries of origin? What are the implications of remaining embedded in the place of origin for alternative forms of defining citizenship, particularly among those who live their lives stretched across national boundaries? Moreover, are these specific practices and their deployment in the construction of translocalism of particular importance when we consider whether they resolved the ambivalence, nostalgia, and feelings of ambiguous loss documented at the outset of this chapter? More broadly, did they affect immigrants' feelings of well-being and emotional states overall?

Co-Presence and Translocal Social Citizenship

The practices of co-presence illustrated here constituted some of the ways immigrants sought to belong simultaneously in communities that were split by international boundaries but joined materially and symbolically in a translocal space. These practices involved embodied mobility as well as virtual and imaginative linkages connecting the *felt experience of home* in the place of origin to what might become a *felt home* if a sense of belonging were established in Miami. Jørgen Carling believes these interactions are part of a "moral economy of social belonging" that produces reciprocal manifestations of group membership and loyalty.[39] The visits, phone calls, and gifts embodied emotional reciprocity creating psychic resources that continuously bound together members of social groupings separated by physical distance.

The moral obligations of translocality are strongly present in Miami's immigrant population. As we have shown, although women are somewhat more likely to feel that keeping in touch and visiting the country of origin are very important, both women and men developed strategies that allowed them to remain involved in the lives of those they left behind. These efforts were not just individual strategies to maintain emotional well-being or mitigate the effects of ambiguous loss as we have shown; they also represented efforts to hold on to vernacular forms of citizenship in home society groupings. For example, Yanira, a Puerto Rican, had strong emotional links to the island and remained in touch with kin through the telephone and letter writing, but these specific actions were part of a larger agenda that involved "being there" for her family: "I would say that they [ties] are strong. I write to my friends pretty often . . . and I also communicate with my family, and if they need anything, we are there. My husband has both of his sisters there, so I would say that they [ties] are and continue to be strong."

Although Yanira did not visit the island very often, her husband went at least twice or thrice a year for business. Additionally, although they did not send money home, as she indicated, they were "there" if their family needed anything. The notion of "being there" is a form of sentient resource that immigrants provide to those left behind. M. Bianet Castellanos argues that sentiments such as love and concern transmitted within a migrant network to improve the lives of others work toward the construction (and reproduction) of a multisite community. [40] Moreover, "being there" also acts as a proxy for a link in a broader social safety net. That her family in Puerto Rico could rely on her for assistance spoke to Yanira's contribution to the social infrastructure of residents of Puerto Rico, an island that more and more is witnessing population loss due to out-migration. Like Yanira, many others in our sample expressed similar sentiments regarding kin back home and their desires to "be there" for them. As a type of care work, "being there" does not just benefit those left behind but is reciprocal across space. Thus, we argue that it is a manifestation of civic engagement in the country of origin as it contributes to the work of social reproduction within transnational households. Does this mean that copresence and its consequences—particularly being on the receiving but also giving end of care—translate into an alternative form of citizenship?

Feminist citizenship theories have problematized the masculinist assumptions undergirding legal definitions of citizenship:

> According to feminist theory, the emphasis on citizenship as legal rights reflects male concerns for legitimacy and individualism. The concern for legitimacy may also be tied to the "competitive norms of capitalist culture" (Jones 1990, 807), since property rights of inheritance traditionally belong to legitimate heirs alone. When male concerns for rights and legitimacy dominate the discourse about citizenship, the focus becomes less on maximizing citizen participation and more on deciding which groups should be recognized as citizens and which should be excluded. [41]

Carol Hardy-Fanta argues for a version of feminist citizenship based on broad-based participation that promotes full inclusion of diverse groups and an approach in which difference does not preclude equal treatment. She asserts that community is maintained through relationships, but also balances mutuality with protections to individuality. Importantly, she states, "Community is built out of personal relationships, and citizenship is more than a set of interactions between individuals and state institutions."[42] Hardy-Fanta's perspective on feminist citizenship means that being part of a community is more than a legal right or entitlement bestowed upon some populations and not others, but really, it is built upon relationships among individuals, the level of equality in these relationships, and opportunities for fulfilling relationships, not just with individuals but among groups.

Feminist theorists Pamela Herd and Madonna Harrington Meyer believe that varying kinds of unpaid care work, which they define as the "daily physical and emotional labor of feeding and nurturing citizens," are vital forms of civic activity.[43] Grounded in this premise, we argue that expressing care within a migrant network embodies a form of social citizenship, in which the relationship to the place of origin and those who inhabit and constitute it for the departed immigrant is defined more by immigrant practices, often rooted in affect, than by their legal relationships to the state. Thus, a form of translocal social citizenship results from immigrants' sustained involvement in mundane shared practices of caring, belonging, or sentiment spread geographically across borders, or, as Nina Glick Schiller and Ayse Caglar state, "incorporative forms of daily participation in the social life" of a geographically distantiated collective.[44]

Full citizenship, thus, can be measured by more than one's legal papers. Immigrants' strategies of expressing social citizenship involved nurturing relationships over long distances and contributing to the work of social reproduction at various scales—tasks that often are accomplished through co-presence strategies. These citizenship practices reflect the moral economy of belonging that immigrants experience as embodied globalists.

Thus, returning to the example above, Yanira's care work—which benefited members of the home society—was a form of participatory social citizenship.[45] Immigrants such as Yanira are part of a translocal community of sentiment through social citizenship efforts that span borders. Even though immigrants are not physically present, they maintain involvement in the affairs of their multisite communities through these expressions of care. Unclear, though, is whether expressing involvement and forms of care across borders facilitates immigrant well-being. We turn to this question in the next section.

Co-Presence and Feelings of Well-Being

As we have seen, the emotions that shape the experiences of migration and settlement invoke a mix of practices to participate physically, virtually, imaginatively, or by proxy in stable and nurturing relationships with loved ones, while also surrounding immigrants symbolically in the comforting cultural landscapes of the homeland. In this section we examine the statistical relationship between the strategies of co-presence we have documented, which represent forms of transnational civic engagement, and the emotional states of immigrants. Although some of the indicators we employ are not ideal measures of co-presence strategies, and in many cases, they are not exhaustive of the concepts they seek to operationalize, our intent is to better understand whether and which strategies of co-presence are significantly related to immigrants' emotional states, particularly emotional well-being and the presence of positive affect (also referred to as happiness).

In the analysis, our outcome is a modified version of the Bradburn Affect Balance Scale (ABS), used to assess emotional well-being or happiness.[46] This scale has equal numbers of questions gauging positive and negative affect; the scale is determined by subtracting scores on negative affect from positive affect scores yielding a measure of affect balance or "happiness." We begin by documenting immigrants' reports of happiness by country or region of origin and gender to later interpret whether strategies of co-presence change these at all. Figure 7.1 charts a means comparison of scores for the ABS by origin and gender. Higher scores indicate a greater prevalence of positive affect or happiness.

Comparing positive affect across origin and gender reveals that Cuban women and men have among the highest levels of happiness, only trailing South American and non-Spanish Caribbean men. Among those with the lowest happiness scores are Haitian men and women and Spanish Caribbean men and women but especially the men, who have the lowest scores of all groups. Cubans' higher scores on positive affect may reflect the fact that they do not need to visit the homeland to feel the comfort evoked in embodied co-presence. While a longing for Cuba (nostalgia) remains for many Cuban immigrants, compared to other groups, Cubans may be better able to cope with ambiguous loss by reconstituting their family and friendship networks in Miami. On the other hand, Haitians were less likely to migrate with family members than other nationality groups and instead worked very hard to reconstitute families in Miami through reunification provisions in US immigration law after at least one family member secured residency. Many of the Haitians in our qualitative sample were brought over by parents who first migrated and then sent for them as children and were seeking to sponsor the visas of other family members at the time of their interview. The remaining analyses test whether strategies of creating co-presence increased or decreased happiness.

267

Figure 7.1 ABS (Happiness) Scores by Country/Region of Origin and Gender

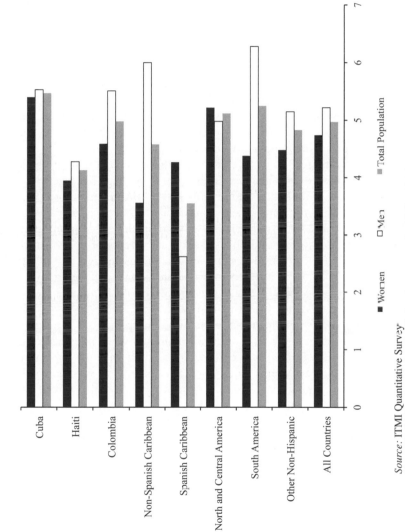

Source: ITMI Quantitative Survey
Note: The higher the number, the higher the score on the AES, which indicates positive affect, or happiness.

Embodied Co-Presence and Happiness

In Table 7.3,[47] Model 1 shows that compared to never having visited the home country, visiting only once in the last twelve months was related to decreased happiness. When controlling for country of origin in Model 2, we found that those who had visited, but not necessarily in the last twelve months, were happier than those who had never visited since they left. Regardless of the number of visits, Haitians, non-Spanish-speaking Caribbean immigrants, and people from the Spanish Caribbean (Dominicans and Puerto Ricans) showed overall less happiness compared to Cubans. In Model 3, when the rest of the controls are included, Model 2's results on visits remain significant, suggesting that sporadic visits (e.g., maybe once every two years) may be better for maintaining happiness than never visiting. Also, the country-of-origin differences remained, and the "other non-Hispanics" group also reported lower happiness than Cubans. These country-of-origin patterns are illustrated in Figure 7.1.

Based on these findings we speculate that sporadic visits to the homeland are associated with increases in happiness, perhaps because trips home are important symbolically and also facilitate other forms of co-presence, including conversation and imagination about prior trips or any future trips. At the same time, *never* going home may diminish participation in kinship networks of reciprocity and dull the ancillary effects of conversation and imagination. While our findings and interpretations suggest that integration in homeland networks is important for emotional well-being, future research should also include queries on the effects on happiness from visits from family and friends from the homeland.

Our qualitative evidence supports these interpretations. Embodied co-presence helped ease the ambivalence Natalia felt when missing her family in the Dominican Republic, even though she knew that she was more economically secure in Miami. She brought her parents to visit when she felt sad, sent money monthly, and called them weekly. She also stayed in touch with childhood friends, exchanged birthday calls with them, and visited Santo Domingo with her children. As the quantitative results show, however, the frequency of visiting is important to understanding how embodied co-presence relates to happiness. Natalia stated, "When I visit I feel a sentiment, like nostalgia, like sadness, when I think of them, when I see, you know, so much poverty. Though in my country I can be with my family, and there are many pretty things to see and appreciate, many pretty things in my country, the beaches, nature."

This quote suggests contradicting effects of visiting that might shed light on why more frequent visits seem to have no significant effects on happiness. On the one hand, embodied co-presence can infuse immigrants with positive feelings that come from being amidst family and friends as

Table 7.3 Effect of Embodied Co-Presence on Happiness (OLS regression)

	Model 1			Model 2			Model 3		
	Estimate	SE		Estimate	SE		Estimate	SE	
Corporeal co-presence variables									
Visits to the home country									
Never visited since leaving[a]									
No visits in last 12 mos.	—	—		0.61	0.31	*	0.73	0.31	**
One visit in last 12 mos.	−0.61	0.35	†	—	—		—		
Two visits in last 12 mos.	—	—		—	—		—	—	
Three visits in last 12 mos.	—	—		—	—		—	—	
Country/region of origin									
Cuba[a]									
Haiti				−1.35	0.52	**	−1.08	0.55	*
Colombia				—	—		—	—	
Non-Spanish Caribbean				−0.98	0.47	*	−1.38	0.54	**
Spanish Caribbean				−1.94	0.48	***	−1.78	0.49	***
North and Central America				—	—		—	—	
South America				—	—		—	—	
Other non-Hispanic				—	—		−1.73	0.6	**
Control variables									
Female							—	—	
Age							—	—	
Married							0.51	0.26	*
Years in the United States							—		
Years of education							—	—	
Citizen							—	—	
Perceived English fluency									
Does not speak English well/at all							−1.16	0.43	†
Speaks English well							−1.03	0.35	**
Speaks English very well[a]									
Receiving differential treatment because of phenotype is									
No problem[a]									
A small problem							−1.36	0.39	***
Somewhat of a problem							−1.11	0.46	**
A major problem							−1.91	0.68	**
Yearly income (US$)									
Less than 20,000							−1.81	0.64	**
20,000–39,999							—	—	
40,000–59,999							—	—	
60,000–79,999							—	—	
80,000 +[a]									
Intercept	4.97	0.21	***	5.27	0.23	***	6.61	1.02	***

Source: ITMI Quantitative Survey.

Notes: a. Reference group.

Predictors lacking any significant effect are excluded from the table, even though they were included in the models.

† = p ≤ 0.10; * = p ≤ 0.05; ** = p ≤ 0.010; *** = p ≤ 0.001.

well as in the cultural and physical environment of the country. At the same time, Natalia made reference to the poverty in the country that introduced feelings of sadness—embodied co-presence put her in greater proximity to this social problem. From these comments, we can speculate that although the trips helped her to manage the ambiguous loss and nostalgia that she felt by being away from her family and country, the frequency of these visits matters for what they reveal about immigrants' struggles. Sporadic visits may be manifestations of symbolic ethnicity or a form of ethnic involvement in which "ethnic identity needs" are not intense; thus, the connections to one's ethnicity, or, in this case, the country of origin, are more symbolic in nature.[48] Herbert Gans argues that symbolic ethnicities can persist across generations.[49] We argue that symbolic ethnicity, as manifested through visits, is associated with enhanced well-being, as these visits may be related to leisure and reuniting with kin. Taking more frequent trips, although not statistically significant, might suggest that immigrants have greater "identity needs" and, thus, are homesick and travel to seek comfort. Alternatively, frequent trips may suggest that immigrants must return to take care of family issues (e.g., an illness). These visits ultimately may not significantly increase happiness. Moreover, if one considers the case above, frequent visits may result in decreased happiness given repeated exposure to the country of origin's problems, perhaps even the same problems that originally led to immigrants' departures. This reminder could introduce negative emotions, such as sadness. Although the sadness might have dissipated when Natalia returned to Miami from her visit, some of these feelings possibly remained, similar to the survivor guilt that refugees report, albeit to a lesser extent.

Virtual Co-Presence and Happiness

Table 7.4 presents results from the analysis exploring how virtual co-presence relates to happiness. Using frequency of communication as an indicator of virtual co-presence, Model 1 shows that people who rarely communicate with anyone in the home country are happier than those who never communicate with anyone in the home country. When country of origin is controlled for in Model 2, those who sometimes or rarely communicate have higher levels of happiness than those who never communicate. Model 3, which includes the full set of controls, reveals that any level of communication increases happiness compared to never communicating at all, although the highest gains belong to those who communicate less often.

The clearest finding is that communication with people back home is associated with greater happiness. Although we cannot speak directly to causality based on these tests, we can show that communicating with home is associated with being happy. However, as with trips home, communicating sometimes or rarely is associated with higher levels of happi-

Table 7.4 Effect of Virtual Co-Presence on Happiness (OLS regression)

	Model 1			Model 2			Model 3		
	Estimate	SE		Estimate	SE		Estimate	SE	
Virtual co-presence variables									
Frequency of communication with home country									
Always communicates	—	—		—	—		0.94	0.45	*
Sometimes communicates	—	—		0.69	0.43	†	1.22	0.43	**
Rarely communicates	0.78	0.46	†	1.02	0.47	*	1.36	0.46	**
Never communicates[a]									
Country/region of origin									
Cuba[a]									
Haiti				−1.44	0.51	**	−1.25	0.53	**
Colombia				—	—		−0.75	0.51	†
Non-Spanish Caribbean				−0.95	0.46	*	−1.51	0.52	**
Spanish Caribbean				−1.9	0.48	***	−1.84	0.48	***
North and Central America				—	—		—	—	
South America				—	—		−0.67	0.43	†
Other non-Hispanic				—	—		−1.81	0.58	***
Control variables									
Female							—	—	
Age							—	—	
Married							0.44	0.25	†
Years in the United States								—	
Years of education							—	—	
Citizenship							—		
Perceived English fluency									
Does not speak English well/at all							−1.12	0.41	**
Speaks English well							−1.08	0.33	***
Speaks English very well[a]									
Receiving differential treatment because of phenotype is									
No problem[a]									
A small problem							−1.39	0.39	***
Somewhat of a problem							−1.11	0.46	**
A major problem							−1.85	0.66	**
Yearly income (US$)									
Less than 20,000							−1.79	0.59	**
20,000–39,999							—	—	
40,000–59,999							—	—	
60,000–79,999							—	—	
80,000 + [a]									
Intercept	4.76	0.33	***	4.94	0.34	***	5.71	1.02	***

Source: ITMI Quantitative Survey.
Notes: a. Reference group.
Predictors lacking any significant effect are excluded from the table, even though they were included in the models.
† = p ≤ 0.10; * = p ≤ 0.05; ** = p ≤ 0.010; *** = p ≤ 0.001.

ness than communicating constantly. This apparent contradiction suggests two possibilities.

First, frequent conversations may serve as constant reminders of problems in the country of origin or Miami, or frequent conversations may be needed to solve these problems. Conversely, perhaps to avoid the negative effects of hearing about these problems, immigrants purposefully avoid contact to spare themselves the heartache. For example, a Haitian immigrant, Mirta, told us she only called when she had money or gifts to send because the needy situation of her family members in Haiti made her feel bad: "It's hard because you know when you call, you will be asked, 'When can you send something to me?' and such. Because you don't have [money] to send, you make very few calls. You call when you can send something back home. . . . When I know I have nothing to send, I don't call. When I do have, then I call to let them know that I am sending something. If things are bad, I'll know [they will call], so I do what I have to do, work more, sell something or whatever to send something. But I don't like this type of suffering."

A second interpretation is that consistent communication is symptomatic of immigrant struggles, whether they involve homesickness, trouble adapting or integrating, or something else. The qualitative evidence we presented throughout this chapter suggests that immigrants reach out to loved ones because they need the comfort or support that comes from remaining active in these relationships. Recall Camila, the Peruvian, who said, "The emotional part is the hard part." Or take Carlos, a Dominican father who left his son with his mother and grandmother in the home country so he could earn enough to better care for him materially. Carlos said he called his son every day in order to remain active in his life. "An emotional bond was going to break," he explained. Carlos may be calling daily to assuage the boy's loss of the physical presence of his father. He additionally may be calling to assuage his own guilt and, especially, to manage his mixed emotions at leaving. In Carlos's interview, he discussed the possibility that the bond might break, the boy's feelings about losing the physical presence of his father, and Carlos's own conviction that the boy was better off with his father working abroad and sending money for his care. So immigrants who call daily may be those who are separated from family and close friends and who feel higher levels of ambiguous loss, or ambivalence to begin with, and therefore are less happy in Miami. In other words, a selectivity effect may be taking place among those who regularly call. For immigrants who are better integrated in both Miami and in the homeland, and who have come to terms with their migration decisions, including the contradicting feelings that can result, moderate communication may keep them active enough in homeland relationships to feel its positive effects.

Imaginative Co-Presence and Happiness

The stories by the immigrants interviewed confirm that the happiest immigrants live translocal lives, mitigating loss, ambivalence, and ontological insecurity by remaining important and relevant to those left in the country of origin. The quantitative results thus far add nuance to our conceptual framework by showing the possibility that enmeshment, beyond just involvement in support networks from the country of origin, may detract from immigrant well-being rather than enhance it. What does the evidence about imaginative co-presence and co-presence by proxy add to these findings?

Our survey did not include measures we considered sufficiently valid as indicators of imaginative co-presence. This area of research deserves further development. However, we do have qualitative evidence that immigrants in our sample used media content from the homeland or produced by the Miami-based coethnic community for imaginative co-presence. Remember Luis, the Dominican, who went to the beach (which he remarked felt and looked like home) to listen to the political news from the Dominican Republic. There he felt like the "*papá de los pollitos*," the father of the chicks in the farmyard, a metaphor for the retired doctor's sense of being a leader in the Dominican nation. Mirta, the Haitian immigrant who avoided painful phone calls, happily recalled her younger days in a better-off Haiti when she listened to music on Creole-language radio stations. She used media consumption to create a translocal space that additionally compressed time, while imagining, feeling, and physically sensing the social embeddedness of a past moment in her life in Haiti.

When asked why she listened to Haitian radio in Miami, Mirta responded, "So I can know what is going on. Like I said, I feel good when I hear some Haitian music, happy music, and they are telling you about your country and what's going on. You feel as though you are there [in your own world]" The answer initially suggests an information-seeking motivation, but quickly apparent is that Mirta's desire to hear news and other programming in Creole is driven by the affective and experiential dimensions of media consumption, which create a feeling that she is in her own world, where she feels safe, calm, and happy. The following interview excerpt links her feelings about Haiti to her emplaced relationships as well as to a sense of public security she associated with a time prior to neoliberal dislocations of production discussed in Chapter 2.

RESEARCHER: How do you feel when you listen to the radio? Happy, sad, nostalgic, informed, something else, nothing special really? Why?

MIRTA: Let's see, the program *Bengie* plays some music that makes me remember the last time I was in Haiti. Some of the music is nostalgic because you are remembering that the time these songs/music were being performed was when Haiti was okay [literally, "was standing on both its legs, standing upright"]. It was like you can be lying in bed and feel like going somewhere and you get up, get dressed, and go out without fear of leaving your home. You get dressed to go out with your boyfriend, fiancée, husband, or whatever. No matter the time, because you simply call up someone and say, "I am not sleepy. Do you want to go out?" . . . If you decided to go, it could be midnight. You get dressed and there are some nice places to walk and see in Haiti, like La Cave, La Detant. You know you could get something to eat, and walk. It's not like you would run into questionable characters, although there are people like that everywhere, but you know there are others as well. Like places like Ca Mawon,[50] these people are in the streets the entire night. Why can't things be that way again? People in the streets all night, folks playing games, and others playing music and people dancing (sighs). Although at that time, there was never enough food, never enough money, except that our agriculture was good, and people would find food through that to eat, a place to sleep; I am not sure what happened.

Mirta turned to Creole-language radio to stimulate imaginary co-presence with people and places that provided her tranquility, stability, and predictability at a time when other forms of co-presence were blocked to her. At the time of her interview in 2008, she had been back to Haiti once in the past year for a funeral and was working to bring her father over to help her care for her son. As mentioned previously, she called infrequently because she only liked to call when she could send money. Therefore, Haitian radio programs in Creole were among those things associated with Haiti that took her back in time to experience feelings of comfort linked to better times.

Co-Presence by Proxy and Happiness

To measure co-presence by proxy, a number of indicators were used to test the relationships between embodied proxy and happiness. Table 7.5 presents regression analysis in which five different indicators of co-presence by proxy were examined. Having best friends from the home country and the frequency of sending remittances were not significantly related to immigrants' levels of happiness. In contrast, always attending festivities and celebrating holidays related to the country of origin were associated with increased happiness, when all else was held constant (see Model 3). Similarly, immigrants' involvement in organizations related to the home country was significantly (albeit marginally so) associated with increased happiness. We need to note here, though, that auxiliary analyses showed that when participation in *any* organization was included in the model, it absorbed the effect of participation in ethnic organizations on happiness. In other words, civic engagement and participation in organized group settings are most important to immigrants' happiness, regardless of whether the organization is related to the home country. Paradoxically, attending conational churches was associated with a decrease in happiness. However, this finding is possibly a product of self-selection. Those who are in

Table 7.5 Effect of Co-Presence by Proxy on Happiness (OLS regression)

	Model 1			Model 2			Model 3		
	Estimate	SE		Estimate	SE		Estimate	SE	
Co-presence by proxy									
Best friends are from home country	—	—		—	—		—	—	
Attends festivities related to home country									
Always	—	—		0.8	0.42	†	0.87	0.43	*
Sometimes	—	—		—	—		—	—	
Never[a]									
Attends religious services with conationals	−0.73	0.4	†	−0.73	0.35	*	−0.82	0.37	*
Frequency of participation in home country organizations									
Always	1.46	0.79	†	1.5	0.79	*	1.34	0.77	†
Sometimes	—	—		—	—		—	—	
Rarely	—	—		—	—		—	—	
Never[a]									
Sends remittances									
Frequently	—	—		—	—		—	—	
Sometimes	—	—		—	—		—	—	
Rarely	—	—		—	—		—	—	
Never[a]									
Control variables									
Country/region of origin									
Cuba									
Haiti				−1.09	0.55	*	−0.89	0.56	†
Colombia				—	—		−0.81	0.5	†
Non-Spanish Caribbean				−1.24	0.46	**	−1.65	0.51	***
Spanish Caribbean				−2.11	0.46	***	−1.97	0.48	***
North and Central America				—	—		—	—	
South America				—	—		0.79	0.44	†
Other non-Hispanic				−1.06	0.56	†	−2.01	0.58	***
Female				—	—		—	—	
Age				—	—		—	—	
Married				—	—		0.56	0.26	*
Years in the United States				—	—		—	—	
Years of education				—	—		—	—	
Citizenship				—	—		—	—	

(continues)

Table 7.5 continued

	Model 1			Model 2			Model 3		
	Estimate	SE		Estimate	SE		Estimate	SE	
Perceived English fluency									
Does not speak English well/at all							−0.99	0.43	*
Speaks English well							−0.92	0.34	**
Speaks English very well[a]									
Receiving differential treatment because of phenotype is									
No problem[a]									
A small problem							−1.32	0.39	***
Somewhat of a problem							−1.09	0.46	*
A major problem							−2.00	0.68	**
Yearly income (US$)									
Less than 20,000							−1.52	0.57	**
20,000–39,999							—	—	
40,000–59,999							—	—	
60,000–79,999							—	—	
80,000 + [a]									
Intercept	5.28	0.24	***	5.87	0.3	***	6.64	0.98	***

Source: ITMI Quantitative Survey.
Notes: a. Reference group.
Predictors lacking any significant effect are excluded from the table, even though they were included in the models.
† = p ≤ 0.10; * = p ≤ 0.05; ** = p ≤ 0.010; *** = p ≤ 0.001.

most emotional angst could be the ones seeking out conational churches. Alternatively, attendance at such churches could be an indicator of a lack of social integration, which itself could lower happiness. In short, of all the indicators that were tested, the only one that solidly confirms our theory that co-presence by proxy increases happiness is attendance at festivities related to the home country.

When examined in combination with the other two indicators that were significantly related to happiness, a broader picture of social integration appears. Considering the positive effects of embodied and virtual co-presence, and the mixed effects of proxies, we can conclude that ways of integrating into US society matter (e.g., civic engagement, social engagement through cultural activities), but also that complete disconnection from home society networks is detrimental to immigrants' happiness (e.g., never visiting and never communicating). Thus, the statistical evidence available reveals that some strategies for co-presence are more effective than others regarding the maintenance of emotional well-being, with the weakest support being for co-presence by proxy. At the same time, immigrants must carefully navigate and straddle their involvement across locales, given that US social integration is also vital to sustaining emotional well-being, and too much enmeshment in the home society may not mitigate the ambivalence and ambiguous loss that migration spurs; in fact, it could make it worse.

Conclusion

In this chapter we analyzed the emotions immigrants experienced and the practices immigrants engaged in to preserve feelings of membership in family, kinship, and friendship groups as well as the wider hometown or home region's cultural groups. For many, the ultimate goal was to improve how they coped with the emotions associated with migration, particularly the ambiguous loss, nostalgia, and ambivalence associated with leaving the natal home, even if the outcomes of migration were positive in other ways (e.g., social mobility, greater physical security). These conflicting emotions and, more generally, perceptions of ontological insecurity led immigrants to sustain practices and ways of being that emphasized co-presence with emotionally significant people and places in the communities of origin. Co-presence strategies served as mechanisms to shrink time and space distantiation. These involved family visits, phone calls, electronic chat and e-mail, the consumption of media produced by the ethnic community and the homeland, the use of embodied proxies, and evocations of homeland culture through food, music, dance, and culturally encoded commodities. Although immigration meant that immigrants were physically anchored to one physical space, through strategies of co-presence they become mentally and emotionally anchored to more than one geographic place, which, in their minds, converged into one social space.

These strategies, to varying degrees, facilitated civic engagement across borders and helped to construct a translocal form of social citizenship that helped migrants manage emotional ambiguity and ontological insecurity. Additionally, they helped immigrants cope with and adapt to the material realities of migration, including the marginality that we spoke of in previous chapters.

Not all immigrants had the same capacities to utilize co-presence strategies to foster translocal social citizenship or increase emotional well-being given the unequal access to communication technologies in the country of origin and in the United States and the inability to travel, among other factors. Our quantitative analyses revealed that remaining active in relationships formed in the places of origin and finding the right balance between preserving ties and creating new social attachments in Miami had important implications for happiness. Indeed, making a balanced life in a translocal space was associated with the highest levels of emotional well-being.

Practices of translocal social belonging provide evidence that perceptions of immigration guided by legally defined citizenship and the exclusionary legal practices constituting the modern nation-state fail to capture the multiplicity of sites and modes of belonging endemic to the populations of the world's globally connected cities. Formal legal frameworks associated with practices such as naturalization, voting, and deportation determine boundaries for belonging and exclusion in the modern nation-state, but the more informal ways of belonging that are constructed through daily local practices that sustain social reproduction, or what Deborah Reed-Danahay and Caroline B. Brettell call "the 'on the ground' vernacular practices employed by immigrants and those in contact with them," create other forms of citizenship that are socially and culturally constructed across and within geographic borders.[51]

As we have maintained throughout this book, place matters. We argue that Greater Miami facilitates another strategy of translocal social citizenship given the physical and cultural compatibilities that enable immigrant adjustment and integration. In other words, just as certain strategies of co-presence help immigrants sustain social citizenship in the country of origin, settlement in a minority-majority city on the edge of the Caribbean facilitates belonging in the destination country. By examining immigrants in Greater Miami, we show how they achieve translocal belonging, in addition to co-presence, by actively re-creating the social environments of the home country in a place that supports their efforts to resolve the range of emotional responses to migration that we have identified. From a broader perspective, practices of social co-presence are combined with translocal placemaking to produce a hybrid notion of negotiated citizenship in which the self seeks to belong at various scales. We examine these placemaking efforts next.

Notes

1. Gieryn 2000; Leach 2002.
2. Giddens 1990, p. 92.
3. Ibid., p. 92.
4. Gergen 1994.
5. Skrbiš 2008, but see Faier 2011.
6. Matt 2011.
7. Ibid., p. 266.
8. Ibid.
9. Boss 1999, 2006.
10. Aranda 2003, 2007; Hochschild 1979.
11. Smelser 1998, p. 6 (emphasis in original).
12. Ibid., p. 8.
13. Aranda 2007; Vaquera and Aranda 2011.
14. Peruvian kinship culture has a broader definition of nieces and nephews than the Anglo American culture. Emilia's cousin's children are also considered her nieces and nephews.

15. Smith 2006.
16. Duany 2011.
17. Vertovec 2009, pp. 974–975.
18. Aranda 2003, 2007; Baldassar 2008; McKay 2006b; Urry 2000; Vargas 2008.
19. Baldassar 2008; Mason 2004; Urry 2000, 2002, 2007.
20. Georgiou 2006; Sampedro 1998; Vargas 2008.
21. Scannell 1995; Moores 2004; Silverstone 1993; IJsselsteijn, van Baren, and van Lanen 2003.
22. Smith 2006.
23. Conradson and McKay 2007, p. 168.
24. Baldassar 2008; Mason 2004; Urry 2002.
25. IJsselsteijn, van Baren, and van Lanen 2003.
26. Biocca and Harms 2002, p. 14, cited in IJsselsteijn, van Baren, and van Lanen 2003, p. 925.
27. Baldassar 2008.
28. Scannell 1995.
29. Aksoy and Robins 2003. Transnational television in this case is produced in the immigrant homeland and consumed abroad. Consumption of transnational television is different from most uses of global television, which is typically produced in a developed country and received in sites all over the world.
30. Baldassar 2008; Hughes et al. 2012.
31. Sampedro 1998.
32. Vargas 2008, p. 50.
33. Silverstone 1993. See also Scannell 1995.
34. Sampedro 1998; Silverstone 1993; Vargas 2008.
35. Along with Internet newspapers, many locally produced Creole-language radio programs for Haitians, and Caracol radio's substantial production for Miami-based Colombians, participants mentioned radio programs produced by the local Dominican community, Miami-based Canal Sur's real-time offering of homeland television news from around South America on cable, and Dominican Republic–based Dominicana TV, also available on local cable. Local cable provider Comcast offers a "Cable Latino" package with real-time news and entertainment channels from around the Americas, including Colombia, Venezuela, Chile, Ecuador, Peru, the Dominican Republic, and Mexico. Additionally, Canal Sur rotates news programs on a single channel. Haitian television programming at the time of the interviews consisted of local Haitian-produced Island TV but expanded to a digital channel with locally produced news in Creole and English for a wider pan-Caribbean audience.
36. Silverstone 1993.
37. Ajiaco and sancocho are traditional Colombian soups.
38. Baldassar 2008; McKenzie and Menjívar 2011.
39. Carling 2008, p. 1458.
40. Bianet Castellanos 2009.
41. Quote within the quote comes from Jones 1990, p. 807. Main quote from Hardy-Fanta 1993, p. 100.
42. Hardy-Fanta 1993, p. 100.
43. Herd and Meyer 2006, p. 325.
44. Glick Schiller and Caglar 2008, p. 205.
45. Herd and Meyer 2006.
46. The original version of the ABS consists of five items measuring positive

affect and five items measuring negative affect (Bradburn 1969; Van Schuur and Kruijtbosch 1995). However, a condensed version of this scale was used during the current investigation: one item from each affective subscale was excluded before data collection commenced given that the items were deemed by the authors to be culturally inappropriate for this population. More clearly, in order to quantify negative affect, participants were asked to respond to the following inquiries: "During the past few weeks, have you . . . (1) felt bored, (2) felt depressed or very unhappy, (3) felt upset because someone criticized you, and (4) felt lonely or isolated from other people." Positive affect was assessed using the following four items: "During the past few weeks, have you . . . (1) felt pleased about accomplishing something, (2) felt particularly excited about something, (3) felt proud because someone complimented you on something you have done, and (4) felt that things were going your way." In alignment with the existing literature, positive and negative affect scores were calculated by adding up the number of affirmative responses to items making up each affective subscale; the resulting values for both positive and negative affect ranged from 0 to 4. Following Bradburn's recommendations, negative affect scores were subtracted from positive affect scores in order to obtain a more comprehensive measure of emotional well-being or happiness; the values that result from these calculations ranged from −4 to 4.

47. In terms of operationalizing our conceptual model, we were limited in measuring embodied co-presence as an independent variable because we did not have data on the visits of family members or friends to Miami. We therefore operationalized embodied co-presence only as immigrants' visits to the home country, examining the relationship between these visits and happiness using nested models.

48. Gans 1979, p. 1.

49. Ibid.

50. While the interviewer did not ask the participant for clarification about these places, from the context and after consultation with Haitian colleagues we believe these to be popular nightspots that Mirta is recalling from younger days in Haiti.

8

Translocal Placemaking and Belonging

Unlike any other state in the United States, [in Miami] you feel like home. Whatever mood strikes you, you can speak either Spanish or English. You can have parrandas¹ during the Christmas season without having to explain its meaning. The people do not look at you as if you are crazy because they understand the Latino culture.

—Yanira, Puerto Rican migrant

My home base is Miami. I have everything here. . . . When I go to Puerto Rico, I enjoy it, the atmosphere and the food. You realize that you are from there. [But] I always liked the Latino environment [in Miami] but with facilities. Like everything is clean and open and relaxed. I can do everything easily. Like to install a phone line. And there is more security. And you realize the differences.

—Marco, Puerto Rican migrant

The statements above from Yanira and Marco illustrate two widespread perceptions that convince migrants from Latin America and the Caribbean that Miami is a place where they can reconstruct their lives. They believe that in the United States, they have the foundations for economic advancement and a peaceful life many lacked in their countries of origin, while at the same time, in Miami in particular they also can remain embedded in a world of cultural understandings and social relationships that affirm their personal and collective identities. Thus, Miami seemed to contain an optimal combination of what they left and what they sought, as many immigrants attained the economic and physical security the United States had to offer along with the feelings of ontological security that Miami provided. Miami helped them to re-create a sense of stability and trust in their place in the world.

In the previous chapter, we explained how immigrants engaged in

281

strategies to maintain social co-presence with people and places in the homeland. A certain level of continued social embeddedness in the natal home helped immigrants to manage ambivalence and other emotions that accompanied the migration process. In this chapter, we show that for many immigrants, another strategy for well-being lies in the selection to live in Miami itself. In this global city they are reminded of their places of origin, where their personal and group identities were originally formed and nurtured. Miami's cultural and sometimes built landscape, as well as its geographic proximity to Latin America and the Caribbean, facilitate a translocal process of emplacement that involves creating sustainable sociocultural environments in which prevailing practices, interpretations, or attitudes evoke emotions, memories, and sensory perceptions that are associated with the place of origin. By combining translocal placemaking with co-presence strategies that allowed immigrants to feel the security of active embeddedness in relationships from the natal home, immigrants evoked the comforts of the natal home in their everyday lives in Miami.

Together, both of these strategies make claims for a more complete process of translocal social citizenship, which is ultimately based on participation in and contribution to social collectives that span international boundaries. Just as men and women "do gender"[2] (or engage in gendered practices) in their everyday lives, so do immigrants "do" or "create" belonging; however, in doing so they weave together common membership practices into a version of everyday belonging that draws from and contributes to multiple social spaces spanning country boundaries (hence, translocal social citizenship). Spanish speakers from around the Caribbean expressed the strongest feelings of belonging in Miami, yet with few exceptions, all of our study participants described a sense of comfort that came from living in a culturally or materially inscribed area with at least some markers of home. For them, Miami produced sensory perceptions and a cultural feel of home and made them believe it could be a place where they found security in the continuing viability of their self-identities and group memberships that are not bound to the nation-state.

Some researchers view the increasing ethnic concentration and cultural retention of immigrants in Miami as a rejection of assimilation.[3] By assimilation we mean the absorption of the US dominant culture and integration into its primary institutions. Others have examined the case of Cuban immigrant incorporation in Miami and advanced the idea that immigrants could assimilate without necessarily acculturating to US dominant norms and culture.[4] In this chapter, we illustrate how the possibility of securing a sense of place and belonging attracts immigrants to settle in Miami and stimulates processes of incorporation based on a daily life enacted in a translocal place that is culturally and socially a hybrid of immigrant homeland and (native) US norms and culture. This is especially true for Spanish-speaking immigrants, but Haitians also enacted some of the processes of placemaking even if not always achieving the same levels of satisfaction with their results. Our results thus call into question the simplistic notion that ethnic concentration represents a "failure to become American" through separation from the "mainstream" and also cast doubts on the underlying assumptions of spatial assimilation research that equates minorities' integration with native whites in white social spaces as the only form of beneficial integration.[5]

Felt and Pragmatic Home: The Attraction of Miami

Immigrants perceive Miami as offering a developed world context of economic opportunity, order, and physical security, like many areas of the United States. But what uniquely attracts immigrants to Miami is the security that comes from continuity in relationships and understandings of their position in the world. The city's newer immigrant residents believe that in Miami, they see a possibility to extend the comfort they felt in their natal homes—in other words, their "felt homes" of emotional security and support[6]—to a developed-world context of physical security and economic opportunity.

Immigrants experience conditions of opportunity, order, and physical security in shops, government offices, and public spaces such as streets or airports. While natives might criticize service, efficiency, and civility in Miami, satisfaction with this orderliness was pervasive among our participants because they compared Miami to what they experienced as public insecurity and bureaucratic inefficiency in their countries of origin. To them, the city felt orderly and materially developed, and they thought of it as a place where they could achieve their pragmatic goals involving multiple dimensions of human security. The control they may reclaim over their lives because of this order and development is part of what makes them say they are happier in Miami than in their places of origin. They believed they could combine the emotional security of the felt home with the economic and physical security they sought through immigration.

Alonso, a concert producer in the Dominican Republic who designed and sold sound equipment in Miami, explained why he believed the city provided an almost perfect context in which to rebuild his life after an economic collapse bankrupted him in the late 1980s.

INTERVIEWER: What impression did you have of life here before you came?

ALONSO: Exactly what I am still living. More tranquility. There is a level of stress as there is everywhere, but a level of stress you can resolve. . . . In our countries at that time there were no options. You couldn't do this; you couldn't do that. It completely shook you up. You could cut your veins, or turn the page, and so I turned the page. . . . Miami has many good things, many open spaces, few high-rises over 100 stories. The air is fresh and clean, my goodness. And there is a Latino environment. Miami is what we would want for our countries. If you think about it clearly, it is an economic system that is super stable, a system for the acquisition of things. It has everything. You have a job in which you earn a living, although you do not necessarily earn a whole lot, but you earn well enough and you speak Spanish . . . [and] this is what people in any country would dream of. What I would want for the Dominican Republic is that it would be like Miami, although that would be impossible.

Alonso lived with his wife and children in Miami and kept in touch with his extended family in the Dominican Republic through weekly telephone calls and regular visits. In Miami, his friends were Dominican, Cuban, and Puerto Rican, all from the Caribbean, as well as Nicaraguan, like his second wife (his first wife died of cancer after moving with him to Miami). His boss was a Cuban immigrant he knew when he worked in the Dominican Republic; his clients included international performers he worked for in his country of origin as well. Thus, for Alonso and many others, Miami was a beautiful, orderly, and clean place where he could mostly earn enough to advance materially within a stable and culturally reaffirming environment that represented an extension of home.

A few things bothered Alonso and other immigrants about Miami, however. When asked about "the bad" in Miami, Alonso identified the government's inability to resolve traffic congestion. He also associated government incapacity with the Latin American origins of most local officials: "Miami is a sweet beauty (*una chulería*)," he said. "The only bad thing about Miami is that everyone, the bad and the good, comes through here (laughs). But really, I love Miami. The bad here is the traffic that these local officials can never fix. Well, almost all are Latinos. That's the problem. If they resolve the traffic problem, this city would be divine." For Alonso, Miami is what he would want for his country, except for the traffic and "bad" immigrants, including public officials, who come in with the good.

The reference to Latino public officials as the source of local urban problems tapped into perceptions that public corruption of civil servants abounds and is something endemic to the Latino politician. This feeling is similar to that of many immigrants about home country politicians, often blamed for causing the conditions of insecurity that prompted their need to immigrate in the first place. Thus, the Latino culture of Miami reminded Alonso of home in both good ways that attract him to Miami and "bad" ways that bothered him, but not enough to cause him to resettle elsewhere.

In numerous interviews, immigrants expressed similar feelings: on the one hand, an appreciation for Miami's public security, orderliness, economic opportunities, and consumer culture as compared to the places of origin, and, on the other, complaints about inconveniences and problems like traffic, rudeness, and comparatively low salaries. Statements linking immigration to the city's problems—the feeling that the city suffers from urban sprawl, lack of civility, and corrupt Latino politicians—in part reflects the reality of urban problems in a city that is more than half immigrant. It also suggests that our study participants were associating public incivility and corruption in Miami with memories of what they did not like about their home countries' urban services, political corruption, and street-level culture, which, at the same time, felt familiar. For example, a recently arrived Puerto Rican graduate assistant for one of the authors of this book, Sallie Hughes, mentioned that parties on the weekends in his lower-middle-class neighborhood disrupted his study, but he shrugged and admitted that he wouldn't move because the noise made him feel like he was back home.

Another example was Cristobal, a journalist and political asylee who left Bogotá, Colombia's capital and largest city, after being threatened by paramilitary members. Cristobal told us in an interview that the good thing about Miami was "everything that has to do with respecting others, simply [respecting another's] life." Yet seconds later, in the same part of the interview, Cristobal said what bothered him most about Miami was that immigrants felt like they could bend or break the law. "Latinos have a problem with authority. We feel that the police are just there to harass us," he said. He cited as examples shoplifting in Kmart or complaints by street vendors about regulation of their food stands. Cristobal believed this behavior was related to "precisely these cultural values that one brings with him, that makes one disrespectful of the life of another." However, statements about incivility in Miami were overshadowed by statements about the appreciation of the area's public order and bureaucratic efficiency as compared to the home country. In the end, our participants chose Miami over other places in the United States with potentially higher salaries and better urban services—and perhaps more urban civility, as suggested by popular polls that rank Miami high on the list of cities with the rudest drivers.[7] Despite its problems, Miami offers immigrants something other places do not: a sense of security associated with the familiarity of home.

Amelia, a forty-four-year-old from Colombia, openly discussed this trade-off and was happy with her decision. Amelia moved from a Caribbean coastal city in Colombia after getting divorced and beginning to feel squeezed out of both the labor market and the market for a new intimate partner. Her descriptions of Miami were gendered by her status as a woman living alone but also reflected trends that held for both women and men alike:

The good thing about Miami is that I feel close to my country. Geographically I feel very close to my country because in two hours I am in my house. From here to Cartagena on the plane it's more or less two hours and fifteen minutes. It is really close. So really everyone comes to visit. I see my girlfriends constantly, my relatives. A lot of people come. I cannot even see them all because I cannot be visiting everyone all the time. Personally, I also love the climate, the heat. I feel secure. Even though people don't like the quantity of people the city has, and all of the traffic, to me, because I live alone, for me this makes me feel like there is life around me. And if I lived further up north, that difficulty, that solitude, would be terrible.

Amelia decided that the multiple dimensions of security she felt in Miami, including the ability to construct a form of multisited belonging, compensated for the city's urban problems and low salaries. As such, she made Miami her home. She continued, "The bad part of Miami, I think, is that because it is a city that is so overpopulated, so obviously the salaries are lower, the things are more expensive, the opportunities I believe are a little less than they could be further up north. But I won't trade the tranquility I feel here. I am very close [to Colombia] and I know a lot of people. . . . My cousin lives in New York and she makes more than I do and pays more for her apartment than I do. She lives more alone. So I prefer to have less money and live peacefully and happy."

Despite inequality and urban stress, eight in ten Miamians from all Latin American and Caribbean nationality groups in our quantitative sample agreed or strongly agreed that living in the United States had made them happier. Amelia, Alonso, Yanira, and Marco attributed their happiness to their experiences of the area as a place that felt like home. The institutional capacities of the city were probably necessary, but not sufficient, to attract immigrants to Miami. As Marco said, Miami was "a Latino environment but with facilities."

Data from our quantitative survey support the attraction of Miami above and beyond the economic reasons immigrants most often offered for decisions to immigrate to the United States. In other words, immigrants decided to move to the United States to seek economic security and advancement,[8] but they chose Miami because of social networks, warm weather, and a number of other conditions that facilitated translocal placemaking such as proximity to the country of origin, ease of travel, and ability to use their native languages. Table 8.1 presents a means comparison of immigrants' reasons for coming to the United States and reasons why they chose to settle in Miami specifically. While about 55 percent of men and 51 percent of women reported they immigrated to the United States for economic

Table 8.1 Reasons for Migrating to Miami Compared to Reasons for Migrating to the United States (percentage)

	Miami		United States	
	Men	Women	Men	Women
Economics	10.1	7.7	30.3	26.7
Job or investment opportunity	12.0	8.7	24.4	24.3
Education	4.7	4.7	13.4	11.4
Having friends or family there	58.1	57.8	17.7	16.4
Quality of life	9.3	8.9	15.1	16.4
Retirement	1.0	1.4	n.d.	n.d.
Proximity to country of origin	10.7	10.0	n.d.	n.d.
Easier travel	4.2	2.9	n.d.	n.d.
Use of native language	5.7	3.1	n.d.	n.d.
Weather	23.8	19.9	n.d.	n.d.
Less crime	2.3	0.6	n.d.	n.d.
Politics	n.d.	n.d.	38.3	32.1
The "American Dream"	n.d.	n.d.	7.8	5.9
Violence in home country	n.d.	n.d.	4.5	5.1
Curiosity	n.d.	n.d.	1.4	2.6
Not my decision	n.d.	n.d.	3.9	3.0
Other	9.0	12.3	6.6	14.1

Source: ITMI Quantitative Survey.
Notes: Percentages do not add up to 100 because respondents were allowed to select multiple answers.
n.d. = no data.

reasons or because of a job or investment opportunity, only 22 percent of men and 16 percent of women said they chose Miami as their destination for these reasons. Global city salary pressures and the perceptions of workplace favoritism discussed below may contribute to these comparatively lower numbers.

At the same time, however, roughly 58 percent of both men and women said they moved to Miami because they had family and friends living there, while just about 18 percent of men and 16 percent of women said they chose to move to the United States to live near family and friends. Contrary to what one might expect, choosing Miami because of family and friendship networks did not vary widely across national-origin groups, but gender differences did emerge within certain groups (see Table 8.2). Of Cubans, 59 percent of men and 68 percent of women said one of the reasons they moved to Miami was because family and friends lived there. Only Haitian women (42 percent) and other non-Hispanics (25–26 percent) responded at substantially lower rates than Cubans and the overall sample.

Miami's tropical weather was also important in the decision to immigrate to Miami (24 percent of men and 20 percent of women listed it as a reason for choosing Miami as a settlement destination), but weather was not

Table 8.2 Reasons for Moving to Miami by Country/Region of Origin and Gender (percentage)

	All		Cuba		Haiti		Colombia		Non-Spanish Caribbean	
	Men	Women	Men	Women	Men	Women	Men	Women	Men	Women
Economics	10.1	7.7	8.6	6.2	10.7	11.9	11.7	6.8	2.4	6.2
Job or investment opportunity	12.0	8.7	6.1	2.1	13.4	8.2	15.4	9.3	11.4	12.6
Education	4.7	4.7	2.1	3.2	11.9	9.9	8.6	7.8	3.4	10.0
Friends or family in South Florida	58.1	57.8	58.8	68.4	58.5	41.6	53.8	52.8	54.2	52.9
Weather	23.8	19.9	26.8	17.9	17.9	21.8	26.5	31.2	25.5	21.2
Less crime	2.3	0.6	1.1	0.0	7.8	4.4	2.3	1.4	0.0	0.0
Quality of life	9.3	8.9	8.5	7.4	20.9	27.8	7.1	6.9	9.6	10.3
Retirement	1.0	1.4	2.0	1.3	0.0	1.6	3.4	0.0	0.7	0.0
Proximity to country of origin	10.7	10.0	13.0	8.0	20.0	14.0	9.5	21.6	5.9	14.3
Easier travel	4.2	2.9	2.6	1.3	19.3	23.5	0.0	0.6	11.4	0.4
Use of native language	5.7	3.1	7.6	5.1	2.0	0.0	5.3	6.9	0.7	0.0
Other	9.0	12.3	10.7	7.3	11.1	16.6	7.1	7.8	10.5	16.9

(continues)

Table 8.2 continued

	Spanish Caribbean		North/Central America		South America		Other Non-Hispanic	
	Men	Women	Men	Women	Men	Women	Men	Women
Economics	5.0	9.4	20.3	15.1	13.5	2.7	9.4	3.2
Job or investment opportunity	0.0	11.7	18.1	9.7	11.1	12.6	45.8	23.4
Education	3.7	4.7	2.8	2.2	7.3	2.2	8.4	6.0
Friends or family in South Florida	68.4	59.0	65.4	62.0	66.0	54.1	25.4	26.5
Weather	44.5	20.0	7.2	15.3	14.3	17.6	29.3	26.8
Less crime	0.0	1.9	5.3	0.4	1.3	0.0	4.8	0.0
Quality of life	5.1	2.4	8.0	6.4	7.9	7.6	11.2	16.2
Retirement	0.0	4.8	0.0	2.1	0.0	0.0	0.0	1.9
Proximity to country of origin	4.6	7.2	9.9	12.9	12.2	5.0	0.0	2.4
Easier travel	0.0	0.0	0.0	3.5	5.5	1.2	0.0	2.4
Use of native language	1.4	0.0	3.7	3.7	14.5	2.7	0.0	0.0
Other	4.4	10.3	3.5	13.6	8.8	16.7	11.3	24.3

Source: ITMI Quantitative Survey.
Notes: N = 1,268.
Totals do not add up to 100 percent because respondents were given the option of choosing multiple reasons.

universally important. It mattered to more people from the Spanish Caribbean and Colombia, with its Caribbean coastline, than to people from mainland Latin America (gender variations also emerged within subgroups). At the same time, few Haitians (2 percent of men and no women) and people from the non-Spanish Caribbean (about 1 percent of men and no women) thought that being able to speak their native languages was important for choosing Miami as a settlement destination. Also, fewer non-Cuban Spanish speakers from the Caribbean cared about language when choosing Miami as a destination (1 percent of men and no women). Comparatively, language use was a settlement factor for Cubans (8 percent of men and 5 percent of women), Mexicans, and Central Americans (4 percent of men and women) and South Americans (about 15 percent of men, but only 3 percent of women).[9]

While generally less important, proximity to the homeland did not produce large differences among groups (except for Haitian men and Colombian women), but ease of travel did. Many more Haitians were likely to have chosen Miami as their US destination because of ease of travel than people from other countries, 19 percent for men and 24 percent for women, compared to an overall average of 4 percent for men and 3 percent for women. This was also important to non-Spanish Caribbean men (11 percent).

These differences suggest Latin American and Caribbean immigrants who settle in Miami view the city as qualitatively different from the rest of the United States. Our interpretation of why this is so is developed in the rest of this chapter.

Placemaking and the Importance of Home

Places, as opposed to unconstructed geographic or physical spaces, are socially constructed and culturally inscribed through previous and ongoing practices, relationships, and worldviews that are "emplaced." In other words, places "are spaces made culturally meaningful" through human action, interaction, and interpretation.[10] They also are part of what constitutes personal and collective identities; they not only evoke identity but also become an ingredient that forms identity.

The mechanism through which places are made culturally meaningful and at the same time also help to constitute cultural identity is inscription. Neil Leach explains the duality of the inscription process as follows: someone identifies with a place and develops a feeling of belonging there, and an identity becomes forged against the physical backdrop of a place, such as its architecture or the natural landscape of a beach.[11] The physical form of a built or natural place thus becomes intricately associated with understandings, emotions, and behaviors in such a way that it may "facilitate a form of identification, and help engender a sense of belonging."[12] The process, then, is iterative. Places are socially constructed as they are inscribed with cultural meaning, and once inscribed, places can facilitate cultural identification and a sense of belonging, and so on.

The form of a built or natural place is inscribed with meaning by the activities that have occurred there. Buildings are inert, but built places are invested with symbolism through performances of ritualistic or repeated behaviors that become associated with the form of a place.[13] "Through repetition in rituals, these spaces are remembered, with participants reinscribing themselves into the space, evoking corporeal memories of previous enactments. The rituals are naturalized through these corporeal memory acts, and the places in which they are enacted become spaces of belonging."[14] Places linger in the minds and bodies of those who experienced them through direct participation in an emplaced activity, such as praying a rosary at a particular shrine or drinking a *cortadito* at a coffee stand window. Additionally, places linger in individuals through understandings, sensations, and emotions associated with the behaviors enacted in those places.

Memory lingers because we do not simply pass through or reside in places.[15] We inhabit them. Inhabiting a place means acting within it, but also "holding" it within us through "body memories" that can be awakened by sensorial or behavioral cues—for instance, remembering past experiences on a humid morning or while listening to music from the homeland. Places are also carried in language, as in regional dialects, jokes, or phrases, as well as in habitual attitudes and behaviors that, while moldable, are also enduring. Places, therefore, stay with us as we move physically across space and time. Places, writes Edward S. Casey, "come to us lastingly":

> Once having been in a particular place for a considerable time—or even briefly if our experience there has been intense—we are forever marked by that place. . . . The whole brute presence of the place. What lingers most powerfully is this presence and, more particularly, *how it felt to be in this presence:* how it felt to be [in that place at that time]. . . . The essence of a place can be compressed into a single sensation that, being reawakened, can bring place back to us in its full vivacity.[16]

Language, body memory, and habitual attitudes and behaviors embed experience as predispositions in thought and action. While individualistic, the general parameters of predispositions hold across groups that share a culture or economic position. These predispositions are what Bourdieu has labeled "habitus" and others might call ways of being and understanding the world that are associated with collective identity. The body's customary actions and the mind's predispositions help to create stability, a "coherent and lasting world to which return can be made again and again."[17] Shared, coherent, and lasting predispositions lay the foundation for the emotional and psychic security Anthony Giddens calls ontological security.[18]

Human attachment to place, and especially the home, has long been studied by psychologists, but only recently has this area garnered the interest of other social scientists.[19] This lag is curious because home is an important place for the formation and maintenance of identity and belonging. Home is where our most intimate relationships are experienced and where our identities are initially formed and nurtured. We express identities through personalization of our material homes, and for most people, home is where we feel most secure physically and ontologically.[20] As J. Douglas Porteous and Sandra Smith have stated, "It is one of the obvious facts of life, so often overlooked, that people are not merely attached to other people but to familiar objects, structures, and environments that nurture the self, support the continuity of life, and act as props to memory and identity. . . . Place is meaningful to people and the place called home is the most meaningful place of all."[21]

Leaving home can be a journey of self-actualization, but forced displacement from home can be traumatic and involves feelings of emotional loss and ontological bewilderment when a place that helped constitute intimate relationships, significant memberships, and personal identities is lost.[22] Immigrants and travelers alike thus try to evoke the home to alleviate loss and dislocation with mementos or symbolic memorials built in ethnic enclaves.[23] Like all human beings, immigrants traveling with families may include the built space of familial intimacy in their idea of home. But for the immigrant, home is more complicated.[24] As we show in this chapter and the previous one, home for the immigrant can be located across more than one territorial space—a translocality that is constituted through enactments and extension of cultural memberships or evoked through "real-time" communication technologies and media that are created in the country of origin and received in the immigrant destination.

Studies of first-generation immigrants have shown that home can be constructed translocally: one's intimate and familiar places, as well as the memories and relationships that constitute them, are situated in two geographic spaces at the same time.[25] Immigrant placemaking extends familiar surroundings and creates mobile subjectivities that are bifocal. As discussed in previous chapters, bifocality includes a "dual frame of reference through which expatriots constantly compare their home and host countries" and the activities and relationships "migrants routinely engage in . . . that bind them to both 'here' and 'there' in their everyday lives."[26] Translocal placemaking creates a continually constructed place "where culture and social relations are recuperated and refigured," writes Deirdre McKay of Filipina domestic workers' placemaking in Hong Kong.[27] For our participants, translocal placemaking in Miami is the act of merging the new home and old home within the mind, body, and structure of experience.

J. Douglas Porteous has argued that displaced people experience a "felt home" of the hearth and a "euphemistic home" of temporary location.[28] Globalization theorists such as Jan Nijman have made similar arguments about the "ephemerality" of Miami.[29] Contrary to Nijman's argument that Miami is a euphemistic home, the lived experiences of Latin American and Caribbean immigrants show that they engage in practices that extend the felt home, rather than euphemistically experience the area as a place they consume and leave behind.

Indeed, from the quantitative data in our study we know that, of those who gave a definitive yes or no answer about future intentions (about one-fifth reported they did not know), the percentage of immigrants who articulated plans to remain living in Miami at least ten years contradicts the idea that the city is a transient one. Table 8.3 reports responses.[30]

Thus, while certain segments of the white and African American populations continue to exit Miami,[31] and while the extent to which the Latin American and Caribbean populations leave the Miami area annually given the continual gains in their numbers (which could represent increasing immigration to the region) is unclear, most of the Latin American and Caribbean immigrants who stay appear to be fully invested in their relationship with Miami. However, exclusionary laws, the increased cost of living, and the most recent housing market crash, among other dynamics, could eventually jeopardize their plans if these factors have not done so already. What we do know is that Miami is a place in which immigrants have made their lives and homes. The following sections illustrate the ways in which immigrants have accomplished this.

Table 8.3 Definite Plans to Stay or Not in South Florida for Ten Years or More (percentage)

Country/Region of Origin	Men		Women	
	Yes	No	Yes	No
Cuba	95.6	4.4	94.3	5.8
Colombia	88.8	11.2	92.9	7.1
Haiti	78.0	22.0	75.3	24.7
Non-Spanish Caribbean	82.0	18.0	79.7	20.3
Spanish Caribbean	74.2	25.8	94.3	5.7
North and Central America	90.7	9.3	96.8	3.2
Other South American	89.0	11.0	88.8	11.2
Other non-Hispanic	92.7	7.3	91.5	8.5

Source: ITMI Quantitative Survey.
Note: N = 917.

(Re)Enacting and (Re)Experiencing Home

Our participants inhabited their places of origin in the full sense Casey described.[32] They acted within them during their formative years, and their minds and bodies carried their natal homes—emotionally, experientially, expressively, and sensorially—in a state of readiness for cues that bring those memories to the surface. In Miami, these cues are frequent because the ambiance of the city is so similar to home places around the Caribbean basin. The environment makes them feel as if they are in both places.

Much work has documented Cubans' reconstruction of their native home in Miami over the last decades, but our data show that immigrants of many national origins extend their homes to multiethnic Miami. Consider Esteban, a Colombian from one of the country's coastal cities. Esteban said he could not live in the US Northeast because of the cold and what he described as "the American way of life there." The feeling of being in Colombia and Miami at the same time persuaded him to choose Miami as his place of settlement: "We cannot deal with the cold. We cannot deal with the American way of life there. Here [Miami] we are in a big Barranquilla. I feel like I am in a bigger version of my city—here in Miami."

Odalys, a Cuban immigrant, described how she experienced multiple temporal and spatial layers of connection that join her natal home in Cuba with Miami: "I would call my mother on the phone and would talk to her and she would tell me, 'It's raining here.' [I would tell her,] 'Here too.' So there are things that bind you. . . . There were many things that remind you, I mean your past, and that bound me a bit to the city. . . . So to adapt I prefer to be in a place where I can, on average, move in between adapting [to the United States] and things that kept me in contact with my past."

Miami acts as a "mnemonic place" for Latin American and Caribbean immigrants that evokes a particular history, culture, and place-bound identity.[33] But immigrants are not only reminded of home through sensory cues but also experience and enact home through performance of or participation in behaviors that are customary, learned, or otherwise associated with their places of origin. The relationship between performance and the sensory feel of place is repetitive and builds on itself, as is the relationship between performance, sensory memory, and the material or built forms of a place. In other words, all three are components of this process.

Performance and sensory memory create a multifaceted experience of being at home that can be a powerful force. Consider Claudia, a Dominican woman who lived first in New York and found the experience dislocating. For Claudia, the feeling of home in Miami is captured through her senses and embodied in customary practices from her homeland. She engaged in what she described below—what we consider to be homeland performances—such as going to the beach or doing her shopping in Spanish, at the same time that sensory cues, such as the temperature and architecture styles in Miami and the Dominican Republic, merged her two territorial homes into one enacted and experienced felt home:

> The best thing that Miami has is that it seems like the Dominican Republic in the sense of the temperature, the beach. We Dominicans, on the weekend one goes to the beach, and it is really close, and like he said, the houses look the same. There are a lot of houses that look like in the Dominican Republic, and in the Dominican Republic now they are constructing high-rises just like here in Miami. And also when I came here for the first time, it seemed good. There was no problem with language, with communication. Here when you go to a store you do not have to think about it. When you go in New York, you have to think in English to ask the person how much something costs. In other words you have to be thinking in English to know how much. Not here. Here people don't bother asking in English. You say, "¿Cuanto cuesta?" [How much is this?], and that is it. Here you have the language, the same temperature as the Dominican Republic. Here the identification is we are all Latinos, and the majority is Hispanic.

Cultural Inclusion and Exclusion

Claudia's last sentence—"Here the identification is we are all Latinos, and the majority is Hispanic"—highlights the widely held notion among Latinos and the wider US populace that Miami offers immigrants unique opportunities for belonging based upon their Iberian or Latin American cultural heritage. Indeed, forming memberships based on shared cultural knowledge, practices, and worldviews is an important way that immigrants engaged in translocal placemaking and created a sense of belonging in Miami. The cultural compatibility that made subgroups of Latinos feel like members of a pan-Latino majority group in Miami occurred both because they found and connected with culturally similar others, and because the worldviews, beliefs, and behaviors of many subgroups were not marginalized in Miami's mainstream cultural landscape. In turn, they felt culturally included and that they belonged.

Yet the concept of cultural citizenship, which Renato Rosaldo refers to as "the right to be different and to belong in a participatory democratic sense,"[34] originally referred to Latinos as a US minority group, viewed in contrast to the native white majority reference group and referring to claims making in the legal sphere of citizenship through cultural practices. In the case of Miami, a minority-majority city, inclusion and membership are sought by subgroups of Latino and non-Latino immigrants who are stratified with regard to country of origin, race, social class, and gender. Immigrant stratification is one of the reasons why a pan-immigrant political movement in favor of immigration reform has not emerged to the same extent in Miami as it has in other major cities. A general sense of cultural inclusion for Latinos can be found, but because it coexists with other forms of immigrant differentiation, cultural inclusion does not lead to pan-immigrant or even pan-Latino political solidarity.

Miami's cultural forces do not work in the same way for all of its immigrant residents, and to the degree that a sense of cultural belonging exists in Miami, it is most strongly identified with Latinos who have perceived exclusion in other parts of the United States and who share the same language as well as some cultural traditions. Language, cultural traditions, and racial norms are part of frameworks of identity learned in an immigrant's place of origin that mark inclusion in a group, but as we saw in Chapter 6, they also stratified immigrants in Miami in multiple ways. In broad brushstrokes, immigrants who were not from the long-established white Cuban subgroup, did not speak Spanish, or were negatively racialized among Latinos and others did not feel the level of inclusion in Miami that other Latinos found strongly appealing and comforting. For immigrants from culturally demoted groups, Miami was perceived to be culturally ambiguous and often exclusionary.

The discussion of language and racialization norms that follows suggests that culturally disadvantaged immigrants can extend homeland memberships to their own conational group in Miami but have trouble finding connections and belonging in the hierarchical ethnic landscape of global Miami. Miami may feel like home to them in certain senses and in some practices that enact embodied memories, but the ability to forge cultural memberships is tenuous when these immigrants move outside of their own coethnic groups. Thus, while translocal placemaking through cultural shareability is real and significant, the ability to create cultural memberships in Miami is also available differentially.

Inclusion, Exclusion, and the Use of Spanish

Our Spanish-language participants discussed the importance of using their native language more often than any other aspect of culture. These immigrants believed that the ability to use their native language was necessary for achieving pragmatic goals, like finding a well-paid job. However, the significance of being able to use Spanish in Miami is more extensive. Use of the native language in everyday life was an activity that provided a sense of comfort because it extended homeland cultural memberships and reinforced personal identities. We noticed this aspect of native-language use for our Spanish-language participants, as well as our Creole-dominant Haitian participants.

Amanda, who is Puerto Rican, discussed how the use of Spanish connects her with a wider Latino collective in Miami and made her feel "at home" at the same time that the area's climate and food blended the ongoing feeling of being in Miami with her embodied memories of Puerto Rico: "The good thing about Miami is that it is very Hispanic . . . and I feel more or less at home because I speak Spanish most of the time. The climate is similar to Puerto Rico, the food, and the way people are is more similar to Puerto Rico."

The association of language with home aesthetically and culturally is important to consider when trying to understand what societal factors contribute to a sense of belonging. Rafael, a Cuban, also felt like use of his native Spanish contributed to his feelings of well-being and of being at home—or in the case of an exile, a better version of home: "You speak in Spanish and that makes you feel, like I was going to say, 'as if you're at home,' but I feel better here than at home if home is Cuba. It makes you feel real good." Language also plays a role in constructing pan-*Latinidad* by easing the process of immigrant adaptation. For example, Guadalupe, a Dominican, stated, "I had an easier time [adapting] . . . because everyone spoke Spanish. . . . I felt closer to my country, to my people, and so I felt a lot better."

Haitians expressed similar feelings about the emplacement capacity of native language when they heard spoken Creole on community radio programs produced in Miami. Haitian Creole is a language that is marginalized by both Spanish and English use in Miami. It is the primary language of most Haitians in Miami, followed by English as a second or third language. The most easily accessible Creole-language media in Miami is on AM radio, which carries dozens of informational, cultural, and musical programs targeting the Haitian community audience. In this case, language is constitutive of membership in a cultural collective because it is communicating information in a way that group members understand, and also because the information is about what is happening to members of the geographically dispersed Haitian nation.

Qualitative interviews suggest that Haitians seek out Creole-language radio both for information about Haiti and the positive emotional effects of embedding themselves in their own language and cultural references, which explains why about eight in ten Haitians in our survey said they preferred to get news from the home country on radio, compared to an average of about three in ten for all Latin American and Caribbean immigrants.

Haitian participants, such as Mirta in Chapter 7, explained that hearing Creole on the radio, and occasionally on a locally produced cable television program, made them "happy," or "feel good." Antoine, a male Haitian participant, explained that both language and news from home evoked a positive emotional experience. "When they give the news in Creole, I am happy. I watch television, I watch 'Island TV' magazine, [listen to] Haitian radio, as long as I have time [literal expression used—"as long as time does not fight me"]. I hope to hear them because I am happy. Information that comes directly from Haiti, I am pleased especially when they are giving the Haitian news. I enjoy hearing that."

Immigrants Ben and Greg discussed Creole-language radio as a way to participate in everyday relations with kin in Haiti. Ben explained, "There is a radio station called Radio Dimanche Ton Nouvel [Your Sunday Newscast], which gives all the news from Haiti. I listen every Sunday morning and it tells me the news so that I can talk to people in Haiti as though I am there."

"It connects you to Haiti, but it is not it," Greg said.

"But it allows me to know what is going on in my home country," said Ben.

Wallace, a sixty-two-year-old man who speaks only Creole, listens to Creole radio to help him get through troubled, sleepless nights. "Because it is what I most understand. I use it all night long; I listen to everything that is going on all night long, you understand, because I don't sleep. It is at night that I listen to the radio."

Use of Creole in Miami helps Haitians connect to a national cultural collective spanning Miami and Haiti, but not to the wider diasporic populations of Miami. This point illustrates one way in which language forms part of what makes an area feel like home, but it also emphasizes that issues of language and belonging are not clear-cut. Language also can serve as a mechanism of exclusion, not just among native whites, African Americans, and Latinos, but within the Latino and Caribbean immigrant populations.

An obvious way that language divides Miami's immigrant population is through the dominance of Spanish. Language politics were furious in Miami during the Cuban ascendance to political power in the 1980s, resulting in an English-only movement that diminished in visibility and power once a Cuban majority was elected to the largest local government boards.[35] By the 2000s, the area had settled into what appears to be a pervasive English-Spanish bilingualism, with Spanish serving as the de facto primary language in many public encounters. The dominance of Spanish remains significant for ethnic relations and in the daily lives of people who do not speak Spanish. The feelings of exclusion caused by this dominance can be found not only among monolingual English-speaking natives, many of whom have left Miami in large numbers since the 1980s, but also Creole-speaking Haitians, along with Jamaicans and others from the English-speaking Caribbean.

Unlike Jamaicans, Haitians are linguistically isolated outside of their diaspora community if they only speak Creole. For some Haitians, the Creole language thus signifies a double marginalization in Miami, both by English and Spanish speakers. This isolation became apparent in a focus group discussion with bilingual and English-dominant Haitian and Haitian American college students in 2009, when Michelle joked that Spanish speakers are "ruling almost everything," and Sheryl complained she was encouraged in school to learn Spanish rather than perfecting her Creole. Both young women were daughters of Haitian immigrants and grew up in Miami.

SHERYL: In the United States Spanish is like the second, like if you are applying for a job, or in school, or whatever the place may be, it is like the second language that you have to learn. And I still don't understand that to this day. Even in high school you have to take up Spanish. Elementary, middle school, you have to take up Spanish. I'm like, "Why Spanish?" At home, like when I was little in elementary school, at home we speak Creole. Why do I have to learn to speak Spanish?
INTERVIEWER: That's what your teachers told you in high school?
SHERYL: Elementary school. I remember learning Spanish in elementary school and I was like, "But I already speak Creole. Why do I have to learn Spanish? I don't understand." You know no one ever explained that to me. Even now when you go in for a job, like most places that you go to down here in Miami, some of the people who work in the stores do not speak English. They only speak Spanish. And I don't understand. Why is it so, like, that we are diverting to this one specific culture when there is more than one culture here?

As the daughter of Haitian immigrants, Sheryl felt that her culture was marginalized within a minority-majority city and pleaded for either the use of English as a common language or a multicultural approach to language in public education and the job market. While Spanish-English-Creole divides are fairly obvious to insiders and outsiders, language differences among Spanish speakers can also be perceived as boundaries that determine cultural membership. Among Spanish speakers, differences in vocabulary, accent, and appropriateness of slang that are associated with country of origin and class status created divisions and perceptions of exclusion. For example, Paulina, who is from Mexico, did not necessarily like living in Miami and expressed a desire to move to the western part of the United States. She addressed the issue of language specifically as one of the factors that created feelings of animosity with other groups: "I haven't liked it. There is just such a mixture of people that I feel . . . I don't even know in what language to speak. Because you speak in English and they don't understand you, but you speak in Spanish and they do not [understand you either] because the words are different from what they are speaking. It is not that I do not like it. It's that I am not drawn towards it. . . . It is not like the rest of the US."

Mexican Spanish vocabularies and accents are quite different from the variants spoken in the Caribbean, and both are noticeably different from the Spanish spoken in various South American countries. For example, a Brazilian graduate student married to a Cuban with South American clients, who was working with one of the authors, Sallie Hughes, on another project, assumed that a business owner with a northern Mexican accent was a ranch hand rather than an agrobusiness owner: "Listen to his accent," was her explanation. Similarly, our participants found variations in appropriateness of slang and humor as markers of difference rather than unity, as a focus group discussion about Spanish-language radio in Miami, recounted below, demonstrates. These linguistic differences remind Spanish-speaking immigrants of ways in which they are placed in multiple Miami-based social hierarchies, sometimes to their disadvantage. An analysis of perceptions of language, news topics, and representations of national groups and countries of origin in mass-market Spanish-language media in Miami supports this conclusion.

First, consider this focus group discussion among Colombians and Peruvians about risqué Cuban-style humor on Spanish-language radio in Miami. While a common language should have enhanced the cultural "shareability"[36] of programming—meaning its ability to be accepted across national-origin groups—differences in language use and appropriate use of language in humor created disjunctures. María, a Colombian who listened to radio all day as she chauffeured her children to their activities, explained energetically how she was offended by what she heard on local radio in Spanish on stations owned by major US networks or local Cuban radio entrepreneurs (who, in one case, identifies his ownership on the air). The exception for María are programs aired by the Colombian broadcaster Radio Caracol, which retransmits news from Colombia as well as an increasing amount of locally produced news for Miami's Colombian and South American communities. Radio programs from her own country or community of coethnics in Miami elicited a very different reaction:

> What I want to say very clearly is it is an absurd Spanish. They
> [radio disc jockeys] use the regional words from each country, the
> worst that can be found. They use them as if it were nothing, on
> the air. And, well, I also listen to the radio programs from
> Colombia—there are fortunately like three in the morning—and I
> know who anchors them. They are good-quality programs, and

they don't have to discuss only sexual themes and use bad words, because apparently some part of the Hispanic population likes to listen to those types of words, but for the rest of us it is insulting. So they run these stations as if they were small village stations [of poor quality]. Not a town from one of our countries, no, but where that guy comes on and says, "This is my station." How stupid. I don't care who owns the station. . . . [Spanish-language radio in Miami] is just a low-quality small-town business.

Mass-market US television produced in Spanish provides more insight into how shared language cannot overcome in-group differences. Despite US network attempts to create a uniform dialect for the purpose of homogenizing a national audience of Latino consumers in the United States,[37] immigrants in our study perceived the content of Spanish-language television news as based upon the national cultures and concerns of Cubans in local media and Mexicans for national television. Spanish-speaking immigrants who were not from Cuba or Mexico experienced displacement when watching because of the differences between the dominant cultural codes and news topics embedded in US Spanish-language television and their informational interests and homeland cultural norms. These disjunctures seemed to increase discomfort with these media outlets.

In our survey, Puerto Ricans, Colombians, and other South Americans consumed English-language television more than US-based Spanish-language television, even though English was a second language for all except some of the Puerto Ricans. Anyone with a television set receives channels in Spanish and English in Miami, so the effects of class differences are somewhat muted. Focus group discussions further suggested that non-Cuban, non-Mexican Spanish speakers preferred homeland news and informational content on homeland media instead of mainstream US-based Spanish-language broadcasting. Further, we found the preference for homeland media over Spanish-language US media to reflect two dynamics—the media content's connection to immigrants' homeland cultural group and negative emotional reactions to how US-based mainstream media reflected ethnic power hierarchies in Miami. Not only did cultural dissonance make Spanish-speaking immigrants' attempts to embed themselves in cultural familiarity impossible when viewing news on Spanish-language US media, but the programming reminded them of their subordinate statuses in Miami, creating anger and angst. These immigrants experienced alienation from culturally dissonant symbols and rituals, stereotyping of their country of origin or nationality group, and unmet informational needs. Again, even the use of Spanish was sometimes alienating in itself because of differences in accents, meanings of words, humoristic styles, and relative standards of good grammar.

Carlos, a Dominican, is typical of the trends in much of the discussion about US-based Spanish-language television. "Hispanic television is totally biased, all Cuba and Mexico. Telemundo and Univision are complete nonsense. Maybe Channel 41 [affiliated with Colombia's RCN (National Broadcasting Network)] is a little better, but not much, because they know what sells is Cuban. There's a report about Fidel and they talk incessantly. If there is news from Santo Domingo, it crawls across in the running headline and keeps going. Because they think that the only person on the other side of the screen is a Cuban."

Diego, a Peruvian, explained his use of English-language television as the result of feeling "overwhelmed" by news about Cuba. "I put a lot of channels in English on," he said. "I like to listen to the news in English and, well, Channel 23 [a local affiliate of national US Spanish-language broadcaster Univision], but it also saturates the news with Cuban news, the same as the others. The excess of Cuban news overwhelms me." Daisy, a Peruvian, echoed others when she said the stereotypes of her country bothered her. "It makes me a little angry . . . [how much] they ridicule."

While communications research suggested telenovelas and melodramatic entertainment programming travel better across national-origin groups, they are not always well received. Xiomy, a Colombian, said the variety program *Don Francisco* on the Univision network only interviews Mexicans (even though Don Francisco himself is Chilean). "There are not only Mexicans who have things to say. I can assure you that in Peru there are people with things to say, that there are marvelous Colombians, but they don't exist. What exists are Mexicans. Or if they show a Colombian, it is because he did something bad." Dominicans likewise complained of *Don Francisco* and the Cuban talk show host Cristina, also on Univision for many years.

For the immigrants in our study who were not from Cuba or Mexico, the two groups that dominate the local and national media markets, respectively, consumption of US commercial media in Spanish was thus a jarring experience that reminded them of their distance from home and subordinate status in Miami's Latino hierarchy. Cultural encoding and thematic choices not only distanced them: on many occasions they seemed alienated, describing the content with energetic vocabulary charged with negative emotions. They described themselves as bored, insulted, or overwhelmed by the content. Entertainment formats that communications research suggests are more culturally compatible, such as telenovelas, seemed more accepted, although acceptance was muted by the negative talk about news and variety show hosts perceived as biased against immigrants' countries or as lowbrow, exploitative culture.

Another way that the inclusionary potential of language is limited involved class and the perception that a form of bilingualism was necessary to succeed in social arenas in Miami that are associated with the Cuban American segment of local society or the English-language culture of the wider United States. "Sometimes I feel like I am a lesser person because I get stuck with English," said Sofia, an upper-class Peruvian. "But other than that I feel fine [in Miami]." Recall in Chapter 4 that knowledge of English had positive effects for social mobility and self-esteem. Thus, although Miami is a Spanish-dominant city where Latin American and many Caribbean immigrants can get by without knowing English, in arenas of social life that overlap more closely with US institutions and white social spaces, including highly skilled professional work environments, immigrants felt they needed to master a high level of English (preferably unaccented) along with Spanish, since fluent bilingualism is considered an important marker of inclusion in Miami's upper middle and upper classes. This interpretation also is supported by the quantitative analysis on employment discrimination in Chapter 6 that found that those who reported speaking English "well" also reported higher levels of employment discrimination compared to those who described speaking English "very well." The expectation of fluent bilingualism is also similar to being part of a globalized elite in immigrants' countries of origin, where good English is a social status marker of attending the best private schools.

Race, Place, and (Latino) Belonging

Just as people circulate among Miami, the Caribbean, and Latin America, so do cultural norms such as those involved in deciphering racial meanings, particularly in encounters with native whites as shown in Chapter 6. The presence of a large Latino population that spans multiple economic classes attracted migrants to Miami who previously had settled in other parts of the United States. These secondary migrants told tales of facing racial discrimination based on dichotomous black-white norms elsewhere in the United States.

As we argued in Chapter 6, patterns of racialization among immigrant populations reflected nationally based Latin American and Caribbean racial schemas and US racial ideologies. The patterns of discrimination and ethnic rivalries that emerged in Miami coexisted with immigrants' efforts to create cultural belonging in the city. At first blush, this coexistence appears to be a paradox. However, the explanation for this paradox becomes clearer when we compare secondary migrants' perceptions and experiences of race and racism elsewhere in the United States with their perceptions and experiences in Miami. More specifically, when we examine how immigrants who have lived elsewhere in the United States speak of racism and language use, we see that Miami has offered them opportunities for inclusion that they perceived to be unavailable in many other areas of the United States, as their past experiences with white racism suggest. Thus, in spite of experiencing racialization in Miami, for some, cultural membership in the city attenuated the perceptions and possibly the effects of other forms of exclusion.

We first consider Puerto Rican Amanda and her reflections about race, language, and belonging. Like many participants in our study, Amanda discussed experiences with the US white racial frame that occurred in other parts of the country. These experiences were sometimes considered more egregious forms of discrimination and racism when compared with experiences of racialization in Miami. Amanda, who identified as black, reported that "the worst experience that I've had here in the United States was when a group of neo-Nazis threw a bottle at me in Cambridge [Massachusetts]. I was in Harvard Square, and they threw a bottle that hit my heel."

In addition to this experience with overt racism, Amanda discussed the condition of marginality she felt in the US Northeast when she found herself on the sidelines of the multiple groups with whom she associated in Boston: "Being black, blacks there did not accept me at first because they would say that I was not really black because I was Hispanic and my best friend was white. And the whites obviously did not accept me very much because they did not know how . . . how to make sense of me since I was black but my best friend was white. And either way, she was Hispanic. So they did not know how to classify me."

This experience illustrates the ambiguous position that individuals such as Amanda occupy in the cognitive racial mappings of non-Latinos, particularly outside of Miami. When faced with multiracial members of the same ethnic group, the question of where Latinos fall along the color line becomes more complex and can have an impact on their ability to sustain group memberships. Recent literature suggests that general boundaries are forming around Latinos, separating them from both white and black categories,[38] although other research suggests that upwardly mobile light-skinned Latinos may identify with whites while darker-skinned Latinos may be more likely to identify with other black and nonblack minorities.[39] The returns on class status, however, seemed to be less when Latinos from middle- or upper-middle-class backgrounds found themselves in cities where the socioeconomic position of the local Latino groups was one of disadvantage and where little class heterogeneity existed. In these cases, they were combating not just racial stereotypes but stereotypes that conflated Latinos and poverty.

Amanda's decision to move to Miami reflected her experiences in Boston. She decided to move to Miami because she wanted a different environment for her children: "Well, I have two kids, and I lived in Boston for thirteen years. . . . [I]t was very cold; there were few Hispanics from varying social classes and different opportunities for Hispanics, and I wanted my children to grow up bilingual. The warmth [in Miami] is similar to Puerto Rico's—better. There are more opportunities than in Puerto Rico."

Amanda liked that Miami was home to Latinos from different class backgrounds, and she saw more opportunities for her children to grow up in a context where they were not automatically assumed to be poor because of their ethnoracial background. Amanda's own experiences with marginalization in Boston shaped her views regarding the kind of environment in which she wanted to raise her children. Thus, the context in which she made her decision to come to Miami is important. She was attracted to Miami and formed an image of Miami as a city in which she could find more diversity and, thus, acceptance: "Miami is like the model Hispanic city here. Not like Chicago or New York that they are Hispanic, but there is . . . not so much [socioeconomic] diversity within the Hispanic community, and that is why I wanted to come here."

The diversity she implied pertains to social class. Karla, also Puerto Rican, found the Latino environment in Miami to be appealing as well, particularly after she had experienced the opposite when she first migrated and settled in Washington, DC. Although Karla laughed off her experiences with discrimination, they encouraged her to seek out a different kind of context in which she would be less likely to face racism against Latinos. Like Amanda, this search led Karla and her husband to settle in Miami: "One of the reasons why we decided to come to Miami, aside from the weather being so horrible there [Washington, DC] and much better here, is because we had a son and we did not want to raise him in an area in which, apparently in the Washington area there is so much racism, much more than what I would have ever encountered in the [US] South. We did not want our son to grow up in that environment. We wanted him to be accepted as if he were any other child."

In examining the experiences of immigrants from Latin America and the Caribbean who have multiple frames of reference regarding life in various parts of the United States, we see that they perceived Miami as a more culturally familiar and inclusive environment that enhanced feelings of security and well-being. Miami offered them a place in which membership based on cultural inclusion was attainable to a greater extent than in other places in the United States. The settlement decisions that these individuals made, in which they weighed the costs of racism, resemble the forms of strategic assimilation that Karyn Lacy found in her study of middle-class blacks' neighborhood preferences. These preferences involve deliberate decisions to minimize racism yet still expose children to the culture of their ethnic/racial group.[40]

Ariana, a Colombian, expressed similar motivations for moving to Miami after first settling elsewhere in the United States: "Ah, well, I like Miami because of the people, the togetherness. I like the social environment. I would like that my children perhaps could grow up surrounded by Latinos." Like Amanda and Karla, Ariana wanted her children to grow up amidst Latinos and Latino culture. Although this exposure could be accomplished in other major cities or new destinations with Latino communities or ethnic enclaves, the three did not want their children to grow up as "the other," not just in terms of race and culture but also with regards to class status, which is often conflated with race in places where Latinos are mostly disadvantaged. This desire was enough motivation to relocate their families to a place where they perceived less white racism, fewer racial stereotypes, and a generally warmer social and aesthetic climate, even if racialization among Latinos existed.

The general finding that emerges from our interviews is that places are perceived as exclusionary to varying degrees and that the particular context of settlement within the United States (e.g., the demography of race, diversification of ethnic groups, and power of particular ethnic groups) is a significant mediator of race relations and an influence in long-term settlement decisions. In addition to the racial and ethnic contexts, political and economic power also matter.[41] The power of an ethnic group in a certain region can serve the purpose of lessening the stigmas attached to the corresponding race/ethnic group. The tendency to associate Latinos with groups in poverty is mitigated when class variation exists in the particular area of settlement and a large enough community that Latinos in general are not alone on the front lines of racial integration. We see this tendency in play with Sixto, a Mexican, when he compared Atlanta to Miami:

SIXTO: There is discrimination in the way that people judge you, especially Anglos. They see that you are really different, and they think you are another person. And the truth is that we are equal. We are all equal.
INTERVIEWER: Where did you perceive this the most?
SIXTO: In Atlanta.
INTERVIEWER: Do you think that racism exists here [Miami]?
SIXTO: In South Florida, no.
INTERVIEWER: Why do you think there is more racism in Atlanta and not so much here?
SIXTO: In Atlanta, because there are not many Latinos there.

In Sixto's case, the demographics of the city are held responsible for the likelihood of experiencing racism. Rodrigo, a Peruvian, also subscribed to the perspective that racism and the white racial frame were more prevalent outside of Miami. His experiences in Colorado shaped his perceptions of racism in the United States vis-à-vis Miami:

RODRIGO: I think that there is racism in Miami, but it is less. In fact, I think that racism can be noticed more in the North than here in Miami, since there are so many cultures that it might make it more difficult for them to attack one another. But definitely, in the North there is racism. . . . One small experience was that a person, knowing that I was Peruvian, called me a Mexican, and as much as I would repeat to him that I was not Mexican, he continued to tell me that since I spoke Spanish, I was Mexican.

INTERVIEWER: And where did this happen to you?

RODRIGO: In Colorado . . . I think that because of that person's ignorance, he did not take the time to learn about the cultures of Latin America, I suppose. I think it is stupid that he would confuse everyone in the world with only one nationality.

Rodrigo believed that while the man's actions were a result of ignorance, they were also a manifestation of racism that he thought was more prevalent in the rest of the country compared to Miami. In areas in which members of an ethnic minority group differ in terms of their countries of origin, homogenizing them because of the common language spoken—in this case, as Mexican—represented a form of racialization. Moreover, this process implied a sense of superiority over Rodrigo in the way that this person assumed he had the right to ascribe to him any nationality that he deemed appropriate, with little consideration for Rodrigo's own national identity.

The tendency in some areas of the United States to racialize all Latinos as Mexican, the largest and oldest Latino-origin group in the United States, taps into persistent frames of marginalization As Mae M. Ngai has shown, successive historical constructions of Mexicans in US immigration policy and twentieth-century racial segregation laws have enduringly framed them as illegal aliens, whether or not they have legal residency, citizenship, or even a birthplace in the United States.[42] Through extension of the "illegal/Mexican" frame, racially tagged non-Mexican Latinos are turned into "impossible subjects" who can never be culturally white enough to deserve legal membership in the United States.[43] Latinos who cannot pass for white in mainstream US racial constructions because of physical racial markers or speech patterns are assumed to be culturally and ethnically inassimilable, unable to possess Anglo American criteria for membership.

The most publicized and dramatic examples of this racialization are Puerto Rican US citizens who were detained by immigration authorities in Georgia and Illinois because of their last name or accent. In the case of the Chicago man, he was quoted as saying that even though officials knew that Puerto Ricans were US-born citizens, "just because of the way I look—I have Mexican features—they pretty much assumed that my papers were fake."[44] Some of our phenotypically white participants described experiencing similar constructions outside of Miami.

In a context such as Miami, where the Hispanic population is numerically dominant and has diversified in the last two decades, country-of-origin differences are indeed salient and do not homogenize Latinos. If anything, they become shorthand for larger racial, political, and class dynamics that work to socially stratify Miami residents based on their particular national-origin group and the racialization of ethnicity.[45] Thus, the phenomenon that we identify is that, in spite of the racial and ethnic dynamics that fracture Latino and immigrant solidarity in Miami in significant ways, the white racism that those in our sample faced outside of Miami was interpreted as more damaging and sometimes contributed to decisions to resettle in a more multiethnic Latino, global city such as Miami. Differences in perceptions of racism and its consequences inside and outside of Miami show that the experiences of inclusionary discrimination that are hallmarks of Latin American and Caribbean racial dynamics are transformed in the United States, where immigrants must negotiate and make sense of their experiences as insiders and outsiders at multiple levels: as outsiders in predominantly native white spaces or areas, as insiders in Latino immigrant Miami, but altogether as embodied contradictions who face inclusionary and exclusionary forms of discrimination, sometimes simultaneously across contexts, and at different scales.

We have shown throughout this book that popular or scholarly images of cultural inclusion in Miami must be problematized, given the exclusionary structures that sort immigrants based upon national origin, race, gender, legal status, class, and language. Yet the fact remains that Spanish-speaking participants who have lived elsewhere in the United States express feelings of inclusion in Miami that are based on a shared cultural ethos and a sense of cultural power that is absent in most other areas of the country. Immigrants may feel dislocated in parts of the United States where they are a minority, are seen as cultural outsiders, or lack voice, visibility, or power. The reverse often happens in Miami. For natives, Miami may seem foreign—a place filled with unusual foods, foreign languages, and striking landscapes—an exotic place to vacation or extract wealth but not to call home. However, these sentiments illustrate how Miami has become a racialized place in the social imagination of the US nation.

The notion of the "exotic" could easily stand in for the process of racialization. Perhaps this interchangeability is one of the reasons so much white and African American flight has taken place in the last three decades, adding evidence to arguments that foreshadow the racial balkanization of entire regions of the country. William H. Frey has argued that the labor competition introduced by low-skilled immigrant workers in major multiethnic metropolises is associated with the out-migration of white, working-class natives; in other words, immigrants are understood to push wages down, leading to these expulsion factors that account for patterns of native-born "white flight."[46] Although we acknowledge and find evidence to confirm that Miami has indeed become racialized at a regional scale given these demographic shifts, we concur with Mark Ellis and Richard Wright's warnings about the use of the term *balkanization* in describing this phenomenon.[47]

Balkanization suggests permanent instability and conflict and carries as its main assumption that immigrants are responsible for the fragmentation and separatism that can fracture the conception of shared nationhood.[48] However, immigrant Miamians perceive the place they call home quite differently. As we have noted, ethnic concentration, particularly in light of the evidence that shows that secondary migrants to Miami often reported a desire to get away from environments in which they were racialized by whites, indicates that these demographic shifts are not the result of immigrants rejecting Americanism. On the contrary, they are seeking out environments in which they can find sustainable ways of life that minimize the feelings of otherness that settlement in predominantly white areas invokes.

However, we must note that the racialization of Miami does not mean a black-white split, seen in the numbers of African Americans who have also exited Miami. The racialization of Miami as a "Latino" city relies on the use of Spanish as one of the key racial markers that molds it into an "exotic" space, but given the social power that Latinos hold, Miami's racialization becomes threatening to the country's white cultural and national identities, and as such, Miami, from the outside, is seen as a racialized place. Referred to as a "third-world country" by prominent public figures, the region is ceded from US sovereignty even in common parlance. Not more than a week after moving to Miami, one of the authors, Elizabeth Aranda, was told at a new faculty orientation what appeared to be a common joke in the city that was also a frequently seen bumper sticker on cars: that the last American to leave Miami should make sure to bring the American flag. This example is but one of the fact that what was viewed as home to some was viewed as foreign by others. In spite of being a Latino city, the racialization of Latinos nevertheless abounded in white social spaces, in this case, the halls of the ivory tower. Such characterizations of Miami as exotic, foreign, and racially marked have led to scholarly arguments that transience is endemic to the city. But to Latin American and Caribbean immigrants who compare Miami with their places of origin, the city feels orderly and materially developed, like a place where they can pursue their pragmatic goals of material and economic security within a culturally familiar social environment.

Nevertheless, forms of exclusion persist and seem to affect Haitian immigrants the most. Racialization in Miami plays out quite differently for immigrants who do not come from Spanish-speaking countries. We have mentioned how the Creole language creates bonds of membership in the Haitian ethnic community but can be marginalized outside of it. And we have shown how Haitians perceive their exclusion as based upon race and discriminatory immigration policies. They perceive as much racism coming from Latinos in the city (immigrants and native born) as from native Anglos and sometimes even African Americans.

Placemaking, Race, and Exclusion: The Haitian Experience

In some ways, the (re)enactment and (re)experience of home for Haitians is similar to what other immigrants from the Caribbean perceive because of the similarity of Miami's climate to Haiti, the ease of circulation between Haiti and Miami, and the large Haitian population in Miami, which is residentially clustered in the north part of the county. However, as we saw earlier in this chapter, for many Haitians, feelings of cultural inclusion are limited to their own coethnic community.

We explore perceptions of cultural exclusion among Haitians in Miami through an analysis of how they perceive representations of their homeland and the Haitian immigrant community in mass-market media in Spanish and English, as compared to their reactions to mainstream television and media content produced in their own coethnic community. The comparison demonstrates the inclusion they feel in their own community and the depth of the exclusion felt in the city at large, sketching further the racial and ethnic limits to placemaking through shared culture.

While consuming media produced in their own community reinforces Haitians' feelings of inclusion in a transnational Haitian community, reactions to mainstream US representations of their national and ethnic community, as well as their homeland, result in feelings of exclusion that heighten emotional distress. "It makes you feel bad; it hurts because it is your country," said Geoff, a focus group participant. Another participant, Daniel, stated that having legal status in the United States didn't lessen his cultural and sentimental ties to Haiti, nor did it improve how his national group was depicted. So how US media depict Haiti "hurts a lot, because it doesn't matter what I am. Whether I am a citizen [or not], I am still Haitian. I am [a US] citizen on paper, and I am Haitian."

To better understand how a non-Latino, nonwhite immigrant minority straddled the boundaries of inclusion and exclusion in Miami, we present two life stories that are in many ways typical of Miami's Haitian immigrants. They show that avoiding news portrayals of Haitians produced by Miami's dominant cultural groups and seeking the affirmative effects of media content produced in their own community were strategies Haitians engaged in to heighten ontological security and manage the structurally rooted emotional challenges that pervaded their lives.

Jean is a thirty-nine-year-old Haitian immigrant who works at a public utility plant. His father paid a smuggler to bring him from Haiti when he was eleven. Bilingual in Creole and English, he has a junior college degree and is the father of a five-year-old boy. He listens to Haitian radio in Creole, preferring music. For information he listens to National Public Radio broadcasts in English, which participants said rarely talk about Haitians.

Jean read news representations of Haitians in the Miami-based US media as stigmatizing and dehumanizing. Like other Haitians, he consumed local news to understand what was happening in Miami, but he tried to avoid representations of his ethnic group. He preferred to listen to music in Creole and watch sports or science fiction TV shows, on which he felt racial groups got along in an idealized version of the future. When asked about his impression of media coverage on Haiti and Haitians in the United States, he answered, "They make us feel like lowlifes. They make us feel like we don't have any real value; we are not like real people. Just little black folks that come around and just need the white folks around here. . . . Yeah. They treat you like you don't have any class. Second-class citizen and stuff. Not like you are second class; you're like last class of anything." Jean believed that Cubans receive the best treatment in local news. He continued, "I think Cubans get the best news coverage than anybody else and Haitians get the worst. . . . 'Cause every time, once the news is about Cubans, they always give you like either they accomplish this, or they're fighting against Cuba and Castro, or their family is doing great, or one of them got to be governor or another got to be a commissioner. It's always in the news about how great they're doing and how much they give to change the country. But about Haitians all we ever get is they're Haitian, they're dirty, they are no good, and they're not very smart."

Jean's strategy was to withdraw from mainstream news, instead using broadcast media for entertainment. "They do not help me to live a good life in South Florida because they are very contrary to life; they make it seem like we are living in caves."

Mirta's experiences provide further insight into how Haitians in Miami negotiate inclusion and exclusion. Discussed in the previous chapter, Mirta is a nurse's assistant who moved from Haiti in 2001 and at the time of her interview lived on $2,100 a month, which included $700 in child support for her six-year-old son. Mirta is trilingual, although she communicated better in Creole and French than in English. She considered her family's class origins in Haiti when she was growing up to be middle class and described traveling abroad, living in her family's own well-equipped home, and finishing high school. Her father was a cruise ship worker, and her mother, now deceased, was a seamstress. In Miami, her status as a divorced single mother had so far prevented her from finishing an advanced nursing degree so she could make more money and "have a better life."

Mirta described her work environment as pervaded by national-origin hierarchies and discrimination, where people from other nationality groups sought to place their own conationals in jobs. She perceived racial discrimination in hiring, and like her fellow Haitians, Mirta found the media environment in Miami hostile to blacks and Haitians in particular. Like several Haitians interviewed, she wondered what her countrymen and countrywomen did to deserve such treatment. She often wished to return to Haiti, where trusted relatives could watch her son while she went to school, but the criminal insecurity in Haiti prevented her from returning except for once every few years to take part in important rituals and kinship gatherings, the latest being her uncle's funeral. Mirta experienced great stress from a lifestyle that included economic insecurity, social isolation, discrimination, and being overworked: "I am graying, I am getting old, and getting all kinds of sickness because of the stress of being here."

Consumption of news in English in US newspapers and on television channels (Mirta calls them "Cuban" channels although the Haitian interviewer calls them "American") stimulated palpable negative emotions that contrasted markedly with the security, stability, and inclusion that communication researchers have described as the experience of someone in the dominant cultural group watching national television.[49] Like Jean, Mirta consumed news from mainstream US media to know what was going on in Miami, but it alienated and saddened her because she perceived it as focusing on criminal and financial insecurity in the United States while also stigmatizing Haiti, Haitians, and the Haitian community in Miami.

MIRTA: When you hear news of Haiti, you just sit and cry because of what you knew and how they talk about Haiti, as if it's a place where no one lives. Like a desert without a living soul or some cannibalistic place, but it is not like that in the country. But they show it like that so that they can keep you in the situation you are in. If they describe the place like that, you will have no tourists, nothing. Even those from there who live here will be afraid to go back. . . .

INTERVIEWER: What about when you read news about Haitians in the United States?

MIRTA: Well, I'll tell you the stories I like to hear are of a young Haitian going to school, completing a master's degree, working with some big company or doing something big. When you hear of some Haitian going to Tallahassee [Florida's capital], one who becomes a judge or is working at a university. But more often than not you hear of young Haitian Americans who are arrested and are going to jail. Those are things that are not pleasant to hear. Those things are not good because you want to know why a child would come here and do all the bad things. They should look for what is good, especially, those of us who are black—we should take what is good out of this. But I don't see why with us, they only show those things that are negative.

In research on national television reception, Roger Silverstone argues that one of the ways in which news enhances ontological security is by constructing reality in cyclical representations of crisis followed by crisis resolution or diversion to other types of news and patriotic spectacle.[50] For Mirta and most Haitians interviewed, however, US mainstream media present a broken cycle of never-ending crisis. As Mirta stated, "when they talk about Haiti, they portray it as a place that is empty, done for, a destitute place, a place that is completely lost."

The marginalization produced by media representations reinforced feelings of exclusion from the city's institutions generally. They added insult to injury. These generalized patterns of exclusion were recognized and experienced as deeply alienating by our Haitian study participants, and they often took an emotional toll. Kerry, a Haitian immigrant who has been in Miami for twenty years, explained, "If you are not careful you develop an inferiority complex that will be detrimental for you, making you unable to function. It may be very emotional and you may not be able to really live in this country. You know that you have something to offer and you know what you can do, but no one gives you an opportunity or acknowledges your value. Currently, you know that you have to do twice as much as any one else in order to be recognized."

While Haitian immigrants in Miami occupy professional and working-class occupations to a greater extent than many people in the wider United States would assume, in addition to the structures of marginalization we have documented, the context of settlement for this African diaspora from a non-Spanish speaking country includes greater immigration obstacles and higher rates of poverty than other white and Hispanic groups.[51] As we saw in Chapter 6, our Haitian participants also expressed strong perceptions of discrimination by Hispanics, Anglo Americans, and sometimes African Americans. A focus group member exclaimed in frustration at perceived employment discrimination, "This thing has to stop! Someone needs to put a stop to this, to advise the Hispanics that everyone has to eat." While her statement was outspoken, this participant's sentiment of discrimination was widely shared.

In summary, while Miami's context supports the construction of belonging based on shared culture among Spanish-speaking immigrants, who often compared Miami to life in other areas of the United States, Haitians in Miami felt marginalized by US and Latin American racial frames, immigration policies, economic hierarchies associated with the city's functions in global and regional financial flows, and linguistic patterns that conveyed cultural and political authority on both Spanish and English.

Miami is indeed different from other parts of the United States, even older immigrant destination cities, because it is more than a city with a large Latino enclave or even a series of enclaves. Enclaves in the sense of bounded ethnic neighborhoods with coethnic businesses may be found in the areas that remain African American and in some places in the county from which Anglos have retreated.[52] For Latin American residents of Miami, the city is really a Latino metropolis segmented by race, culture, and, particularly, legal status and class: the Latin American wealthy in Key Biscayne and Brickell, the upper middle classes in Doral and Weston, the middle classes in Kendall, the poor and working classes in central county areas such as Hialeah and east Calle Ocho (Eighth Street) in Little Havana, as well as in the southern portion of the county in Homestead and Florida City, and the undocumented in the shadows. Thus, class divisions and race, as well as the issue of legal status, represent the most important sources of divisions confronting multiethnic Miami in years to come. For the time being, those who experienced multiple layers of exclusion often felt as if they had been pushed to the margins of both the society they left behind and the one in which they were supposed to be making a life.

Translocal Denizens

Thus far, we have demonstrated Miami's capacity to generate feelings and practices of belonging at different levels, because in the minds of many of our participants, Miami is a place that is close to home and feels like home. Immigrants can be back home in just a few hours; use their native language for daily activities; engage in familiar leisure, religious, or ceremonial practices; find people from their own country; and, for people from the Caribbean basin, be reminded of home by the architecture, physical landscape, and climate.

Yet at the same time, inclusion is differentially structured. Although Miami's community context was important for many, some exceptions exist, as we have seen. The impact of place on the likelihood of feeling they belonged in the United States, for some, was negligible, though these respondents represent a very small proportion of our quantitative sample. As we illustrated in the previous chapter, ambivalence often characterizes respondents' emotional experiences of migration. Moreover, place did not always mitigate contradicting emotions resulting from the immigrant condition. Fernando, a Mexican, is an example. Fernando felt ambivalent toward his transnational life. He struggled with having left his family in Mexico and being the only one from his home community in the United States. At the same time, even after living twenty years in the United States (eight of those he spent in Miami), he did not feel as though he was part of this coun-

try. Rather than feeling embedded in two countries, he felt painfully alienated from social life in Mexico and Miami, "in a parallel universe in which
you are not part of the United States. But you are also not part of what your
life was those first twenty years . . . [and] we [immigrants] share [this]. It is
a parallel universe, a universe where you are neither here nor there."

The emotional responses to migration described in the last chapter for
some of our participants stretched into the realm of place, and although
they no longer felt they belonged completely in the home country, they
likewise did not feel full social and cultural membership in the United
States. Fernando continued, "I am not totally, I do not feel like I am an
American citizen. I have Mexican citizenship too. My son is obviously
American, my wife is American, but I do not feel part of this country yet.
But when I return to Mexico, I also do not feel totally part of Mexico. I'm
telling you, you find yourself again like in a gray area that you share with
other immigrants but not with Mexico and not with the United States."

Although, for some, these issues were resolved by living in Miami
where they could lead a bicultural lifestyle and engaging in translocal social
citizenship practices, for others like Fernando, ambiguity about immigrant
life remained, even though he admitted that he was more comfortable in
Miami than if he lived in Washington, DC, his other point of reference in
the United States. It many in this sample experienced the simultaneity of
translocalism and US incorporation through the construction of translocal
citizenship practices, Fernando felt like he belonged to neither society. He
lived at the margins of both Mexican and US societies—as a denizen of
both but a member of neither.

In a global city, marginality becomes central to urban life.[53] Thus, those
struggling economically and racially, among them single mothers like Mirta,
had additional barriers when fully incorporating into US society. Regardless
of immigrant preferences regarding Miami's cultural environment, the economic realities of living in an area where the cost of living was growing and
income inequality was increasing affected many. Although connections to
home societies were more often than not made stronger by living in this
global city, economic, social, racial, and legal marginality created limits to
translocal placemaking practices and sometimes even trumped the positive
effects of shared culture, ease of circulation, and the multiple sensory reminders of home in the built landscape and daily social interactions.

In all, immigrants' emotional lives were stretched across borders. Their
attachments to place kept them linked to their natal home communities
through deliberate strategies that allowed them to remain socially embedded in hometown relationships through practices of co-presence, while engaging in placemaking in Miami as part of efforts to feel at home or, more
literally, to extend the felt home to Miami.

Even with the limitations, Miami's embodiment of Latino and
Caribbean cultures, in many cases, eased immigrants into the process of

adaptation to and incorporation into US society. Moreover, the geographic location and Latino/Caribbean ambiance of the city allowed for immigrants to remain immersed in the social horizons of their home countries while they partook in cultural and sensory-based placemaking practices in the global city. Immigrants were active agents in constructing lives that encompassed simultaneous social processes of transborder belonging and US incorporation. As such, citizenship was woven socially in a translocal spatiality that many called home.

Conclusion

In this chapter we have shown how immigrants view Miami as a city where they can find public order and material progress in a place that is both culturally familiar and geographically close to their natal home. We demonstrated that what attracts Latin American and Caribbean immigrants to Miami is how the area, as a space that anchors translocal processes, facilitates belonging in myriad mundane ways. As an immigrant majority city on the edge of the Caribbean, its cultural and physical landscapes remind immigrants of home, and its geographic location facilitates circulations of loved ones, goods, information, and even weather patterns with immigrant homelands. We showed how immigrants engaged in translocal placemaking processes through shared daily cultural practices and embodied memories, allowing immigrants to reenact and reexperience the natal home in Miami. Thus, as a place of settlement, Miami facilitated strategies for resolving ambivalence and improving well-being on multiple scales. While remaining embedded in homeland relationships through co-presence, immigrants layered those comforting relationships on habitual thoughts, behaviors, and experiences that are associated with the homeland but now emplaced in Miami. Immigrants created continuity in relationships, worldviews, and embodied perceptions that anchor the sense of self by engaging in placemaking practices that extend the ontological security rooted in early experiences of the natal home to a context where they have found, or hope to still find, economic, physical, social, and psychic security.

However, immigrants' ability to successfully engage in translocal placemaking was differentiated by socially ascribed traits such as race, as well as language use and national origin. Though almost all of our participants were attracted to the opportunities for inclusion they perceived in Miami, the inclusionary or exclusionary potential of mechanisms such as native language or understandings of race reflected the intraethnic and interethnic hierarchies that prevailed in Miami and that have been discussed in this book.

These hierarchies were also evident in immigrants' perceptions of mass media. Media news agendas, language use patterns, and representations of race and countries of origin are cultural artifacts that vary by which cultural group is responsible for producing the content. Immigrants outside of dominant cultures perceived they were represented in ways that were exclusionary, even insulting. They felt closer culturally to media produced in their Miami-based immigrant communities, which provided a sense of inclusion and even comfort.

Through comparison of immigrants' perceptions of ethnic and mainstream media, we untangle how culture can both include and exclude, depending upon whether one focuses externally toward US society and its structures of power or internally toward the intracthnic hierarchies of the global city. Their patterns of reception untie what may appear to outsiders to be unifying markers of a pan-ethnic or pan-racial community, but for insiders are sometimes severe reminders of marginalization in a city where race, national origin, class, and legal status stratify immigrants.

Feelings of cultural inclusion attenuate perceptions of discrimination and marginalization in Miami when migrants compare the city to other parts of the United States in which they previously resided or visited. While Miami may be exclusionary, it is still perceived as more inclusive than other parts of the country. However, we also uncovered how Haitians, in particular, are blocked from wider belonging given the discrimination they face without the inclusionary mechanisms available to Latinos in Miami. Moving forward, we see the confluence of factors that disadvantage Haitians generally, as symptoms of the broader divisions that will affect immigrants' abilities to successfully make their lives in Miami in years to come.

Notes

1. *Parrandas* in Puerto Rico involve a group of friends serenading another friend's household with Christmas songs. After an hour or so, the party often goes on to another household.
2. West and Zimmerman 1987.
3. Huntington 2004.
4. Portes and Stepick 1993; Stepick et al. 2003.
5. Ellis and Wright 1998.
6. Porteous 1976, p. 388; see also Lattanzi Shutika 2011, p. 84.
7. "Miami Tops Rude Drivers List" 2007.
8. The exceptions are Cubans, who disproportionately immigrate to the United States for political reasons when compared to other national groups, and Haitians, who immigrate for reasons of politics and physical security almost as much as for economic reasons and employment opportunities. See Table 2.4 in Chapter 2 for full breakdown.
9. Varying from other groups' gender differences, South American men stood out from South American women in some ways, including the unequal emphasis they place on economic reasons, language use, and ease of travel. Based on our qualitative data, one hypothesis is that South American women were unable to work in their professions when their husbands' companies transferred them to Miami

since the men migrated to work in companies with homeland connections. However, these gender differences merit further inquiry.

10. Low 1994, p. 66.

11. Leach 2002.

12. Ibid., p. 132.

13. Ibid. Here, Leach relies on the performativity theory of Judith Butler (1990, 1993) and its application to architecture and place by Anne-Marie Fortier (1999).

14. Leach 2002, p. 130.

15. Casey 2001.

16. Ibid., pp. 413–414 (emphasis in original).

17. Ibid., p. 409.

18. Giddens 1990, 1991.

19. Porteous and Smith 2001, p. 6.

20. Porteous 1976.

21. Porteous and Smith 2001, p. 6.

22. Porteous 1976; Porteous and Smith 2001; Vargas 2008.

23. Duany 2011; Porteous 1976; Porteous and Smith 2001.

24. Georgiou 2006.

25. Lattanzi Shutika 2011; McKay 2006b.

26. Duany 2011, p. 2. See also Vertovec 2009.

27. McKay 2006b, p. 275.

28. Porteous 1976, p. 388.

29. Nijman 2007, 2011.

30. The total number of participants whose answers we report in Table 8.3 responded definitively either yes or no to this question ($N = 917$). About 270, or 21 percent, of the sample replied that they did not know if they would remain in Miami.

31. Frey 1996.

32. Casey 2001.

33. Zerubavel 1997, cited in Gieryn 2000.

34. Rosaldo 1994, p. 402.

35. Castro 1992.

36. Straubhaar 2007, p. 201.

37. Dávila 2001.

38. Frank, Akresh, and Lu 2010; O'Brien 2008.

39. Bonilla-Silva 2002, 2004.

40. Lacy 2004.

41. Stepick et al. 2003.

42. Ngai 2004.

43. Ibid.

44. Ramos 2010.

45. Roth 2012.

46. Frey 1996.

47. Ellis and Wright 1998.

48. Ibid.; Wyly 2008.

49. Scannell 1995; Silverstone 1993.

50. Silverstone 1993.

51. Marcelin 2005.

52. Miami-Dade County, Department of Planning and Zoning 2010, see the ethnic distribution maps.

53. Sassen 1998.

9

The Security of Home
in a Global Era

Juan Rodríguez grew up in Miami. Brought there at age six by his Colombian father and other members of his extended family, he adapted quickly
to US society, learning English within a year and attending school there. All
of his life, Juan was told by family members that his job was to excel at
school, even though what he really wanted to do was to help the family by
earning money and joining the men in the orange groves while the women
took jobs taking care of the elderly or as janitors in hotels and office buildings. At first, nobody in his family had work authorization, and their liminal
status lasted for several years. The family pinned their hopes for social mo
bility on Juan. Thus, at his family's request, Juan applied himself at school
and became a stellar student. His dream was to become an aerospace engineer: "All through middle school and high school, that became my mission.
I was going to be an aerospace engineer and so every summer I would take
advance science courses so I could get extra science and mathematics credits in school, to just get ahead faster. And that was my plan. . . . In my junior year of high school I was applying to Embry Riddle [Aeronautical Uni-
versity] to go do aeronautics there."

As he neared his high school graduation, Juan began to make plans to
go to college, including sending out college applications along with his
group of friends. He was among the top ten students of his graduating class.
His friends began to receive college acceptance letters, which was puzzling
to Juan given the difference in the correspondence he was receiving from
the universities to which he had applied. "They needed more information,"
these letters said. In some cases, there was no response at all. Juan came to
learn from his father that he could not provide more information because
Juan was undocumented; he had no official identification. Even his Colombian passport had expired. His guidance counselors were unhelpful, saying,
"Oh, you don't belong here. Go back to your country" and "How can you

exist without government identification?" After the initial shock, Juan became depressed and felt betrayed because he had believed the American mythos that hard work brings rewards. Further, he felt like he had let down his family. Having been told by his father, "Don't talk to anyone about this," he bore it all alone. In an interview, he shared the following:

> Everyone in my family made huge sacrifices to contribute to our collective well-being. I was always told that my contribution would be graduating from high school, going to college, being a good student, getting straight As, and all of that. So when I couldn't do that at the end of high school, I felt like I was just betraying my entire family. It seems so ridiculous because it is like, they had to work in the fields. They had to work eighteen-hour shifts in the sun, be exposed to pesticides, get sick. Their wages got stolen. They had to come home and be able to tell us that they couldn't afford getting groceries for that month. And me, it was like, I couldn't get an acceptance letter to a school. . . . I don't know if they ever believed that they could personally achieve the American Dream but they were certain that I could.

After his bittersweet high school graduation, Juan found himself mowing the lawns of his former teachers who were trying to help him get by. He also helped his grandfather with his work in the informal economy. Around this time, he came out as gay to his family, and his father asked him to leave the home. He barely had enough to rent a room, sometimes eating only avocados from a tree in the backyard where he rented.

Fast forward to the spring of 2013. One of the authors of this book, Elizabeth Aranda, was delivering a lecture to students who were taking a sociology course on Latino/a lives at the University of South Florida in Tampa. The topic was citizenship, and the author showed a YouTube video clip about a group of four undocumented teens who, frustrated with the barriers they encountered when trying to pursue their education and life goals, decided they would walk from Miami to Washington, DC, in what they called the "Trail of Dreams." The students in that class were shocked when they recognized someone in the video. It was Juan Rodríguez, their classmate at the university. Juan had come a long way from gardening for his former teachers.

Eventually Aranda and Juan met, and he explained that he had found his way to an immigrant youth organizer during his deepest moments of despair. He became fully committed to the movement supporting the DREAM Act, a legislative proposal that would grant legal residency and a path to citizenship to students or members of the military who had been brought undocumented to the United States as children, and joined the effort to at-

tract public support for the proposal in Congress. The media spotlight that
the Trail of Dreams attracted caught the attention of Juan's stepmother who,
although out of his life, had never legally divorced his father. A citizen herself, she petitioned for Juan, which resulted in his permanent residency and
a path to citizenship.

Regularizing his status drastically improved Juan's life chances. It allowed him to attend the Honors College at Miami-Dade College and then
transfer to the University of South Florida to complete his bachelor's degree. Juan had fallen into despair when he could not go to college, his aspirations dashed and his economic security imperiled. Yet almost overnight,
he found a renewed sense of hope by joining the immigrants' rights struggle
and, in the process, receiving a lifeline to full membership into the only nation he had known as home.

His family, though, was split in the process. Only his grandparents and
youngest aunt won their asylum petitions. Some went back to Colombia;
his father and disabled sister migrated to Canada, where they eventually obtained refugee status.

When Translocal Social Citizenship Is Not Enough

Making a Life in Multiethnic Miami has told the story of the search for
comprehensive human security through immigration in an age in which
economic upheaval threatens personal sustainability; technological advances facilitate cross-border mobility and communication; and nationally
based legal frameworks, political institutions, and conceptions of the nation
constrict opportunities for formal legal membership. By highlighting the
voices and experiences of Miami's most recent immigrant residents, we
identify how mobility and technologies have opened new opportunities for
belonging that allow immigrants socially and through the use of imagination to merge local spaces across geographic borders in their search for
well-being. Particularly, we have shown how transborder strategies may
create a form of social citizenship that helps immigrants cope with the existential anxieties that may result not only from separation from social relations and identities connected to the place of origin but also from the new
ways in which social stratification and exclusion are experienced in the immigrant destination.

What we have not fully captured in this book are the cases in which
these strategies are ineffective or insufficient to ameliorate the challenges
posed by the process of immigration and settlement in a new country.
Translocal social citizenship for many immigrants is a salve for ontological
insecurity associated with immigration dislocations, but it is not always
enough to allow immigrants to make a home in global Miami. For the un-

documented immigrant, the loss of homeland-based comforts is compounded by frequent feelings of threat, marginalization, and exclusion. Formal legal membership remains the solution they seek. We also have not been able to fully show or come to understand the levels of human insecurity of immigrants who are forced out of the US experience, as eventually happened to members of Juan's family.

Juan's story is about an immigrant who chose to come out of the shadows and fight to make the US political system work for him, in the end securing residency for himself through his stepmother's sponsorship but continuing to fight for the legal security of his spouse and thousands of other undocumented youth. Sofía and Camila, immigrants from Peru introduced in previous chapters and from our original study sample, also returned to their country of origin to seek relief from immigration-related stress. Their experiences illuminate the reasons immigrants leave the United States and the struggles they face during reincorporation into their societies of origin. Sofía's inability to find an intimate partner and start a family in the United States, coupled with being left without a job, and Camila's anxiety and depletion of savings while trying to keep a work visa motivated thoughts of departure, a departure that was spurred on by events in Peru. However, the process of reincorporation that Sofía and Camila experienced was not easy either. Like Juan's struggle for full membership in the United States, their plan to reintegrate in Peru carried risks and ambiguities that affected their sense of security and well-being.

We thus conclude *Making a Life in Multiethnic Miami* with stories of three immigrants navigating the opportunity structures of globalization. Their stories illustrate strategies to enhance human security when translocal social citizenship is not enough to create a home in global Miami, and the trade-offs these strategies entail.

Demanding Inclusion Through Formal Legal Citizenship

Juan's family experienced immigration and settlement challenges in ways similar to others in our study. His story shows how some undocumented immigrants who remain committed to lives in the United States recently have decided to enter the formal arena of politics even with the risks involved. Having grown up in the United States, they understand and identify with previous struggles to expand US citizenship rights.

As one of the most sympathetic faces of the current immigration reform movement, Juan and other "Dreamers" are tapping deeply held American values about protection of the young and the moral right to see hard work pay off. Using these values as a political entrée, Juan and thousands of other undocumented youths are engaging in a head-on political struggle to change the system.

While the decision to participate in the system remains rare because of the risks involved, undocumented immigrants and their citizen relatives have entered the US political stage in great numbers since the crackdowns after 9/11, and more forcefully after the mass protests against a controversial House proposal in 2005–2006. Their voices reverberated in the 2012 election and the immigration policy debates that followed. The US political system historically has expanded the rights of voice, representation, and presence haltingly, unevenly, and sometimes with great costs. Yet as social movements and civil rights struggles of women, African Americans, gays and lesbians, and other less powerful groups have shown, formal membership responds to organized demands, calls for justice, and brute politics.

How Juan came to enter the immigrants' rights struggle is a story born in the criminal violence of Colombia in the 1990s. Juan's grandfather was an executive for a US multinational company and his extended family lived on a property with several neighboring houses, as is common in parts of Latin America. On November 9, 1996, after their home had been burglarized several times, Juan's grandfather received a phone call from a neighbor while the family was out. The neighbor told him that a group of armed men was awaiting their return. Fearing these men would extort money and possibly kidnap him or a member of his family, Juan's grandfather made arrangements to leave the country that very same day. Taking nothing with them to the airport, ten members of Juan's family left for Miami and applied for asylum. Each nuclear family unit with dependents had to apply for asylum separately.

Juan grew up in the many years that the complicated asylum process took. His extended family settled together in a two-bedroom house and began their lives from scratch. At first they did not have work permits and took bottom-rung jobs they considered safe from immigration scrutiny. After a few years, they got work permits and could get somewhat better-paying jobs. Some asylum cases took up to a decade to be resolved, but of those decided before September 11, 2001, all were granted their petitions for asylum. The cases that were not decided until after 9/11 were all denied. Between 2003 and 2008 individual family units received orders of removal, meaning that after years of living in the United States, and in spite of by then having US-born children, they had thirty days to pack their things and leave the country. The last rejection letter was to Juan's father, whose application had included petitions for Juan and his disabled sister. In the end, Juan's family was split apart. Some went back to Colombia while Juan's father and sister fled to Canada, where Juan had an uncle. Juan had little recollection of what life was like in Colombia and decided to stay in Florida, the only place he considered home, to fight for inclusion in a nation that split his family apart.

Juan's turning point came after he had left his family home, his future uncertain. He saw an immigrant youth organizer on Spanish-language TV talking about the DREAM Act and thought he might qualify. He explained in an interview that he had reached out to this organizer, because, as he said, "I had nothing to lose." The organizer became a mentor and eventually hired Juan to work on a project organizing undocumented students to register their citizen classmates to vote before the 2008 election. Juan finally had a job that paid enough to have three meals a day and meet basic living expenses. He subsequently became immersed in the immigrants' rights movement, which led to his involvement in the Trail of Dreams. The catalyst for the walk was the hopelessness palpable in the community. Juan explained, "I guess as someone who has struggled with depression, it really affected me at a very personal level in 2009 when multiple undocumented students took their lives across the country. And that, next to the fact that we had Obama as a president, and that was supposed to be this wonderful new world. Life for immigrants actually became worse in this country after Obama got elected . . . [and] the motivation came from the anger of that."

These issues hit closer to home when one of Juan's peers from the immigrant youth organization he worked with also attempted suicide. "I had to go and meet him at the hospital. I spent the whole night at the hospital with him, and I realized that I couldn't keep waiting." His friend's attempted suicide gave Juan the push he needed to become committed to participate in the 1,500-mile walk aiming to call attention to the plight of Dreamers, the name given to other adolescents like him, who were undocumented but unafraid to challenge the system that was marginalizing them.[1]

Although Juan had found greater security in his life since having his legal status regularized, he continues to fight for other immigrants such as himself, including his husband, Felipe, who although undocumented, benefited from President Obama's 2012 Deferred Action for Childhood Arrivals program that allows adolescents pursuing higher education or serving in the military to stay in the United States on a temporary status. Legally married to Juan in Massachusetts, Felipe will see his work permit and driver's license expire in two years. Although the Senate passed an immigration reform bill in June 2013, the inaction on immigration reform in the House of Representatives as of this writing means that the prospects for meaningful reform of the system are bleak. Without broad-based reform, immigrants such as Felipe will continue to live in an uncertain and temporary state of liminality. Moreover, after the US Supreme Court struck down the Defense of Marriage Act, it is possible that subsequent court challenges might extend immigration status to the spouses of gay US citizens. However, nothing is certain, because much of the momentum on reform seen in the summer of 2013 died down in the fall. Nonetheless, immigrants such as Juan continue to advocate for reform, most recently by participating in an immigration reform protest in Orlando, Florida, on October 29, 2013. Juan and fourteen others were arrested for blocking an intersection to call attention to the plight of immigrant families who are being torn apart by deportation practices.[2]

Seeking Security Through Return

Peruvians Sofía and Camila are immigrants who felt they had better chances to obtain security by returning to their country of origin. Unbeknownst to each other, they both worked in the same digital technology company in Miami in the 2000s. Sofía worked as a financial analyst and Camila in the cafeteria. In the summer of 2013, one of the authors of this book, Elena Sabogal, traveled to Peru. Upon her arrival, her sister shared with her a chance encounter she had with Sofía in a grocery store. Having interviewed Sofía in 2003, Sabogal reestablished contact with her. They met for dinner on a cold, drizzly night in Lima. Over dinner, Sofía told her about how she came to return to Peru.

In the years that transpired since her interview in Miami, Sofía became quite successful. She had achieved three of the four goals she had set for herself in the sixteen years she lived in the United States. She continued her education and attained an MBA, she bought a house several years after settling in Miami, and she became a US citizen. However, the fourth goal she could never manage to quite reach: finding a fulfilling relationship that would last. Although at one point Sofía was involved in a serious relationship, they eventually went their separate ways. Throughout her time in Miami, Sofía had a successful career and never really had any financial struggles. In fact, she made money by buying several homes and selling them once their value had risen. She made enough of a profit that she bought herself an apartment in Lima. Given that she had legal immigrant status and financial resources she visited Peru every year. After over a decade of residing in Miami, Sofía began to feel like she missed Peru, particularly her family. Economic and legal security could not replace the comfort derived from social support and emotional attachments: "For me family is very important because in the United States I was alone. I had a good job, I studied, and I did a lot of things, but I did not have a family. My mother, sister, brother, and cousins were not there. I had no one."

In 2009, the company Sofía worked for closed its headquarters and filed for bankruptcy. Sofía continued to work for them from home until she was finally let go in 2012. For six weeks she looked for another job in Miami, but to no avail. Considering that in recent years she had been drawn to return to Lima, when she heard of a job opportunity there, she wasted no time successfully relocating: "Here in Lima I am happy because I am closer to my mother who is getting older. I see my brother and sister and my childhood friends. In the United States I made friends, but I was older, and to me making friends when you are older is not the same as your lifelong friends to whom you never have to explain anything."

The job that she took in Lima once she returned lasted only ten months. At the time she spoke with us, she was again looking for work. When asked if she would consider returning to the United States to live, she stated, "It is a lot less stressful to search for a job in Lima than it was in Miami. Why? Because I have family and because I have a house that is already paid [for]. In the United States I had a mortgage and I was alone. Here I have my family's support and that is important."

Although the original motivation for Sofía to come to Miami was to escape the physical insecurity that she felt from having been victimized by crime several times back in the early 1990s, she felt that citizen security in the upscale districts in Lima she frequented had improved dramatically. Therefore, that kind of insecurity was no longer a push factor. However, Sofía stated that had she found in Miami someone with whom to be in a long-term relationship, or someone she could start a family and have children with, she would likely have stayed, even though she lost her job: "I think that if I had found emotional security in my life, I would not have come back to Lima." But without a stable relationship, she felt she lacked "firm roots" in Miami. She continued, "If I had been happy there, if I had felt I had roots [with a husband and children] in the United States, I would have searched for a job there, and I would have never thought about returning to Peru."

Now that Sofía is looking for work in Peru, as a woman with financial resources and a US passport, the door to return to the United States remains open. Sofía can act as a mobile agent seeking security across national borders.

Contrary to Sofía's experience of being laid off several years after her employer declared bankruptcy, Camila lost her kitchen job in the same company immediately. She turned to cleaning houses. Having lived in Miami for eight years, first on a tourist visa and then on a series of work-related visas, her largest fear was that she or one of her family members would lose legal immigration status. During those years, they had fought very hard to remain legal. In fact, they spent all of the money they had acquired from selling their apartment in Lima plus the capital they had from her husband's previous job's severance package, on fees related to visa applications, lawyer and clerk fees, and government fees. But after she was laid off, with their applications for a visa extension pending, Camila and her husband had no more money left. She said in no uncertain terms, "So much energy wasted. So much effort to end up with nothing. . . . The six years were over and we had not accomplished anything."

Unlike Sofía, Camila immigrated with her family, and her husband's relatives lived in Miami. Emotional loss was not what drove her to leave

Miami. Instead, insecurity arising from her unstable immigration status drove her away. Camila told us about her family's constant struggle to navigate an immigration system that Susan Bibler Coutin has likened to "the wolf's mouth."[3] She told stories about the employers they encountered who either sponsored them for a brief time or promised to sponsor them but ultimately never did. She also told us about the thousands of dollars they spent on lawyer fees, visa-related fees, and government transactions, all so that their visas could be renewed and their legal status would not lapse. Camila viewed these expenses as "investments, not costs." However, time and again, the lawyers, paralegals, and others hired to help them made careless mistakes when filing their paperwork, to such an extent that at one point in time, their son's legal status lapsed. The paralegal working on their case failed to indicate that the father's name was Pedro Sr. and the son's name was Pedro Jr., therefore it appeared like her son was not on her application at all. "To take away the legal status of a person is like taking their life; it is like declaring that person terminally ill," she said. Camila was horrified that one day the police would show up and cart off her son: "There was a feeling of complete insecurity because of fear of the police. It is not just distrust, but fear of the police because you are in terror that they will not let you explain. Automatically, they are the law and that is it, period. They do not allow you to talk; they do not allow you to explain. . . . They do not ask questions; they handcuff you and take you off."

Her son's status eventually was rectified. But given these fears, and after having spent an estimated $60,000 to $70,000 trying to gain permanent legal status only to still be waiting for their legal extensions as their visa expiration date neared, Camila and her husband decided to leave the United States altogether so as to avoid being out of status. In January of 2010, Camila left for Spain with her son. Since her grandfather was Italian and she had Italian passports, she could legally settle anywhere in the European Union. Her grown daughter remained in the United States and eventually legalized her status through marriage. Camila's husband joined them in Spain two months later, still awaiting the papers that would have given them US visa extensions. Their visa extensions were finally approved in August of 2010, but since they had already left the country, they could not return.

When they settled in Spain, they quickly learned that they could not make a living there given the country's economic crisis. They tried their luck in two cities, Tenerife and Madrid. However, they reached the conclusion that they would do better in Lima: "If we are going to look for work in Madrid, we might as well look in Lima. There we have support." Thus, a decade after deciding to search for security and a sustainable life through immigration, Camila returned to live in Peru with her husband and son.

Reintegrating socially and physically in Lima was not an easy experience, creating ambiguous feelings. These feelings troubled her in ways that suggest she was experiencing ontological insecurity, a disruption of the well-being that stems from trust in relationships and ways of being or understanding the world that anchor personal and group identities. We have shown throughout this book how immigration can disrupt relationships and the sense of place in the world they support; Camila described facing similar feelings upon return and reintegration into life in Lima. Describing the reintegration process, she noted that her original home had changed, and it left her uncomfortable and uncertain that she still belonged: "When you leave your country and then return, you become a little bit of a foreigner. In my case I do not feel comfortable here. At first it was great to see my family again. I had not seen my mother in years. I returned to Peru after ten years away. But [the city has grown] and the traffic is unbearable and Lima is expensive. Much more so than Miami and Madrid. . . . I am a 'bird of passage' here because I do not feel comfortable in Lima. There are so many things I do not understand."

Camila also felt that many of the problems that initially led to her departure remained. She was even exposed to a fake kidnapping scam where a voice on the phone said they had kidnapped her son, a form of extortion common in several Latin American countries. Since her son was home at the time, she did not worry, but it still frightened her.

Her experiences have made Camila want to return once again to the United States if her status should be rectified, if not through a work visa then via family sponsorship once her daughter becomes a US citizen. She still believes the full experience of security she seeks will be found in the United States: "If I do not receive the American residency through my own merit, I am still going to receive it through my daughter. I do not want to miss the opportunity."

Camila's belief that her security ultimately resides in the United States exists alongside the positive aspects of being reunited with her family and old friends in Lima. In this way she very much captures the ambivalence of immigration told in the pages of this book, as well as the inadequacies of virtual and imaginary co-presence strategies for some who are unable to visit the country of origin to see, touch, and hear their closest friends and loved ones: "There is this part that I was unable to find outside of Peru. To see the people you love again, your lifelong friends. It seems incredible to see them and touch them. I tell them that they do not value the ability they have to get together because they do not know what it feels to live far away. They do not understand the importance of friendship and sharing time together."

Camila's story captures the paradoxes of searching for belonging and well-being through immigration, where the goal is to weave together the various dimensions of human security on a foundation of firmly rooted ontological security. Both Camila's and Sofía's stories illustrate the difficulty of finding the full experience of security in immigrants' lives—happiness, well-being, sustainability—in an age of globalization and mobility. The happiest respondents in our study, as we demonstrated in Chapter 7, had managed to combine greater securities in Miami with moderate levels of translocal citizenship through strategies of embodied and absent co-presence (virtual, imaginative, by proxy) and being socially and emotionally embedded in two places. For life to be more secure across borders, the structural causes of insecurity must be addressed in countries of origin, but also, the US context must change as well given the millions of immigrants who have spent years in the United States, sometimes even the majority of their lives, just to remain on the sidelines of US society.

More broadly, concepts of citizenship must be expanded to allow for new global realities. While mobility and communication across borders have accelerated greatly during the decades that Jan Aart Scholte calls the contemporary period of "accelerated globalization,"[4] the legal definition of belonging in nation-states has not kept up and, as we have shown in this book, has resulted in all sorts of inequalities and social suffering that harm individuals and families. As stories of the Dreamers and split families reach a wider US public, the ground is ripe for opportunities for immigrants, children of immigrants, and natives to come together around the cause of immigration reform that addresses these realities. As Dreamer organizations recently told House Republicans—who in mid-2013 discussed legislation that would legalize *only* the children of undocumented immigrants—the activists would oppose any amendments to comprehensive immigration reform that would "divide our families." "Our parents sacrificed everything to bring us here for a better future for us and our families," Cristina Jimenez, managing director of United We Dream, told reporters. "We wouldn't be here without them and we won't leave them behind."[5] A young generation of immigrants, who have lived their lives as US residents—in spite of whatever the formal legal code says of them—is demanding social change that has at its heart the humanistic needs of all people, including the right to be with the people they love in the same physical space. Perhaps this generation will be successful in turning the need for immigration reform into the civil rights issue of this decade.

Future of the Global City

The larger process we addressed in *Making a Life in Multiethnic Miami* is how immigrants swept up in global economic processes create a new form of multisited citizenship to help them negotiate a local landscape where they experience different levels of membership. Remaining active in cross-border social relationships fortified many of the immigrants in our study, allowing them to continue their struggle for formal membership and general well-being in a global city where legal residency, race, national origins, gender, and class represent formidable barriers to full inclusion. Their struggles take place in a city that only recently and very rapidly underwent conversion from a legally segregated US city of the Deep South to one resembling a global city in its economic structure, a city that, in spite of its history, is led by an elite cohort of a Latino immigrant group. At the same time, Miami has become in the social imagination of US nationhood a racialized place in which "mainstream Americans" (read: non-Hispanic whites) are perceived to be marginalized through cultural exclusion.

In the last three decades, Miami has converted from a city on the edge of transformation from a US tourist haven, to a Cuban-led city in the 1980s, to a multiethnic city connecting global regions in the twenty-first century. The immigrant-run global city is culturally more open to Latino immigrants than other areas of the United States where Latinos are a racial and class minority or are negatively racialized; at the same time Miami can be politically, economically, socially, or otherwise exclusionary. This exclusionary nature is one of the central paradoxes that shapes the process of making a life in multiethnic Miami. Experiences of exclusion through racialization, national-origin hierarchies, language use, and, as we have just emphasized again, legal status are juxtaposed with (1) a pan-ethnic Latinidad and the use of the Spanish language that engenders feelings of cultural belonging, and (2) the potential for intergroup immigrant solidarity, such as we see with the Miami Dreamers, that is rooted in the common experience of immigration and social exclusion.

Although other global cities such as New York and Los Angeles have large immigrant populations, this southern-most global city is unique in that most of its immigrant residents are not broadly considered to be cultural outsiders, contrary to immigrant minorities who have settled in other parts of the United States and in global cities where a white US racial frame stigmatizes Spanish speakers. Moreover, the class heterogeneity among immigrant groups in Miami results in an opportunity structure where immigrant origins and Latin American and Caribbean backgrounds are not as commonly conflated with poverty status as they might be in more traditional immigrant gateway cities, yet where these same immigrants struggle to maintain a foothold in the city's shrinking middle class.

Thus, in spite of this local uniqueness, immigrants in Miami cannot escape the multiple inequalities and exclusions that complicate and sometimes block their search for security through immigration. US racial projects have been woven into federal immigration policies that approach immigrant groups generally as a suspect class of people. Such policies, in tandem with local and state-level policies, still exert control over the lives of some immigrants whose legal statuses relegate them to the margins of social life, regardless of where in the United States they live.

Redefining Citizenship

Feminists and other critical citizenship scholars have argued for a rearticulation of the meaning of citizenship. Rather than a legal status that is granted by the state in accordance with regulations that determine entry and membership, immigration policy should be reoriented toward feminist and vernacular approaches that look at the value-added contributions of immigrants in their day-to-day involvement and participation not just in the realm of productive work that sustains the US economy, but also in terms of their contributions to the work of social reproduction—that is, work that sustains families and households and contributes to the social reproduction of generations—in communities around the country and in the varying places of origin. This restructuring, however, requires us to acknowledge that current US immigration policy represents a racial project of the state that clears the way for legal violence and that supports an economic philosophy enhancing polarization. In order to undo this racial project, alleviate the social suffering that it causes, and hopefully sow seeds for a more fair economic system, these phenomena and their implications need to be understood. We have attempted to do just that in this book.

We have argued that the growing pool of undocumented immigrants in the US as well as many immigrants with temporary statuses, including legal residency, are products of neoliberal efforts in which government and business stakeholders benefit from the creation of temporary, mobile, and flexible pools of workers who (1) can be deployed as labor demand increases to benefit state and capitalists' interest, (2) fill the needs of a formal citizenry that also has felt the effects of neoliberal state policies that have deinvested in the social infrastructure that sustains the legally acknowledged populace, and (3) make up a group that has no formal political representation in the United States, even at the local level where, paradoxically, their contributions to and consumption of social goods and services are most notable, yet also where enforcement efforts have recently been most concentrated.[6]

Since the 1980s, the new federalism of the Reagan years—part of "a global movement to neoliberalise government policy"—encouraged a structure of government that "downloads considerable responsibility for social welfare and reproduction costs onto localities and states."[7] In this book, we have shown how in Miami, this neoliberal approach has structured the modes of incorporation of immigrants into the economy as well as into the ethnic landscape of the region. By cutting back the social safety net at the federal level and transferring these responsibilities to state and local governments, the United States has ensured that the needs of its citizenry cannot fully be met given the state's declining contributions toward the social welfare of the nation. Undocumented immigrants and those who have a variety of temporary legal statuses have taken up these responsibilities by performing the jobs that allow the country to continue to run; much like the uncompensated and often invisible reproductive work that women engage in, immigrants, too, often take on jobs in which the primary responsibility is to provide care. Whether caring for the elderly, caring for children, caring for those who are ill or disabled, or even taking low-paying jobs in the public sector, immigrants, both with legal status and without, have taken on many of the responsibilities that the US government formerly took on through social welfare programs but has been increasingly seeking to divest itself of.

Paradoxically, although immigrants have left environments that have been transformed by global structural adjustment policies, particularly in the case of the undocumented, they have come to be regarded as invisible subjects who have become collateral damage of neoliberal policies, but this time in another country and at various scales, including the local level. At the nation-state level, their status as legally nonexistent subjects absolves government from caring for *their* needs or helping to sustain *their* communities. Thus, undocumented immigrants and those who have temporary legal status, in theory, encapsulate profit without investment—eerily resembling, albeit in a different way and with greater margins for agency, attributes of former racial systems of labor exploitation in the United States and elsewhere. By not reforming the current immigration system, the status quo is one that perpetuates this system of oppression.

However ideal this scenario might seem to elite stakeholders, immigrants are not just the totality of their labor or labor potential—they have real needs that have, in essence, been passed on to local and state governments, who also are scaling back financial support for social welfare programs, at the same time that some states enact laws that criminalize the very populations filling the voids left by shrinking social safety nets. From this perspective, efforts to withhold the social rights of citizenship from the undocumented represent yet another aspect of a neoliberal agenda of cutting the costs of social reproduction.

"Downloading" tasks supporting successful immigrant incorporation to state and local governments has reignited the immigration debate in the last couple of decades; however, the localization of immigration politics has also come with an infusion of xenophobic and nativist tones that get to the underlying racial assumptions of who is American and who is not. The full benefits of citizenship historically were reserved for white men who owned property, and the courts have often stepped in to decide who is white.[8] More recently, the Supreme Court has upheld the "papers please" provision of Arizona's Senate Bill 1070 law, which allows law enforcement officials to determine who is undocumented based on judgments of behavior that in many cases would be inseparable from subjective determinations based on appearance. Thus, for a nation that claims to be in a postrace era, requiring proof of legal status and the racial profiling this question entails can be seen as "colorblind" tools to maintain the Anglo American essence of the country.

The lack of major immigration reform that would hold accountable the federal government for the well-being of those who have come to fill the void left by the new federalism has resulted in the not-so-benign neglect of the immigrant population. It also has added a layer of oppression onto them for they have become the scapegoats for many of the social problems afflicting the nation, ranging from income inequality to unemployment to the drawing down of resources to invest in social safety nets as well as divestment in social infrastructure such as education. And as we saw in the discussion of Juan's motivations for activism, documented at the beginning of this chapter, the toll we pay for excluding immigrants from formal membership in the nation-state can take the form of human lives that are lost to hopelessness and despair.

Despite the promises from President Barack Obama upon his 2008 election, during the length of his first term, no real incentive appeared for the immigration system to be reformed, nor did the macroeconomic challenges facing the country suggest any would be found in the immediate future. But since the 2012 presidential election in which Latinos played a large role in the reelection of President Obama, both Democrats and Republicans have come to realize that the Latino vote can no longer be taken for granted. In spite of this recognition, the prospects for any meaningful immigration reform to take place in 2013 are bleak. It is apparent that should a piecemeal effort emerge to reform the system at this time, it will involve further militarization of the border and expansion of US interior enforcement. As we have seen in past election cycles, public officials' desires to appeal to Latino populations tend to be forgotten in the years that are sandwiched in between national elections. This reality leaves a dismal picture for immigrants, unless their life stories can evoke enough empathy from policymakers and the US public so that key officials become invested in ameliorating the social suffering of immigrants who are struggling due to hightened enforcement and lack of meaningful immigration reform.

Our hope in carrying out this research is that the full humanity of immigrants—including their rights to be in physical co-presence with their kin—be recognized. In studying how immigrants search for comprehensive human security in a rapidly changing world, this research attempts to cast light on the lasting consequences of policies that devalue investments in social reproduction for the gain of the global elite. Yet we also aim to show how immigrants are not passive victims of macroscale processes. By illustrating how they engage in translocal social citizenship, we can move closer to reimagining what an approach to citizenship based on human needs, contributions, rights, and potentials might truly look like.

Notes

1. Juan's story has been mentioned in a number of policy briefs and in popular media. See the Florida Immigrant Advocacy Center (2010), Preston (2010), and Morel (2013). See the film *The Dream Is Now,* for documentation of the wider events he discusses, http://www.thedreamisnow.org.

2. Jacobson 2013.

3. Coutin 2003, p. 105.

4. Aart Scholte 2005, p. 101.

5. Avila and Marshall 2013.

6. Donato and Armenta 2011.

7. Ellis 2006, p. 50.

8. Ngai 2004.

References

Aart Scholte, Jan. 2005. *Globalization: A Critical Introduction*, 2nd edition. New York: Palgrave MacMillan.

Abrahamson, Mark. 2004. *Global Cities*. New York: Oxford University Press.

Acosta-Belen, Edna, and Carlos E. Santiago. 2006. *Puerto Ricans in the United States: A Contemporary Portrait*. Boulder: Lynne Rienner.

Aksoy, Asu, and Kevin Robins. 2003. "Banal Transnationalism: The Difference That Television Makes," in *The Media of Diaspora: Mapping the Globe*, edited by Karim H. Karim, 89–104. New York: Routledge.

Alberts, Heike C. 2005. "Changes in Ethnic Solidarity in Cuban Miami." *Geographical Review* 95, no. 2 (April): 231–248.

Albright, Jason. 2008. "Contending Rationality, Leadership, and Collective Struggle: The 2006 Justice for Janitors Campaign at the University of Miami." *Labor Studies Journal* 33, no. 1 (March): 63–80.

Allison, Paul D. 2002. *Missing Data*. Thousand Oaks: Sage.

Almeida, Paul D. 2007. "Defensive Mobilization: Popular Movements Against Economic Adjustment Policies in Latin America." *Latin American Perspectives* 34, no. 3 (May): 123–139.

Alvazzi del Frate, Anna. 2011. "When the Victim is a Woman." *Global Burden of Armed Violence 2011*: 113–144. http://www.genevadeclaration.org/fileadmin /docs/GBAV2011_CH4_rev.pdf (accessed November 10, 2013).

American Association for Public Opinion Research (AAPOR). 2011. *Standard Definitions: Final Dispositions of Case Codes and Outcome Rates for Surveys,* 7th edition. Deerfield: AAPOR. http://www.aapor.org/AM/Template.cfm?Section =Standard_Definitions2&Template=/CM/ContentDisplay.cfm&ContentID =3156 (accessed July 16, 2003).

American Civil Liberties Union of Massachusetts. 2008. *Detention and Deportation in the Age of ICE: Immigrants and Human Rights in Massachusetts*. Boston: ACLU of Massachusetts. http://aclum.org/sites/all/files/education/aclu_ice _detention_report.pdf (accessed July 16, 2013).

Americans for Immigrant Justice. 2011. *Client Profiles*. Miami: AI Justice. http:// aijustice.org/about-us/client-profiles/ (accessed October 5, 2011).

Appadurai, Arjun. 1995. "The Production of Locality," in *Counterworks: Managing the Diversity of Knowledge*, edited by Richard Fardon, 204–225. New York: Routledge.

————. 1996. *Modernity at Large: Cultural Dimensions of Globalization*. Minneapolis: University of Minnesota Press.

Aranda, Elizabeth M. 2003. "Global Carework and Gendered Constraints: The Case of Puerto Rican Transmigrants." *Gender and Society* 17, no. 4 (August): 609–626.

————. 2007. *Emotional Bridges to Puerto Rico: Migration, Return Migration, and the Struggles of Incorporation*. Lanham: Rowman and Littlefield.

Aranda, Elizabeth, and Elizabeth Vaquera. 2011. "Unwelcomed Immigrants: Experiences with Immigration Officials and Attachment to the US." Special issue, "Between Black and White." *Journal of Contemporary Criminal Justice* 27: 299–321.

Aranda, Elizabeth, Elizabeth Vaquera, and Elena Sabogal. 2007. "Immigrant Transnationalism and Modes of Incorporation Study." Funded by the National Science Foundation, Proposal No. 0752644.

Avila, Jim, and Serena Marshall. 2013. "DREAMers Tell Republican House: That's Not Our Dream." ABC News, July 23. http://abcnews.go.com/Politics/dreamers -republican-house-dream/story?id=19742213 (accessed July 23, 2013).

Badenhausen, Kurt. 2012. "America's Most Miserable Cities." *Forbes*, February 2. http://www.forbes.com/sites/kurtbadenhausen/2012/02/02/americas-most -miserable-cities/ (accessed July 16, 2013).

Baker, Susan. 2002. *Understanding Mainland Puerto Rican Poverty*. Philadelphia: Temple University Press.

Baldassar, Loretta. 2008. "Missing Kin and Longing to Be Together: Emotions and the Construction of Co-Presence in Transnational Relationships." *Journal of Intercultural Studies* 29, no. 3 (August): 247–266.

Basch, Linda, Nina Glick Schiller, and Cristina Szanton Blanc. 1994. *Nations Unbound: Transnational Projects, Post-Colonial Predicaments, and Deterritorialized Nation-States*. Langhorne: Gordon and Breach.

Batalova, Jeanne, and Margie McHugh. 2010. *DREAM vs. Reality: An Analysis of Potential DREAM Act Beneficiaries*. Washington, DC: Migration Policy Institute. http://www.migrationpolicy.org/pubs/dream-insight-july2010.pdf (accessed July 16, 2013).

Bennett, W. Lance. 2007. *News: The Politics of Illusion*, 7th edition. New York: Pearson Longman.

Berkowitz, Dan, and James V. TerKeurst. 1999. "Community as Interpretive Community: Rethinking the Journalist-Source Relationship." *Journal of Communication* 49, no. 3 (Summer): 125–136.

Bianet Castellanos, M. 2009. "Building Communities of Sentiment: Remittances and Emotions Among Maya Migrants." *Chicana/Latina Studies* 8, no. 1/2: 140–171.

Biocca, Frank, and Chad Harms. 2002. "Defining and Measuring Social Presence: Contribution to the Networked Minds Theory and Measure." *Proceedings of PRESENCE*, 7–36.

Bogaards, Matthijs. 1998. "The Favourable Factors for Consociational Democracy: A Review." *European Journal of Political Research* 33, no. 4 (1998): 475–496.

Bonilla-Silva, Eduardo. 1997. "Rethinking Racism: Toward a Structural Interpretation." *American Sociological Review* 67, no. 3 (June): 465–480.

————. 1999. "The Essential Social Fact of Race." *American Sociological Review* 64, no. 6 (December): 899–906.

————. 2002. "The Linguistics of Color Blind Racism: How to Talk Nasty About Blacks Without Sounding 'Racist.'" *Critical Sociology* 28, no. 1–2: 41–64.

————. 2004. "From Bi-Racial to Tri-Racial: Towards a New System of Racial Stratification in the USA." *Ethnic and Racial Studies* 27, no. 6: 931–950.

Borjas, George J. 2006. "Making It in America: Social Mobility in the Immigrant Population." *Future of Children* 16, no. 2 (Autumn): 55–71.

Boss, Pauline. 1999. *Ambiguous Loss: Learning to Live with Unresolved Grief.* Cambridge: Harvard University Press.

———. 2006. *Loss, Trauma, and Resilience: Therapeutic Work with Ambiguous Loss.* New York: W. W. Norton.

Bourricaud, François. 1975. "Indian, Mestizo and Cholo as Symbols in the Peruvian System of Stratification," translated by Barbara Bray, in *Ethnicity: Theory and Experience,* edited by Nathan Glazer and Daniel P. Moynihan, 350–387. Cambridge: Harvard University Press.

Brachfield, Pere. 2010. "El 'Dunning Harassment' a los Morosos," Gestores de Riesgo y Morosidad: Blog sobre la Gestión del Riesgo, la *Morosidad y Temas Económicos,* February 12. http://www.gestoresderiesgo.com/colaboradores /pere-brachfield-morosologo/el-%E2%80%9Cdunning-harassment %E2%80%9D-a-los-morosos (accessed July 18, 2013).

Bradburn, Norman M. 1969. *The Structure of Psychological Well-Being.* Chicago: Aldine.

Brannigan, Martha. 2010a. "Jean Monestime Unseats Long-Time Miami-Dade Commissioner Rolle." *Miami Herald,* November 3, B1.

———. 2010b. "Spotlight on Monestime, Rolle as Runoff Nears." *Miami Herald,* October 14, B1.

Brannigan, Martha, and Matt Haggman. 2010. "Monestime, Bell Take Commission Seats." *Miami Herald,* November 17, B3.

Brookings Institution. 2004. *Growing the Middle Class: Connecting All Miami-Dade Residents to Economic Opportunity.* Brookings Institution Center on Urban and Metropolitan Policy. Washington, DC: Brookings Institution.

Browning, Rufus, Dale Rogers Marshall, and David H. Tabb. 2003. "Can People of Color Achieve Power in City Government?" in *Racial Politics in American Cities,* 3rd edition, edited by Rufus Browning, Dale Rogers Marshall, and David H Tabb, 3–16. New York: Longman.

Burawoy, Michael. 1991. *Ethnography Unbound: Power and Resistance in the Modern Metropolis.* Berkeley: University of California Press.

Burawoy, Michael, Joseph A. Blum, Sheba George, Zsuzsa Gille, Teresa Gowan, Lynne Haney, Maren Klawitter, Steven H. Lopez, Seán Ó Riain, and Millie Thayer. 2000. *Global Ethnography: Forces, Connections and Imaginatons in a Postmodern World.* Berkeley: University of California Press.

Burgess, Katrina. 2009. "Neoliberal Reform and Migrant Remittances: Symptom or Solution?" in *Beyond Neoliberalism in Latin America? Societies and Politics at the Crossroads,* edited by John Burdick, Philip Oxhorn, and Kenneth M. Roberts, 177–196. New York: Palgrave Macmillan.

Bush, Gregory W. 1999. "'Playground of the USA': Miami and the Promotion of Spectacle." *Pacific Historical Review* 68, no. 2 (May): 153–172.

Butler, Judith. 1990. *Gender Trouble.* London: Routledge.

———. 1993. *Bodies That Matter.* London: Routledge.

Carling, Jørgen. 2008. "The Human Dynamics of Migrant Transnationalism." *Ethnic and Racial Studies* 31, no. 8: 1452–1477.

Casebeer, Kenneth M. 2008. "Constructing a Story of Law and Class: Cases, Statutes, and Foundational Readings: Of Service Workers, Contracting Out, Joint Employment, Legal Consciousness, and the University of Miami." *Buffalo Law Review* 59 (December): 1059–1093.

Casey, Edward S. 2001. "Body, Self and Landscape. A Geophilosophical Inquiry into the Place-World," in *Texture of Place: Exploring Humanist Geographies,* edited by Paul C. Adams, Steven Hoelscher, and Karen E. Till, 403–425. Minneapolis: University of Minnesota Press.

Cassola, Jose. 2011a. "Incumbents Hold on to Sweetwater Commission Seats." *Miami Herald*, May 10. NewsBank online (accessed July 25, 2013).

———. 2011b. "Sweetwater Commissioners Face Challengers—Sweetwater Elections Are Underway with Three Commissioners Seeking Reelection Against a Total of Six Challengers." *Miami Herald*, April 25. NewsBank online (accessed July 25, 2013).

Castro, Max J. 1992. "The Politics of Language in Miami," in *Miami Now! Immigration, Ethnicity, and Social Change,* edited by Guillermo J. Grenier and Alex Stepick III, 109–132. Gainesville: University of Florida Press.

CBS News/Associated Press. 2009. "GOP Rep. Calls Miami 'Third World Country.'" February 11. http://www.cbsnews.com/2100-250_162-2217944.html (accessed July 18, 2013).

Cerrutti, Marcela, and Rodolfo Bertoncello. 2003. "Urbanization and Internal Migration Patterns in Latin America." Paper prepared for the Conference on African Migration in Comparative Perspective, Johannesburg, South Africa, June 4–7.

Chardy, Alfonso. 2002. "Holding Haitians a Security Issue, INS Brief Details." *Miami Herald*, November 13.

———. 2006. "False Raid Rumors Frighten Immigrants." *Miami Herald*, April 28, 1A.

Charles, Carolle. 2007. "Political Refugees or Economic Immigrants? A New 'Old Debate' Within the Haitian Immigrant Communities *but* with Contestations and Division." In *Immigration, Incorporation and Transnationalism,* edited by Elliott R. Barkan, 175–192. New Brunswick: Transaction.

Charles, Jacqueline. 2002. "Dade's Diversity Displayed on Ballot." *Miami Herald*, October 14, B1.

Charles, Jacqueline, and Tere Figueras Negrete. 2006. "Haitian-American Candidates Faced a Double Challenge." *Miami Herald*, September 10, B1.

Charles, Jacqueline, C. Salazar, and D. Martinez. 2002. "Dade Vote Is Historic for 2 New Legislators." *Miami Herald*, November 6, B1.

Chavez, Leo R. 1997. "Immigration Reform and Nativism: The Nationalist Response to the Transnationalist Challenge," in *Immigrants Out! The New Nativism and the Anti-Immigrant Impulse in the United States,* edited by Juan F. Perea, 61–77. New York: New York University Press.

Chui, Stephen, and Tai-Lok Lui. 2009. *Hong Kong: Becoming a Chinese Global City*. New York: Routledge.

City Mayors Foundation. 2009. "The Most Expensive and Richest Cities in the World." http://www.citymayors.com/cconomics/usb-purchasing-power.html (accessed November 11, 2013).

Clark, Lesley. 2006. "Congressman Calls Miami 'Third World.'" *Miami Herald*, November 28, 1B.

Clavijo, Sergio. 2009. "Social Security Reforms in Colombia: Striking Demographic and Fiscal Balances." IMF Working Paper, Western Hemisphere Department, March.

Cobas, José A., Jorge Duany, and Joe R. Feagin. 2009. *Racializing Latinos: Historical Background and Current Forms*. Boulder: Paradigm.

Cohen, Adam. 2001. "Gloom over Miami." *Time,* June 24. http://www.time.com/time/magazine/article/0,9171,135186,00.html (accessed September 2, 2007).

Cohen, Joseph Nathan, and Miguel Angel Centeno. 2006. "Neoliberalism and Patterns of Economic Performance, 1980–2000." *ANNALS of the American Academy of Political and Social Science* 606 (July): 32–67.

Conradson, David, and Deirdre McKay. 2007. "Translocal Subjectivities: Mobility, Connection, Emotion." *Mobilities* 2, no. 2: 167–174.

Corporación Latinobarómetro. 2005. *Informe Latinobarómetro 2005*. Santiago, Chile: Corporación Latinobarómetro. http://www.latinobarometro.org/latino /LATContenidos.jsp (accessed July 24, 2013).

Coutin, Susan Bibler. 2003. *Legalizing Moves: Salvadoran Immigrants' Struggle for US Residency*. Ann Arbor: University of Michigan Press.

Creswell, John W. 2007. *Qualitative Inquiry and Research Design: Choosing Among Five Approaches*. Thousand Oaks: Sage.

Croucher, Sheila. 1997. *Imagining Miami: Ethnic Politics in a Postmodern World*. Charlottesville: University Press of Virginia.

Dahl, Robert A. 1971. *Polyarchy: Participation and Opposition*. New Haven: Yale University Press.

Dash, Nicole, Walter Gillis Peacock, and Betty Hearn Morrow. 2000. "And the Poor Get Poorer: A Neglected Black Community," in *Hurricane Andrew: Ethnicity, Gender and the Sociology of Disasters*, edited by Walter Gillis Peacock, Betty Hearn Morrow, and Hugh Gladwin, 206–225. Miami: International Hurricane Center, Laboratory for Social and Behavioral Research.

Dávila, Arlene M. 2001. *Latinos, Inc.: The Marketing and Making of a People*. Berkeley: University of California Press.

De Fede, Jim. 1999. "Leadership Abhors a Vacuum." *Miami New Times*, July 22. http://www.miaminewtimes.com/photoGallery/index/240191/0/ (accessed November 11, 2011).

De Genova, Nicholas, and Ana Y. Ramos-Zayas. 2003. *Latino Crossings: Mexicans, Puerto Ricans, and the Politics of Race and Citizenship*. New York: Routledge.

De La Cruz, Ralph. 2007. "Remembering Past Is Key to Compassion." *South Florida Sun Sentinel*, November 4, 1H.

Departamento Administrativo Nacional de Estadística. 2007. *Colombia: Una Nación Multicultural, Su Diversidad Étnica*. Bogotá: Departamento Administrativo Nacional de Estadística. Dirección de Censos y Demografía.

Dominguez, Jorge I., and Michael Shifter. 2003. *Constructing Democratic Governance in Latin America*. Baltimore: Johns Hopkins University Press.

Donato, Katharine M. 1993. "Current Trends and Patterns of Female Migration: Evidence from Mexico." *International Migration Review* 27, no. 4 (Winter): 748–771.

———. 2010. "Processes of Migration in the Americas: US Migration from Latin America: Gendered Patterns and Shifts." *ANNALS of the American Academy of Political and Social Science* 630 (July): 78–92.

Donato, Katharine M., and Amada Armenta. 2011. "What We Know About Unauthorized Migration." *Annual Review of Sociology* 37 (August): 529–543.

Donato, Katharine M., Donna Gabaccia, Jennifer Holdaway, Martin Manalansan IV, and Patricia R. Pesar. 2006. "A Glass Half-Full? Gender in Migration Studies." *International Migration Review* 40, no. 1 (Spring): 3–26.

Dreby, Joanna. 2010. *Divided by Borders*. Berkeley: University of California Press.

Duany, Jorge. 1998. "Reconstructing Racial Identity: Ethnicity, Color, and Class Among Dominicans in the United States and Puerto Rico." *Latin American Perspectives* 25, no. 3 (May): 147–172.

———. 2002. *Puerto Rican Nation on the Move: Identities on the Island and in the United States*. Chapel Hill: University of North Carolina Press.

———. 2004. "Puerto Rico: Between the Nation and the Diaspora—Migration to and from Puerto Rico," in *Migration and Immigration: A Global View,* edited by Maura I. Toro-Morn and Marixsa Alicea, 177–195. Westport: Greenwood.

———. 2006. "Racializing Ethnicity in the Spanish-Speaking Caribbean: A Comparison of Haitians in the Dominican Republic and Dominicans in Puerto Rico." *Latin American and Caribbean Ethnic Studies* 1, no. 2 (November): 231–248.

———. 2011. *Blurred Borders. Transnational Migration Between the Hispanic Caribbean and the United States.* Chapel Hill: University of North Carolina Press.

Dumont, Jean-Christophe, and Olivier Monso. 2007. "Matching Educational Background and Employment: A Challenge for Immigrants in Host Countries," in *International Migration Outlook*, 131–159. Paris: Organisation of Economic Co-operation and Development.

Durand, Jorge, and Douglas S. Massey. 2010. "New World Orders: Continuities and Changes in Latin American Migration." *ANNALS of the American Academy of Political and Social Science* 630 (July): 20–52.

Eckland, Emily T. 2004. "Ankle Lock: Success and Sorrow." *Miami Herald*, January 11, B1.

Eckstein, Susan Eva. 2009. *The Immigrant Divide: How Cuban Americans Changed the US and Their Homeland.* New York: Routledge.

Eckstein, Susan, and Lorena Barberia. 2002. "Grounding Immigrant Generations in History: Cuban Americans and Their Transnational Ties." *International Migration Review* 36, no. 3 (Fall): 799–837.

Economic Commission for Latin America and the Caribbean (ECLAC). 2005. *Preliminary Overview of the Economies of Latin America and the Caribbean 2004.* New York: United Nations. http://www.eclac.cl/cgi-bin/getProd.asp?xml=/publicaciones/xml/0/20480/P20480.xml&xsl=/de/tpl-i/p9f.xsl&base=/tpl/top-bottom.xslt (accessed February 4, 2006).

Ellis, Mark. 2006. "Unsettling Immigrant Geographies: US Immigration and the Politics of Scale." *Tijdschrift voor Economische en Sociale Geografie* 97, no. 1: 49–58.

Ellis, Mark, and Richard Wright. 1998. "The Balkanization Metaphor in the Analysis of US Immigration." *Annals of the Association of American Geographers* 88, no. 4 (December): 686–698.

Entman, Robert M. 1993. "Framing: Toward Clarification of a Fractured Paradigm." *Journal of Communication* 43, no. 4 (December): 51–58.

Esguerra Villamizar, Lola Viviana. 2011. *Instintos de Libertad. Secuestro en América Latina. Historias e Imágenes de Cautiverio.* Investigación para la Conferencia Subregional del CHDS en Santiago de Chile: Fundación País Libre, July 19–23. http://www.paislibre.org/site/images/stories/AMRICA_LATINA.pdf (accessed July 18, 2013).

Espina Prieto, Mayra Paula. 2001. "The Effects of the Reform on Cuba's Social Structure: An Overview." *Socialism and Democracy* 15, no. 1: 23–39.

Faier, Lieba. 2011. "Theorizing the Intimacies of Migration: Commentary on the Emotional Formations of Transnational Worlds." *International Migration* 49, no. 6 (December): 107–112.

Feagin, Joe R. 2006. *Systemic Racism: A Theory of Oppression.* New York: Routledge.

———. 2009. *The White Racial Frame: Centuries of Racial Framing and Counter-Framing.* New York: Routledge.

Feagin, Joe, and Hernan Vera. 1995. *White Racism*. New York: Routledge.

Ferreira, Francisco H. G., Julian Messina, Jamele Rigolini, Luis-Felipe Lopez-Calva, Maria Ana Lugo, and Renos Vakis. 2012. *Economic Mobility and the Rise of the Latin American Middle Class*. Washington, DC: World Bank.

Fiedler, T. 1992. "Challenger Transformed into Front-Runner." *Miami Herald*, February 26, A1.

———. 1997. "South Florida Could Be Hit Hard by Reforms on Campaign Financing." *Miami Herald* (Final ed.), February 28, 1A.

Figueras Negrete, T., and J. Charles. 2006. "Radio Is Key for Haitian Candidates." *Miami Herald*, September 3, B3.

Fischl, Michael. 2007. "The Other Side of the Picket Line: Contract, Democracy, and Power in a Law School Classroom." *N.Y.U. Review of Law and Social Change* 31 (November): 517–536.

Fisk, Catherine L., Daniel J. B. Mitchell, and Christopher L. Erickson. 2000. "Union Representation of Immigrant Janitors in Southern California: Economic and Legal Challenges," in *Organizing Immigrants: The Challenge for Unions in Contemporary California*, edited by Ruth Milkman, 199–224. Ithaca, NY: Cornell University Press.

Florida Immigrant Advocacy Center. 2010. "Unleash the DREAM: End the Colossal Waste of Young Immigrant Talent. Miami." April. http://aijustice.org/dream -act-article/ (accessed November 12, 2013).

Foner, Nancy. 2000. *From Ellis Island to JFK: New York's Two Great Waves of Immigration*. New Haven: Yale University Press/Russell Sage Foundation.

"Foreigners Responsible for a Fifth of Florida Home Sales." 2012. *Miami Herald*, August 27. NewsBank online (accessed July 31, 2013).

Forman, Tyrone A., Carla Goar, and Amanda E. Lewis. 2002. "Neither Black nor White? An Empirical Test of the Latin Americanization Thesis." *Race and Society* 5, no. 1: 65–84.

Fortier, Anne-Marie. 1999. "Re-Membering Places and the Performance of Belonging(s)," in *Performativity and Belonging*, edited by Vikki Bell, 41–64. London: Sage.

Francis, Thomas. 2011. "Security Breach: The US Government Has Deported Thousands of Non-Criminal Immigrants Living in Florida Through a Program Designed to Round Up Violent Offenders." Florida Center for Investigative Reporting, January 31. http://fcir.org/2011/01/31/security-breach/ (accessed July 25, 2013).

Frank, Reanna, Ilana Redstone Akresh, and Bo Lu. 2010. "Latino Immigrants and the US Racial Order: How and Where Do They Fit In?" *American Sociological Review* 75, no. 3 (June): 378–401.

Freedman, Jane. 2003. *Gender and Insecurity: Migrant Women in Europe*. Burlington, VT: Ashgate.

Fregoso, Rosa-Linda, and Cynthia Bejarano. 2010. *Terrorizing Women: Feminicide in the Américas*. Durham: Duke University Press.

Frey, William H. 1996. "Immigration, Domestic Migration, and Demographic Balkanization in America: New Evidence for the 1990s." *Population and Development Review* 22, no. 4: 741–763.

Fussell, Elizabeth. 2010. "The Cumulative Causation of International Migration in Latin America." *ANNALS of the American Academy of Political and Social Science* 630 (July): 162–177.

Gans, Herbert. 1979. "Symbolic Ethnicity: The Future of Ethnic Groups and Cultures in America." *Ethnic and Racial Studies* 2, no. 1 (January): 1–20.

———. 1999. "The Possibility of a New Racial Hierarchy in the Twenty-First Century United States," in *The Cultural Territories of Race: Black and White Boundaries,* edited by Michèle Lamont, 371–390. Chicago: University of Chicago Press.

García, Angela S., and David G. Keyes. 2012. *Life as an Undocumented Immigrant: How Restrictive Local Immigration Policies Affect Daily Life.* Washington, DC: Center for American Progress.

García, María Cristina. 1996. *Havana USA: Cuban Exiles and Cuban Americans in South Florida, 1959–1994.* Berkeley: University of California Press.

García Bedolla, Lisa. 2009. *Latino Politics.* Cambridge: Polity.

García y Griego, Manuel. 1980. *El Volumen de la Migración de Mexicanos no Documentados a los Estados Unidos: Nuevas Hipótesis* (Estudios/Encuesta Nacional de Emigración a la Frontera Norte del País y a los Estados Unidos). México, D.F.: Centro Nacional de Información y Estadísticas del Trabajo.

Garvin, G. 2009. "When Non-US Citizens Vote." *Miami Herald* (Final ed.), April 7, 13A.

Gaventa, J. 1982. *Power and Powerlessness: Quiescence and Rebellion in an Appalachian Valley.* Champaign: University of Illinois Press.

Georgiou, Myria. 2006. *Diaspora, Identity and the Media.* Cresskill: Hampton.

Gergen, Kenneth J. 1994. *Realities and Relationships: Soundings in Social Construction.* Boston: Harvard University Press.

Giddens, Anthony. 1990. *The Consequences of Modernity.* Oxford: Polity.

———. 1991. *Modernity and Self-Identity: Self and Society in the Late Modern Age.* Palo Alto: Stanford University Press.

Gieryn, Thomas F. 2000. "A Space for Place in Sociology." *Annual Review of Sociology* 26: 463–496.

Gilbert, Dennis. 2007. *Mexico's Middle Class in the Neoliberal Era.* Tucson: University of Arizona Press.

Glenn, Evelyn Nakano. 1992. "From Servitude to Service Work: Historical Continuities in the Racial Division of Paid Reproductive Labor." *Signs* 18, no. 1 (Autumn): 1–43.

———. 2011. "Constructing Citizenship: Exclusion, Subordination, and Resistance." *American Sociological Review* 76, no. 1: 1–24.

Glick Schiller, Nina, and Ayse Caglar. 2008. "And Ye Shall Possess it, and Dwell Within: Social Citizenship, Global Christianity, and Nonethnic Immigrant Incorporation," in *Citizenship, Political Engagement, and Belonging: Immigrants in Europe and the United States,* edited by Deborah Reed-Danahay and Caroline B. Brettell, 203–225. New Brunswick: Rutgers University Press.

Goldberg, David Theo, Ramón Grosfoguel, and Eric Mielants. 2006. "Field of Dreams: Cultures of Scholarship and Public Policy on Race in the United States." *International Journal of Comparative Sociology* 47, no. 3–4 (August): 259–280.

Gómez, Laura E. 2007. *Manifest Destinies: The Making of the Mexican American Race.* New York: New York University Press.

González, Juan. 2000. *Harvest of Empire: A History of Latinos in America.* New York: Penguin.

González de la Rocha, Mercedes. 2006. "Vanishing Assets: Cumulative Disadvantage Among the Urban Poor." *ANNALS of the American Academy of Political and Social Science* 606 (July): 68–93.

Goodman, Joshua. 2007. "Immigrant Children Face Deportation—Brothers in Florida Are Test Case." *South Florida Sun Sentinel,* November 20, 26A.

Gootenberg, Paul. 2010. "Latin American Inequalities: New Perspectives from History, Politics, and Culture," in *Indelible Inequalities in Latin America: Insights from History, Politics, and Culture,* edited by Paul Gootenberg and Luis Reygadas, 3–22. Durham: Duke University Press.

Gramsci, Antonio. 1992. *Prison Notebooks.* New York: Columbia University Press.

Grasmuck, Sherri, and Patricia R. Pessar. 1991. *Between Two Islands: Dominican International Migration.* Berkeley: University of California Press.

Greenbaum, Susan D. 2002. *More Than Black: Afro-Cubans in Tampa.* Gainesville: University Press of Florida.

Grenier, Guillermo J. 2006. "The Creation and Maintenance of the Cuban American 'Exile Ideology': Evidence from the FIU Cuba Poll 2004." *Journal of American Ethnic History* 25, no. 2/3 (Winter/Spring): 209–224.

Grenier, Guillermo J., and Max J. Castro. 1999. "Triadic Politics: Ethnicity, Race, and Politics in Miami, 1959–1998." *Pacific Historical Review* 68, no. 2 (May): 273–292.

Grenier, Guillermo J., and Lisandro Pérez. 2003. *The Legacy of Exile: Cubans in the United States.* Boston: Allyn and Bacon.

Grizzle, Gloria A., and Paul C. Trogen. 1994. "Cutback Budgeting in Florida: Causes, Approaches and Consequences." *Politics and Policy* 22, no. 3 (September): 503–523.

Grosfoguel, Ramón. 2003. *Colonial Subjects: Puerto Ricans in a Global Perspective.* Berkeley: University of California Press.

———. 2004. "Race and Ethnicity or Racialized Ethnicities? Identities Within Global Coloniality." *Ethnicities* 4, no. 3: 315–336.

Guarnizo, Luis Eduardo. 1997. "Los Dominicanyorks: The Making of a Binational Society," in *Challenging Fronteras: Structuring Latina and Latino Lives in the US,* edited by Mary Romero, Pierrette Hondagneu-Sotelo, and Vilma Ortiz, 161–174. New York: Routledge.

Hackworth, Jason. 2007. *The Neoliberal City: Governance, Ideology and Development in American Urbanism.* Ithaca: Cornell University Press.

Haggman, M., and L. Figueroa. 2010. "Miami-Dade County Commission: Dorrin Rolle in Race to Save His Political Life." *Miami Herald,* August 26, B1.

"Haitians in America Meet Requirements for TPS." 2006. *South Florida Sun Sentinel,* August 24, 20A.

Hardy-Fanta, Carol. 1993. *Latina Politics, Latino Politics: Gender, Culture, and Political Participation in Boston.* Philadelphia: Temple University Press.

Heaton, Tim B., Renata Forste, and Samuel M. Otterstrom. 2002. "Family Transitions in Latin America: First Intercourse, First Union and First Birth." *International Journal of Population Geography* 8: 1–15.

Henderson, Tim. 2003. "Highest Immigration Rate Belongs to Dade." *Miami Herald,* May 21, 1B.

Herd, Pamela, and Madonna Harrington Meyer. 2006. "Care Work: Invisible Civic Engagement," in *Global Dimensions of Gender and Carework,* edited by Mary K. Zimmerman, Jacquelyn S. Litt, and Christine E. Bose, 324–340. Stanford: Stanford University Press.

Higham, John. 2002 [1955]. *Strangers in the Land: Patterns of American Nativism, 1860–1925.* New Brunswick: Rutgers University Press.

Hoag, Christina. 2005. "Visas for Skilled Noncitizens Who Are US Educated to Rise by 20,000." *Miami Herald,* April 6, 1C.

Hochschild, Arlie Russell. 1979. "Emotion Work, Feeling Rules, and Social Structure." *American Journal of Sociology* 85, no. 3 (November): 551–575.

Hoene, Christopher W. 2009. *Research Brief on America's Cities: City Budget Shortfalls and Responses: Projections for 2010–2012*. Washington, DC: National League of Cities.

Hoffman, Kelly, and Miguel Angel Centeno. 2003. "The Lopsided Continent: Inequality in Latin America." *Annual Review of Sociology* 29: 363–390.

Holston, James, and Arjun Appadurai. 1999. "Cities and Citizenship," in *Cities and Citizenship*, edited by James Holston, 1–18. Durham: Duke University Press.

Hondagneu-Sotelo, Pierrette, and Ernestina Avila. 1997. "I'm Here, but I'm There: The Meanings of Latina Transnational Motherhood." *Gender and Society* 11, no. 5 (October): 548–571.

Hout, Michael. 2008. "How Class Works: Objective and Subjective Aspects of Class Since the 1970s," in *Social Class: How Does It Work?*, edited by Dalton Conley and Annette Lareau, 25–64. New York: Russell Sage Foundation.

HSBC Private Banking. 2011. "About Us." http://www.hsbcprivatebank.com /aboutus/what-is-private-banking.html (accessed October 17, 2011).

Htun, Mala. 2008. "Political Inclusion and Social Inequality: Women, Afro-Descendants, and Indigenous Peoples," in *Constructing Democratic Governance in Latin America*, edited by Jorge I. Dominguez and Michael Shifter, 72–96. Baltimore: Johns Hopkins University Press.

Hughes, Sallie, Yves Colon, Lilia Santiague, and Tsitsi Wakhisi. 2012. *Haitian Community Media in South Florida: Transnational Audiences, Journalists and Radio Programmers*. Miami: University of Miami School of Communication and the McCormick Foundation.

Huntington, Samuel P. 2004. "The Hispanic Challenge." *Foreign Policy* (March/April): 30–45.

Huysmans, Jef. 2006. *The Politics of Insecurity: Fear, Migration and Asylum in the EU*. Abington: Routledge.

Ibrahim, Maggie. 2005. "The Securitization of Migration: A Racial Discourse." *International Migration* 43, no. 5 (December): 163–187.

IJsselsteijn, Wijnand, Joy van Baren, and Froukje van Lanen. 2003. "Staying in Touch: Social Presence and Connectedness Through Synchronous and Asynchronous Communication Media," in *Human-Computer Interaction: Theory and Practice (Part II)*, vol. 2, edited by Constantine Stephanidis and Julie Jacko, 924–928. Mahwah: Lawrence Erlbaum.

Imbusch, Peter, Michel Misse, and Fernando Carrión. 2011. "Violence Research in Latin America and the Caribbean: A Literature Review." *International Journal of Conflict and Violence* 5, no. 1: 87–154.

Inter-American Development Bank Research Department. 2007. "Outsiders? Social Exclusion in Latin America." *Ideas for Development in the Americas* 14 (September–December): 1–16.

Irizarry, Lilliam. 2008. "Más de la Mitad de los Puertorriqueños viven en EE.UU" [More than half of Puerto Ricans live in the United States]. Associated Press, December 29. http://www.primerahora.com/noticias/mundo/nota/masdelamitad delospuertorriquenosviveneneeuu-259717/ (accessed November 11, 2013).

Jacobson, Susan. 2013. "Immigration-Reform Rally Arrestees Released from Jail." *Orlando Sentinel*, October 30. http://www.orlandosentinel.com/news/local /breakingnews/os-immigration-reform-orlando-20131029,0,7464242.story (accessed November 11, 2013).

Janoschka, Michael, and Axel Borsdorf. 2006. "*Condomínios Fechados* and *Barrios Privados*: The Rise of Private Residential Neighbourhoods in Latin America," in *Private Cities: Global and Local Perspectives,* edited by Georg Glasze, Chris Webster, and Klaus Frantz, 89–104. London: Routledge.

Jones, Kathleen B. 1990. "Citizenship in a Woman-Friendly Polity." *Signs* 15, no. 4 (Summer): 781–812.

Jones-Correa, Michael, and Katherine Fennelly. 2009. "Immigration Enforcement and Its Effects on Latino Lives in Two Rural North Carolina Communities." Paper presented at the *Undocumented Hispanic Migration: On the Margins of a Dream* conference, Connecticut College, New London, October 16–18.

Kasinitz, Philip, John H. Mollenkoph, Mary C. Waters, and Jennifer Holdaway. 2008. *Inheriting the City: The Children of Immigrants Come of Age.* New York: Russell Sage Foundation.

Kennedy, Kelli. 2007. "Glitz and Glamour Overshadows Majority of Miami's Population, Adv00, FL." Associated Press News Service, News Sports, January 26. NewsBank online (accessed July 29, 2013).

Killian, Caitlin, and Cathryn Johnson. 2006. "'I'm Not an Immigrant!' Resistance, Redefinition, and the Role of Resources in Identity Work." *Social Psychology Quarterly* 69, no. 1 (March): 60–80.

Kinnvall, Catarina, and Jitka Lindén. 2010. "Dialogical Selves Between Security and Insecurity: Migration, Multiculturalism, and the Challenge of the Global." *Theory and Psychology* 20, no. 5 (October): 595–619.

Kleinman, Arthur, and Joan Kleinman. 1996. "The Appeal of Experience; The Dismay of Images: Cultural Appropriations of Suffering in Our Times." *Daedalus* 125, no. 1 (Winter): 1–23.

Kofman, Eleonore. 2007. "The Knowledge Economy, Gender and Stratified Migrations." *Studies in Social Justice* 1, no. 2: 122–135.

Lacayo, A. Elena. 2010. "Impact of Section 287(G) of the Immigration and Nationality Act on the Latino Community." National Council of La Raza, Issue Brief no. 21. http://www.nclr.org/images/uploads/publications/287gReportFinal_1 .pdf (accessed November 10, 2013).

Lacy, Karyn. 2004. "Black Spaces, Black Places: Strategic Assimilation and Identity Construction in Middle-Class Suburbia." *Ethnic and Racial Studies* 27, no. 6: 908–930.

Laguerre, Michel S. 1998. *Diasporic Citizenship: Haitian Americans in Transnational America.* New York: St. Martin's.

Lattanzi Shutika, Debra. 2011. *Beyond the Borderlands: Migration and Belonging in the United States and Mexico.* Berkeley: University of California Press.

Laurie, Nina, and Alastair Bonnett. 2002. "Adjusting to Equity: The Contradictions of Neoliberalism and the Search for Racial Equality in Peru." *Antipode* 34, no. 1 (January): 28–53.

Leach, Neil. 2002. "Belonging: Towards a Theory of Identification with Place." *Perspecta* 33: 126–133.

Lee, Jennifer, and Frank D. Bean. 2004. "America's Changing Color Lines: Immigration, Race/Ethnicity, and Multiracial Identification." *Annual Review of Sociology* 30: 221–242.

Levitt, Peggy. 2001. *The Transnational Villagers.* Berkeley: University of California Press.

Lewin, Tamar. 2011. "In Puerto Rico, Protests End Short Peace at University." *New York Times,* February 17. http://www.nytimes.com/2011/02/18/education/18 puertorico.html?pagewanted=all&_r=0 (accessed July 25, 2013).

Lewin-Epstein, Noah, and Asaf Levanon. 2005. "National Identity and Xenophobia in an Ethnically Divided Society." *International Journal on Multicultural Societies* 7, no. 2: 90–118.

Life by Dream. 2009. "Camila: An Update," March 4. http://lifebydream.blogspot.com/2009/03/camila-update.html (accessed July 10, 2013).

Lijphart, Arend. 1977. *Democracy in Plural Societies: A Comparative Exploration.* New Haven: Yale University Press.

Lin, Jan. 2011. *The Power of Urban Ethnic Places: Cultural Heritage and Community Life.* New York: Routledge.

Lipset, Seymour Martin. 1967. "Values, Education, and Entrepreneurship," in *Elites in Latin America,* edited by Seymour Martin Lipset and Aldo Solari, 3–60. New York: Oxford University Press.

Little, Cheryl, and Kathie Klarreich. 2005. *Securing Our Borders: Post 9/11 Scapegoating of Immigrants.* Miami: Florida Immigrant Advocacy Center.

Little, Cheryl, and Charu Newhouse al-Sahli. 2004. *Haitian Refugees: A People in Search of Hope.* Miami: Florida Immigrant Advocacy Center.

Loewe, B. 2011. "New Numbers Demonstrate Persisting Problems with ICE's Secure Communities Program." *Uncover the Truth: ICE and Police Collaborations,* March 24. http://uncoverthetruth.org/featured/new-numbers-demonstrate-persisting-problems-with-ices-secure-communities-program-pr/ (accessed July 19, 2013).

Lora, Eduardo, and Johanna Fajardo. 2011. *Latin American Middle Classes: The Distance Between Perception and Reality.* IDB Working Paper Series No. IDB-WP-275. Inter-American Development Bank, Department of Research and Chief Economist, December.

Low, Setha M. 1994. "Cultural Conservation of Place," in *Conserving Culture: A New Discourse on Heritage,* edited by Mary Hufford, 66–77. Champaign: University of Illinois Press.

Lukes, Steven. 2005. *Power: A Radical View,* 2nd edition. New York: Palgrave Macmillan.

Luna, Pablo, and Fernando Filgueira. 2009. "The Left Turns as Multiple Paradigmatic Crises." *Third World Quarterly* 30, no. 2: 371–395.

Lush, Tamara. 2007. "FTAA Settlement Reached." *Miami New Times,* October 4. http://www.miaminewtimes.com/2007-10-04/news/ftaa-settlement-reached/ (accessed July 19, 2013).

Marcelin, Louis Herns. 2005. "Identity, Power, and Socioracial Hierarchies Among Haitian Immigrants in Florida," in *Neither Enemies nor Friends: Latinos, Blacks and Afro-Latinos,* edited by Suzanne Oboler and Anani Dzidzienyo, 209–227. New York: Palgrave Macmillan.

Marrow, Helen. 2012. "When We All Become the Immigration Police." *World on the Move* 18, no. 2: 7–9. Published by the International Migration Section of the American Sociological Association.

Marschall, Melissa J., and Anirudh V. S. Ruhil. 2007. "Substantive Symbols: The Attitudinal Dimension of Black Political Incorporation in Local Government." *American Journal of Political Science* 51, no. 1 (January): 17–33.

Martin, Daniel C., and Michael Hoefer. 2009. "Refugees and Asylees: 2008." *Annual Flow Report, June 2009.* Office of Immigration Statistics, Policy Directorate. Washington, DC: Department of Homeland Security. http://www.dhs.gov/xlibrary/assets/statistics/publications/ois_rfa_fr_2008.pdf (accessed July 19, 2013).

Martínez, Samuel. 2009. *International Human Rights. The Global Repercussions of US Policy.* Berkeley: University of California Press.

Martinez v. Bush, 234 F.Supp. 2d 1275 (S.D. Fla. 2003).

Mason, Jennifer. 2004. "Managing Kinship over Long Distances: The Significance of 'the Visit.'" *Social Policy and Society* 3, no. 4 (October): 421–429.

Massey, Doreen. 1993. "Power Geometry and a Progressive Sense of Place," in *Mapping the Futures: Local Cultures, Global Change*, edited by J. Bird, B. Curtis, T. Putnam, G. Robertson, and L. Tickner, 59–69. London: Routledge.

———. 1994. *Space, Place and Gender*. Cambridge: Polity.

Massey, Douglas, ed. 2008. *New Faces in New Places: The Changing Geography of American Immigration*. New York: Russell Sage Foundation.

Massey, Douglas S., and Katherine Bartley. 2005. "The Changing Legal Status Distribution of Immigrants: A Caution." *International Migration Review* 39, no. 2 (June): 469–484.

Massey, Douglas S., and Chiara Capoferro. 2006. "*Sálvese Quien Pueda*: Structural Adjustment and Emigration from Lima." *ANNALS of the American Academy of Political and Social Science* 606 (July): 116–127.

———. 2008. "The Geographic Diversification of American Immigration," in *New Faces in New Places: The Changing Geography of American Immigration*, edited by Douglas S. Massey, 25–50. New York: Russell Sage Foundation.

Massey, Douglas S., Jorge Durand, and Nolan J. Malone. 2002. *Beyond Smoke and Mirrors: Mexican Immigration in an Era of Economic Integration*. New York: Russell Sage Foundation.

Massey, Douglas S., Magaly Sanchez R., and Jere R. Behrman. 2006. "Introduction: Of Myths and Markets." *ANNALS of the American Academy of Political and Social Science* 606 (July): 8–31.

Matt, Susan J. 2011. *Homesickness: An American Story*. Oxford: Oxford University Press.

———. 2012. "The New Globalist Is Homesick." *New York Times*, March 21. http://www.nytimes.com/2012/03/22/opinion/many-still-live-with-homesickness.html?_r=0 (accessed April 2, 2012).

Mayol, Alberto M. 2012. *El derrumbe del modelo: La crisis de la economía de mercado en el Chile contemporáneo* [The collapse of the model: The market economy crisis in contemporary Chile]. Santiago: LOM Ediciones.

Mazzei, P. 2011. "Legislature: Little Hope Seen for State DREAM Act." *Miami Herald*, January 19, B1.

McHugh, Kevin E., Ines M. Miyares, and Emily H. Skop. 1997. "The Magnetism of Miami: Segmented Paths in Cuban Migration." *Geographical Review* 87, no. 4 (October): 504–519.

McKay, Deirdre. 2006a. "Introduction: Finding 'the Field': The Problem of Locality in a Mobile World." *Asia Pacific Journal of Anthropology* 7, no. 3 (December): 197–202.

———. 2006b. "Translocal Circulation: Place and Subjectivity in an Extended Filipino Community." *Asia Pacific Journal of Anthropology* 7, no. 3 (December): 265–278.

McKenzie, David, and Hillel Rapoport. 2006. *Migration and Education Inequality in Rural Mexico*. Working paper no. 23, November. Buenos Aires: Institute for the Integration of Latin American and the Caribbean.

McKenzie, Sean, and Cecilia Menjívar. 2011. "The Meanings of Migration, Remittances and Gifts: Views of Honduran Women Who Stay." *Global Networks* 11, no. 1 (January): 63–81.

Meléndez, Edwin. 2007. "Changes in the Characteristics of Puerto Rican Migrants to the United States," in *Latinos in a Changing Society*, edited by Martha Montero-Sieburth and Edwin Meléndez, 112–131. Westport: Praeger.

Mendelson, Margot, Shayna Strom, and Michael Wishnie. 2009. *Collateral Dam-*

age: An Examination of ICE's Fugitive Operations Program. Washington, DC: Migration Policy Institute.

Menendez, Ana. 1995. "11 Seeking 5 Council Seats in Sweetwater." *Miami Herald,* May 4, 3.

Menjívar, Cecilia. 2006. "Liminal Legality: Salvadoran and Guatemalan Immigrants' Lives in the United States." *American Journal of Sociology* 111, no. 4 (January): 999–1037.

Menjívar, Cecilia, and Leisy Abrego. 2009. "Parents and Children Across Borders: Legal Instability and Intergenerational Relations in Guatemalan and Salvadoran Families," in *Across Generations: Immigrant Families in America*, edited by Nancy Foner, 160–189. New York: New York University Press.

———. 2012. "Legal Violence: Immigration Law and the Lives of Central American Immigrants." *American Journal of Sociology* 117, no. 5 (March): 1380–1421.

Metellus, Gepsie, Leonie Hermantin, Gislaine Toussaint, and Sophia Lacroix. 2004. *Analysis of Service Gaps in Little Haiti and the Haitian/Haitian-American Community in Miami-Dade County,* Working Paper Series SL WPS 01. Miami: Haitian Neighborhood Center, Sant La.

"Miami Tops Rude Drivers List." 2007. *USA Today*, May 15. http://usatoday30 .usatoday.com/news/nation/2007-05-15-rude-drivers_N.htm (accessed September 30, 2012).

Miami-Dade County, Department of Planning and Zoning. 2007. "An Overview of the Socio-Economic Condition of Miami-Dade County." Social and Economic Development Council, Miami-Dade County Department of Planning and Zoning: Planning and Research Section, May. http://www.miamidade.gov/business /library/reports/socio-economic-condition-overview.pdf (accessed July 19, 2013).

———. 2010. "'Where Hispanics Live, 2010,' 'Where Non-Hispanic Blacks Live, 2010,' and 'Where Non-Hispanic Whites Live, 2010.'" Miami-Dade County Department of Planning and Zoning: Planning and Research Section. http://www .miamidade.gov/planning/maps-census.asp (accessed July 18, 2013).

Miami-Dade County, Department of Sustainability, Planning, and Economic Enhancement. 2011. "Miami-Dade County Economic and Demographic Profile." http://www.miamidade.gov/business/library/reports/2011-economic-demographic -profile.pdf (accessed January 13, 2013).

Miami-Dade County, Economic Development and International Trade. 2011. "Miami-Dade Labor Market Report, November 2011 Release." Department of Sustainability, Planning, and Economic Enhancement, November. http://www.miami dade.gov/oedit/library/11_11_lmr.pdf (accessed February 23, 2012).

Milkman, Ruth. 2000. *Organizing Immigrants: The Challenge for Unions in Contemporary California*. Ithaca: Cornell University Press.

Mohl, Raymond A. 1989. "Shadows in the Sunshine: Race and Ethnicity in Miami." *Tequesta: The Journal of the Historical Association of Southern Florida*, no. 49: 63–80.

———. 1990. "On the Edge: Blacks and Hispanics in Metropolitan Miami Since 1959." *Florida Historical Quarterly* 69, no. 1 (July): 37–56.

———. 1995. "Making the Second Ghetto in Metropolitan Miami, 1940–1960." *Journal of Urban History* 21, no. 3 (March): 395–427.

———. 2001. "Whitening Miami: Race, Housing, and Government Policy in Twentieth-Century Dade County." *Florida Historical Quarterly* 79, no. 3 (Winter): 319–345.

Monestime, Jean. 2010. "Verbatim: As American a Story As It Gets." *Miami Herald,* November 20, A20.

Moore, James. 2004. "50 Years After Brown: Segregation in the Miami-Dade County Public Schools." *Equity and Excellence in Education* 37, no. 3: 289–301.

Moores, Shawn. 2004. "The Doubling of Place: Electronic Media, Time-Space Arrangements and Social Relationships," in *Media Space: Place, Scale and Culture in a Media Age*, edited by Nick Couldry and Anna McCarthy, 21–36. London: Routledge.

Morel, Laura C. 2013. "Immigration Debate Critical for Same-Sex Couples." *Tampa Bay Times*, May 21, 5A.

Moreno, Dario. 1997. "The Cuban Model: Political Empowerment in Miami," in *Pursuing Power: Latinos and the Political System*, edited by F. Chris García, 208–226. Notre Dame: University of Notre Dame Press.

Moreno, Dario, and Nicol Rae. 1992. "Ethnicity and Partnership: The Eighteenth Congressional District in Miami," in *Miami Now! Immigration, Ethnicity, and Social Change*, edited by Guillermo J. Grenier and Alex Stepick, 186–203. Gainesville: University Press of Florida, 1992.

Morley, David. 2004. *Home Territories: Media, Mobility and Identity*. New York: Routledge.

Morris, Ruth. 2005. "Detention Center Wins Accreditation." *Sun Sentinel*, January 22, 1B. http://articles.sun-sentinel.com/2005-01-22/news/0501220107_1_krome-accreditation-immigration (accessed July 29, 2012).

———. 2007. "Split Decision—As More Longtime Residents Are Deported Many Are Forced to Choose Whether to Leave Their US Born Children Behind." *South Florida Sun Sentinel*, February 25, 1A.

Muñoz, Heraldo. 2011. "Don't Turn Away from the World's Most Violent Region." United Nations Development Programme. http://www.undp.org/content/undp/en/home/ourperspective/ourperspectivearticles/2011/08/29/don-t-turn-away-from-the-world-s-most-violent-region.html (accessed September 28, 2012).

Murguia, Edward, and Edward E. Telles. 1996. "Phenotype and Schooling Among Mexican Americans." *Sociology of Education* 69, no. 4 (October): 276–289.

Nackerud, Larry, Alyson Springer, Christopher Larrison, and Alicia Issac. 1999. "The End of the Cuban Contradiction in US Refugee Policy." *International Migration Review* 33, no. 1 (Spring): 176–192.

Naples, Nancy A. 2007. "The Social Regulation of Community: An Intersectional Analysis of Migration and Incorporation in the Heartland." *Journal of Latino-Latin American Studies* 2, no. 3 (Spring): 16–23.

National Immigration Law Center. 2010. *The DREAM ACT: Good for Florida's Economy; Good for Florida's Future*. Washington, DC: National Immigration Law Center, December. http://v2011.nilc.org/immlawpolicy/DREAM/Florida-DREAM-fact-sheet-11-30-10.pdf (accessed October 9, 2012).

Navarrette, Ruben, Jr. 2010. "Illegal Aliens Are Not Criminals." *PJ Media*, January 21. http://pjmedia.com/blog/illegal-aliens-are-not-criminals/ (accessed February 21, 2011).

Nevins, Joseph. 2002. *Operation Gatekeeper: The Rise of the "Illegal Alien" and the Making of the US-Mexico Boundary*. New York: Routledge.

Newall, Michael. 2006. "Backed by Church, Janitors Push for Union." *National Catholic Reporter*, May 19. http://natcath.org/NCR_Online/archives2/2006b/051906/051906i.php (accessed July 25, 2013).

Ngai, Mae M. 2004. *Impossible Subjects: Illegal Aliens and the Making of Modern America*. Princeton: Princeton University Press.

Nijman, Jan. 2007. "Locals, Exiles and Cosmopolitans: A Theoretical Argument About Identity and Place in Miami." *Journal of Economic and Social Geography* 98, no. 2 (April): 176–187.

————. 2011. *Miami: Mistress of the Americas*. Philadelphia: University of Pennsylvania Press.

Noriega, Chon, and Francisco Javier Iribarren. 2011. *Quantifying Hate Speech on Commercial Talk Radio: A Pilot Study*. Chicano Studies Center Working Paper Series, No. 1. University of California, Los Angeles. http://www.chicano.ucla.edu/files/WP1QuantifyingHateSpecch_0.pdf (accessed August 25, 2012).

O'Brien, Eileen. 2008. *The Racial Middle: Latinos and Asian Americans Living Beyond the Racial Divide*. New York: New York University Press.

Ojito, Mirta. 2009. "Doctors in Cuba Start Over in the US." *New York Times*, August 3. http://www.nytimes.com/2009/08/04/health/04cuba.html (accessed August 4, 2009).

Omi, Michael, and Howard Winant. 1994. *Racial Formation in the United States*, 2nd edition. New York: Routledge.

Organisation for Economic Co-operation and Development (OECD). 2010. *Latin American Economic Outlook 2011: How Middle-Class Is Latin America?* Paris: OECD Publishing.

Padgett, Tim. 2006. "There's Trouble—Lots of It—in Paradise." *Time*, November 19, 38.

Parenti, Michael. 1970. "Power and Pluralism: A View from the Bottom," *Journal of Politics* 32 (1970): 501–530.

Parrado, Emilio A., and René M. Zenteno. 2002. "Gender Differences in Union Formation in Mexico: Evidence from Marital Search Models." *Journal of Marriage and Family* 64, no. 3 (August): 756–773.

Parreñas, Rhacel Salazar. 2001. *Servants of Globalization: Women, Migration and Domestic Work*. Stanford: Stanford University Press.

————. 2005. *Children of Global Migration: Transnational Families and Gendered Woes*. Stanford: Stanford University Press.

Passel, Jeffrey S. 2006. *The Size and Characteristics of the Unauthorized Migrant Population in the US: Estimates Based on the March 2005 Current Population Survey*. Washington, DC: Pew Hispanic Center, Pew Research Center.

Passel, Jeffrey S., and D'Vera Cohn. 2009. *A Portrait of Unauthorized Immigrants in the United States*. Washington, DC: Pew Hispanic Center, Pew Research Center.

————. 2011. *Unauthorized Immigrant Population: National and State Trends, 2010*. Washington, DC: Pew Hispanic Center, Pew Research Center.

————. 2012. *Unauthorized Immigrants: 11.1 Million in 2011*. Washington, DC: Pew Hispanic Center, Pew Research Center.

Passel, Jeffrey S., and Roberto Suro. 2005. *Rise, Peak and Decline: Trends in US Immigration 1992–2004*. Washington, DC: Pew Hispanic Center, Pew Research Center.

Pedraza, Silvia. 1996. "Cuba's Refugees: Manifold Migrations," in *Origins and Destinies: Immigration, Race, and Ethnicity in America,* edited by Silvia Pedraza and Rubén G. Rumbaut, 263–279. Belmont: Wadsworth.

————. 2004. *"Los Marielitos* of 1980: Race, Class, Gender, and Sexuality," *Cuba in Transition,* Volume 14. Papers presented at the Fourteenth Annual Meeting of the Association for the Study of the Cuban Economy (ASCE), Miami, Florida, August 5–7.

Pelissero, John P., David B. Holian, and Laura A. Tomaka. 2000. "Does Political Incorporation Matter? The Impact of Minority Mayors over Time." *Urban Affairs Review* 36, no. 1 (September): 84–92.

Perea, Juan F. 1997. *Immigrants Out! The New Nativism and the Anti-Immigrant Impulse in the United States*. New York: New York University Press.

Pérez, Lisandro. 1990. "Cuban Miami," in *Miami Now! Immigration, Ethnicity, and Social Change,* edited by Guillermo J. Grenier and Alex Stepick, 83–108. Gainesville: University of Florida Press.

Pérez, Louis A., Jr. 2003. *Cuba and the United States: Ties of Singular Intimacy.* Athens: University of Georgia Press.

Pérez-Stable, Marifeli, and Miren Uriarte. 1997. "Cubans and the Changing Economy of Miami," in *New American Destinies: A Reader in Contemporary Asian and Latino Immigration,* edited by Darrel Y. Hamamoto and Rodolfo D. Torres, 141–162. New York: Routledge.

Perlmann, Joel. 2005. *Italians Then, Mexicans Now: Immigrant Origins and Second-Generation Progress.* New York: Russell Sage Foundation.

Petras, James. 1981. "Dependency and World System Theory: A Critique and New Directions." *Latin American Perspectives* 8, no. 3/4 (Late Summer–Autumn): 148–155.

Plaza, Orlando, and Nelly P. Stromquist. 2006. "Consequences of Structural Adjustment on Economic and Social Domains: Two Decades in the Life of Peru." *The ANNALS of the American Academy of Political and Social Science* 606 (July): 95–115.

Porteous, J. Douglas. 1976. "Home: The Territorial Core." *Geographical Review* 66, no. 4 (October): 383–390.

Porteous, J. Douglas, and Sandra E. Smith. 2001. *Domicide: The Global Destruction of Home.* Montreal: McGill-Queen's University Press.

Portes, Alejandro. 1969. "Dilemmas of a Golden Exile: Integration of Cuban Refugee Families in Milwaukee." *American Sociological Review* 34, no. 4 (August): 505–518.

———. 2013. "A Bifurcated Enclave: The Peculiar Evolution of the Cuban Immigrant Population in the Last Decades." Keynote address at the 9th conference on Cuban and Cuban-American studies, "Dispersed Peoples. The Cuban and Other Diasporas." Miami, May 23–25.

Portes, Alejandro, and Robert L. Bach. 1985. *Latin Journey: Cuban and Mexican Immigrants in the United States.* Berkeley: University of California Press.

Portes, Alejandro, Luis E. Guarnizo, and Patricia Landolt. 1999. "The Study of Transnationalism: Pitfalls and Promise of an Emergent Research Field." *Ethnic and Racial Studies* 22, no. 2 (March): 217–237.

Portes, Alejandro, and Kelly Hoffman. 2003. "Latin American Class Structures: Their Composition and Change During the Neoliberal Era." *Latin American Research Review* 38, no. 1 (February): 41–82.

Portes, Alejandro, and Rubén G. Rumbaut. 1996. *Immigrant America: A Portrait,* 2nd edition. Berkeley: University of California Press.

———. 2001. *Legacies: The Story of the Immigrant Second Generation.* Berkeley: University of California Press.

———. 2006. *Immigrant America: A Portrait,* 3rd edition. Berkeley: University of California Press.

Portes, Alejandro, and Alex Stepick. 1993. *City on the Edge: The Transformation of Miami.* Berkeley: University of California Press.

Portocarrero, Gonzalo, ed. 1998. *Las Clases Medias: Entre la Pretensión y la Incertidumbre.* Lima: SUR Casa de Estudios del Socialismo.

Pratts, Mary Louise. 1991. "Arts of the Contact Zone." *Profession:* 33–40.

Preston, Julia. 2010. "To Overhaul Immigration, Advocates Change Tactics." *New York Times,* January 2. http://www.nytimes.com/2010/01/02/us/02immig.html?ref=polit (accessed November 11, 2013).

Prieto, Yolanda. 1987. "Cuban Women in the US Labor Force: Perspectives on the Nature of the Change." *Cuban Studies* 17: 73–94.

Purcell, Susan Kaufman. 1996. "The Cuban Illusion: Keeping the Heat on Castro." *Foreign Affairs* 75, no. 3 (May–June): 159–161.

Purkayastha, Bandana. 2005. "Skilled Migration and Cumulative Disadvantage: The Case of Highly Qualified Asian Indian Immigrant Women in the US." *Geoforum* 36, no. 2 (March): 181–196.

Ramdin, Albert R. 2008. "Haiti's Myriad Problems Require Bold Solutions." *Miami Herald*, September 30, 15A.

Ramji-Nogales, Jaya, Andrew I. Schoenholtz, and Phillip G. Schrag. 2007. "Refugee Roulette, Disparities in Asylum Adjudication." *Stanford Law Review* 60, no. 2 (November): 295–410.

Ramos, Victor. 2010. "Puerto Rican Man Detained as Illegal Immigrant." *Orlando Sentinel*, May 25. http://blogs.orlandosentinel.com/news_hispanicaffairs/2010/05/puerto-rican-man-detained-as-illegal-immigrant.html (accessed October 10, 2012).

Reed-Danahay, Deborah, and Caroline B. Brettell. 2008. "Introduction," in *Citizenship, Political Engagement, and Belonging: Immigrants in Europe and the United States*, edited by Deborah Reed-Danahay and Caroline B. Brettell, 1–17. New Brunswick: Rutgers University Press.

Reese, Stephen D., August Grant, and Lucig H. Danielian. 1994. "The Structure of News Sources on Television: A Network Analysis of 'CBS News,' 'Nightline,' 'MacNeil/Lehrer,' and 'This Week with David Brinkley.'" *Journal of Communication* 44, no. 2 (June): 84–107.

Reichert, Josh, and Douglas S. Massey. 1980. "History and Trend in US Bound Migration from a Mexican Town." *International Migration Review* 14, no. 4 (Winter): 475–491.

Renshon, Stanley A. 2008. *The Debate Over Non-Citizen Voting: A Primer*. Washington, DC: Center for Immigration Studies.

"Return to Sender: Ice Operations Nab 53 Foreign Nationals." 2007. *Miami Herald*, April 2, 3B.

Reygadas, Luis. 2010. "The Construction of Latin American Inequality," in *Indelible Inequalities in Latin America: Insights from History, Politics, and Culture*, edited by Paul Gootenberg and Luis Reygadas, 23–49. Durham: Duke University Press.

Rhodes, Leara. 2001. *Democracy and the Role of the Haitian Media*. New York: Edwin Mellen.

Rivera-Batiz, Francisco L., and Carlos E. Santiago. 1996. *Island Paradox: Puerto Rico in the 1990s*. New York: Russell Sage Foundation.

Rivero, Yeidy. 2011. "Interpreting *Cubanness, Americanness*, and the Sitcom: WPBT-PBS's *¿Qué pasa USA.?* (1975–1980)," in *Global Television Formats: Understanding Television Across Borders*, edited by Tasha Oren and Sharon Shahaf, 90–107. London: Routledge.

Rocco, Raymond. 2006. "Transforming Citizenship: Membership Strategies of Containment, and the Public Sphere in Latino Communities," in *Latinos and Citizenship: The Dilemma of Belonging*, edited by Suzanne Oboler, 301–328. New York: Palgrave Macmillan.

Roediger, David. 2005. *Working Toward Whiteness: How America's Immigrants Became White*. New York: Basic.

Rosaldo, Renato. 1994. "Cultural Citizenship and Educational Democracy." *Cultural Anthropology* 9, no. 3: 402–411.

Rose, Chanelle N. 2012. "Tourism and the Hispanicization of Race in Jim Crow Miami, 1945–1965." *Journal of Social History* 45, no. 3: 735–756.

Ross, K. 2000. "Curbelo First to Declare for County Commission Vacancy." *Miami Herald*, April 8, 3B.

Roth, Wendy D. 2012. *Race Migrations: Latinos and the Cultural Transformation of Race*. Stanford: Stanford University Press.

Rubio, Mauricio. 2004. "Kidnapping and Armed Conflict in Colombia." Paper presented at the PRIO Workshop, "Techniques of Violence in Civil War," Oslo, August 5. http://uniset.ca/terr/art/colombiakidnapping.pdf (accessed July 25, 2013).

Rytina, Nancy. 2002. *IRCA Legalization Effects: Lawful Permanent Residence and Naturalization Through 2001*. Washington, DC: Office of Policy and Planning, Statistics Division, Immigration and Naturalization Service.

Sabogal, Elena. 2005. "Viviendo en la Sombra: The Immigration of Peruvian Professionals to South Florida." *Latino Studies* 3, no. 1 (April): 113–131.

———. 2012. "Denaturalized Identities: Class-Based Perceptions of Self and Others Among Latin American Immigrants in South Florida." *Latino Studies* 10, no. 4 (Winter): 546–565.

Sabogal, Elena, and Lorena Núñez. 2010. "*Sin Papeles:* Middle- and Working-Class Peruvians in Santiago and South Florida." Special issue, "Peruvian Migration in a Global Context." *Latin American Perspectives*, issue 174, vol. 37, no. 5 (September): 88–105.

Safa, Helen. 1998. "Introduction." *Latin American Perspectives* 25, no. 3 (May): 3–20.

Sampedro, Victor. 1998. "Grounding the Displaced: Local Media Reception in a Transnational Context." *Journal of Communication* 48, no. 2 (June): 125–143.

Sánchez, Rosaura. 2011. "The Toxic Tonic: Narratives of Xenophobia." *Latino Studies* 9: 126–144.

Sanchez R., Magaly. 2006. "Insecurity and Violence as a New Power Relationship in Latin America." *ANNALS of the American Academy of Political and Social Science* 606 (July): 178–195.

Sanders, Jimy M., and Victor Nee. 1987. "Limits of Ethnic Solidarity in the Enclave Economy." *American Sociological Review* 52, no 6 (December): 745–773.

Santa Ana, Otto, and Celeste González de Bustamante. 2012. *Arizona Firestorm: Global Immigration Realities, National Media, and Provincial Politics*. Lanham: Rowman and Littlefield.

Santiso, Carlos. 2004. "The Contentious Washington Consensus: Reforming the Reforms in Emerging Markets." *Review of International Political Economy* 11, no. 4 (October): 828–844.

Sassen, Saskia. 1998. *Globalization and Its Discontents: Essays on the New Mobility of People and Money*. New York: New Press.

———. 2009. "The Specialised Differences of Cities Matter in Today's Global Economy," in *Reforming the City: Responses to the Global Financial Crisis*, edited by Sam Whimster, 209–236. London: Forumpress.

———. 2011. *Cities in a World Economy*, 4th edition. Thousand Oaks: Pine Forge.

Sawyer, Mark Q. 2004. *Racial Politics in Post-Revolutionary Cuba*. New York: Cambridge University Press.

Scannell, Paddy. 1995. "For a Phenomenology of Radio and Television." *Journal of Communication* 45, no. 3 (September): 4–19.

"Se Dispara el Paseo Millonario." 2000. *El Tiempo*, May 20. http://www.eltiempo.com/archivo/documento/MAM-1245549 (accessed September 28, 2012).

"Secuestro al Paso." 1996. *Caretas,* February 22. http://www.caretas.com.pe/1402 /secuestros/secuestros.html (accessed September 28, 2012).

Shumow, Moses. 2010. "'A Foot in Both Worlds': Transnationalism and Media Use Among Venezuelan Immigrants in South Florida." *International Journal of Communication* 4: 377–397.

Silverstone, Roger. 1993. "Television, Ontological Security and the Transitional Object." *Media, Culture and Society* 15, no. 4: 573–598.

Simon, D. 2006. "Candidates Discovering Caribbean Americans." *Miami Herald,* November 4, 1A.

Sinclair, John. 2003. "'The Hollywood of Latin America': Miami as Regional Center in the Television Trade." *Television and New Media* 4, no. 3 (August): 211–229.

Sirkeci, Ibrahim. 2005. "War in Iraq: Environment of Insecurity and International Migration." *International Migration* 43, no. 4 (October): 197–214.

Sisken, Alison. 2013. "Visa Waiver Program," *Congressional Research Service,* Order Code RL32221, January 13. http://www.fas.org/sgp/crs/homesec /RL32221.pdf (accessed July 10, 2013).

Skrbiš, Zlatko. 2008. "Transnational Families: Theorising Migration, Emotions and Belonging." *Journal of Intercultural Studies* 29, no. 3 (August): 231–246.

Small Arms Survey. 2012. "Femicide: A Global Problem." Research Notes. *Armed Violence,* no. 14 (February): 1–4. http://www.smallarmssurvey.org/fileadmin /docs/H-Research_Notes/SAS-Research-Note-14.pdf (accessed May 13, 2012).

Smelser, Neil J. 1998. "The Rational and the Ambivalent in the Social Sciences: 1997 Presidential Address." *American Sociological Review* 63, no. 1 (February): 1–16.

Smith, Robert Courtney. 2006. *Mexican New York: Transnational Lives of New Immigrants.* Berkeley: University of California Press.

Sontag, Deborah. 1994. "Haitian Migrants Settle In, Looking Back." *New York Times,* June 3. http://www.nytimes.com/1994/06/03/nyregion/haitian-migrants -settle-in-looing-back.htm (accessed October 13, 2012).

South Florida CEO. 2004. *FTAA Free Trade Area of the Americas Miami. A Special Report by Latin CEO Magazine.* Miami: Americas Publishing Group.

Stasiulis, Daiva, and Abigail Bakan. 1997. "Negotiating Citizenship: The Case of Foreign Domestic Workers in Canada." *Feminist Review,* no. 57 (Autumn): 112–139.

Stepick, Alex. 1992. "The Refugees Nobody Wants: Haitians in Miami," in *Miami Now! Immigration, Ethnicity, and Social Change,* edited by Guillermo J. Grenier and Alex Stepick, 57–81. Gainesville: University of Florida Press.

———. 1998. *Pride Against Prejudice: Haitians in the United States.* Needham Heights: Allyn and Bacon.

Stepick, Alex, Guillermo Grenier, Max Castro, and Marvin Dunn. 2003. *This Land Is Our Land: Immigrants and Power in Miami.* Berkeley: University of California Press.

Stepick, Alex, and Carol Dutton Stepick. 2009. "Diverse Contexts of Reception and Feelings of Belonging." *Forum: Qualitative Social Research* 10, no. 3, art. 15 (September). http://www.qualitative-research.net/index.php/fqs/article/view/1366 /2863 (accessed November 13, 2013).

Stepick, Alex, Carol Dutton Stepick, and Philip Kretsedemas. 2001. *Civic Engagement of Haitian Immigrants and Haitian Americans in Miami-Dade County.* Miami: Immigration and Ethnicity Institute, Center for Labor Research and Studies.

Stowers, Genie N. L., and Ronald K. Vogel. 1994. "Racial and Ethnic Voting Patterns in Miami," in *Big-City Politics, Governance and Fiscal Constraints,* edited by George E. Peterson, 63–84. Washington, DC: Urban Institute Press.

Straubhaar, Joseph D. 2007. *World Television: From Global to Local.* Los Angeles: Sage.

Suárez-Orozco, Marcelo M. 2005. "Right Moves? Immigration, Globalization, Utopia and Dystopia," in *The New Immigration: An Interdisciplinary Reader,* edited by Marcelo M. Suárez-Orozco, Carola Suárez-Orozco, and Desirée Baolian Qin, 3–19. New York: Routledge.

Sutton, Jane. 2002. "Haitians Flee Boat, Make Dash for Florida Shores." *Philadelphia Inquirer,* October 30, A02.

Swartz, Mimi. 2007. "Shop Stewarts on Fantasy Island?" *New York Times,* June 10. http://www.nytimes.com/2007/06/10/magazine/10fisher-t.html?pagewanted =all&_r=0 (accessed July 31, 2012).

Telles, Edward E. 2004. *Race in Another America: The Significance of Skin Color in Brazil.* Princeton: Princeton University Press.

———. 2007. "Race and Ethnicity and Latin America's United Nations Millennium Development Goals." *Latin American and Caribbean Ethnic Studies* 2, no. 2 (September): 185–200.

Telles, Edward E., and Vilma Ortiz. 2009. *Generations of Exclusion: Mexican Americans, Assimilation, and Race.* New York: Russell Sage Foundation.

Teproff, C. 2009. "Mayoral Victory Shifts Power." *Miami Herald,* June 3, 1B.

Terrazas, Aaron. 2010. *Haitian Immigrants in the United States,* Washington, DC: Migration Information Source. http://www.migrationinformation.org/USfocus /display.cfm?id=770 (accessed June 17, 2011).

Tilly, Charles. 1999. *Durable Inequality.* Berkeley: University of California Press.

Tirman, John. 2006. *Immigration and Insecurity: Post-9/11 Fear in the United States.* Cambridge: MIT Center for International Studies Audit of the Conventional Wisdom.

Transactional Record Access Clearinghouse (TRAC Immigration). 2010. *Asylum Denial Rate Reaches All Time Low: FY 2010 Results, a Twenty-Five Year Perspective.* TRAC Reports, September 2. http://trac.syr.edu/immigration/reports /240/ (accessed July 10, 2013).

United Nations Development Programme. 2008. *Human Development Indicators, 2008.* New York: United Nations. http://hdr.undp.org/en/statistics/data/ (accessed July 7, 2009).

Urry, John. 2000. *Sociology Beyond Societies: Mobilities for the Twenty-First Century.* London: Routledge.

———. 2002. "Mobility and Proximity." *Sociology* 36, no. 2 (May): 255–274.

———. 2007. *Mobilities.* Cambridge: Polity.

US Bureau of Labor Statistics. 2013. "Local Area Unemployment Statistics." http://www.bls.gov/lau/home.htm#cntyaa (accessed July 15, 2013).

US Census Bureau. 1990. "1990 Summary Tape File 3 (STF 3)—Sample Data." Washington, DC: US Census Bureau.

———. 2000. "Table FBP-1. Profile of Selected Demographic and Social Characteristics: 2000. Population Universe: People Born in Haiti. Geographic Area: Florida." Washington, DC: US Census Bureau.

———. 2009–2011a. American Community Survey, 3-year estimates. "ACS Demographic and Housing Estimates" for Coral Gables, Florida. Washington, DC: US Government.

———. 2009–2011b. American Community Survey, 3-year estimates. "Selected Economic Characteristics" for Coral Gables, Florida. Washington, DC: US Government.

————. 2010. "Profile of General Population and Housing Characteristics, 2010 Demographic Profile Data, Homestead City." Washington, DC: US Government.

————. 2011a. American Community Survey, 1-year estimates, "Selected Characteristics of the Foreign-Born Population by Period of Entry into the United States" for Miami-Dade County. Washington, DC: US Government.

————. 2011b. American Community Survey, 1-year estimates, "Total Ancestry Reported" for Miami-Dade County. Washington, DC: US Government.

————. 2011c. American Community Survey, 1-year estimates, "Selected Population Profile in the United States" for Haitians in the US. Washington, DC: US Government.

————. 2011d. American Community Survey, 1-year estimates, "Selected Population Profile in the United States" for Haitians in Florida. Washington, DC: US Government.

————. 2011e. American Community Survey, 5-year estimates, "Total Ancestry Reported" for North Miami city, Florida. Washington, DC: US Government.

————. 2011f. American Community Survey, 5-year estimates, "Total Ancestry Reported" for El Portal village, Florida. Washington, DC: US Government.

————. 2011g. American Community Survey, 5-year estimates, "Total Ancestry Reported" for North Miami Beach city, Florida. Washington, DC: US Government.

————. 2011h. American Community Survey, 1-year estimates, "Selected Population Profile in the United States" for Cubans, Haitians, Colombians, and Nicaraguans for Miami-Dade County, Florida. Washington, DC: US Government.

————. 2011i. American Community Survey, 3-year estimates, "Nativity and Citizenship Status in the United States" for Sweetwater city, Florida. Washington, DC: US Government.

————. 2011j. American Community Survey, 3-year estimates, "Selected Social Characteristics in the United States" for Sweetwater city, Florida. Washington, DC: US Government.

————. 2011k. American Community Survey, 5-year estimates, "Hispanic or Latino Population by Specific Origin" for Sweetwater city, Florida. Washington, DC: US Government.

————. 2011l. American Community Survey, 1-year estimates, "Selected Social Characteristics in the United States" for Miami-Dade County, Florida. Washington, DC: US Government.

————. 2012. American Community Survey, 1-year estimates, "Selected Social Characteristics in the United States," for Miami-Dade County, Florida. Washington, DC: US Government.

————. 2013. "Quick Facts: Florida." http://quickfacts.census.gov/qfd/states/12/1232275.html (accessed July 15, 2013).

US Citizenship and Immigration Services. 2014. "TPS Designated Country: Haiti." http://www.uscis.gov/portal/site/uscis/menuitem.eb1d4c2a3e5b9ac89243c6a75 43f6d1a/?vgnextchannel=e54e60f64f336210VgnVCM100000082ca60a CRvgnextoid=e54e60f64f336210VgnVCM100000082ca60aRCRD (accessed January 13, 2013).

US Department of Health and Human Services. HHS Poverty Guidelines. 2005. http://aspe.hhs.gov/poverty/05poverty.shtml (accessed November 11, 2013).

————, Administration for Children and Families. Office of Refugee Resettlement. 2012. "Asylee Eligibility for Assistance and Services." July 12. http://www.acf.hhs.gov/programs/orr/resource/asylee-eligibility-for-assistance-and-services (accessed October 1, 2012).

US Department of Homeland Security. 2007. *An Assessment of United States Immigration and Customs Enforcement's Fugitive Operations Teams.* Washington, DC: US Department of Homeland Security, Office of the Inspector General.

———. 2012. *Characteristics of H-1B Specialty Occupation Workers. Fiscal Year 2011 Annual Report to Congress, October 1, 2010–September 30, 2011.* http://www.uscis.gov/sites/default/files/USCIS/Resources/Reports%20and%20 Studies/H-1B/h1b-fy-11-characteristics.pdf (accessed November 11, 2013).

US Department of Justice. 1997. *1997 Yearbook of the Immigration and Naturalization Service.* Washington, DC: US Department of Justice, Immigration and Naturalization Service.

US Department of Justice, Executive Office for Immigration Review. 2005. "Asylum Protection in the United States." News Release, April 28. http://www .justice.gov/eoir/press/05/AsylumProtectionFactsheetQAApr05.htm (accessed July 10, 2013).

US Department of Labor and Human Resources, Bureau of Labor Statistics, Household Surveys 2003–2013. "Data, Tables and Calculators by Subject." Local Area Unemployment Figures for Puerto Rico. http://data.bls.gov/timeseries /LASST43000003 (accessed November 10, 2013).

US Department of State. 2010. "Visa Wait Times—for Interview Appointments and Processing." US Department of State, Bureau of Consular Affairs, Travel.State .Gov. http//travel.state.gov/visa/temp/wait/wait_4638.htm (accessed November 6, 2010).

———. 2013a. "Advice About Possible Loss of US Citizenship and Dual Nationality." US Department of State, Bureau of Consular Affairs, Travel.State.Gov, January 11. http://travel.state.gov/law/citizenship/citizenship_778.html (accessed July 18, 2013).

———. 2013b. "Visa Waiver Program (VWP)." http://travel.state.gov/visa/temp /without/without_1990.html (accessed July 10, 2013).

———. 2013c. "Visitor Visas—Business and Pleasure." US Department of State, Bureau of Consular Affairs, Travel.State.Gov. http://www.travel.state.gov/visa /temp/types/types_1262.html (accessed July 20, 2013).

US Immigration and Customs Enforcement (ICE). 2011. "Fact Sheet: ICE Fugitive Operations Program," March 25. http://www.ice.gov/news/library/factsheets /fugops.htm (accessed June 26, 2012).

———. 2012. "Secure Communities: Frequently Asked Questions (FAQs)." http://www.ice.gov/secure_communities/faq.htm (accessed June 26, 2012).

Van der Werf, Martin. 2001. "How Much Should Colleges Pay Their Janitors? Student Protests Force Administrators to Consider Issues of Social Justice and Practicality." *Chronicle of Higher Education,* August 3, A27.

Van Schuur, Wijbrandt H., and Martine Kruijtbosch. 1995. "Measuring Subjective Well-Being: Unfolding the Bradburn Affect Balance Scale." *Social Indicators Research* 36: 49–74.

Vaquera, Elizabeth, and Elizabeth Aranda. 2011. "The Multiple Dimensions of Transnationalism: Examining Their Relevance to Immigrants' Subjective Well-Being." *Journal of Social Research and Policy* 2, no. 2 (December): 47–72.

Vargas, Lucila. 2008. "Ambiguous Loss and the Media Practices of Transnational Latina Teens: A Qualitative Study." *Popular Communication* 6, no. 1: 37–52.

Vertovec, Steven. 2009. *Transnationalism.* London: Routledge.

Wade, Peter. 2010. *Race and Ethnicity in Latin America,* 2nd edition. New York: Pluto.

Warren, Christopher L., and Dario V. Moreno. 2003. "Power Without a Program:

Hispanic Incorporation in Miami," in *Racial Politics in American Cities,* 3rd edition, edited by Rufus P. Browing, Dale Rogers Marshall, and David H. Tabb, 281–308. New York: Longman.

Wasem, Ruth Ellen. 2007. *Immigration: Legislative Issues on Nonimmigrant Professional Specialty (H-1B) Workers.* CRS Report for Congress, August. http://assets.opencrs.com/rpts/RL30498_20070823.pdf (accessed August 5, 2013).

———. 2010. *US Immigration Policy on Haitian Migrants.* CRS Report for Congress. January 15. http://trac.syr.edu/immigration/library/P4230.pdf (accessed July 29, 2013).

———. 2011. *US Immigration Policy on Haitian Migrants.* CRS Report for Congress. May 17. http://www.fas.org/sgp/crs/row/RS21349.pdf (accessed July 29, 2013).

Waters, Mary. 1999. *Black Identities: West Indian Immigrant Dreams and American Realities.* Boston: Harvard University Press.

West, Candace, and Don H. Zimmerman. 1987. "Doing Gender." *Gender and Society* 1, no. 2 (June): 125–151.

Whitefield, Mimi. 2012. "July Sizzles for Brazilian Visitors to Miami—Even Though the Brazilian Economy Is Cooling Off, Brazilian Visitors to South Florida Are Expected to Set New Records. July Is a Peak Time for Visits." *Miami Herald,* July 23. NewsBank online (accessed July 31, 2013).

Wides-Munoz, Laura. 2006. "Raid Rumors Spark Fear Among Immigrants." Associated Press, April 28. http://www.washingtonpost.com/wp-dyn/content/article/2006/04/28/AR2006042801575_pf.html (accessed November 12, 2013).

Williams, David R., Yan Yu, James S. Jackson, and Norman B. Anderson. 1997. "Racial Differences in Physical and Mental Health: Socioeconomic Status, Stress, and Discrimination." *Journal of Health Psychology* 2, no. 3 (July): 335–351.

Williamson, Robert C. 1997. *Latin American Societies in Transition.* Westport: Praeger.

Winsberg, Morton D. 1979. "Housing Segregation of a Predominantly Middle Class Population: Residential Patterns Developed by the Cuban Immigration into Miami, 1950–1974." *American Journal of Economics and Sociology* 38, no. 4: 403–418.

———. 1983. "Ethnic Competition for Residential Space in Miami, Florida, 1970–1980." *American Journal of Economics and Sociology* 42: 305–314.

Woods, C. 2007. "Colombians Aim for Political Unity." *Miami Herald,* September 24, 1A.

World Bank. 1996. *World Bank Development Report 1996. From Plan to Market.* Table 5: Distribution of Income of Consumption. New York: Oxford University Press.

———. 2007. *World Development Indicators 2007.* Table 2.7: Distribution of Income or Consumption. Washington, DC: World Bank.

———. 2013. *Annual Remittances Data: Inflows.* Washington, DC: World Bank.

WorldCity. 2003. *Trade Americas: The Guide to US Trade and Business in the Western Hemisphere.* Miami: WorldCity.

———. 2008. *South Florida Global Economic Impact Study.* Miami: WorldCity, Beacon Council.

Wright, Erik Olin. 1979. *Class Structure and Income Determination.* New York: Academic.

Wright, Todd. 2010. "Marlins Have Cheap Seats, Most Pricey Eats." NBC Miami, April 7. http://www.nbcmiami.com/news/sports/The-Cheap-Seats-Marlins-Tickets-Among-the-Lowest-in-MLB-90128217.html (accessed May 16, 2012).

Wright Austin, Sharon D. 2008. "Black Political Incorporation in Miami-Dade County." Paper presented at the annual meeting of the Western Political Science Association, San Diego, March 20.

Wyly, Elvin. 2008. "Urban Geographies of Immigration and the 'Balkanization' Debate." Unpublished manuscript, November 18. http://www.geog.ubc.ca/~ewyly/g350/balkanization.pdf (accessed July 29, 2013).

Yúdice, George. 2003. *The Expediency of Culture: Uses of Culture in the Global Era.* Durham: Duke University Press.

Zabin, Carol, and Sallie Hughes. 1995. "Economic Integration and Labor Flows: Stage Migration in Farm Labor Markets in Mexico and the United States." *International Migration Review* 29, no. 2 (Summer): 395–422.

Zavella, Patricia. 1997. "The Tables Are Turned: Immigration, Poverty, and Social Conflict in California Communities," in *Immigrants Out! The New Nativism and the Anti-Immigrant Impulse in the United States,* edited by Juan Perea, 136–163. New York: New York University Press.

Zerubavel, Eviatar. 1997. *Social Mindscapes: An Invitation to Cognitive Sociology.* Cambridge: Harvard University Press.

Zillow. 2013. "The U.S. Housing Crisis: Where Are Home Loans Underwater?" http://www.zillow.com/visuals/negative-equity/#8/25.691/-80.516 (accessed July 15, 2013).

Zolberg, Aristide R., and Long Litt Woon. 1999. "Why Islam Is Like Spanish: Cultural Incorporation in Europe and the United States." *Politics and Society* 27, no. 1 (March): 5–38.

Index

Agenda setting, 162–164
Albright, Madeleine, 2, 150
Alvarez, Carlos, 153, 171
American Dream, 1; achievement of, 47,
    320; (Latino) American Dream, 15–
    16; pursuit of 16, 26–27, 31;
    unattainability, 81, 235
Argentina: economic output, 50–51;
    economic security, 13; government,
    72; population increase, 54; visa
    waivers, 108–109. See also Tango
    Effect in Argentina
Aristide, Jean-Bertrand, 11, 183
Arizona Senate Bill 1070 law, 332–333
Ashcroft, John, 21
Asylum, 42, 95–96, 323; affirmative
    asylum, 98; asylum seekers, 67, 96,
    98, 190; defensive asylum, 99;
    denials, 71, 88, 93, 180, 181–182;
    denials as racism, 214; process of,
    96–98; as terrorism threat, 21, 82,
    180, 214

Balkanization, 23, 308–309
Barreto, Prisca, 188
Beck, Ulrich, 6
Blackness, 20, 202, 208, 226–228, 236
Bolivia: economic output, 51
Border enforcement, 115. See also
    Border security
Border Patrol, 85, 214
Border security, 82. See also Border
    enforcement

Bosch, Juan, 48
Brazil: economic hardships, 49;
    economic output, 50–51; economic
    security, 13; kidnappings, 68;
    migration flow, 63; population
    increase, 54; social political party, 49.
    See also Samba Effect in Brazil
Bush, George W., 85, 91
Bush, Jeb, 14, 85

Carey-Shuler, Barbara, 183
Carter, Jimmy, administration, 178, 181
CASA. See Colombian American Service
    Association
Castro: anti-Castroism, 175, 178;
    regimen, 19, 175
Centeno, Deborah, 188
Chartwells, 150–151, 155. See also
    Unionization
Chavez, Cesar, 153
Chile: social political party, 49
Citizen insecurity, of Latin America, 65,
    70
Citizenship, 82, 331. See also Translocal
    social citizenship
Citizenship and Immigration Services, 96
Classism. See Racialization, social class
    discrimination
Clinton, Bill, 49; administrations, 176;
    reelection campaign, 192
Colombia: asylum seekers, 98; economic
    insecurity, 62–63; economic output,
    50–51; embodied proxies, 259;

environment of insecurity, 11; gender differences, 39; kidnappings, 67–69; migration admission, 92–93; migration decision, 290; migration flow, 63; naturalization, 188; political insecurity, 71; population increase, 54; social mobility, 126. *See also* Political incorporation, Colombian model; Zapata, Juan Carlos

Colombian American Service Association (CASA), 188

Conditioning settlement, 5

Costa Rica: economic output, 51

Cross-border locality. *See* Locality

Cuba: class location 143–145; communist ideology, 204, 224; Cuban revolution, 19, 143, 212; culture, 9, 14; economy, 76; predominant minority, 8, 14, 19, 165, 212, 222–223; social class, 125; social mobility, 126; transformation of Miami, 18–19, 20, 114, 119; upward mobility, 130, 156. *See also* Castro; Cuban-Haitian Entrants program; Cubans; Political incorporation, Cuban model

Cuban Adjustment Act, 175

Cuban American National Foundation, 175

Cuban-Haitian Entrants program, 181

Cubans: asylum seekers, 240; community mobilization, 177; discrimination, 223–224; effects of Cold War, 165, 174; electoral powers of, 162, 165, 167, 171; embodied co-presence, 266–268; embodied proxies, 259; initial wave of immigration, 19, 21–22, 143–144, 161, 174, 208; in the labor force, 119; migration decisions, 57–59, 74, 287, 317; national identity, 204; political dominance, 179, 225; reception, 248; second wave of immigration, 119, 143–144, 174; sociopolitical profile of Cubans, 20, 164, 214; transnational embeddedness, 255; travel restrictions, 252. *See also* Cuba

Cumulative causation, 16

DACA. *See* Deferred Action for Childhood Arrivals

Defense of Marriage Act, 324

Deferred Action for Childhood Arrivals (DACA), 95, 324

Definitional power, 163–164, 193

Department of Homeland Security, 85, 106. *See also* Electronic Monitoring Program; National Fugitive Operations Program; Operation Endgame; Secure Communities

Deportation, 29, 95, 107, 108, 278; fear of, 87, 90, 95, 152; of gang members, 10–11; self-deportation, 82; threat of, 27, 37, 80–81, 84, 88. *See also* Asylum; Raids

Development Relief and Education for Alien Minors (DREAM) Act, 94–95, 320, 324

Diaz-Balart, Lincoln, 178

Diaz-Balart, Mario, 178

Domestic migration, 61. *See also* Global migration

Dominican Republic: economic insecurity, 9, 13, 64; migration, 13, 48–49; population increase, 54. *See also* Dominican

Dominican: imaginative co-presence, 258; racial roots, 202. *See also* Dominican Republic

Downward mobility, 27, 59, 64, 125, 126; class location, 143, 146; perceptions of, 138–140; as social insecurity, 156

DREAM Act. *See* Development Relief and Education for Alien Minors Act

Dreamers, 322, 324, 329. *See also* Development Relief and Education for Alien Minors Act

Duvalier, Francois, 179

Duvalier, Jean-Claude, 179, 181

Earthquake (Haiti, 2010), 21

Ecuador: economic output, 51; environment of insecurity, 11; government, 72; migration, 50, 63; population increase, 54

El Salvador: asylums seekers, 240; economic output, 51; economic stabilization, 11; Hurricane Stan (2005), 51; population increase, 54

Electronic Monitoring Program, 88

Environments of insecurity, 11–13, 27, 47, 74–76, 106; exiting, 71–72;

globalization of, 35; link to migration, 15, 45–46
Estevez, Felipe, 152

Faculty for Workplace Justice, 151, 160
Family reunification policy, 101, 181, 185
FARC. *See* Fuerzas Armadas Revolucionarias de Colombia
Feminicide, 69–70
Fuerzas Armadas Revolucionarias de Colombia (FARC), 67
Fujimuri, Alberto, 63

Gender inequality, 3, 126, 132–133, 156; effects of upward mobility, 132–134
Giddens, Anthony, 6, 12, 16
Global migration, 1, 5; and education, 131, 246; ambivalence toward, 245–246, 248, 273; effects of migration, 132–133, 250; gender differences, 133–134; inability to return to home country, 247–248; increase in, 62–63; migration reasons, 13, 57–59, 64–65, 146, 272; and weather, 287. *See also* Domestic migration; Immigration
Global mobility, 16, 38
Global population movement, 5, 14
Globalization, 12, 32, 115, 322, 329; economic globalization, 4, 15, 27; economic restructuring, 113; impacts of, 143
Gonzalez, Elian, 176
Guantanamo Bay Naval Base, 182
Guatemala: economic output, 51; Hurricane Stan (2005), 51; population increase, 54

H-1B visa, 99, 109
Haiti: earthquake (2010), 21, 179, 185, 215; economic output, 50; Haitian immigration, 20–21, 47–48, 71, 175, 179; hurricanes, 215; increase in population, 180, 181; local office, 161; migration reasons, 57, 67, 290, 317; political incorporation, 172, 179, 180; political insecurity, 71–72, 179; social mobility, 126. *See also* Cuban-Haitian Entrants program; Duvalier, Francois; Duvalier, Jean-Claude;

Haitian Refugee Immigration Fairness Act of 1998; Haitians; Political incorporation, Haitian model
Haitian Refugee Immigration Fairness Act of 1998, 181
Haitians: asylum seekers, 21, 98, 179, 214, 240; census 2010, 42; cultural exclusion, 310, 313, 317; deportation, 20; embodied co-presence, 268; embodied proxies, 259, 261; feelings of isolation, 299; media stereotypes, 179–180, 311–312; naturalization, 180, 182; perceived discrimination, 216, 219; political boundaries, 182; political representation, 183; racialization, 309–310; racial social systems, 212; reception of, 20–21, 179; reunification provisions, 266. *See also* Haiti
Homesickness, 2; stigmatized emotion, 3, 29, 244–245. *See also* Social co-presence
Honduras: economic output, 51; environment of insecurity, 11, 13; Hurricane Mitch (1998), 51; migration flow, 63; population increase, 54
Huerta, Dolores, 153
Hurricane Mitch (1998), 10, 51, 215
Hurricane Stan (2005), 10, 51

ICE. *See* Immigration and Customs Enforcement
Illegal Immigration Reform and Immigrant Responsibility Act of 1996, 14, 41
Immigrants' rights movement, 324
Immigration, 10; increase in, 92; as threat to terrorism, 13–15; visitor visa, 92–93, 99. *See also* Global migration
Immigration and Customs Enforcement (ICE), 41, 80, 84–87. *See also* Operation Return to Sender; Raids
Immigration policies, 15, 29, 212, 213, 238, 310; changes, 80–83; criminalization of immigrants, 85, 94, 105, 234, 330; and employment, 100; entry policies, 79, 214; post–September 11, 90–91, 104, 323; reform, 162, 190, 214, 323–324, 329,

331, 333; trends, 54, 84, 225, 307.
　　See also Family reunification policy
Immigration Reform and Control Act of
　　1986, 181, 190
International Monetary Fund, 49

Janitors, justice for. See Service
　　Employees International Union
Jones-Shafroth Act, 102

Legalization, 32, 94, 162, 165, 231
Liminal legality, 80, 97, 104
Little Havana. See Miami, Little
　　Havana
Locality, 8, 30, 38, 230. See also
　　Translocality
Loneliness, 3, 29, 248, 254, 260

"Magic City," 15, 41
Maroño, Manuel M., 186–188
Medina, Eliseo, 153
Meek, Kendrick, 153
Menendez, Ana, 154
Mestizaje, 200–201, 227
Mexicans: migration flow, 241;
　　perceived discrimination, 216, 219;
　　stereotypes, 222, 231–232. See also
　　Mexico
Mexico: economic insecurity, 9, 61–62;
　　economic output, 51; education
　　inequality, 130; environment of
　　insecurity 11, 13, 67; gender
　　segregation, 126; Hurricane Stan
　　(2005), 51; immigration trends, 54;
　　kidnappings, 68; migration reasons,
　　59, 290; population increase, 54;
　　social mobility, 126; upward mobility,
　　130. See also Mexicans; Tequila
　　effect in Mexico
Miami: as a sociocultural environment,
　　282, 313–314, 330; attraction of,
　　283–286, 293, 295, 313–314, 316;
　　displacement among groups, 298,
　　301; income inequality, 116–118, 120,
　　159–160, 218, 286; increase of
　　poverty, 120, 122; internationalization
　　of, 115, 118; Latinization, 113–114,
　　303; Little Havana, 177–178, 206,
　　208, 314; racially segregated city, 19,
　　39, 199, 208, 308; racial social
　　system, 207, 213, 229, 309;

unemployment, 112, 157. See also
　　Cuba; Racialization
Modernity, 3, 6, 7
Monestime, Jean, 184
Movimiento Democracia (Movement for
　　Democracy). See Sanchez, Raul Saul

NAFTA. See North American Free Trade
　　Agreement
National Fugitive Operations Program,
　　86–87
National Labor Relations Board, 152
National security, threats to, 15, 81–82
Natural spaces, 6, 213
Naturalization, 31, 161–162, 186, 189,
　　278. See also Legalization;
　　Naturalized citizens
Naturalized citizens, 102, 106, 162, 190.
　　See also Legalization; Naturalization
Neoliberal economic restructuring, 5, 49,
　　112
Neoliberal economic strategies, 27
Neoliberal policies, 12, 27; effects of,
　　116, 238, 331; effects on economic
　　insecurities, 50, 54, 62, 70, 146;
　　economic policies, 46–47, 104
Neoliberal transformation, 10
Neoliberalism, 5, 8, 11; effects on social
　　infrastructure, 12, 59, 113, 124;
　　implementation, 53, 115; shift away
　　from, 13
Nicaragua: population increase, 54; wave
　　of migration, 175. See also
　　Nicaraguan Adjustment and Central
　　American Relief Act of 1997;
　　Political incorporation, Nicaraguan
　　model
Nicaraguan Adjustment and Central
　　American Relief Act of 1997, 190
North American Free Trade Agreement
　　(NAFTA), 9, 49

O'Brien, Hugh, 167
Obama, Barack, 85, 86, 95; and
　　immigration reform, 190, 324, 333
Occupational mobility, 6
Ontological security: definition, 6–7,
　　243, 281, 292, 311; enhanced by
　　news, 313; increasing, 250, 257, 273,
　　316; perceptions of, 13, 277; sense of
　　assurance, 7; threats to, 8, 328

Operation Endgame, 85
Operation Return to Sender, 89
Ozzie, Guillen, 2

Panama: economic output, 51
Paraguay: economic output, 50–51
Personal Responsibility and Work
    Opportunity Reconciliation Act of
    1996, 14
Peru: economic hardships, 49; economic
    output, 51; economic security, 13, 62–
    63; kidnappings, 68; migration
    reasons, 59, 67; political insecurity,
    71
Pierre, Andre, 185
Pluralism, in electoral power, 162–164
Political incorporation: 167; Colombian
    model, 186–187, 189; Cuban model,
    172–174, 186, 189; Haitian model,
    179–182, 189; Nicaraguan model,
    186–187, 189–190
Portes, Alejandro, 5
Private banking, 114
Proposition 187, 14
Psychic insecurity, 76, 83, 87–91, 104–
    106, 247
Puerto Rican: discrimination, 236, 307–
    308; drug violence 11; economic
    insecurity, 53; environment insecurity,
    64, 104; imaginative co-presence,
    258; industrial development, 53;
    migration, 48–49, 54, 102–103;
    migration decisions, 13, 63–64; urban
    unemployment, 53; US citizenship,
    103, 106, 231
Puerto Rico Farm Labor program, 48

Racial mapping, 304
Racial profiling, 85–86, 105, 233, 333
Racialization: definition, 199–200; and
    immigration policies, 225, 231; racial
    discrimination, 216–218, 226–228,
    230; racial formations, 212, 303;
    racial hierarchy, 233–234, 300;
    relational hierarchies, 201, 204, 218,
    228, 296; social class discrimination,
    202, 205, 218, 228, 236; triracial
    stratification system, 213, 216; white
    racial framing, 205, 208, 221, 235,
    304
Raids, 90, 93. *See also* Immigration and

Customs Enforcement; Operation
    Return to Sender
Reagan, Ronald, administrations, 20,
    178, 181
Reception, 79–81, 112, 130, 138, 247,
    317; and media, 250–251, 257; new
    arrivals, 175; sociological
    dimensions, 106
Redistricting, 18
Regalado, Tomas, 153
Republican presidential nomination of
    2008, 14
Resettlement. *See* Secondary migration
Ros-Lehtinen, Ileana, 178

Salinas, Carlos, 49
Samba Effect in Brazil, 11
Sanchez, Raul Saul, 153
Save Our State. *See* Proposition 187
Secondary migration, 49, 246
Section 287(g), 41, 85
Secure Communities, 86, 91
SEIU. *See* Service Employees
    International Union
September 11, 2001, 81; anti-immigrant
    movement, 83; post–September 11,
    91, 105, 152, 323. *See also* National
    security, threats to
Service Employees International Union
    (SEIU), 149–150, 153
Shalala, Donna, 149, 150, 152
Social co-presence: embodied co-
    presence, 251–252, 262; embodied
    co-presence and happiness, 268;
    embodied proxies, 259–260;
    embodied proxies and happiness, 274;
    imaginative co-presence, 257–258;
    imaginative co-presence and
    happiness, 273–274; monetary
    remittances, 262, 274; as translocal
    practice, 250, 277, 329; virtual co-
    presence, 252–255; virtual
    co-presence and happiness, 270–272
Social insecurity, 12, 71–74, 79, 134, 146
Social mobility, 112–113, 123–124, 126–
    128, 136, 159; contributing factors,
    37; downward social mobility, 146;
    and education, 130, 134; and legal
    status, 138; perceived, 154–156;
    upward social mobility, 129, 149,
    319. *See also* Reception

Spanish language: mechanism of
  exclusion, 298
Stepick, Alex, 5
Stern, Andy, 153
Students Toward a New Democracy, 151,
  153
Suarez, Xavier, 167

Tango Effect in Argentina, 11
Tequila Effect in Mexico, 11
Thompson, Elsa, 188
Trail of Dreams, 320–321, 324
Translocal placemaking, 292–293, 316;
  homeland performances, 294;
  language use, 296–297, 316. *See also*
  Spanish language, mechanism of
  exclusion
Translocal social citizenship, 8, 30–31,
  265, 277–278; practices, 315, 333;
  process of, 38, 282; tradeoffs, 321–
  322
Translocality, 263, 292. *See also* Locality
Transnational perspectives, 28; racial
  ideology, 327

UNICCO (US cleaning service
  company), 147–155
Unionization, 150, 155. *See also* Service
  Employees International Union;
  UNICCO
Univision, 302
Upward mobility, 128–130, 138, 140,
  145; facilitators to, 132; gender
  differences, 133–134, 156;
  opportunities for, 124; perceived, 126,
  131, 133–134
Uruguay: economic security, 13;
  population growth, 51; social political
  party, 49; visa waivers, 108–109

Venezuela: debt collectors, 77–78;
  economic hardships, 49; economic
  output, 50–51; environment of
  insecurity, 11, 13; migration 50
Villaraigosa, Antonio, 167

World Bank, 49, 51, 76

Zapata, Juan Carlos, 188–189

About the Book

With more than a million immigrants from Latin America and the Caribbean, Miami, Florida, boasts the highest proportion of foreign-born residents of any US city. Charting the rise of Miami as a global city, Elizabeth Aranda, Sallie Hughes, and Elena Sabogal provide a panoramic study of the changing dynamics of the immigration experience.

The authors move easily between an analysis of global currents and personal narratives, examining the many factors that shape the decision to emigrate and the challenges faced in making a new home. Offering a wealth of new insights, their work demonstrates why Miami is such an exceptional laboratory for studying the social forces and local effects of globalization on the ground.

Elizabeth M. Aranda is associate professor in and chair of the Department of Sociology at the University of South Florida. **Sallie Hughes** is associate professor of journalism and Latin American studies at the University of Miami. **Elena Sabogal** is associate professor of women's and gender studies at William Paterson University of New Jersey.